Capitalism's Favorite Child

Capitalism's Favorite Child

Global Fashion Business since 1850

Pierre-Yves Donzé and Ben Wubs

BLOOMSBURY VISUAL ARTS
LONDON · NEW YORK · OXFORD · NEW DELHI · SYDNEY

BLOOMSBURY VISUAL ARTS
Bloomsbury Publishing Plc, 50 Bedford Square, London, WC1B 3DP, UK
Bloomsbury Publishing Inc, 1385 Broadway, New York, NY 10018, USA
Bloomsbury Publishing Ireland, 29 Earlsfort Terrace, Dublin 2, D02 AY28, Ireland

BLOOMSBURY, BLOOMSBURY VISUAL ARTS and the Diana logo are trademarks of
Bloomsbury Publishing Plc

First published in Great Britain 2026

Copyright © Pierre-Yves Donzé and Ben Wubs, 2026

Pierre-Yves Donzé and Ben Wubs have asserted their right under the Copyright, Designs and Patents Act, 1988, to be identified as Authors of this work.

For legal purposes the Acknowledgements on p. xvii constitute an extension of this copyright page.

Front cover image: A Cotton Office in New Orleans (Le Bureau de coton à La Nouvelle-Orléans), 1873, by Edgar Degas Musée des beaux-arts de Pau. Fine Art Images/Heritage Images/Getty Images.

Back cover image: Imported Silk Reeling Machine at Tsukiji in Tokyo, Utagawa Yoshitora. Courtesy of Metropolitan Museum of Art/Gift of Lincoln Kirstein, 1959.

All rights reserved. No part of this publication may be: i) reproduced or transmitted in any form, electronic or mechanical, including photocopying, recording or by means of any information storage or retrieval system without prior permission in writing from the publishers; or ii) used or reproduced in any way for the training, development or operation of artificial intelligence (AI) technologies, including generative AI technologies. The rights holders expressly reserve this publication from the text and data mining exception as per Article 4(3) of the Digital Single Market Directive (EU) 2019/790.

Bloomsbury Publishing Plc does not have any control over, or responsibility for, any third-party websites referred to or in this book. All internet addresses given in this book were correct at the time of going to press. The author and publisher regret any inconvenience caused if addresses have changed or sites have ceased to exist, but can accept no responsibility for any such changes.

A catalogue record for this book is available from the British Library.

A catalog record for this book is available from the Library of Congress.

ISBN: PB: 978-1-350109-80-3
HB: 978-1-350109-81-0
ePub: 978-1-350109-83-4
ePDF: 978-1-350109-82-7

Typeset by RefineCatch Limited, Bungay, Suffolk
Printed and bound in Great Britain by Bell & Bain Ltd, Glasgow

For product safety related questions contact productsafety@bloomsbury.com.

To find out more about our authors and books visit www.bloomsbury.com and sign up for our newsletters.

Contents

List of figures	ix
List of tables	xv
List of boxes	xvi
Acknowledgements	xvii

Introduction — 1

1 The emergence of the modern fashion business — 7
- The global expansion of the commodity trade—wool, cotton, and silk — 8
- Technological innovation—textile machinery, sewing machines, and artificial colors — 14
- Standardization of sizes — 19
- New consumption temples—department stores — 20
- Conclusion — 24

2 The rise of haute couture or high-end fashion — 25
- The inventor of a new business: Charles Frederick Worth — 27
- The heyday of French haute couture (1880–1939) — 32
- Haute couture as a transnational industry — 37
- Trade associations in haute couture — 42
- Conclusion — 43

3 Fashion for the masses — 45
- Change in consumption habits — 46
- Clothing industry around the world — 49
- Networks and large factories — 51
- Producing fabrics for the European colonies — 58

	The internalization model in apparel retail: C&A	59
	The outsourcing model: M&S	61
	Conclusion	63
4	**West meets East and the Rest**	65
	How British cotton conquered the world and deindustrialized India	66
	Japan's Meiji Restoration, selective Westernization, and uniforms	68
	Forced opening of China, the Opium Wars, and the Westernization of Chinese culture	73
	Chinese and Japanese influences on Western fashion	75
	Wax fabrics connected Asia, Europe, and Africa	77
	Conclusion	80
5	**American fashion**	83
	Fur, cotton, and slavery	84
	Industrialization and textiles	85
	Ready-to-wear	87
	The rise of New York fashion	89
	The rise of denim	90
	Leisure and sportswear	92
	Conclusion	96
6	**Fashion, fascism, and the Second World War**	101
	Italian fascism, fashion, and fibers	102
	Nazi autarky, Aryanization, and artificial fibers	106
	Japan's fashion during the military dictatorship	110
	Paris fashion during the German occupation	112
	British-controlled fashion	114
	American independence from Paris	117
	Conclusion	122
7	**Postwar fashion systems**	123
	A new business model for Parisian haute couture	124
	US fashion industry—mass production, creativity and imitation	128

	The emergence of Italian fashion	131
	Western fashion and garments in Japan	133
	Growth of global apparel industry	136
	Conclusion	138
8	**Global fashion: Outsourcing and the end of the production paradigm**	**141**
	Global shifts in the textile and apparel industries	142
	The rise of global fashion companies	147
	Mediatization of fashion	152
	The Japanese way	154
	Fashion in developing economies	157
	Conclusion	159
9	**Fashion conglomerates and fast fashion**	**161**
	The rise of LVMH	162
	Financialization of luxury fashion brands	164
	Fast fashion—retail and production	167
	(Un)sustainability and fashion	173
	Conclusion	176
10	**Sports to fashion**	**179**
	Sportswear and casual style in the United States	180
	A German sports-shoemaker conquers Germany—and then the world	182
	Game changers—the rise of Nike and Reebok	184
	Near-death experience and revival of adidas	188
	Marketing of sportswear	191
	Fashionalization of adidas	193
	Conclusion	196
11	**Digital fashion and global production networks**	**199**
	Globalization and global production networks	200
	Fashion forecasting: WGSN (London) and Stylesight (New York)	202
	E-commerce, fast fashion, and the destruction of traditional retail	206

Mediatization, bloggers, and influencers	210
The Fourth Industrial Revolution in fashion	212
Conclusion	216

Conclusion 219

Notes	225
References	255
Index	277

Figures

1.1	Cotton weighers in Bombay, British India, before 1860.	10
1.2	Imported Silk Reeling Machine at Tsukiji in Tokyo, 1872. Japanese artist: Utagawa Yoshitora , active ca. 1850–1880. Gift of Lincoln Kirstein, 1959.	12
1.3	Silk Factory in Japan, 1890.	12
1.4	Two Young Boys Climbing on Spinning Frame to Mend Broken Threads and Put Back Empty Bobbins, Bibb Mill No. 1, Macon, Georgia, USA, Lewis Hine for National Child Labor Committee, January 1909.	15
1.5	Advertising for Singer Machines, 1892.	17
1.6	Printemps Department Store in Paris, France Nineteenth Century.	21
1.7	Cover for Shanghai Manhua, July 1, 1928.	23
2.1	Marie-Antoinette Josèphe Jeanne (1755–1793), Queen of France, engraving after a design by Jean-Michel Moreau le Jeune (1741–1814); engraver unknown.	26
2.2	Anglo-French costumier and dress designer Charles Frederick Worth (1825–1895).	27
2.3	Evening ensemble, French, 1887. Artist Charles Frederick Worth.	28
2.4	Russian actress and ballerina Ida Lvovna Rubinstein (October 5, 1885–September 20, 1960) during the performance of "La Dame aux Camélias" (Alexandre Dumas fils), standing on stage, a bouquet of camellias in her hand. She is dressed in a black dress by Worth, over which a garland of camellias is draped. As jewelry a tiara and a necklace.	32
2.5	Two women in summer dresses, the beach in the background. Left: sundress of white mousseline printed in multiple colors, by Martial et Armand. Right: "Robe de sport" of green crêpe "Fantasia" A.G.B. by Lucien Lelong. Part of a page from the fashion magazine Art-Goût-Beauté (1920–1933).	34
2.6	French fashion designer, Gabrielle Coco Chanel, in profile reclining on a chaise lounge with cigarette, wearing a dark dress with gold medallion necklaces and a ribbon in her hair; photographed in Paris in 1937.	35

2.7	French Exports of Clothing and Lingerie, in Tons, 1913–1936. G. Deschamps, La Crise dans les Industries du Vêtement et de la Mode à Paris pendant la Période de 1930 à 1937.	36
2.8	Poster: Paul Poiret in Vienna. From November 27–29, 1911.	41
2.9	Woman in cape designed by Madeleine Vionnet. Plate from Gazette du Bon Ton, Brentano's, Paris, 1922.	41
3.1	Front cover of Cosmopolitan magazine for November 1917.	47
3.2	Advertisement for La Belle Jardinière, 1933.	49
3.3	Advertising poster for a clothing shop showing a man wearing a suit inset into a view of Place du Château d'Eau, location of the shop.	50
3.4	Advertisement for Raynster raincoats, 1918. Washington State Apple Commission / New York Botanical Garden, LuEsther T. Mertz Library.	51
3.5	Conservation of fur products in freezer room to combat moths, Rudolf Hertzog, Berlin, 1914. Rudolph Hertzog / Kollection Kuhn.	53
3.6	Garment workers seated at their sewing machines around a long workbench in an unspecified workshop in the garment district of New York City, New York, 1936. Image used to illustrate the threat of strike action by the Amalgamated Ladies' Garment Workers' Union.	55
3.7	Au Pauvre Jacques Clothing Fashions Poster, circa 1900.	58
4.1	Emperor Meiji and his Consort in the Plum Garden, by Kobayashi Kiyochika, Japan, 1887.	68
4.2	Young moga (modern girls) walk down a Ginza street in 1928 dressed in "Beach Pyjama Style." Kageyama Kōyō.	70
4.3	Fabric selection for Christian Dior's new designs, in Tokyo, Japan on December 7, 1964.	72
4.4	A studio photograph of a group of young society women in 1930s Shanghai proudly and confidently showing off their unbound feet and modern, Western footwear.	73
4.5	Chinese-style garments in 1913, US. Abby E. Underwood / Meredith Corporation / Serials in Microfilm Collection (SIM).	74
4.6	Silk dress with silk embroidery, 1933, attributed to Callot Soeurs. Tim Evansion via Flickr.	76
4.7	Image of three cotton factories in Haarlem, Prévinaire & Co, in the 1840s. The top two factories are placed opposite each other in the image, while they were located at the extreme edges of the city. In 1875 the company was renamed Haarlemsche Katoen Maatschappij (HKM).	78

List of Figures

4.8	"Materials Our Grandmothers Never Knew." Advertisement for pine oil products manufactured and sold by the Hercules Powder Company for use in the production of textiles. Hercules Incorporated.	82
5.1	California fashions of furs for 1868 and 1869.	84
5.2	Young Spinner—Indian Orchard Cotton Mill. Photograph from the records of the National Child Labor Committee (U.S.), 1916.	86
5.3	Advertising for Levi Strauss: "It's no use they can't be ripped." Included in the exhibit "Levi Strauss: A History of American Style," Feb 13, 2020–Aug 8, 2021 at the Contemporary Jewish Museum in San Francisco.	91
5.4	Vogue 1928. Model, holding a pole and reaching for gymnastic rings, wearing a two-piece bathing suit with a belted striped sweater top and wool jersey shorts with a white bathing cap, by Jean Patou.	93
5.5	Actress Greta Garbo poses for a publicity photo for the MGM movie "A Woman Of Affairs" which was released in 1928.	95
5.6	Mid-twentieth century postcard showing an aerial view of the American Viscose Corporation Plant in Front Royal, Virginia, USA.	98
6.1	Blackshirts taking part in a meeting in Naples. Naples, October 24, 1922.	103
6.2	Italian menswear 1930s.	104
6.3	Frauen-Warte, the only official woman's nazi magazine, 1942.	107
6.4	Milk wool manufacturing: stand of AKU, Arnhem (Algemene Kunstzijde Unie NV) at the Jaarbeurs in Utrecht.	110
6.5	Lucien Lelong at his desk in Paris, France, around 1940.	113
6.6	Utility Clothes- Fashion Restrictions in Wartime Britain, 1943.	114
6.7	Woman worker in the Douglas Aircraft Company plant (Oct 1942).	118
6.8	The worn out nylon [and silk] stockings in this barrel full of salvaged stockings will be reprocessed and made into parachutes for army fliers, tow ropes for gilder planes and other war material.	120
6.9	Lunchtime brings a few minutes of rest for these women workers of the assembly line at Douglas Aircraft Company's plant, Long Beach, California, October 1942. Sand bags for protection against air raid form the background.	121
7.1	A woman holding a bottle of Miss Dior perfume by Christian Dior, December 1954.	125
7.2	Mondriaan Fashion from Paris, dresses made by Yves Saint. Laurent, the models in The Hague Municipal Museum, 1966.	128

7.3	Men pulling racks of clothing on busy sidewalk in Garment District, New York City, 1955.	129
7.4	Italian fashion designer Biki (Elvira Leonardi Bouyeure) in the fashion show room at her atelier with two models. Beside her, her son-in-law Alain Renaud. Milan, 1968.	132
7.5	Designers Sonia Rykiel, Karl Lagerfeld and Kenzo Takada seated in Rykiel's Paris apartment to discuss fashion in the 1970s for WWD (Nathalie Rykiel stands in the background leaning forward). Article title: "French Fashion Talk."	134
7.6	The gift display in a ladies fashion shop on Saville Row, Newcastle upon Tyne, 1966.	138
7.7	Pierre Balmain Show in Victoria Hotel, Amsterdam, 1951.	139
7.8	Magazine advertisement for DuPont Lycra, the brand name for the polyester-polyurethane copolymer invented by Joseph Shivers in 1958 at the DuPont laboratory in Waynesboro, Virginia. The advertisement was published in the September 22, 1961 edition of *Life* magazine.	140
8.1	Share in World Production of Man-made Fibers, by Region, as a Percentage (1975–2015).	143
8.2	A Chinese female worker in a textile factory in Huaibei, Anhui province, 2015.	144
8.3	Bangladeshi women sewing clothes, 2013. Fahad Faisal.	145
8.4	Launch of "Opium" Perfume, Yves Saint Laurent and models, 1978.	147
8.5	Karl Lagerfeld fits one of his designs on top model Ines de la Fressange at Chloe's Paris studio, 1983.	148
8.6	Giorgio Armani with Models, 1982.	151
8.7	Issey Miyake, spring/summer 1995.	156
8.8	Chaoyue Sportswear—China Fashion Week, 2007. kris krüg via Flickr.	158
8.9	Model Naomi Campbell backstage at the Donna Karan Spring 1997 Ready to Wear Runway Show on November 1, 1996, in New York City.	160
9.1	Johann Rupert the CEO of the Richemont group lines up a putt on the first hole during the third round of the 2018 Alfred Dunhill Links Championship on The Old Course at St Andrews on October 6, 2018 in St Andrews, Scotland.	165
9.2	People awaited the arrival of British Queen Elizabeth II near a giant 1,500 square meter advertisement for Swedish fashion retailer H&M that shows German-born fashion designer Karl Lagerfeld and U.S. model Erin Wasson November 2, 2004 in central Berlin, Germany.	169

List of Figures

9.3	Oscar Garcia Maceiras, chief executive officer of Inditex SA, during a full year earnings news conference at the company's headquarters in Arteixo, Spain, on Wednesday, March 13, 2024.	171
9.4	UNIQLO store in Okeaniya Shopping and Entertainment Complex, Slavyanka, Russia, representative of the breakthrough of the Japanese apparel industry outside of Japan, 2016.	172
9.5	World Production of Man-made and Natural Fibers, 1975–2015 (in 1,000 Tons).	174
9.6	European and Chinese textile and plastic waste at Dandora dump site in Nairobi.	175
9.7	Behind the bar during a party to celebrate the one year anniversary of Studio 54, with special decorations from fashion designer Issey Miyake (apple blossom-like plants and gold screens) along with a combination entertainment/fashion show with an 'East meets West' theme on April 26, 1978 in New York.	177
10.1	Men's Leisure wear. Fashion plates, men's 1880–1939.	180
10.2	Vintage color historic souvenir photo postcard published circa 1942 as part of a series titled, 'Greetings from California,' depicting the vibrant beach and boardwalk and amusements pier, here showing an aerial view of the crowded beach boardwalk and amusements of Santa Cruz beach and boardwalk.	181
10.3	View of the Dassler shoe factory, 1928.	183
10.4	Nike factory workers take a nap at lunchtime below the conveyor belt where they work. Ho Chi Minh City, Vietnam, 1997.	185
10.5	Michael Jordan sits in a space ship being filmed with a camera on a crane arm against a green screen on a soundstage for a Nike "Aerospace Jordan" television commercial for Super Bowl XXVII in September, 1992 in Los Angeles, California.	186
10.6	Joseph Simmons, Darryl McDaniels and Jam Master Jay of the hip-hop group "Run DMC" pose for a portrait session wearing Addidas sweat suits in front of the Empire State Building in May 1985 in New York, New York.	189
10.7	Nike Chief Executive Officer Phil Knight at the US Open men's tennis finals, NYC, September 10, 1995.	192
10.8	Three-divisional Structure of adidas, 2002.	194
10.9	Zinedine Zidane and Yohji Yamamoto attend a cocktail reception celebrating the opening of the new Y-3 Flagship store hosted by Yohji Yamamoto and adidas on March 10, 2011 in London.	195
11.1	WGSN senior director Greer Hughes is seen on stage during the Texhibition Istanbul 2023 at Istanbul Expo Center on March 10, 2023 in Istanbul, Turkey.	203

11.2	A speech about IBM Watson is delivered during the Release Ceremony for World Leading Internet Scientific and Technological Achievements as part of the third World Internet Conference (WIC) at Wuzhen Internet International Conference and Exhibition Center on November 16, 2016 in Jiaxing, Zhejiang Province of China.	205
11.3	Logistic distribution center of the Zara Company. Sabon. Arteixo. la Coruna. The Spanish Fashion Company, INDITEX, owned by Amancio Ortega.	207
11.4	Shein pop-up store at the Square One Shopping Centre, December 2023 in Mississauga.	209
11.5	Computerized Flat Knitting Machine (Jacquard Machine), Japan.	214
11.6	Paris—3D Printed Stilettos for Dyson Showroom Exhibition. Jiri Evenhuis via Wikimedia Commons	215
11.7	Young girls working in a sweatshop in Bangladesh, November 18, 2015. Solidarity Center via Flickr.	216
11.8	Picture taken on December 12, 2012 shows employees of the internet retail company Zalando working at a logistics center in Erfurt, Eastern Germany. Zalando, is facing criticism after the broadcast of a television documentary in Germany denouncing working conditions in one of its logistics centers.	217

Tables

1.1	World Production of Silk, Metric Tons, 1833–1910	11
3.1	Tailoring Workers in England and Wales, 1851–1911	56
5.1	Ten Leading Industries in America 1860–1920, by Value Add, 1914 Prices (Millions of 1914 American Dollars)	88
6.1	Major Rayon-producing Countries 1921–1939 (in 000 Tons)	109
7.1	Haute Couture Houses in Paris, 1954	124
7.2	Gross Sales (FF), Profit (FF) and Profitability (%) of Maison Christian Dior, 1977	126
8.1	Armani Group Turnover, in Millions of Euros, 2004	150
9.1	Largest Listed Companies Worldwide within the Apparel and Fashion Industry, in Billion Dollars	173
10.1	Global Sports Shoe Market and Market Shares, 1991–1999	187
10.2	Fashion Brand Position and Brand Value, in Million US Dollars	196

Boxes

Box 1.1	The silk merchants Siber & Brennwald	13
Box 1.2	The global expansion of the Singer Sewing Machine Corporation (1851–1914)	16
Box 2.1	The birth of fashion models	31
Box 2.2	Wiener Werkstätte: How Viennese design and fashion influenced Paris and Berlin	40
Box 3.1	A La Belle Jardinière (France) and the distribution of fashion for the working class	48
Box 3.2	Berlin as the European capital of confection (1880–1933)	52
Box 4.1	The birth of designer schools in Japan	71
Box 4.2	Chinese and Japanese raw silk and the European and US silk industry before the Second World War	81
Box 5.1	Hollywood and fashion: How the movies changed the way we dressed	94
Box 5.2	The rise of synthetic fibers and foreign direct investment in the United States	97
Box 6.1	Jewish fashion district in London during the war	116
Box 6.2	Rosie the Riveter: How leisurewear and denim liberated American women	118
Box 7.1	Licensing strategies of Western fashion companies in Japan	135
Box 7.2	The nylon revolution and the emergence of synthetic fibers	139
Box 8.1	From trench coats to fashion: Burberry	151
Box 8.2	Japanese capital and American designers: Donna Karan New York (DNKY)	156
Box 9.1	H&M's collaboration with Karl Lagerfeld: High end meets fast fashion	168
Box 9.2	Issey Miyake's fashion business	177
Box 10.1	Hip hop, sportswear, and fashion	188
Box 10.2	Soccer shirts as fashion items	197
Box 11.1	IBM Watson and fashion forecasting	204
Box 11.2	Zalando: Europe's leading online fashion platform	217

Acknowledgements

The idea for this book started some ten years ago and is the result of a long journey researching and discussing the dynamics of the global fashion industry. We, the two authors, met at the annual conferences of the European Business History Association (EBHA) and during a European research project (HERA) on the fashion industry, the Enterprise of Culture. Our shared interest in the historical development of multinational companies and creative industries led us to research the emergence and transformation of the luxury conglomerate LVMH since its foundation, as well as Christian Dior and the sportswear business. We also shared an interest in asking big historical questions and looking globally and broadly at fashion as one of the largest businesses in the world. While Ben Wubs was a visiting professor at Kyoto University in 2015, we launched, together with Rika Fujioka, the Kansai Workshop on Global Fashion Business (six editions to date) to bring together academic researchers and business people around various aspects of fashion business history in Japan and Asia. In the meantime, similar workshops and events have been organized in Europe. We have also co-organized several seminars at the Erasmus University in Rotterdam, joint sessions at international conferences and participated in various workshops. We would like to express our deepest gratitude to all those who participated in these events, exchanged ideas with us and helped us to refine our framework for a global business history of fashion. We would like to thank the following people in particular: Takeshi Abe, Bethan Bide, Regina Lee Blaszczyk, Ninke Bloemberg, Patrizia Casadei, Eugene Choi, Wirawan Dony Dahana, Franck Dardenne, Colette Depeyre, Thomas Doebeli, Rika Fujioka, Roger Gerards, Daphne Geveke, Ingrid Giertz-Mårtenson, David Gilbert, Tomoko Hashino, Latchezar Hristov, Naoko Inoue, Alice Janssens, Michelle Jones, Christian Kleinschmidt, Roman Köster, Tereza Kuldova, Sophie Kurkdijan, Takafumi Kurosawa, Mariangela Lavanga, Wessie Ling, W. David Marx, Elisabetta Merlo, José Antonio Miranda, Yasuhiro Ohta, Francesca Polese, Véronique Pouillard, Magdalena Popowska, Giorgio Riello, Alba Roldán, Ana Uribe Sandoval, Emanuela Scarpellini, Luciano Segreto, Sonnet Stanfill, Mark Spoerer, Miki Sugiura, Keiko Suzuki, and Susanne Vegter. None of them are of course responsible for any errors, misjudgments, or omissions in this book.

The completion of this book was also made possible by the financial support of several institutions, whom we would like to thank for their generous sponsorship. We benefited from grants from the Japan Society for the Promotion of Science (Grant-in-Aid for Scientific Research no. 22K01592 and 23K22136) and HERA II: Humanities in the European

Research Area (12-HERA-JRP-CE-OP-050). Pierre-Yves Donzé benefitted from a visiting professorship at Erasmus University Rotterdam in 2024, which enabled a fruitful stay for the final preparation of the manuscript. We would also like to express our gratitude to the research interns at the Erasmus School of History, Culture and Communication Lexy Remij and Elina Ziehm for their invaluable help in the iconographic research and the preparation of the boxes in the various chapters of the book. Finally, many thanks to Bloomsbury Publishing for their interest, patience, and support in finalizing the manuscript.

Osaka and Rotterdam, April 7, 2025

Introduction

> We take leave of the charming chapter on the "à la mode devil" and the way in which he often behaves in a funny way in the present day, with the feeling that our explanations have clearly demonstrated the connection that also exists between the phenomenon of fashion and our economic organization. There is no need to fear being accused of exaggeration if one claims: Fashion is capitalism's favourite child: it has sprung from its innermost being and expresses its peculiarity like few other phenomena of the social life of our time.[1]

These are the final words of an article titled *Wirtschaft und Mode* ("Business and Fashion"), written by the German economic historian and sociologist Werner Sombart in 1902. It made a "contribution to the theory of modern demand management" and, according to Sombart, saw fashion as an essential part of capitalism in that it mobilized consumption. As taste and demand constantly change, companies must adapt to the market instantly; otherwise, they will lose their market share or, worse, go under. Changing fashions force companies to keep adapting their offerings.

Another important aspect of the fashion industry was its international intertwining of design, production, and consumption. From designs in Paris and Vienna to production in Berlin, to supply in the furthest corners of Germany, the fashion industry was connected in all its facets. Sombart realized at the time that you cannot study the fashion industry from the material production side alone because taste and symbolic values not only play a major role in the creation of high-end luxury fashion but also in mass-produced clothing. Fashion was thus at the heart of the economic system and even one of the drivers of modern capitalism.

It took more than a hundred years to follow the insights of Sombart and study fashion as a global economic and business activity, instead of just a sociological or cultural phenomenon. This book on the global history of the fashion industry draws on research in the new culturally informed field of business history and examines its ever-altering supply chains and changing production and consumption relations and locations over the last 170 years. The main actors in the fashion industry are explored, including manufacturers, designers, intermediaries, trade associations, trade shows, fashion forecasters, and retailers. We follow Sombart's logic and take fashion as a capitalistic phenomenon that mobilizes consumption and constantly changes tastes to increase sales and profits. In addition, the fashion industry constantly changes its global production locations and follows the economic logic of diminishing factor prices, particularly labor costs. According to Sombart, "fashion is capitalism's favourite child."[2]

This book explores the global fashion business from the middle of the nineteenth century till the twenty-first century. While Sombart fell into obscurity, mainly due to shifts in his ideological trajectory during the First World War and the interwar period, a fellow city dweller and contemporary, Georg Simmel, had an enormous influence on the sociology of fashion.[3] In his seminal article in 1904, Simmel stated:

> Fashion is a form of imitation and so of social equalization, but, paradoxically, in changing incessantly, it differentiates one time from another and one social stratum from another. It unites those of a social class and segregates them from others. The elite initiates a fashion and, when the mass imitates it in an effort to obliterate the external distinctions of class, abandons it for a new mode—a process that quickens with the increase of wealth.[4]

Although Simmel's observation has frequently been repeated in fashion studies, it is only one part of the fashion process, even if the new elites that emerged in the twentieth century—celebrities in sports, movies, and music—influenced the tastes of millions all over the world. We are not the first to show that the trickle-down effect has transformed into a trickle-up effect for certain fashion items such as denim, sneakers, and sportswear. However, we also show that, although the new sartorial styles were often invented on the street, it was the industry and its marketers that further developed the styles, extended the demand for them, and made them into fashion for the masses. We do, therefore, doubt the interpretation of the sociologists Patrik Aspers and Frédéric Godart, who define fashion "as an unplanned process of recurrent change against a backdrop of order in the public realm."[5] Possibly, the introduction of new fashion styles was a spontaneous development; however, this interpretation leaves out the role of fashion forecasters and the marketing departments of fashion companies.[6]

In the 1960s, Roland Barthes argued that fashion was not just the result of designers or a spontaneous bottom-up process. According to Barthes, fashion magazines were key intermediaries in connecting producers and consumers. The exchange through media gave birth to a modern fashion system and to fashion itself.[7] We agree with him that fashion can only be studied as a system—not only nationally but internationally and transnationally.

Yuniya Kawamura developed Barthes' ideas to argue there are many different intermediaries in the fashion system:

> Fashion is a system of institutions, organizations, groups, producers, events, and practices, all of which contribute to the making of fashion, which is different from dress and clothing. It is the structural nature of the system that affects the legitimation process of designers' creativity. A systemic differentiation can be made between clothes and fashion, which are two independent, autonomous entities.[8]

According to Kawamura, clothing and fashion are thus two separate things. Clothing manufacturing involves different institutions and is the material production process, while fashion is the construction of an idea. However, she also states: "Although fashion is not about clothing, without it, fashion cannot exist. They are not mutually inclusive nor are they mutually exclusive."[9]

This book not only examines the different forms of fashion production but also the connections between these different forms, from catwalk to street fashion and vice versa, especially the role that different actors in the fashion industry have played in this. We aim to show also that it is hard to distinguish between clothes and fashion. Although we recognize that fashion is an "ideology" or "myth," as Kawamura claims,[10] and it must be seen as a cultural product with symbolic value, clothing or apparel also has this symbolic value. Street and sportswear, in particular, express the identity of the wearer. We believe that the differentiation between *high* fashion (couture) and *low* fashion (mass-manufactured clothes) is simplistic and ahistorical. It is a narrative created by designers in the nineteenth century to promote themselves and create a basis for the distinction of the elite, be it the bourgeois (middle class) or aristocrats. In the twentieth century, several sartorial styles were adopted by the upper class and luxury fashion brands (e.g., denim, sneakers, and leisure and sportswear) and this bottom-up evolution of styles was a global movement.[11]

That brings us to another aspect of this book—the fact that global fashion had begun already in the nineteenth century when markets were integrating rapidly. To understand the business history of fashion, a global approach is needed. International connections created international fashion styles but also dependencies on raw materials, manufacturing, and markets. The Industrial Revolution was primarily based on manufacturing cotton yarn and cloth. It is always portrayed as a success story of the West, but the consumption of cotton from Asia created mass demand in Western Europe in the seventeenth and eighteenth centuries, proving that the world was connected long before the first globalization wave in the late nineteenth century. This book starts around the mid-nineteenth century because this period represents a major change in the history of fashion, with the emergence of a Western, mostly European, phenomenon. According to Gilles Lipovetsky, modern fashion is intimately linked to the development of individualism and personal taste. The idea of individual consumption based on permanent change, which is the essence of modern fashion, appeared first in Europe, from where it spread across the globe.[12] However, around the mid-nineteenth century, a new production system arose based on a rapid increase in the exchange of commodities globally, ground-breaking technological innovations (like the sewing machine, artificial dyes, and power looms), and the introduction of mass production based on factory work and the rise in demand for finished clothing for the new city-dwellers. Modern imperialism and the rise of fashion capitals like Paris, Vienna, and London made fashion a Western middle- and upper-class phenomenon; however, at the same time, the masses in the metropoles and colonies were demanding cheap Western-style clothes.[13] In the twentieth century, with the rise of the middle class around the world, Western-style clothes became the dominant fashion style.

We are inspired by Sanjay Subrahmanyam's ideas about "connected histories."[14] He seeks to move away from comparative history, which has prevailed in the past and is regarded by Subrahmanyam as a simplistic and overly isolated and mechanistic framework for writing global histories. Fashion has always been a global business—hence, its history in different countries has always been connected. Raw materials and final products such as silk (China and Japan), printed cotton (India), and kimonos (Japan) spread to the West. The development of chartered companies such as the Dutch East India Company (or *Vereenigde Oost-Indische Compagnie*, "the VOC") and the English (later British) East India Company (EIC) depended in part on trade in fabrics to the West and the East. The use of cotton, for example, was not a Western invention but came from the East.[15] The consumption of cotton fabrics stimulated production in the West and eventually led to the Industrial Revolution. This, in turn, kicked off a new plantation economy in North America, one based on slavery.[16] Global supply chains always played a part, but these changed constantly. The fashion system consisted roughly of production, distribution, consumption, and mediation. The role played by these different elements changed in different periods. While fashion is often equated with clothing, the industry is composed of complex supply chains, from textile manufacturing to the organization of trade shows and fashion weeks.[17] Despite a certain continuity, production networks of the fashion industry have thus varied from historical period to historical period, and between cities, regions, nations, and continents.[18]

We are aware that "the West" is a historical construction and an ideology; however, we have tried to use the terms West and East as value-free as possible and in a geographical sense, for lack of any other clear indication.[19] Switching to "Global South" (developing countries) and "Global North" (developed countries) may sound less Eurocentric but is less well suited to describing the historical evolution of the global fashion industry over the last two centuries.[20]

Fashion was, and still is, not only a matter of creation, design, and culture but also one of the largest industries in the world. Yet it is too often approached as a static business when it is, in fact, constantly in flux. Locations and supply chains are subject to constant change. Historical evolution matters a great deal when it comes to understanding the dynamics of this global industry. Using a business and economic history approach, we endeavor in this book to overcome these major shortcomings and provide a new history of the fashion industry. In particular, the book will stress the truly global nature of the fashion business since the 1850s and attempt to explain how and why the fashion industry changed from then on. What were the main drivers of change? Was it technology that determined the constantly changing supply chains? Or were the ever-changing relative factor costs forcing the industry to change its manufacturing, distribution, and consumption structure? What was the role of private businesses and entrepreneurs? Did governments stimulate or impede the fashion industry through legislation or trade policies? To what extent were capital markets decisive for the emergence of large fashion conglomerates? What was the role of symbolic capital and intangible factors like creativity and human capital? Lastly, how is it possible for the West to still be playing such an integral role in the industry despite the constantly changing economic and geopolitical conditions?

In this book, we use several different but related concepts. We have already discussed the complex and multifaced idea of fashion. The word nowadays is used in so many ways and contexts that it has lost much of its meaning. However, we still think it a useful word to describe the more symbolic part of the industry related to the way we dress. We do not just use it as a synonym for *haute couture* (which literally means "high sewing" and is also a French legal concept). In the nineteenth century, couture was also called *confection* and referred to tailored clothes. However, in the twentieth century, the meaning of confection changed to cheap mass-manufactured clothes or ready-to-wear. Ready-to-wear includes all types of mass-produced standardized clothing, both expensive and cheap. *Prêt-a-porter*, the direct French translation of ready-to-wear, refers specifically to standardized clothes sold by French luxury fashion companies. "Apparel," a formal American-English term for clothing or garments, spread globally in the twentieth century. The word "textile" originally came from woven cloth but is today an umbrella term that includes any kind of fiber, yarn, or fabric. This small exploration of fashion-related concepts, material or immaterial, shows how complicated it is to make a clear distinction between these different aspects of the industry.

The objectives of the book are to offer a global perspective on the business history of fashion and to contribute to a better understanding of the long-term evolution of this industry. By adopting this long-term historical approach to the global fashion business, we aim to identify patterns usually overlooked when using short-term research perspectives. Fashion experiences have changed fundamentally over the last two centuries: from the introduction of factories to global sourcing of raw materials and expansion into new markets, from the rise of global supply chains to the development of e-commerce, from the transformation of haute couture to the rise of multinational conglomerates, from the opening of new markets in Asia to the advent of ultra-fast fashion. Nevertheless, despite the globalization of manufacturing and consumption, which started in the nineteenth century, Western Europe and the United States have maintained their competitive advantage regarding the production of fashion in terms of creation and added value.

Meanwhile, today's fashion industry is still one of the world's key economic sectors. In 2021, global apparel sales were estimated at $1.7 trillion by Euromonitor and $2.3 trillion by McKinsey,[21] about the same amount as the global automobile market (about $2.1 trillion in 2022).[22] The transformation of this industry and its success stories have attracted the attention of many scholars in the fields of management and marketing, cultural studies, and history.[23] Such works do, however, have two significant shortcomings if a proper understanding of the dynamics of the global fashion industry is to be achieved. First, they largely neglect the global dimension of the modern fashion industry from its start in the mid-nineteenth century. They usually focus on France, the United States, Italy, and the United Kingdom, with the rest of the world generally approached as a mere outlet or manufacturing location. Second, the business dimension is often underestimated. Fashion is essentially discussed as an activity carried out by genius creators, legitimated by fashion shows and media, and consumed by a broad range of people. The firms and the business models behind the visible side of fashion are largely absent from the discussion.

It is only recently that business historians have begun to research and write about the fashion industry. The historical emergence of intermediaries and the formation of fashion systems around the world have been the focus of a broad range of works worldwide. They have contributed to showing that fashion as an industry should be considered a business system that includes a broad range of actors and that the nature of this system has changed over the years.[24] The role of institutions in shaping fashion systems has, in particular, caught the attention of historians.[25] Another major stream of research in the business history of fashion focuses on the growth of apparel and fashion companies from a transnational and global perspective. Business historians have analyzed the process of expansion of fashion companies since the mid-nineteenth century, demonstrating that the globalization of styles, values, and consumption has relied on a large variety of enterprises.[26] The present book builds on this scholarship. Its preparation has been possible because business historians have carried out innovative research over the past two decades. We believe it is time to offer a general synthesis of the long-term global evolution of fashion from a business history perspective.

This book follows a twofold chronological and thematic narrative. We start with a chapter that explains why the mid-nineteenth century marked a major break in the global history of the fashion business, demonstrating that the modern fashion industry was born in this context (Chapter 1). Next, we discuss the formation and development of the haute couture business model (Chapter 2) and the industrialization of clothing (Chapter 3) between the mid-nineteenth century and the interwar years. While these chapters mostly focus on Europe, the material and cultural exchanges between the West, the East, and the Rest during this same period are explored in Chapter 4. Then, Chapter 5 focuses on the emergence of a specific fashion industry in the United States. Nationalism, fascism, and the Second World War caused a major disturbance to the business history of fashion around the world, and these changes are tackled in Chapter 6. The following three chapters analyze the transformation of the apparel and fashion industries globally in the decades following the end of the war (Chapter 7), in the 1970s and 1980s (Chapter 8), and during the second globalization wave (Chapter 9). The end of the twentieth century was characterized by the extension of the scope of fashion to a broad range of industries and businesses. In Chapter 10, we explore the "fashionalization" of business through the example of sportswear. Chapter 11 offers a discussion of current issues—specifically, digitalization and sustainability—from historical and business perspectives. The final chapter sums up the book's overall conclusions.

Chapter 1

The emergence of the modern fashion business

[...] the situation of Japanese women is pitiful, for all the housework falls on their shoulders, as does the burden of serving parents and caring for children, so that the burden of Japanese women for the sake of the progress of the nation is too great to bear. If Japanese women used Singer machines, they could do in an hour the work that normally took a day. So, selling machines in Japan will not just service the cause of corporate profits, but will contribute to the advance of Japan's material civilization.[1]

The quotation above is from a report written in 1903 by Toshiyuki Hata, manager of Singer Company in Japan, to the Japanese Ministry of Agriculture and Commerce. The objective was to convince the authorities that Singer would be an excellent partner for building a modern nation by contributing to making Japanese women "good wives and wise mothers." This anecdote falls at the crossroads of multiple influences that illustrate the various dimensions of an emerging new industry in the second half of the nineteenth century: the modern fashion business. The arrival of Singer sewing machines in Japan reflects the global spread of new technologies by Western multinationals, their use by local elites to help build modern nations and their impact on local material culture. In many countries, such as Japan, Singer not only relieved women's domestic work but also played a part in changing the type of clothes people wore. This multinational contributed to the Westernization of lifestyles in Japan. And sewing machines were not just used in the home—hundreds of them equipped factories that began to mass-produce garments.

Beyond the case of the sewing machine, the Industrial Revolution, characterized by the massive production of cotton products and the development of machinery for increasing the productivity of manufacturing, had a dramatic impact on the way people consumed and wore garments. This chapter demonstrates how, in the middle of the nineteenth century, a modern fashion business emerged. It goes against the idea developed by some social scientists who argue that the expression of social identity through dresses and accessories goes back to the beginnings of civilization and was a global phenomenon from its origins.[2] The need for clothing has indeed always been a basic need of humans. Scholars have discussed the emergence of fashion as the consumption of clothes in the context of a permanent change that makes it possible to stress one's belonging to a specific social class and to distinguish oneself from other social groups. While some argue that the birth of fashion occurred in the court of Louis XIV in France, when the symbolic power of fashion was used by the French court to expand its soft power, for others, the roots of fashion go back to Italy during the late Middle Ages or even Ancient Egypt or Prehistory.[3] Discussing the beginnings of fashion is endless because it depends on the approach and the focus used by scholars for their arguments. However, considering fashion as a business, one must acknowledge that the middle of the nineteenth century represents the turning point. Modern global fashion business was formed during this period, based on the encounter between the symbolic value of fashion and the new means of production that resulted from the Industrial Revolution. It emerged as an industry organized globally but largely controlled by European entrepreneurs and firms. It relied on a fourfold transformation: the global expansion of commodity trade, technological innovation related to clothing, the standardization of sizes, and the birth of a new consumption culture. This chapter addresses the question of how these four different dimensions contributed to the formation of the modern global fashion business.

The global expansion of the commodity trade—wool, cotton, and silk

For ages, wool, cotton, and silk were the basic materials for clothing and fashion. The trade of these commodities, both in raw form and as fabrics, experienced a dramatic change in the middle of the nineteenth century, characterized by a fast-growing expansion and the extension of production networks throughout the globe. Wool, cotton, and silk perfectly embodied the advent of the first global economy.[4] However, the trade dynamic of these three commodities developed slightly differently.

From ancient times, wool had been one of the traditional natural fibers used throughout Europe for making clothes. In the Middle Ages, with the rise of sheep farming, the UK became a major producer of raw wool. Wool was notably exported to Italy and Flandres, where weavers produced fabrics and sheets. However, in the nineteenth century, the production of wool faced ecological constraints in Europe. British entrepreneurs, therefore, moved production to their colonies in Australia and New Zealand, where extensive farming was possible. Despite this increase in supply, wool fabrics and garments did not experience the big growth that cotton experienced. Low cost, large supplies, and ease of processing with machines ensured cotton's success as the main commodity for clothing during the Industrial Revolution. While cotton fabrics were used for the manufacture of clothing for the masses, wool remained more focused on pricy garments. The supply chain of wool was globalized during the second part of the nineteenth century. Large trading companies imported wool from Australia and New Zealand, as well as Pakistan and India for specific products such as cashmere, and they supplied mostly small producers based in Europe that made high-quality goods for niche markets.[5]

Cotton used to be one of the most used natural fibers for making textiles. It led to an important industry in India during the seventeenth and eighteenth centuries when Indian calico printers exported their goods to Europe. Cotton goods accounted for more than half of all commodities traded to Europe by the English EIC between 1665 and 1780.[6] The calico-printing business also started in Europe during this period, notably in Germany, Italy, Spain, and Switzerland, while some countries, like France, banned the manufacturing and sale of calico because it challenged the position of local woolen producers. The control of global trade networks and the entrepreneurship of British merchants made possible the massive import of raw cotton to the UK. In this country, the consumption of raw cotton amounted to 1 metric ton in 1750 and 24 in 1800. It grew to 267 by 1850 and 788 by 1900.[7] This was followed by several other countries in Europe and then by the United States, as the Industrial Revolution spread throughout the West. While only France had a consumption of raw cotton over 50 metric tons in 1850, in Continental Europe, five other countries passed this level fifty years later (Austria, Germany, Italy, Russia, and Spain).

Raw cotton imported to Europe came essentially from Caribbean, Brazilian, and especially American plantations, where slavery made it possible to produce high quantities cheaply. The volume of raw cotton production in the United States grew from 1.5 million pounds in 1790 to 36.5 million by 1820, and more than 2,000 million by the late 1850s.[8] By the middle of the nineteenth century, the United States had become the world's largest provider of cotton. Liverpool (UK), Bremen (Germany), and Le Havre (France) became major harbors and hubs for the distribution of raw cotton to manufacturers in the UK and mainland Europe. The Civil War in North America had a major impact on the global cotton industry. With most European manufacturers relying on imports from US plantations, the urgent need for raw cotton led merchants and local authorities to grow it in other places such as Brazil, Egypt, Turkey, and especially India.[9] Worldwide cotton production doubled from 1860 to 1890.[10]

The cotton trade was largely controlled by a few trading companies organized globally, which connected plantations, mills, and manufacturers, some of them investing directly in cotton mills, especially in India or China. Among the largest companies, there were enterprises from raw-cotton-producing centers, like the American merchant firm John Fraser & Company, from South Carolina, or Killick, Nixon & Company, founded in 1857 in Bombay, as well as importers based in Liverpool (e.g. Rathbones Brothers) and other major European ports. One can also mention the presence of global trading firms like Gebrüder Volkart, a company founded in 1851 by two Swiss brothers and established in Bombay and Winterthur, at the heart of the cotton industry in Switzerland.[11] This company extended its activities in China and Pakistan in the 1860s and became a major supplier of raw cotton to European manufacturers during the American Civil War. It transferred its headquarters to London in 1893 and, by the end of the nineteenth century, had become a major supplier of Indian cotton to Japanese spinning companies.[12] Moreover, the expansion of the worldwide trade in cotton led to the opening of a new kind of organization that provided capital to merchants through the trade of future contracts and other financial products: the New York Cotton Exchange (1869) and the New Orleans Cotton Exchange (1871).[13]

As for the consumption of silk, it had already been an important material for fashion products manufactured for the elites, especially during the Middle Ages and France's

Figure 1.1 Cotton weighers in Bombay, British India, before 1860.
Source: Johnson, W./KITLV, Leiden University Libraries.

Ancien Régime. The Silk Road was developed to answer the needs of European aristocrats and the bourgeoisie for Asian silk.[14] The consumption of silk also experienced massive development during the second half of the nineteenth century. The opening of China and Japan was the driving force behind this development. World production of silk rose in volume by about 25 percent between 1833 and 1873, then doubled by 1900, and grew again in the early twentieth century (cf. Table 1.1). Between 1833 and 1910, world production went from 8.3 to 30.1 metric tons, while a major shift from Europe to Eastern Asia took place at the same time. Italy represented more than half of world production in 1833. Its share dropped gradually to about 20 percent in the early twentieth century despite increased production after 1880. France (11.7 percent in 1833 and 2.6 percent in 1910) and India (8.3 percent in 1833 and 0.8 percent in 1910), which had facilitated access to the British market (8.3 percent in 1833 and 0.8 percent in 1910), also lost their positions.

As for China and Japan, they became the main suppliers of silk for world markets. In 1833, their presence was still insignificant. China had only 3.5 percent of world production, and Japan was still not integrated with the global economy. Forty years later, in 1873, China had become the largest producer of silk (37.5 percent of world production), far ahead of Italy, with Japan number three (13.2 percent). The forced opening of several ports after the First Opium War and the Treaty of Nanking (1842) strengthened the integration of China in the world economy and had a direct impact on the domestic silk industry, which entered a period of rapid growth. The export of silk grew from 100 tons in 1844 to

Table 1.1 World Production of Silk, Metric Tons, 1833–1910

	1833	1873	1880	1890	1900	1910
Italy	4,235	2,981	2,712	4,473	5,529	6,482
France	970	918	690	614	777	769
India	690	394	253	247	291	226
China	290	3,693	4,965	4,904	5,873	8,476
Japan	–	1,297	1,999	3,458	7,102	11,905
Others	2,135	572	659	1,047	1,463	2,281
Total	8,320	9,855	11,278	14,743	21,035	30,139

Source: Giovanni Federico. *An Economic History of the Silk Industry, 1830–1930*, vol. 5 (Cambridge: Cambridge University Press, 2009), 202.

more than 5,000 tons per year by the 1890s.[15] These volumes represented a high volume of domestic production—more than half of the total output of Chinese silk was exported in the 1880s.[16] However, during this decade, the relative position of China started to stagnate at about one-third of global production, while Japan experienced fast growth, taking the lead in the 1890s—see Table 1.1.

The development of the Japanese silk industry resulted from the actions of the Meiji government, private entrepreneurs, and foreign merchants. Silk reeling was a traditional activity going back at least to the third century and growing constantly until the end of the shogunate era and the opening of the country to global markets in the 1860s. It had, however, to be modernized to produce cost-competitive silk threads and fabrics for the world. As it did in several key sectors for the industrial development of the country, the government invested directly in the establishment of a silk mill in Tomioka, equipped with machines imported from France. It was opened in 1872 and became a model factory that showed Japanese entrepreneurs the power of modern technology. The company itself was not profitable, however, and was taken over in 1893 by Mitsui, one of the largest financial conglomerates (*zaibatsu*) in Japan at that time.[17]

Moreover, foreign merchants contributed to the modernization of the equipment through the import of machines and the action of engineers. Hence, in 1870, the Swiss merchant company Siber & Brennwald sent an engineer to Japan to introduce silk reeling machines.[18] Silk exporters knew the pressure of price on world markets and needed to improve the productivity of silk-making. Finally, since the late 1870s, most local entrepreneurs in this industry did not invest in large-scale factories. Instead, they introduced machinery in small firms and employed young girls as factory workers. A limited modernization of the equipment and the use of cheap labor became the competitive advantage of the Japanese silk industry.

The fast growth of the Japanese silk industry since 1880 relied also on a new market: the United States. Until that time, Japan had focused on the production of high-quality luxury silk for Lyon (France) silk makers, but the huge American market appeared much more promising. Manufacturers refocused on mass-produced, low-quality silk.[19] Silk then became Japan's main export good until the 1920s and consequently a major source of

Figure 1.2 Imported Silk Reeling Machine at Tsukiji in Tokyo, 1872. Japanese artist: Utagawa Yoshitora, active ca. 1850–1880. Gift of Lincoln Kirstein, 1959.
Source: The Metropolitan Museum of Art Open Access Collection.

Figure 1.3 Silk Factory in Japan, 1890.
Source: Photo by Universal History Archive/Universal Images Group via Getty Images.

foreign currency, which was needed for the economic development of the country.[20] It also had an impact on Japanese agriculture. Many farmers specialized in the production of cocoons and so benefited from the high demand for Japanese silk. This dependence on world markets was, however, not without risk. When the price of silk collapsed due to a world crisis brought on by competition from artificial fibers, Japanese agriculture entered a period of deep depression.

Box 1.1 The silk merchants Siber & Brennwald

In 1862, a few years after the forced opening of Japan to foreign trade, the Swiss government sent its first diplomatic and commercial mission to this country under the leadership of representatives of the textile and watch industries. A treaty of commerce was signed between the two countries in 1864. Caspar Brennwald (1838–1899), a young merchant who was a member of this mission, set up a joint business with the son of an entrepreneur from Zurich, who had a silk factory in Northern Italy, Hermann Siber (1842–1918). In 1865, they founded the trading company Siber & Brennwald in Yokohama, which specialized in foreign trade between Japan and Europe. It also brought Western technology to Japan, such as the first gaslight installation in the country at the port of Yokohama (1872).

One of their most traded products was Japanese silk. In 1868, the company recruited a British merchant who specialized in this field, James Walter, and had been trading for an Italian silk manufacturer. The managers and associates of Siber & Brennwald were able to build a dense network of relations with industrialists and politicians in Meiji Japan. They also contributed to the modernization of silk manufacturing and supported the introduction of machines in Japanese workshops. The first mechanized silk factory in Japan was organized in Maebashi in 1870 by a Swiss mechanist who was introduced to local producers by Hermann Siber. Siber & Brennwald benefited then from an increased supply of cheap silk. It strengthened the competitiveness and position of the firm. By 1873, it had already become the largest exporter of Japanese silk, although still only with a share of 8 percent (Ishii, 1984, p. 176). It kept its leading position during the following decades, reaching a market share of 40 percent in 1890. Many other Western silk exporters (mostly, British and Swiss) engaged in this business, but none of them was able to challenge the dominant position of Siber & Brennwald. The company also had a branch in London that became the most important intermediary between Japanese silk producers and European clients during the last third of the nineteenth century before Japanese trading companies took over this business in the early twentieth century. The control of Japan's foreign trade by national firms was considered vital for economic independence, and the government adopted various initiatives to support it.

In the early twentieth century, after this change, the company, renamed Siber, Wolff & Co. (1899) and Siber, Hegner & Co. (1910), diversified to a broad range of goods and services, becoming a general trading company. Its headquarters were destroyed during the Great Kanto Earthquake (1923), moving to Zurich in 1932 after the reorganization of the firm following a long financial crisis. It continued its global expansion in general trading, with a strong focus on Asia, after the Second World War and merged in 2002 with two other Swiss trading companies to form DKSH, a company listed on the Zurich Stock Exchange.

Source: Kanji Ishii, *Kindai Nihon to Igirisu shihon* (Tokyo: Tokyo University Press, 1984); Wolfgang Schanzenbach, "From Siber & Brennwald to DKSH Japan K.K.: More than 140 Years of Building Bridges between East and West," in *Handbuch Schweiz-Japan,* ed. Patrick Ziltener (Zurich: Chronos, 2010), 259–269.

The fast growth of commodity trade around the globe was made possible by the implementation of a worldwide communication and transportation infrastructure. Between the 1830s and 1860s, the development of a global telegraph system, based on electric telegraphs, Morse code, and transatlantic cables, contributed to the creation of a worldwide market and the unification of prices. The total length of submarine cables increased from 4.400 kilometers in 1865 to more than 400,000 in 1903.[21] Investors and traders could know nearly instantly the price of cotton and silk in any market. As for transportation, the shipping industry, dominated by British firms, experienced huge growth, particularly after the development of steamships in the 1830s and the opening of the Suez Canal in 1869, when it became faster and cheaper to export commodities. In 1911, the world's fourteen largest shipping companies included nine British companies, two German, two French, and one Japanese. These companies played a major role in the supply of wool, raw cotton, and silk to European and Japanese textile manufacturers.[22] In Japan, the development of the cotton-spinning industry during the last decades of the nineteenth century led in 1893 to the opening of a direct shipping liaison between Osaka and Bombay.[23] Finally, institutional changes made the formation of a global economy possible. Free trade, following the end of the monopoly of the Dutch (1796) and the British (1833) EICs, and the spread of bilateral agreements after the Cobden-Chevallier agreement (1860), as well as the adoption of the gold standard, which spread from Britain to the European Continent and the rest of the world, set up an institutional order that favored the formation of the first global economy. All these institutional and technological changes were dominated by Western nations and companies. These were also the main drivers for modern imperialism, the scramble for African and Asian markets, and the beginning of the spread of Western fashion to the rest of the world.

Technological innovation—textile machinery, sewing machines, and artificial colors

The Industrial Revolution had, of course, a major impact on the development of the global fashion industry. Industrialization in the UK, and later, in Continental Europe and the United States, and then throughout the world, started with the growth of the textile industry. Textile machinery, sewing machines, and artificial colors embodied the influence of the Industrial Revolution on fashion.

At first, textile machinery had an impact on the productivity and growth of production volumes in the textile industry. More and cheaper fabrics could be manufactured thanks to the conception and improvement of new kinds of machines. Ring spinning machines were developed in the United States in the 1830s and revolutionized cotton spinning, and weaving machines were gradually developed during the first third of the nineteenth century in the UK after the invention of the power loom by Edmund Cartwright (1743–1823) in 1785. The production of fabrics was also boosted by the development of the mechanical Jacquard loom. Produced in France in 1804 and improved over the following years, it used punched cards to automatize the manufacture of yarn with specific designs.

Punched cards enabled the mass production of changing fashion designs.[24] Introduced in Lyon workshops, it caused one of the first social movements against the industrialization of textiles. French workers revolted several times in the 1830s against the use of machinery and destroyed Jacquard looms.[25] The production of textile machinery led to the emergence and growth of large and powerful corporations, such as the British firms Platt Brothers (founded in 1770), John Hetherington & Sons (1830) and Howard & Bullough (1856), the Sulzer Brothers in Switzerland (1834), and Mason Machine Works in the United States (1845).[26] Platt Brothers was considered the world's largest textile machinery company in the mid-nineteenth century. It employed several thousand workers and played a key role in the transfer of technology related to textile machinery to many countries, including India, Japan, and Norway.[27]

The second technology to have a major impact on the growth of the global fashion industry in the mid-nineteenth century is the sewing machine. It was co-developed during the 1850s by a group of American entrepreneurs who shared a patent pool.[28] Among the companies that launched this new business, the most successful was undoubtedly the Singer Machine Company (see Box 1.2). The roots of this company go back to the firm founded by Isaac M. Singer (1811–1875) in New York in 1851. It adopted the mass-production system in the 1860s and opened a plant in Glasgow, Scotland, in 1867. This boosted the number of machines manufactured every year, going from 883 in 1855 to 127,833 in 1870 and around 500,000 in 1880.[29] In 1905, Singer employed some 30,000 workers in its eight factories around the world. They mass-produced standardized models, which were then distributed by a huge sales force: more than 60,000 people

Figure 1.4 Two Young Boys Climbing on Spinning Frame to Mend Broken Threads and Put Back Empty Bobbins, Bibb Mill No. 1, Macon, Georgia, USA, Lewis Hine for National Child Labor Committee, January 1909.
Source: Photo by GHI/Universal Images Group via Getty Images.

working in more than 4,000 sales branches.[30] Moreover, Singer was an innovative company in the development of new marketing techniques. In each country where it was implanted, it employed many salesmen and women who visited homes and gave customers credit in order to increase sales. Sewing machines had a threefold impact on the formation of a global fashion industry. First, these machines diffused new ways to manufacture clothes in households throughout the world. As it was easier to make new garments using a sewing machine than doing it by hand, the working class started to change their clothes more often and adopt new colors, shapes, and materials. The sewing machine had made fashion accessible to the masses. Second, these machines contributed to the diffusion of Western fashion around the globe, particularly in East Asia, where sewing was not an important part of the process of making traditional clothes, as it was in Japan with kimonos. It thus accompanied cultural change. Thirdly, sewing machines were also developed for clothing companies. Introduced into factories, they boosted the productivity of manufacturing garments and hence made possible the industrial production of cheap clothes for the masses.

Box 1.2 The global expansion of the Singer Sewing Machine Corporation (1851–1914)

The company Singer & Co. was founded in 1851 by Isaac Singer (1811–1875) and renamed Singer Machine Corporation in 1865. Isaac was an inventor and entrepreneur who engaged in various firms after working as an actor for a few years. Aged 40, he obtained a patent for a sewing machine and focused on this new business. It was the first firm to implement mass-production methods for manufacturing sewing machines. The "Family" model, developed in 1865, enjoyed huge success. It was improved over the following decades but did not fundamentally change, becoming the basis for mass production and distribution.

Singer expanded first in the American market but soon opened branch offices in France (1855), Scotland (1856), Brazil (1858), and Germany (1863). These branches were important for supervising the import and distribution of sewing machines outside America. The second stage of internationalization was the opening of factories abroad. The first attempt to relocate production was made in 1855. Four years after the founding of the firm, Singer planned to open a factory in Paris, but this project was aborted for unknown reasons. Singer's first successful foreign direct investment was realized in Scotland, with the opening of a large manufacturing facility in Glasgow (1867). Other overseas factories were then opened in Canada (1882), Austria (1882), Russia (1902), and Prussia (1904).

At the same time, the sales network extended throughout the globe, from South America to East Asia. In 1890, Singer had about 80 percent of the world market for sewing machines. This expansion relied heavily on a global selling organization. Singer built a broad network of shops and warehouses in all countries where it was installed. Its salesmen visited homes and sold machines to individual households.

At the Centennial Exhibition of Philadelphia, Singer dispatched women to show the public the various kinds of products they could make with a sewing machine. As put by Paula de la Cruz-Fernandez, "Rather than highlighting mass manufacturing of clothing, Singer maintained its preference to display how and what women sewed and embroidered for private purposes" (2020, p. 412). The company worked together with "Singer women"—that is, female sales workers who showed consumers what kinds of new products it was possible to manufacture with these machines, such as embroidery and house linens. Singer also organized sewing schools, mostly within its own shops, in many countries, where young girls could learn how to use such machines. Global marketing was supervised by Singer's headquarters, where an embroidery department was established in the 1890s. This business contributed to changing the culture of sewing and clothing around the world. Until the Second World War, Singer had no localization strategy. It sold its goods anywhere, along with the cultural image linked to them: "good wife and wise mother sewing for the family" (Gordon, 2012, p. 63). In countries like India and Japan, where sewing had been until then an activity carried out by men, it became a female activity.

Source: Andrew Godley, *Fabricating Consumers: The Sewing Machine in Modern Japan* (Berkeley: University of California Press, 2012); Paula de la Cruz-Fernandez, "Manufacturing and the Importance of Global Marketing," in *The Routledge Companion to the Makers of Global Business*, eds Teresa da Silva Lopes, Christina Lubinski and Heidi J. S. Tworek (New York: Routledge, 2020), 410–423.

Figure 1.5 Advertising for Singer Machines, 1892.
Source: Bibliothèque Nationale de France.

Finally, the development of artificial dyes was another major technological innovation. It drastically extended the range of colors available for making clothes and had a huge impact on the development of fashion. The first artificial color was a synthetized mauve, discovered accidentally in 1856 at the Royal College of Chemistry in London by a student, Henri William Perkin, who used coal tar to manufacture gas for streetlamps.[31] He cofounded with his father and brother the company G. F. Perkin & Sons.[32] Following the development of the synthetic organic chemical industry, a large number of new artificial colors were invented during the second part of the century. The total number of artificial dyes on the market was lower than fifty before 1870; by 1913, there were about 1,300.[33] Most of them were developed during the 1880s and 1890s. German companies took the lead in this new business.[34] Competition was, however, fierce. As companies had to make large investments in research and production facilities, only a handful of firms dominated the industry. In 1907, the six largest employed around 90 percent of the workforce, among which were three giants: BASF, Hoechst, and Bayer. In 1925, they merged into IG Farben, one of the world's largest chemical companies, which engaged primarily in the production of artificial dyes (*Farben* means "color" in German). These firms employed hundreds of engineers and chemists to supervise R&D and production. There was also some production in the UK and particularly in Switzerland, where some firms (Ciba and Geigy) copied German innovations as patent application was not possible for chemical processes in Switzerland until 1907.

Artificial dyes were used by manufacturers of fabrics throughout the world to diversify their supplies to customers. Japan is a case in point. Several silk manufacturers started using imported artificial dyes to strengthen their competitiveness against imported fabrics. The ability to respond quickly to changes in consumer tastes was important.[35] The new colors made it possible to produce cheap fashion for the urban middle classes. As soon as Japan opened to foreign trade, silk producers imported new dyes. In 1864, they started importing natural dyes from China, gradually shifting to chemical goods, mostly from Germany but also from Switzerland, the UK, France, and Belgium. This trade grew in the 1880s and became standard practice in the 1890s. Aniline was the most widely exported dye; 78.4 tons was exported to Japan in 1880, rising to 223 tons in 1890 and 645 in 1897.[36] The use of artificial dyes, however, was not uniformly adopted throughout Japan. The most enthusiastic districts, such as Isesaki and Tokamachi, enjoyed subsequent growth thanks to their repositioning in luxury fashion, while reluctant districts entered a period of stagnation or even decline.[37]

Finally, one must stress that the development of artificial colors had a major social impact that went far beyond the apparel industry. It contributed to shaping a new consumption society during the interwar years. The historian Blaszczyk talks about a "color revolution" driven by chemical firms. Moreover, color advisors appeared in the United States during the 1920s as consultants from the chemical industry (color producers) to the manufacturing industry (consumers of colors). General Motors was among the first and established an Art and Color Section in 1926.[38] The manufacturers of home electric appliances and furniture followed this trend. The multiplication of artificial colors developed by the chemical industry was also one of the reasons for the emergence of fashion forecasting in the United States during and after the First World War. Various actors that were engaged in chemicals, textile, and apparel companies started to gather to discuss color forecasting.[39]

Standardization of sizes

The transformation of the clothing industry and the expansion of fashion for the masses did not result only from technological innovation. Apart from new machinery, one must emphasize the determinant role played by the adoption of standard sizes. The idea of dividing a specific population, usually at the national level, into various-sized groups made possible the industrialization of garment production.[40] Standardization enabled mass production. This principle is not unique to the clothing industry—it can be broadly observed in the manufacturing industry since the mid-nineteenth century.[41] However, in the fashion industry, differentiation through color, shape, or material limited the scope of standardization. Rather than mass production, batch production was implemented in industrial firms.

The practice of producing standardized garments can be traced back to the manufacturing of military uniforms. This was the origin of the ready-to-wear industry—like armories gave birth to mass-production methods in fine mechanics. The manufacturing of standardized uniforms was attested already at the end of the seventeenth century in southern England and developed throughout the eighteenth century.[42] In the United States, one of the oldest clothing factories is the US Army Clothing Establishment, founded in Philadelphia in 1812.[43] However, outside the military, the demand for ready-to-wear clothes was limited until the mid-nineteenth century and did not lead to standardization. Hence, military production played a major role in the adoption of a mass-production system in garment manufacturing. The case of Japan shows a clear continuity between the production of uniforms for the army during the Pacific War and the growth of a domestic industry in Western clothing after 1945 (see Chapter 6).

The first attempts to adopt standardized sizes for civilian clothes can be observed in the UK during the 1840s. The first-mover entrepreneurs were mostly sellers of second-hand clothes who understood the new demand of customers for ready-to-wear garments. They invested in production technology and engaged in the manufacturing of standardized goods. The tailor E. Moses & Son, based in Aldgate, was a pioneer and became one of the largest British apparel manufacturers.[44] The company opened its first shop in East London in 1829 and experienced fast growth, becoming the largest clothing outlet in England by 1846. Its expansion continued throughout the UK over the following decades, the company becoming established as a major men's fashion retailer by using new marketing techniques. Laura Jones argues that "E. Moses and Son significantly contributed to a process of democratization within men's fashion during the period, by providing affordable, accessible and desirable clothing for a mass market."[45] The success of this company relied essentially on its network of a few large stores, the definition of a clear target (men from lower and middle classes), and intense advertising campaigns in newspapers. They also invested massively in advertising to support the growing demand of the urbanized middle class for ready-to-wear clothes. In the mid-nineteenth century, apparel producers were among the largest advertising spenders in the UK.[46]

In 1860, E. Moses & Son published a small leaflet arguing that the company was "the first House in London, or, we may say, in the World, that established the system of New Clothing Ready-made."[47] They explained that the high price of handmade suits and clothes limited the scope of the market and that reducing the unit price through standardization expanded the market and met a demand unanswered until then:

> We filled large store-rooms with cheap and new ready-made clothes, quite as well finished as those made to order at the most fashionable houses in town. Our prices, both in the ready-made and bespoke departments of our establishments, were so low as to excite universal astonishment; and perhaps it was at first suspected, that really good articles could not possibly be supplied on such terms. [. . .] Now eighty percent of the population purchase ready-made clothing, because the prejudice against it has been conquered by the reputation of our firm. Thousands of tailors have followed our example.[48]

The adoption of ready-to-wear production methods was made possible by the emergence in the early nineteenth century of a new way to consider the human body. Geometry, numbers, and body measurement were the basic tools of tailors. Now, they started following a scientific approach based on mathematics and standards. Pattern-cutting manuals and specific tools like inch tapes were developed in the 1820s and 1830s.[49] In the middle of the century, some Jewish entrepreneurs launched new businesses based on the industrial application of this new way to make clothes. They started and soon dominated the ready-to-wear industry, which became known in the UK in 1889 as "Jewish tailoring."[50] The success of Jewish entrepreneurs arose notably from the Haskalah, an intellectual movement that emerged in the eighteenth century in Germany that encouraged the adoption of scientific and modern ideas to consider both religion and secular applications.[51] One of these Jewish tailors in the UK was Elias Moses.

The E. Moses & Son model was followed in Continental Europe. In Paris, Pierre Parissot, a mercer who opened his first store in 1824 and founded the chain store *A La Belle Jardinière,* engaged in manufacturing and employed hundreds of tailors at home. By the mid-nineteenth century, thousands of tailors were working for ready-to-wear companies in large cities like Berlin, London, and Paris.[52] The apparel industry took various forms throughout Europe and contributed strongly to the spread of fashion for the masses (see Chapter 3).

New consumption temples—department stores

Finally, the birth of a global fashion industry in the middle of the nineteenth century resulted from the emergence and diffusion of a new kind of outlet in large cities: department stores. Targeting consumers from the urban middle and upper classes, department stores offered a broad range of products, from fashion to dry goods, furniture, and household accessories, which were displayed and labeled with a fixed price. These "palaces of consumption" had electric lights. They offered all the goods manufactured by modern industry and embodied a new culture of consumption. Moreover, customers did not only enter department stores to buy something, as they would a tailor shop or a general store—seeing and being seen in these places was also part of the experience. Shopping became a new form of entertainment, and department stores played a major role in this new trend.[53]

The exact moment these new kinds of stores in European cities appeared is still debated by historians, some of them observing similar patterns of stores in London in the early eighteenth century.[54] However, modern department stores appeared in Western cities in the middle of the nineteenth century. Harrods, in London (1834), Bainbridge's, in Newcastle (1838), Au Bon Marché, in Paris (1838), and Macy's, in New York (1858) are commonly considered the promoters of the new urban consumer culture.

The Parisian store Au Bon Marché is undoubtedly one of the most famous, particularly because it inspired French novelist Emile Zola in the writing of his book *Au Bonheur des Dames*, published in 1883.[55] Au Bon Marché was at first a boutique of dry stores, opened by two brothers, Paul and Justin Videau, in Paris in 1838. In 1852, a new associate joined the firm: Aristide Boucicaut. Born in Normandie in 1810, Boucicaut started his career as an independent peddler and settled in Paris in 1835, working for various stores. When he joined the brothers Videau, Au Bon Marché was just a small store with only twelve employees and four departments. He made it France's first department store and took over the company alone in 1863. When Boucicaut died, in 1877, Au Bon Marché was considered the largest retail enterprise in the world. It employed more than 1,700 people and gross sales amounted to

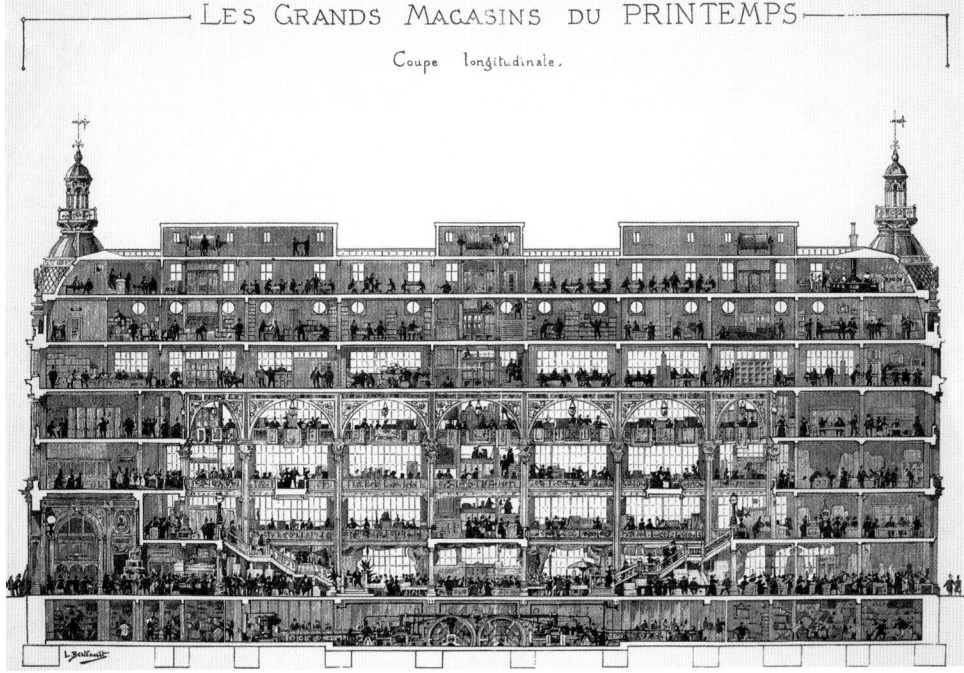

Figure 1.6 Printemps Department Store in Paris, France Nineteenth Century.
Source: Photo by DeAgostini/Getty Images.

73 million francs.[56] His widow, Marguerite Boucicaut, continued managing the store until her own death in 1887—that year, Au Bon Marché had more than 3,100 employees and gross sales of 123 million francs.[57] The company was continued by French investor Bernard Arnault in 1984 before being taken over by the financial group Agache-Willot in 1970.

Boucicaut was an innovator. He transformed the concept of the store and adopted a new retailing model based on an extremely wide range of products, fixed prices with low margins, and displays that made customers feel like buying. He also attracted female consumers through intensive advertising campaigns and sending out millions of catalogs. He also developed mail-order sales, including to foreign markets, which contributed largely to the success of Au Bon Marché. Mail-order sales grew from 5 million francs in 1871–72 (15 percent of gross sales) to 33.3 million in 1902–03 (17.5 percent).[58] Finally, the diversification of goods offered was a major basis for the growth of the firm. Boucicaut organized many new departments—a total of thirty-six in the early 1880s.[59] Regarding clothing and fashion, a ready-to-wear department was added in the 1860s. It started with cloaks, overcoats, shirts, and ties and expanded to prêt-à-porter in the 1880s.[60] However, Bon Marché did not have its own manufacturing facilities for all its production. The company had a few workshops to produce specific items, like coats, cloaks, skirts, and blouses, and relied for other goods on the numerous small workshops that developed throughout Paris during the second half of the nineteenth century.[61]

The new business model developed by Boucicaut, similar to what appeared at the same time at Harrods in London or Macy's in New York, for example, was so successful that it was adopted by many other entrepreneurs, both in the same cities and elsewhere in the world. In Paris, for example, one can mention the opening of the department stores Printemps (1865), La Samaritaine (1869), and Galeries Lafayette (1893). The French model was also exported to other large European cities, like Milan, in Italy. In this city, the brothers Bocconi founded a store in 1865, which was renamed Alle Città d'Italia in 1880 and La Rinascente in 1917. It opened branches throughout the country and became a major place for the diffusion of ready-to-wear fashion.[62] French department stores also became a model in Central and Eastern Europe. Austrian Jews copied and adapted this kind of outlet in Vienna and other cities of the Austro-Hungarian Empire. The process was similar in Russia, the Ottoman Empire, and the Middle East.[63] The over-representation of Jewish entrepreneurs in the department store business resulted from a combination of factors, including historical restrictions on other professions, a tradition of commerce and trade within Jewish communities, and their innovative approaches to retail.[64]

In Eastern Asia, department stores also played a major role in the diffusion of new consumption habits and, more specifically, introduced European fashion to culturally different places. This was particularly the case in East Asia. In Japan, they contributed to the introduction and diffusion of modern consumer culture, particularly Western fashion, since the late nineteenth century.[65] Japanese department stores have a long history, linked to the development of an urban culture in Edo (Tokyo). Several dry goods stores, where people could come and buy various products, were opened during the seventeenth century, the

The emergence of the modern fashion business 23

most famous being Mitsukoshi (1673) and Daimaru (1717). They had cooperative arrangements with silk producers and supplied wealthy customers with high-end silk draperies for their kimonos. However, until the end of the nineteenth century, these stores were closed to common people. They had no window displays and were only open to people who were going to buy something. In 1895, under the management of a new director who had studied in the United States, Mitsukoshi was the first to introduce Western sales innovations like window displays and opening the store to the public. Other dry goods stores quickly followed this example. In the 1900s, they adopted the same organization and management as American and Western department stores. Mitsukoshi took Harrods, for example, as a model. Moreover, these stores started at the same time to diversify their merchandise and offer a broad range of imported goods, from cosmetics to clothing and accessories. During the first half of the twentieth century, they became key actors in introducing European fashion, and this role continued after the Second World War (see Chapter 7).[66]

Figure 1.7 Cover for Shanghai Manhua, July 1, 1928.
Source: Public Domain. MCLC Resource Center via Wikimedia Commons.

As for China, the emergence and expansion of the first department stores took a path strongly different from Japan's.[67] They did not follow the model of the transformation of traditional outlets. They were rather the creation of Western entrepreneurs who were established in the international settlements following the First Opium War and the Treaty of Nanking (1842). They opened department stores first for the foreign community living in the settlements. During the second half of the nineteenth century, Hall & Holtz was opened in Hong Kong and Shanghai, while Weeks & Co. had an outlet in Shanghai. Together with a few other foreign-owned companies, they controlled the department store business in China until the First World War but then lost their competitiveness due to the emergence of new generations of department stores organized and controlled by Chinese entrepreneurs who started businesses abroad and were keen on coming back home. Their companies, like Sincere, a department store founded in Hong Kong in 1900 by Ma Ying Piu, started to dominate upmarket retail during the interwar years and took the form of a diversified conglomerate. They played a major role in the distribution of fashion and luxury in Hong Kong throughout the twentieth century.

Conclusion

There is no specific event or turning point that made fashion a global business in the middle of the nineteenth century. Rather, one can observe a conjunction of very different but interrelated factors that transformed the way companies manufactured clothes and the individuals who consumed them. The spread of Western fashion was a result of the first global economy, based on a communication and transportation revolution and major institutional innovations. The globalization of commodity trade (cotton and silk), technological innovations related to the Industrial Revolution, the standardization of sizes, and the birth of ready-to-wear, as well as the development of department stores in large urban centers, all contributed to the formation of a global fashion system.

The notion of the emergence of a modern, global fashion system is clearly embodied in the world exhibitions, at which new actors in the global fashion industry were present and active. Artificial dyes and sewing machines stood alongside Japanese silk and textile machinery. The most important world exhibitions for culture and industry became popular in the mid-nineteenth century (London 1851; Paris 1855; Vienna 1873; Philadelphia 1876), where the cosmopolitan bourgeoisie, which included the owners of factories, bankers, art lovers, and professors, could exhibit technological progress and new products. Fashion had become one of the tools of Western domination across the world. European and American companies dominated the value chain of fashion production, from the trading companies that controlled the export of wool, cotton, and silk to the producers of artificial dyes and the manufacturers of ready-to-wear garments. Consumption of fashion also became driven by new practices, such as shopping in department stores, that appeared in American and European capitals. Finally, high-end fashion was an individual instrument that enabled the cosmopolitan elites in the imperial capitals to demonstrate their power, status, and wealth.

Chapter 2

The rise of haute couture or high-end fashion

The ensemble of dresses is very rich this winter, I might even say that it is more sumptuous than elegant, and that the women clothe themselves with too many ornaments of all kinds. They lose their grace under this accumulation of lace, gold and silver, mixed with flowers and jewels; in adopting the fashions of the Ancien Régime, they should have done away with what was heavy and overloaded. It seems to me that with a mind as shrewd as that which distinguishes French women, they should have taken from the old customs only what was good about them; for example, the costume of the old women of the Ancien Régime had the great advantage, for them, of not being in any way similar to that of young women: an immense advantage, since it did not allow us to establish a point of comparison that was always unfavourable to the former.[1]

Beyond the critic addressing the clothing habits of women, this quotation from an article published in 1838 in the French fashion and lifestyle magazine *Journal des Dames et des Modes* reminds us that fashion and dressing before the French Revolution were not the result of individual choice. The people had to follow strict rules and social codification. Since the end of the seventeenth century, the French magazine *Le Mercure Galant*, founded in 1672 and considered one of the earliest fashion publications, advised its readers of how best to dress in accordance with one's status.[2] Innovation and change in matter of style, color, and material were not impossible but had to fit within social margins—so there was no *fashion* in the modern sense.

The couturiers who worked at the French court, for example, were not fashion creators. They did not propose new styles and dresses but fulfilled their customers' requests, who understood perfectly when and how to follow, or not, the etiquette. The most famous *modiste* in pre-revolutionary France was Rose Bertin (1747–1813). She worked mainly for Madame Pompadour (1721–1764), the chief mistress of Louis XV, and Queen Marie Antoinette (1755–1793), Louis XVI's wife. Bertin became famous beyond French borders when she opened a store in London in the 1780s.[3] Although she was nicknamed "the fashion minister" at the French court, Rose Bertin was not a creator—she responded to the demands of her clients.

Moreover, the sumptuary laws in Europe had the objective to struggle against the social diffusion of dressing practices, particularly the adoption by the populace and the middle class of dressing styles inspired by the aristocracy. The objective of these laws,

Figure 2.1 Marie-Antoinette Josèphe Jeanne (1755–1793), Queen of France, engraving after a design by Jean-Michel Moreau le Jeune (1741–1814); engraver unknown.
Source: Pairs Musées / Carnavalet Museum, History of Paris.

which was religious in origin, shifted to maintaining social order during the eighteenth century.[4] Then, although the French Revolution abolished privilege, its impact on the social consumption of fashion was very limited, and dressing continued to be a way of expressing social order and one's individual position in it.[5] Outside Europe, dressing also followed strict rules as an expression of social status and position. During the Edo period in Japan, for example, sumptuary laws limited the use of specific materials to certain social groups. Wearing silk was forbidden to non-samurais,[6] for example, and the design of kimonos and other clothes expressed clear social status.

A major change occurred in Paris in the middle of the nineteenth century under the influence of a British couturier usually celebrated as the inventor of haute couture, Charles Frederick Worth (1825–1895). Although he was not alone in this new industry, he built an innovative business model in dressmaking for women and ran the largest fashion enterprise in Paris. Worth was the first "fashion dictator" in the sense that he was a creator who made dresses without hearing the requests of customers. He became the benchmark of fashion in Paris and the Western world at a time when the French capital was the largest and most vibrant city in Continental Europe. Hence, the objective of this chapter is to discuss how haute couture emerged as a business in the middle of the nineteenth century and continued to operate until the Second World War.

The inventor of a new business: Charles Frederick Worth

The entrepreneur who created a new business model based on the creation of dresses was a tailor born in 1825 in the UK.[7] In 1838, Charles Frederick Worth started an apprenticeship at the draper Swan & Edgar, in London, specializing in the sales of fabrics to women from the middle class and the aristocracy who wanted to make dresses themselves.[8] After his apprenticeship, he worked for about a year for the silk mercer Lewis & Allenby, also in London. These businesses were fast expanding, in the context of a developing urban consumption society. Worth benefited from working during his youth in the "retailing revolution."[9] Learning about fabrics and consumers would guide him in organizing his new business in Paris, where he understood which dresses had to be developed to catch the attention of his wealthy customers.

In 1845, Worth decided to cross the Channel and try his luck in Paris. He was engaged as a sales assistant by Maison Gagelin-Opigez & Cie, a draper who specialized in luxury fabrics, particularly silk from Lyon. However, Worth did not limit himself to selling fabrics. He started making dresses for a salesgirl of the company, Marie Vernet, who later became his wife. These creations attracted the attention of his clients, which led Worth to ask his employers to open a small dressmaking workshop. At first, they refused, considering dressmaking unsuited to luxury haberdashery. However, as there was a growing demand for such creations, Gagelin finally allowed Worth to engage in designing dresses.[10]

Figure 2.2 Anglo-French costumier and dress designer Charles Frederick Worth (1825–1895).
Source: Photo by Hulton Archive/Getty Images.

Worth met with great success. He won awards for his innovative designs at the World Fairs in London in 1851 and Paris in 1855. Meanwhile, in 1853, he become Gagelin's partner. The fast growth of his dressmaking business led, however, to tensions between the partners. In 1858, Worth founded his own enterprise with the Swedish financier Otto Gustav Bobergh (1821–1882), who had been, like Worth, a sales assistant in several draper companies throughout Europe. While Worth focused on creation and production, Bobergh took on finance and administrative tasks. The Worth–Bobergh partnership embodied the international dimension of the fashion business at the time, as well as the role immigrants played in the manufacture of high fashion. At the same time, it showed off the golden combination of creativity and business acumen. Haute couture was thus transnational and related to finance from its beginnings.

Worth & Bobergh was a very successful enterprise. Five years after its foundation, in 1863, it employed about 700 workers and had a turnover of 20 million francs (about 60 million euros in 2020).[11] The number of employees increased further to 1,200 in 1870.[12] This rapid expansion essentially relied on the demand from women of the aristocracy and the new bourgeoisie, who lived in an age of economic expansion during Napoleon III's Second Empire (1852–1870). Worth's wife and former model, Marie Augustine Vernet (1825–1898), was the link to the French Empress Eugénie, a Spanish beauty with a passion for fashion.[13] Marie Vernet was at least as entrepreneurial as her husband (see Box 2.1). Finally, in 1864,

Figure 2.3 Evening ensemble, French, 1887. Artist Charles Frederick Worth.
Source: Photo by Heritage Art/Heritage Images via Getty Images.

Worth became even the exclusive supplier of official garments to Empress Eugénie. He gained a great international reputation after dressing the Tsarina of Russia, the Queen of Italy, the Empress of Austria, and Victoria, Queen of England. French writer Emile Zola wrote that Worth was the couturier "in front of whom the queens of the Second Empire kneeled."[14] This was a strategy to enlarge the customer base: dressing the best-known women in Paris and abroad was a way to make Worth's creations known and famous. Worth & Bobergh also adopted a marketing strategy that enabled answering the demands of an international clientele. For example, they employed British sales girls to communicate with wealthy American and British customers in Paris.[15] Moreover, the cooperation with department stores in the United States and the UK, as well as advertisements in foreign fashion magazines such as *Harper's Bazaar*, supported the internationalization of Worth's creations.[16] Thus, from the very beginning of haute couture, the fashion media contributed to the fame of the creators.

In 1870–1871, at the end of the Second Empire, the revolutionary Commune in Paris and the Third Republic were a major shock to French and European aristocracies and a challenge for business, which relied intensively on supplying goods to these people. Bobergh did not believe in a possible continuation of business in France. The partnership he had signed with Worth in 1858 came to an end in July 1870, and he decided not to renew it. He went back to Sweden in 1872 and offered financial support to the first Swedish couturier established in Stockholm, Augusta Lundin (1840–1919). He died in 1882.[17]

Worth continued the company, together with his two sons, Gaston-Lucien (1874), for the management, and Jean-Philippe (1875), for the creation. After the fall of the Second Empire, a Second Republic was proclaimed in France on 4 September 1870. The republican regime, however, did not put an end to luxury consumption. Women from the wealthy bourgeoisie and social elite in Paris and from elsewhere in Europe replaced aristocrats from the imperial court, and the firm continued to flourish. Moreover, the new industrial and financial bourgeoisie in American cities of the East Coast, shopping in department stores, also became important consumers. When he died in 1895, Charles Frederick Worth was the uncontested leader of the haute couture industry in Paris and the world.

The success of Worth was not the mere outcome of his talent to design dresses with a style that attracted the envy of his clients. He was a businessman who implemented several innovations that made his company particularly competitive. At first, he transformed the status of the dressmaker from that of an anonymous craftsman to a designer whose name and taste mattered. Worth was one of the first to label his fashion items, which can be seen as the beginning of branding, or, at least, as the expression of his understanding that his name embodied luxury fashion. As mentioned earlier, Worth did not answer requests from his clients but created dresses that he then offered in his shop. He can be seen as one of the first celebrity designers, as a fashion tastemaker or "fashion dictator" as some authors have argued.[18] Moreover, he understood the need to organize the profession, setting the foundation for the institutionalization of fashion. As we will discuss below, many other dressmakers followed his example and opened fashion houses. To defend their common interests, these designers, led by Charles Frederic Worth, founded in 1868 a trade association, the *Chambre Syndicale de la Couture, des Confectionneurs et des Tailleurs pour Dames*, which became the *Chambre Syndicale de la Couture Parisienne*.

Worth's second strength was his extensive knowledge of textiles and fabrics, owing to his training and first years of business in London and Paris. As his fashion department was within a mercer shop, he was able to meet and get to know representatives from the Lyon silk mills.[19] He was able not only to order fabrics but also to let manufacturers know what he wanted regarding materials, patterns, and colors. The textile producers met his demands and started producing what Worth wanted. Hence, he had a direct influence on fabrics. Women working as dressmakers in Paris did not have this direct relationship with manufacturers.[20] Moreover, Worth used new technology to improve the speed of production and enlarge the possibility of quickly changing a fashion: the sewing machine. He used sewing machines made by Singer and other manufacturers to streamline production. His workers produced interchangeable components of dresses like sleeves or bodices, which were then assembled with other pieces of fabrics to form a dress. Worth also extensively used synthetic dyes.[21] He had a modern business model equipped with the latest technology.

Third, Worth was the first to have the idea to ask young women to wear his creations to show them off to clients. His first model was his beautiful wife, Marie Vernet. He wanted to present his dresses in a realistic atmosphere so that customers could imagine how they could wear them, and not just show them on poor young men or fashion dolls, called *mannequins*.[22] Worth's female models are considered the first live models in fashion history. His wife Marie also used to wear his latest creations when attending receptions and dinners in Paris.

Finally, Worth consciously adopted a luxury position in the fashion industry. He did not base the price of goods on the calculation of raw materials and hours of work. Instead, he intentionally set astronomical prices for his dresses to create and emphasize a distance between women who could afford to purchase them and women who could not. At the same time, adopting prices much higher than other couturiers in Paris positioned him at the top of luxury fashion and legitimated him as the best representative of haute couture. Being very expensive was a way to strengthen his prestige among wealthy customers.[23]

On Charles Frederick Worth's death in 1895, the company was valued at about 50 million francs (about 150 million euros in 2020).[24] His two sons, Gaston (1853–1924) and Jean-Philippe (1856–1926), continued the company and pursued the strategy adopted by their father. However, the firm entered a period of stagnation and decline after 1900 due to growing competition from other couturiers and a change in consumer tastes under the influence of modern art and entertainment. The Worth brothers focused on traditional elites and did not understand much about social change. For example, in 1901, they employed Paul Poiret (1879–1944), a promising young couturier, aged 22, who had worked previously for a few years for the couturier Jacques Doucet (1853–1929). He had an innovative style characterized by the creation of more comfortable dresses for women. This led to tensions with Jean-Philippe Worth, who pursued the traditional style of his father. Poiret decided to leave and set up his own business in 1903. He became one of the promoters of Art Deco and one of the most prominent couturiers during the first decades of the twentieth century.[25]

The company was taken over in 1920–1921 by Gaston's two sons, Jean-Charles (1881–1962) and Jacques (1882–1941), who transformed the family business into a stock company in 1926: Worth SA.[26] It was taken over by the fourth generation in 1936. The company had, however, lost its pre-eminence in Paris haute couture. Maison Paquin, who had already purchased Worth's branch in London in the 1940s, took over the entire firm in 1954. However, financial difficulties led to the closure of Paquin and Worth in Paris in 1956 and of the London branch of Worth in 1967.[27] Endeavors to reawaken the "sleeping beauty" had, for now, failed.[28]

Box 2.1 The birth of fashion models

Charles Frederick Worth is considered the first couturier to use live models to show his creations to customers. When he worked at Maison Gagelin-Opigez & Cie, in Paris, he asked some shop assistants to wear his dresses. He married one of them, Marie Vernet. Born in 1825, she is often considered the first fashion model in history. She entered Gagelin in her twenties and worked as a *demoiselle de magasin*. She oversaw wearing shawls and mantles to be sold to wealthy customers and worked especially for Worth, becoming his wife in 1851. She was not only his model but also an entrepreneurial business partner. She attended lots of public events in Paris dressed in her husband's latest designs and created linkages to the Imperial Court.

The fashion show was a practice that started after 1910 in Paris. Shows were organized four times a year for journalists, private clients, and important buyers like the representatives of department stores. The Winter collection, presented in August, was the most important event of the year, during which new trends were made public. Some shows were held in famous department stores, like Le Printemps. In this context, couturiers used more and more models. In the mid-1920s, Jean Patou employed a total of 32 girls, and, when he sailed to New York, he recruited six American models to show his creations.

Providing models to couture houses became a business during the interwar years. It appeared in the United States in relation to the development of Hollywood. The American actor John Robert Powers (1892–1977) opened the first modelling school in New York in 1923 and started working for fashion shows in the early 1930s. Other companies were created in the following years, the most known being the Ford Model Agency founded in 1946. Fashion, theatre, movies, and commerce were intimately linked during these years. These agencies contributed to making the American beauty a global standard.

Source: Diana de Marty, *The History of Haute Couture, 1850–1950* (Manchester: Anchor Press, 1980); Veronique Pouillard, "Design Piracy in the Fashion Industries of Paris and New York in the Interwar Years," *Business History Review* 85.2 (2011): 331–337; Joanne Entwistle and Elizabeth Wissinger, eds, *Fashioning Models: Image, Text and Industry* (London: A&C Black, 2013); Caroline Evans, *The Mechanical Smile: Modernism and the First Fashion Shows in France and America, 1900–1929* (New Haven and London: Yale University Press, 2013).

The heyday of French haute couture (1880–1939)

Beyond the emblematic case of Worth, haute couture experienced rapid expansion in Paris and throughout Europe during the second half of the nineteenth century. The number of couturiers in Paris grew from 158 in 1850 to 684 by 1872, while the number of ready-to-wear fashion companies increased from 67 to 307.[29] Not all of them were creators of haute couture like the House of Worth, and a large number included half-independent subcontractors and tailors who manufactured basic garments for the middle class. The distinction between couturier and ready-to-wear fashion was anyway artificial. Contemporaries did not distinguish between fashion creation and industrial manufacturing, and the first trade association created in 1868 catered to both professions until 1910.

The success of the House of Worth attracted several other fashion designers in this business. Jacques Doucet (1853–1929), Jeanne Lanvin (1867–1946), Madeleine Vionnet (1876–1975), Paul Poiret (1879–1944), Gabrielle Chanel (1883–1971), Jean Patou (1887–1936), and Lucien Lelong (1889–1958) remain the most famous.[30] A common point of all the designers of haute couture in the early twentieth century is that they did not want to shock their customers. Although they were fashion creators, as Worth was, they developed dresses and clothes that answered the tastes of their elite customers—namely, wealthy

Figure 2.4 Russian actress and ballerina Ida Lvovna Rubinstein (October 5, 1885–September 20, 1960) during the performance of "La Dame aux Camélias" (Alexandre Dumas fils), standing on stage, a bouquet of camellias in her hand. She is dressed in a black dress by Worth, over which a garland of camellias is draped. As jewelry a tiara and a necklace.

Source: George Barbier / Rijksmuseum, Amsterdam.

people from the aristocracy and haute bourgeoisie—who wanted to distinguish themselves from the masses.[31] The creations these couturiers and their position in the fashion system are nonetheless far from the contemporary idea of fashion creation as an original expression of art.

The fast development of haute couture in Paris between the 1880s and the late 1920s was, however, not the only outcome of the presence of a large consumer base. During this period, the French capital was the major center of art creation in Europe and the United States, gathering a broad range of artists, musicians, intellectuals, and creators. The luxury business also developed in the city during this period, with the appearance of numerous small companies such as Cartier, Guerlain, and Vuitton. Fashion and luxury were intimately related businesses that targeted the same customers. The links between both industries even took the form of matrimonial relationships, which were facilitated by the family nature of these companies. For example, Andrée Caroline Worth (1881–1939), daughter of Jean-Philippe and grand-daughter of Charles Frederik, married Louis Cartier (1875–1942), who was the director of the jewelry family firm, together with his father.[32]

In the early twentieth century, haute couture in Paris was based both on the heritage of Charles Worth, for the business model, and an extension of the market beyond aristocracy. As mentioned, the new industrial and financial bourgeoisie in the United States had become important consumers. Similarly, the wealthy classes from Latin America, particularly from Argentina, which was one of the richest countries in the world at the turn of the twentieth century, started to import French haute couture.[33] The demand caused by new riches in new countries supported the growth of Parisian couture.

One of the best expressions of this new positioning of haute couture business during this time is undoubtedly Paul Poiret (1879–1944).[34] He started his career working for Doucet and Worth and launched his own house in Paris in 1903. Two years later, he married the daughter of a textile manufacturer. Poiret is one of the couturiers who altered the shape of corsets in the 1900s, liberating the bodies of women.[35] He also reduced the number of pieces of clothing worn by women. However, Poiret's activities went beyond fashion itself. Close to artists and to the Parisian jet-set, famous for the parties he hosted in his house, he was a promoter of new styles, particularly Art Deco, which inspired his own creations. In 1911, he founded a school for decorative arts, followed by a shop to sell its products in 1912. Sales subsidiaries of the school were later opened in London, Philadelphia, and Berlin. Poiret was, however, not only a fashion *creator* but also a successful businessman who took various steps to ensure the financial stability of his enterprise. In 1911, he was one of the first couturiers to launch his own perfume, named "Rosine" after his daughter. He did not outsource this business—as would soon become the norm in the fashion industry. He owned a laboratory that employed about forty people to manufacture perfume, glass bottles, and boxes. Moreover, Poiret did not become fixated upon Paris. He had an international approach to fashion and developed business relations beyond French borders. He had close contacts to Vienna (Wiener Werkstätte, see Box 2.2) and Berlin, and was among the first to go to the United States. During a trip to New York in 1913, he observed

Figure 2.5 Two women in summer dresses, the beach in the background. Left: sundress of white mousseline printed in multiple colors, by Martial et Armand. Right: "Robe de sport" of green crêpe "Fantasia" A.G.B. by Lucien Lelong. Part of a page from the fashion magazine Art-Goût-Beauté (1920–1933).

Source: Donation of the MA Ghering-van Ierlant Collection, Rijksmuseum, Amsterdam.

unlicensed copies of French fashion in department stores and, when he arrived back in France, became a leader in organizing the reaction of French couturiers to piracy.

A major characteristic of Parisian haute couture during its golden age is the large number of female designers. Jeanne Lanvin opened her business in 1885, Jeanne Paquin in 1891, Soeurs Callot in 1895, Gabrielle Chanel in 1910, and Madeleine Vionnet in 1912. Most of these women were feminists, eager to make their own decisions about their career and private life—a large number were single or divorced. They contributed not only to the emancipation of women in French and European society but also created dresses and clothes women found comfortable to wear. The case of Chanel is undoubtedly the most representative of these female fashion creators.

Gabrielle (Coco) Chanel was born in 1883 and raised in an orphanage where she learned tailoring, making a living in this activity during her youth. Supported by a rich lover, she started making hats in Paris in 1909 and opened her first shop the next year. In 1913, she opened a new store in Deauville in Normandie, a favorite resort for the Parisian elite, dedicated to clothes and dresses. Although Poiret was the first to abandon the

Figure 2.6 French fashion designer, Gabrielle Coco Chanel, in profile reclining on a chaise lounge with cigarette, wearing a dark dress with gold medallion necklaces and a ribbon in her hair; photographed in Paris in 1937.
Source: Photo by Horst P. Horst/Conde Nast via Getty Images.

corset, she remains famous as the liberator of women because she designed simple, comfortable clothes. Fashion historian Valerie Steel argues that "the real secret of Chanel's success was not that her clothes were practical and comfortable, but that they made the rich look young and casual."[36] Moreover, in 1921, she launched a perfume, the famous No. 5, which was one of the first perfumes with an artificial fragrance to be marketed by French couturiers. It strengthened her position as a modernist creator. Chanel No. 5 was originally sold only in Coco boutiques but, in 1924, Pierre Wertheimer, the son of the owner of the company Bourjois, one of the largest perfume companies at that time, convinced her to establish a separate company, Parfums Chanel, to enlarge production and sales. Wertheimer took 70 percent of the capital and Théophile Bader, founder of the department store Galeries Lafayette, 20 percent. Coco received 10 percent of the capital of this new venture, and it gave her the financial support to develop her couture business further.[37] According to the agreement signed with Wertheimer, she continued independently producing fashion but had to use the brand "Chanel" to sell her creations.[38] Perfume and clothes became the two pillars of her successful business. In the 1930s, Chanel was the owner of one the three largest haute couture houses in Paris, employing more than five hundred workers, next to Lelong and Vionnet.

The example of Chanel sheds light on two major characteristics of Parisian haute couture during the interwar years. First, although many women established themselves as creators of fashion, they often relied on men for administrative and financial aspects.

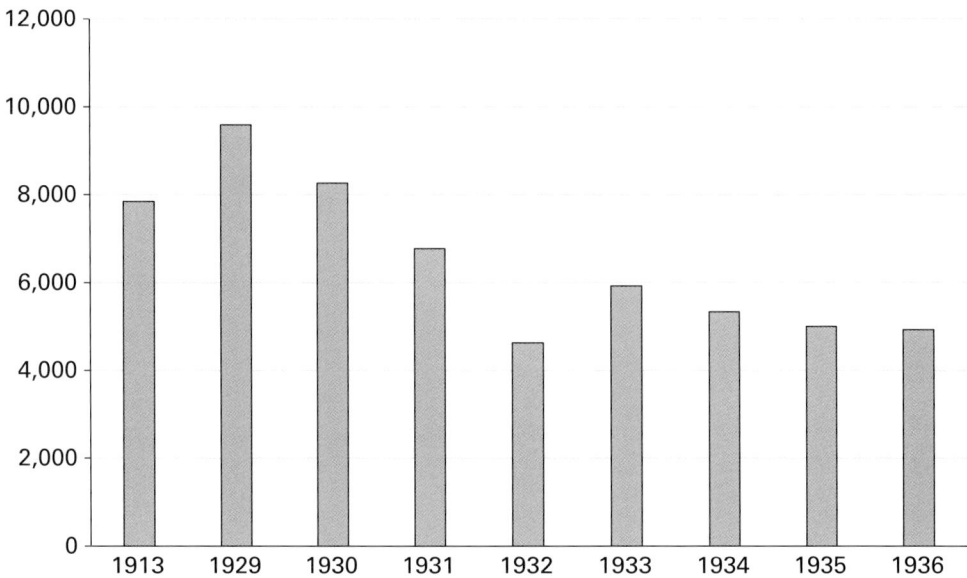

Figure 2.7 French Exports of Clothing and Lingerie, in Tons, 1913–1936.
Source: G. Deschamps, La Crise dans les Industries du Vêtement et de la Mode à Paris pendant la Période de 1930 à 1937 (Paris: Librairie technique et économique, 1937), 35.

During the 1920s and 1930s, men represented most female haute couture entrepreneurs in the trade association of the fashion industry, the Chambre Syndicale de la Couture Parisienne.[39] Second, haute couture was demonstrably not a financially stable business. Most of the couturier houses were tiny companies that lacked cash flow, mainly because some customers were late paying their debts. Various strategies were adopted to make the fashion business more profitable.

The diversification strategy toward unrelated products became a widespread activity, particularly with the launch of perfume collections. Poiret (1911), Chanel (1921), Worth (1924), Jeanne Lanvin (1925), Patou (1925), Lelong (1926), and others expanded into the perfume business. They benefited from the reputation of the fashion brand and made it possible to enlarge sales and profits. Couturier Jean Patou largely pursued this strategy.[40] In 1925, he opened a section for fashion and sport accessories in his shop in Paris. During the 1920s, he also developed collections of hats and cosmetics.

Another way to enlarge sales was to engage in ready-to-wear business. Ready-to-wear was particularly pursued in the 1930s in the context of an economic recession. The crisis that followed the Wall Street crash in 1929 led to a major drop in demand not only in France but in foreign markets where Parisian fashion had expanded dramatically since the late nineteenth century. Figure 2.7, which includes haute couture and other garments, shows the impact of the crisis.

After peaking at more than 9,500 tons in 1929, French exports of clothing and lingerie lost more than half their volume, reaching a low of 4,600 tons in 1932. The years

1933–1936 were consistently below 6,000 tons. In this period, fashion houses shifted from luxury to the mass market to increase their sales. For example, in 1929, Jean Patou established a new division dedicated to the manufacturing of ready-to-wear for the American market, with the line *Jane Paris*.[41] Although it lasted only a few months, this effort expressed a will to develop new business activity with the aim of increasing the company's profits. The Jane Paris line, however, was stopped for unknown reasons, probably a lack of sales. From 1930 onward, Patou refocused on accessories to boost his presence in the United States, opening a new subsidiary that year in New York, Jean Patou Inc., which specialized in the distribution of perfumes. During the 1930s, other couturiers launched their own ready-to-wear collections: Paul Poiret in 1933, with the design of a collection manufactured by the department store Le Printemps, and Lucien Lelong in 1934, with the launch of his own collection, Edition. This practice became quite common after the Second World War (see Chapter 7).

Haute couture as a transnational industry

Although Paris was the major city of haute couture from the 1880s to the 1920s, the business was not restricted to French nationals. It was organized as a real transnational industry with numerous foreign couturiers established in Paris while French nationals expanded their career in other countries, particularly in the United States and the UK.[42] Among the numerous foreigners who established their headquarters or a branch in Paris, in addition to the founding father of haute couture, Charles Frederick Worth, one should mention Lucy Lady Duff Gordon (1863–1935), a British couturier who founded Lucile Ltd, a successful fashion house opened in London in 1900 with branches in New York and Paris; Christoph von Drecoll (1851–1933), a Belgian tailor trained in Germany who opened his house in Vienna in the 1880s before moving to Paris in the early twentieth century; and Gustav Beer (1855–1908), a German couturier established in Paris since 1886. These foreign couturiers came to France to strengthen their reputation as fashion designers, to access a vibrant market and to benefit from the rich resources Paris had to offer in terms of fabrics and specialized labor. Some of them brought major innovations that contributed to the making of Paris as a fashion capital. For example, Lady Duff Gordon became famous for being the first to present new creations under the form of a show with models walking, one by one, to a music soundtrack. This innovative practice was soon adopted by numerous other couturiers in Paris and is considered the origin of the modern fashion show.[43] During the interwar period, the arrival of foreign couturiers continued: Elsa Schiaparelli (1890–1972), from Italy, opened her house in 1927; Robert Piguet (1888–1953), from Switzerland, in 1933; Cristobal Balenciaga (1895–1972), from Spain, in 1936.

Among these numerous couturiers, the family firm Redfern & Sons is another excellent example of transnational couturiers.[44] It was founded in 1855 on the Isle of Wight by the wool draper John Redfern (1820–1895), who became a silk merchant and established a tailor house in London in the 1870s before opening an haute couture house in Paris, with the help of his sons, in 1881. Redfern & Sons built its fame in the French capital through cooperation with the British designer Charles Poynter—who later added "Redfern" to his name—and specialized in the design of womenswear for sport, leisure, and travel. The company then opened a branch in New York in 1884, followed by various locations in the UK, the United States, and France, becoming a real haute couture multinational enterprise. Paris and London were the manufacturing basis of the business. Dresses and clothes sold in the United States were imported, sometimes through smuggling to avoid the high taxes introduced by the American government (McKinley Tariff 1890). After the death of the founder in 1895, the company, which had become a limited liability firm in 1892, continued under the artistic direction of Charles Poynter Redfern. In 1909, the *New York Times* introduced him as "the famous couturier of Paris, London and New York."[45] Until his death in 1929, he embodied the transnational character of French haute couture.

Another international dimension of haute couture at the time was the expansion of French couturiers to foreign markets. The UK and the US were major markets for couture. The UK represented the first stage of the internationalization of French couture houses.[46] The objective of opening a business in London was, however, not just to be closer to the customers of the largest foreign outlet. The British capital was not only a major market but also the world's largest financial center. French couturiers, who were always in need of money, moved to London to gather capital. The House of Paquin took the lead, moving its headquarters to London in 1897 and making the Paris house a branch of a British company. The management of the firm, most workshops, and design nonetheless remained in Paris. Jeanne Paquin did not cross the English Channel (La Manche), and its new headquarters had no design studio. They had a pure financial function. The capital of the London firm amounted to £500,000, and the board included seven directors, among whom was Isidore Paquin, Jeanne's husband and the managing director of the house. Other board members were mostly London financiers, such as Sir Alfred J. Newton, Chairman of Harrods.

Even if they did not all move their headquarters to London, numerous Parisian couture houses followed the pioneering example of Paquin. Worth (1902), Beer (1903), Boué Soeurs (1906), and Doeuillet (1907) opened subsidiaries in London. Like Paquin, their boards included British financiers from the clothing industry and department stores. French haute couture was hence considered a good investment for British manufacturers and distributors. For haute couture businesses, moving to the UK was a way to solve the problem of the lack of capital. However, the most accomplished example of financialization of haute couture through the establishment of a British firm is undoubtedly Vendome Syndicate Ltd, a financial company founded in London in 1907 by the French banker Georges Aubert (1869–1933).[47] He had made a fortune in banking and international trade and had invested in the fashion business. Thirteen shareholders owned a capital of £6,000. Sir Alfred Newton, Chairman of Harrods, was one of them. Vendome Syndicate was an investment company that allowed Aubert to invest in several Parisian fashion houses, among which were Beer, Doeuillet, Doucet, Drecoll, and Poiret. Although the investment company was liquidated in 1909, Aubert reinvested its capital in French garment and couture companies. During the 1920s, he took over Agnès, Doeuillet, Doucet, Drecoll & Beer, Patat, and Poiret. His actions, however, went beyond the injection of capital; he essentially reorganized the fashion industry in Paris. Aubert merged many firms—for example, Drecoll and Beer (1928), Doeuillet and Doucet (1929), Agnès, Drecoll & Cie (1931)—and closed some houses such as Poiret (1929). However, the bankruptcy of the Oustric Banking Group in 1930, in which Aubert was engaged, put an end to his ambitions in the fashion business.

At the same time, during the interwar years, inflation and fluctuating exchange rates after the end of the gold standard made carrying out French haute couture business from London uncertain and unsafe.[48] Most houses, following the example of Aubert, left the UK and came back to Paris, while some others, particularly Paquin and Worth, kept their headquarters across the Channel. Paquin was an exceptionally successful example of a Parisian haute couture business that internationalized its creative activities during the interwar years through cross-border acquisitions. Around 1923, it took over Elspeth Phelps Ltd, one of the major London dressmakers, which was liquidated at that time. The merger led, however, to conflicts between Fox Pitt, former designer of the merged British firm, and French management, resulting in their cooperation ending during the second half of the 1920s.

The transnational expansion of Parisian couture was not limited to the UK. The United States was seen as a promising market from the early twentieth century. At that time, famous French couturiers like Paquin and Poiret went to the United States, accompanied by models, to show their latest creations to American customers. In 1915, Boué Soeurs, a house founded in Paris in 1899, was the first to open a branch in New York. One of the main objectives was to keep doing business after the First World War broke out in Europe.[49]

The expansion into the American market took a step forward during the interwar years with the production, in the United States, of copies of French fashion.[50] While Parisian couturiers did not accept licensing the manufacturing of their creation in Europe, they started selling designs to American department stores and clothing companies to increase their sales in this valuable market. In the mid-1930s, the cost of a legal copy for New York buyers was about one-third cheaper than buying a dress in Paris. Moreover, department stores paid cash to couturiers, while private customers were slow to pay. Although this transatlantic business did not include royalties, it was very profitable for Parisian fashion designers because it increased their sales. However, the negative side of such a practice was that it led to the development of unauthorized copies—counterfeits of haute-couture garments. Copying fashion, however, did not originate in the United States. It started in Paris, where it was an illegal activity, as designs were legally protected. Yet the law was different in America. Designs were not considered intellectual property and hence could not be protected. Copying fashion was consequently not an illegal business, and it flourished. As it was not possible to go to the court to protect fashion creations, Parisian couture houses organized a collective response to fight piracy. This became one of the major activities of the trade association of couturiers during the interwar years.

Box 2.2 Wiener Werkstätte: How Viennese design and fashion influenced Paris and Berlin

The Wiener Werkstätte was a company founded in 1903 by progressive artists and designers in Vienna, following the artistic movement of Vienne Secession. It gathered people engaged in applied arts in architecture, ceramics, furniture, jewelry, and metalwork. Most participants were Austrian decorative artists. Financial support was provided by the businessman Fritz Wärndorfer (1868–1939), whose family had made a fortune in the textile industry, and the banker Otto Primavesi (1868–1926). The objective of Wiener Werkstätte was to promote creativity in the field of applied arts and transform daily life through the diffusion of modern design. It opened branches in Berlin, New York, and Zurich, and exhibited in London. However, after the end of the First World War, it suffered from the collapse of the Austrian–Hungarian Empire, losing markets and financiers. Then, severely hit by the world recession, it was declared bankrupt in 1932.

Figure 2.8 Poster: Paul Poiret in Vienna. From November 27–29, 1911.
Source: Photo by Imagno/Getty Images.

Wiener Werkstätte had several workshops and, within a few years of launching, opened new divisions for textiles (1909) and fashion (1910). Designers engaged in these divisions promoted a style that broke with commercial fashion and emphasized "health-dress"— that is, a way to make dresses that followed the nature of materials and were handmade.

Embodying artistic ideas in clothes was the core idea of Wiener Werkstätte's fashion. One of its major ambitions was to establish Austria as the new center for fashion and luxury against France. Austrian designers like Eduard Josef Wimmer-Wisgrill (1882–1961) presented their dresses to the public during a first show held in 1911. The impact was especially important in Germany, where these artists displayed their dresses in major department stores. It influenced German apparel manufacturers, who understood the possibility of mass-producing stylish clothes to seduce the middle class and compete against the French clothing industry. Outside Austria and Germany, Wiener Werkstätte's fashion met with success in the United States, notably through articles in *Vogue*, London, and Paris. The couturier Paul Poiret, himself a promoter of modern art in France, was, before the First World War, an important customer of Wiener Werkstätte, whose fabrics he used for his creations. He even purchased a dress made by Wimmer for his wife during a visit to Vienna in 1911. The case of Wiener Werkstätte demonstrates that a successful fashion business is not only a matter of creativity and design but also depends on healthy finances and the ability to mobilize the resources necessary for growth. Austrian designers were recognized internationally as innovative creators at the beginning of the twentieth century, but they failed after 1918 due to a lack of financial support.

Source: Hess, Heather, "The Wiener Werkstätte and the Reform Impulse," in Regina Lee Blaszczy, ed., *Producing Fashion: Commerce, Culture, and Commerce* (Philadelphia: University of Pennsylvania Press, 2008), 111–129.

Figure 2.9 Woman in cape designed by Madeleine Vionnet. Plate from Gazette du Bon Ton, Brentano's, Paris, 1922.

Source: Photo by Florilegius/Universal Images Group via Getty Images.

Trade associations in haute couture

Haute couture was an industry based on individual entrepreneurs and firms in a fiercely competitive environment and constant pressure to make profits. However, competition was not the only characteristic of this business. Couturiers cooperated with each other when it was necessary to act collectively.[51] A trade association was founded in 1868 by Charles Frederick Worth under the name of *Chambre Syndicale de la Couture et de la Confection pour Dames et Fillettes*. At first, it catered for both fashion designers and clothing manufacturers. However, the specific and diverging interests of these two groups led to a separation in 1911 and the creation of the *Chambre Syndicale de la Couture Parisienne* (CSCP), the trade association of Parisian high fashion. Until the Second World War, CSCP had only a few rules to define who could be accepted as a "couturier." The basic idea was that they had to make dresses according to the measurements of their clients, while the ready-to-wear industry manufactured goods based on standardized sizes.

CSCP was a large and powerful association that had 104 member firms employing around 13,000 people in 1937.[52] Joining the association was free, and most couturiers were members, with very few exceptions, the most known being Coco Chanel. CSCP carried out various actions that can be divided into two main fields. First, there were general activities usually executed by trade associations in France. These activities involved lobbying public authorities regarding legislation and taxes, offering members legal services and exchange or information about fraudulent customers, improving the skills of workers through the creation of funding to support apprentices, and the foundation of a school in 1931. Furthermore, it organized collective participation in fashion and decorative arts exhibitions (e.g. London and San Francisco in 1923; Paris in 1924), promoting the collective national brand "Unis-France" in the early 1920s.

Second, in the specific field of fashion, the CSCP fought against unauthorized copies of designs.[53] In France, it was possible to go to court and sue copyists as it was an illegal activity. In 1921, the CSCP organized a Service of Defense against the Copying of Models, to fight counterfeits. Madeleine Vionnet played a key role in this process. She organized, in cooperation with the lawyer Louis Dangel, general manager of her company, the *Association pour la Protection des Arts Plastiques et Appliqués* ("Association for the Protection of Visual and Applied Arts"), which encouraged the registration of models and fought against copies in courts. She was also involved in creating a new organization with similar goals in 1930, the *Protection Artistique des Industries Saisonnières* (PAIS) ("Artistic Protection of Seasonal Industries"). Although these organizations fought piracy in France, domestic copiers were often in cahoots with foreign buyers, mostly from the United States. As it was difficult to go to court in the United States, it was necessary to negotiate with local manufacturers and department stores. American sellers of imported dresses and legal copies were keen to protect their own business. They set up their own organizations, such as the Society of American Fashions (1912) and, later, the Fashion Originators' Guild of America (FOGA, 1932), and the Dress Creators League (1932). At its foundation, FOGA included 130 members, mostly manufacturers from New York engaged in the regulation of their activities. It aimed to promote American design and struggled against copies from Paris. This was a private response to piracy, while in France the state offered a legal provision. FOGA was able to establish a powerful organization against the interests of the manufacturers of cheap clothing and some retailers. Negotiations between FOGA and PAIS, which had become a division of CSCP, started in 1939, but the outbreak of the Second World War and the weakening of FOGA, after it was found guilty of violations against the Sherman Anti-Trust Act (1941), put an end to discussions.[54]

Conclusion

Haute couture emerged as a new business in mid-nineteenth century Paris, characterized by couturiers not following strictly the orders of their clients, unlike the tailors of royal courts in the *Ancien Régime*. They developed their own dresses and clothes for wealthy customers and thus became fashion creators. This change was made possible by a social transformation with the advent of the bourgeoisie and less rigid social stratification based more on wealth than status. There was, however, a limitation to the creativity of couturiers—they had to attract their clients, not shock them, so they developed dresses that met customers' tastes and expectations. Fashion was a creative business, not an art.

However, although Paris was the uncontested capital of high fashion, this business was not exclusively French. For the Englishman Charles Frederick Worth, it was from the start a transnational industry. Throughout Europe, couturiers established themselves in Paris to carry out and develop their activities. They also had branches in London and travelled to New York, Buenos Aires, and Caracas to sell their creations. Moreover, London was not only an important market for couture but also a financial center for French couturiers.

Haute couture experienced fast growth between the 1880s and 1920s. There were more than a hundred couture houses in Paris before the Second World War.[55] Yet this industry was intrinsically weak. Except for a few cases, like Chanel, fashion houses were small, lacked the financial means to expand, and faced economic downturns. The need to diversify revenues led some entrepreneurs to diversify their products, especially toward perfumes and ready-to-wear, and sell patterns to American buyers. However, this did not help make the fashion industry more sustainable. Many of the haute couture businesses disappeared between the 1930s and the 1950s, and a new model, embodied by Christian Dior, emerged after the Second World War.

Chapter 3

Fashion for the masses

> The production of "wearing apparel" is carried on partly in manufacturing workshops within which there is merely a reproduction of the division of labor whose membra disjecta were already to hand; partly by small master-craftsmen, who do not, however, work as before for individual consumers, but for factories and warehouses, and to such an extent that often whole towns and stretches of country carry on certain branches, such as shoemaking, as a specialty; finally, on a very large scale, by the so-called domestic workers, who form an external department of the factories and warehouses, and even of the workshops of the smaller masters.[1]

This quotation, taken from the first volume of Karl Marx's *Capital*, published in 1867, shows that clothing had become a major industrial sector in Europe by the middle of the nineteenth century. Beyond the various types of industrial workers described by Marx, clothing employed a high number of people: more than one million people in England and Wales in 1861.[2] Other countries on the Continent, such as France and Germany—but also the United States—would follow the British example in the second half of the nineteenth century.

This demonstrates that haute couture was not the only phenomenon of the fashion industry during the last decades of the nineteenth century and the first part of the twentieth century. The clothing industry experienced a transformation that led to the rise of two new interconnected businesses: mass-produced clothes for the working class (who predominantly used to make clothes themselves or buy second-hand items) and ready-to-wear, including clothes produced for the emerging middle class. The period between the 1880s and the Second World War can be characterized as the classical age of fashion, as described by theorists like Simmel.[3] The upper class and designers of haute couture were the absolute reference regarding "fashion" for the whole society. Styles and designs were imitated by ready-to-wear manufacturers, who then distributed the clothing through a dense network of shops in the growing urban areas. Sometimes there was a clear social distinction between shops for the middle class, like Parisian or New Yorker department stores, and shops for the working class, like the warehouses opened by C&A in the Netherlands and Germany or dry goods stores in the United States selling workwear (denim) to gold miners, farmers, and slaveowners in the South. However, social distinction tended to vanish, or at least become less clear, during the 1930s. The Great

Depression led high-end department stores to invest in second lines of outlets, with fixed-price stores, while retailers once focused on clothing for the working class expanded their customer base to all of society. Mass consumption of fashion became a new social phenomenon during the first decades of the twentieth century. This chapter analyses the conditions of the birth of a modern apparel industry based on industrial production. It addresses the question of why the demand for industrial clothing grew in the middle of the nineteenth century and looks at how entrepreneurs took this opportunity to build new business models.

Change in consumption habits

Fashion for the masses was a social phenomenon that resulted from a change in consumption habits. Urbanization led to the emergence of a new kind of demand by the growing middle class both in large cities and smaller towns. Between 1850 and 1910, the urban population grew from 38 to 127 million in Europe, and from 3 to 41 million in North America. Over the same time, the share of the population living in cities increased from 37 to 69 percent in the UK, from 16 to 36 percent in Continental Europe, and from 13 to 41 percent in North America.[4] This social transformation had a major impact on consumption habits. The new consumer culture that had appeared in London and Paris during the eighteenth century spread throughout the Western world and developed very rapidly during the second half of the nineteenth century. Fashion products became one of these new consumer goods purchased by the masses.

Victorian middle-class women embodied this new culture of consumption. Their social status became ambivalent, as they were "marked culturally both as commodity and consumer."[5] Women were major customers of fashion retailers, criticized by moralists and writers for their weakness toward and greed for novelty. But, at the same time, women were a way for bourgeois men to express their wealth, status, and taste.

The consumption of fashion relied on the development of new forms of retail and the birth of the advertisement. The Victorian periodical press was full of fashion advertisements targeting middle-class women with a broad choice of novelties, from dresses to accessories, inspired by French style and distributed by numerous manufacturers and stores. Fashion was part of the ideal image of household material culture, along with carpets, furniture, clocks, tableware, etc.[6] Mass consumption of fashion was, however, not limited to women. Menswear followed a similar path. The consumption of suits, accessories, and clothing by urbanized middle-class men was a way to express social identity.[7] Nor was this new culture of consumption limited to Victorian Britain. Very similar patterns were observable in Continental Europe and the United States.

During the second half of the nineteenth century, a new kind of magazine for women appeared, whose content mixed general information, housekeeping advice, and fashion plates. Their large print runs made them a major media outlet to diffuse information and knowledge throughout society. In France, *Le Moniteur de la Mode* (launched in 1843) and

Figure 3.1 Front cover of Cosmopolitan magazine for November 1917.

Source: Harrison Fischer / International Magazine Company.

La Mode Illustrée (1860), among others, had a broad readership. In the United States, the dominant magazines were *Harper's Bazar* (1867),[8] *Cosmopolitan* (1886), and *Vogue* (1892). *Vogue* was the first major fashion magazine to expand abroad. Its internationalization started before it shifted its focus toward the mass promotion of ready-to-wear. Before the Second World War, national editions were launched in the UK (1916) and France (1920).[9]

Mass consumption of fashion by the middle class relied also on a change in style toward simpler clothes. During the first decades of the twentieth century, the fashion of the upper class, which was still a major referent, moved to less sophisticated dresses and suits, while the advent of sportswear facilitated the standardization of clothing and the imitation by ready-to-wear manufacturers for the mass market. The Depression of the 1930s strengthened this trend when it led to department stores opening one-price shops that offered clothing and other goods for more affordable prices to the impoverished middle class. Woolworths in the United States, Marks & Spencer in the UK, and Galeries Lafayette in France developed a secondary line of shops to meet this demand.

Outside Europe, the consumption society and culture also developed, particularly in Japan, one of the most urbanized societies in the world. From the seventeenth century on, Edo (Tokyo) and Kyoto were major consumption centers. Large-scale stores were opened in Edo, like Mitsukoshi (1683) and Shirokiya (1662). The consumption of kimonos was not restricted to luxury items for the upper class. Cotton kimonos, like *kasuri*, and cloth sold in small batches enabled the middle class to follow fashion trends and participate in the consumption society. The growth of fashion consumption by the wives and daughters of merchants challenged sumptuary laws, which ceased to be clearly enforced in the early nineteenth century. During the 1850s and 1860s, the forced opening of Japan by American ships and the inflow of cheap cotton and artificial dyes boosted consumption but did not create it.[10] Between 1874–1883 and 1912–1921, the share of private consumption expenditure dedicated to clothing nearly doubled: it grew from 7.8 to 13.3 percent.[11] Japanese people essentially wore traditional clothes until the Second World War, except for military and school uniforms, and Western suits for politicians, some executives in large firms, and bureaucracies. Thus, the increase in expenditure on clothing during that time was not driven by a Westernization of clothing culture. This social change started during the interwar period but was a slow and long process (see Chapter 4).

Box 3.1 A La Belle Jardinière (France) and the distribution of fashion for the working class

Although Parisian department stores are usually considered an expression of the new consumption society focused on the upper and middle classes, some also targeted the working class at the outset. The most famous example is undoubtedly *A La Belle Jardinière (BJ)*. The roots of this store go back to 1824 when the haberdasher Pierre Parissot (1790–1860) opened a shop in Paris with fixed-price garments for workers. One year later, he diversified his collection into uniforms. Professional garments were an important step in the development of the firm because they made it possible to introduce standard sizes and mass production, due to the focus on utility rather than design or style. This manufacturing knowledge was then applied to civilian garments to allow cheap ready-to-wear clothes. BJ also introduced womenswear when moving outside of working clothes.

BJ met with great success. Sales grew very fast in the mid-nineteenth century, and the store moved to new premises in 1867, becoming one of the largest department stores in the French capital. Unlike other stores, however, BJ specialized in clothing and kept focused on this activity throughout the twentieth century. From early on, it adopted a franchise strategy to expand throughout the country, with more than 300 outlets by 1860. Thus, it contributed to the democratization of fashion consumption in the whole country.

BJ relied both on in-house production and supplies from external workshops. By 1855, it already employed 50 cutters in its own building while sewing and finishing were carried out by some 2,000 homeworkers. The increase in demand led the company to invest directly in a factory in Lille, in the north of France, to mass-produce shirts and overalls (1866), then another factory in Paris (1889).

Figure 3.2 Advertisement for La Belle Jardinière, 1933.
Source: Photo by API/Gamma-Rapho via Getty Images.

In 1857, BJ's founder organized a new company, Pierre Parissot & Cie, to prepare for the transmission of his business to his family. After he died in 1860, BJ was managed by his brother and his brother's descendants and was transformed into a joint stock company in 1930. The firm stopped its activities in 1972, three years after it was purchased by the Agache-Willot Group, a company that specialized in textiles and distribution and aimed to take control of BJ's considerable real estate assets—which were taken over by Bernard Arnault in the mid-1980s when he began to invest in luxury fashion and before he took over LVMH.

Source: François Faraut, *Histoire de "La Belle Jardinière"* (Paris: Belin, 1987).

Clothing industry around the world

The mass consumption of fashion throughout Western countries and their colonies since the late nineteenth century, and in Japan since the interwar years, relied on the industrialization of the clothing industry. Providing cheap fashion goods for the masses required the standardization and mechanization of production. This was a long-term phenomenon that appeared in different nations, including the UK, France, Germany, the United States, Russia, and Japan. It relied on two major factors: 1) the setting up and management of global supply chains for raw cotton (especially from the United States, India, and Egypt), wool (from

Figure 3.3 Advertising poster for a clothing shop showing a man wearing a suit inset into a view of Place du Château d'Eau, location of the shop.
Source: Jules Chéret / Library of Congress Prints and Photographs Division.

Australia, New Zealand, and India), and silk (from China and Japan), as well as for German-made artificial dyes, leading to the availability of the material required for the mass manufacture of clothes anywhere in the world; and 2) production technology, particularly mass-production methods, spinning, weaving, and sewing, which reduced the cost of clothes and made it possible to increase personal consumption by changing styles more often and becoming accustomed to changing fashions. Mass production was accompanied by the standardization of sizes. Meanwhile, the First World War and the consequent production of military uniforms also had a significant impact on the emergence of the fashion industry.

Until the mid-nineteenth century, garments were mostly made at home or manufactured by local tailors and craft workshops. The growing demand for cheap ready-to-wear clothing was an opportunity to organize new business models. At the beginning of the nineteenth century, merchants outsourced the manufacture of clothing to small workshops and home workers, particularly women in the countryside and small towns, in a production system close to the "putting-out system" we can observe in many other industries. The merchant distributed raw materials to workers and gathered finished garments against wages, selling the garments to retailers. He was an intermediary between production and the market. The system was based on low labor costs in the countryside. This competition led to complaints from the traditional craft tailors in large cities. For example, in 1834, 9,000 tailors in London

Figure 3.4 Advertisement for Raynster raincoats, 1918. Washington State Apple Commission / New York Botanical Garden, LuEsther T. Mertz Library.

Source: Public Domain via Wikimedia Commons.

went on strike for higher wages and better working conditions.[12] It had no effect, except to strengthen the tendency of merchants to focus their production on small workshops with female workers rather than working with artisans.

The advent of the industrialization of clothing, thanks to the introduction of standardized sizes and the development of sewing machines, challenged this production system in the last third of the nineteenth century. The need to provide cheap fashion led to a production system balanced between mass production in large factories (to achieve low prices) and the flexible production of specialized goods by networks of small workshops (to offer a broad variety of goods). Each country and region had its own dynamics, but we can identify two main organizational forms around the world: networks of small firms and the industrial factory.

Networks and large factories

The first form—networks of small firms—could be observed in large cities like Berlin, London, New York, and Paris, where hundreds of homeworkers and small family workshops produced clothing. These places were at the center of the garment industry in their respective countries until the mid-twentieth century. In 1901, London had more than 64,000 workers in this industry

(27 percent of the national employment in this sector—see Table 3.1. In 1900, New York had a total of 90,000 workers in the clothing industry and a total of 206,000 in the country (44 percent).[13] As for Berlin, it housed hundreds of small ready-to-wear companies in the 1920s, which were part of the largest employment sector of the German capital. This industry was dominated by Jewish entrepreneurs, who held about half of all firms, especially the largest one. Finally, Paris was the home of hundreds of small workshops producing, under outsourced contracts, a broad variety of clothing and fashion accessories for department stores. The number of independent dressmakers in Paris grew from 158 in 1850 to 1,636 in 1896.[14]

Box 3.2 Berlin as the European capital of confection (1880–1933)

The apparel industry in Germany was a large sector, mostly based on small firms that experienced rapid development from the late nineteenth century. Expansion, however, led to a gradual concentration within a few medium-sized and large firms. Between 1882 and 1925, the number of employees in this industry went from 1.1 million people to 1.4 million, while the number of companies decreased from 767,000 to 600,000. In 1907, 1,390 clothing companies (0.2 percent of the total) had more than fifty employees. They represented, at that time, 25 percent of the workforce in the German clothing industry.

Berlin occupied a key position in the German apparel industry, and Jewish entrepreneurs played a major role in this business. They owned about half of all clothing workshops, whatever their size, and dominated most of the largest companies. For example, Valentin and David Manheimer opened a men's coat factory in 1837 and engaged later in the mass production of ready-to-wear clothing, working with numerous independent tailors, who were also mostly Jewish. This firm became one of the biggest clothing companies in Germany but was liquidated in 1931 due to the Great Depression.

Department stores were also major actors in the development of Berlin as a fashion capital. Herrmann Gerson (1812–1861) opened his store in 1836. It became one of the most important in the city. At the end of the 1840s, it had about 1,000 tailors working as outside contractors. The company was the largest fashion company in Germany during the second half of the nineteenth century. It adopted practices like Worth in Paris to attract women from the middle class—for example, supplying the local aristocracy with fancy dresses and organizing catwalk shows in the department store. Other major retailers included fixed-sale-price stores opened by Rudolph Hertzog (1839) and David Leib Levin (1840), both owned by Jewish families.

Clothing companies, department stores, designers, and trade associations worked together at the beginning of the twentieth century to strengthen the creativity of the Berlin confection industry. Among the few designers who became famous, one can mention Kurt Ehrenfreund (1907–1994), who worked as an independent outfitter in Berlin before emigrating to Amsterdam in 1933 and the United States in 1952. The training of designers was also encouraged by the opening of a fashion design department in the school of the Museum of Applied Arts (*Unterrichtsanstalt des Kunstgewerbemuseums*) in 1920.

Some entrepreneurs founded specific organizations to support these activities, like the German Institute for Men's Fashion (*Deutsches Institut für Herrenmode*), founded in 1928. A fashion press (*Elegante Welt* and *Die Dame*, both launched in 1912) and fashion shows, and above all, a lively nightlife in dancing halls and salons, contributed to the influence of Berlin, with the objective of challenging the dominant position of Paris. During the 1920s, fashion was considered the second-largest activity in the city in terms of employment. It had achieved international recognition embodied by the purchase of high-end garments by French department stores, which were re-labeled "Made in France" afterward, and the organization in 1926 of a fashion show by Parisian designers at the Hotel Kaiserhoff.

However, the Berlin apparel and fashion industry was hit severely by the Great Depression and then by the Nazi's Aryanization policy, as many entrepreneurs in this sector were Jewish. These two developments ended the golden age of German fashion (see Chapter 6).

Source: Roman Köster, *Hugo Boss, 1924–1945: Die Geschichte einer Kleiderfabrik zwischen Weimarer Republik und Dritten Reich* (Munich: C.H. Beck, 2011), 19–23; Roberta S. Kremer, ed., *Broken Threads: The Destruction of the Jewish Fashion Industry in Germany and Austria* (Oxford and New York: Berg, 2007).

Figure 3.5 Conservation of fur products in freezer room to combat moths, Rudolf Hertzog, Berlin, 1914. Rudolph Hertzog / Kollection Kuhn.
Source: Public Domain via Wikimedia Commons.

The competitive advantages of these cities were the presence of cheap labor and proximity to the market. The concentration of hundreds of small companies, often specializing in few products or operations, made it possible to manufacture a broad range of clothes and react to changes in consumer demand. The high competition between these workshops and the need to keep production costs as low as possible led to the employment of many immigrant workers. These independent workshops often supplied large retailers and department stores. In London, for example, besides the luxury tailors of the West End district, there were hundreds of small workshops producing customized suits and dresses for the middle class. They supplied wholesalers and retailers with a broad range of goods.[15] The district of Le Sentier, in Paris, based a few hundred meters north of the Louvre palace, is also a case in point. In the eighteenth century, it housed the headquarters of the *Compagnie des Indes* and the place where Indian cloth for the nobility was printed. This activity attracted numerous textile entrepreneurs who employed provincial immigrants. From the mid-nineteenth century, a cluster of clothing entrepreneurs developed and repositioned to supply department stores, making the district the home of numerous homeworkers and sweatshops in which a miserable immigrant population, particularly Jews from Central and Eastern Europe, worked to manufacture garments. It was geographically close to department stores so that coordination between demand and production was easily realized.[16] In Berlin, the creation of various trade associations at the beginning of the twentieth century encouraged the exchange of information between manufacturers, wholesalers, representatives of department stores, and artists, like the *Verband der deutschen Modeindustrie* ("Association of the German Fashion Industry"), an organization whose roots go back to the First World War and which gathered 1,500 members during the interwar years.[17]

The second form was the industrial factory. Unlike the network of small workshops, the industrial factory did not provide a broad variety of goods but cheap, mass-produced garments. It concentrated labor and equipment, mainly sewing machines, in large halls and often cooperated with large-scale retailers that needed a large quantity of clothes. This model can first be observed in the UK, where the manufacture of tailored outwear for men led to the formation of a huge industry clustered in a few large cities like Glasgow, Leicester, London, and Leeds. Leeds specialized in this activity, becoming one of the largest production centers in the UK.[18] Table 3.1 shows the emergence of Leeds as the main manufacturing center for industrial clothing in this country in the context of a fast-growing national industry between 1851 (132,918 workers in England and Wales) and 1911 (249,467 workers). In the mid-nineteenth century, London employed about one-quarter of the total workforce in the national tailoring industry, and the rest of the workers were dispatched throughout England. Cities like Bristol, Essex, Leeds, and Manchester had around 1,000 to 2,000 workers. During the last quarter of the century, Leeds started to emerge and establish itself as a first-mover in the industrial manufacturing of clothing in England. It outpaced Manchester by the early 1880s, and its share of national employment in the tailoring industry, which was lower than 1 percent in 1851 and

Figure 3.6 Garment workers seated at their sewing machines around a long workbench in an unspecified workshop in the garment district of New York City, New York, 1936. Image used to illustrate the threat of strike action by the Amalgamated Ladies' Garment Workers' Union.
Source: UPI/Bettmann Archive/Getty Images.

1861, reached close to 10 percent by 1911. The advantages of this city relied on its location in a wool-production region, a tradition of textile manufacturing, the presence of a dense network of merchants and local financiers, and the ample availability of labor. Moreover, Leeds had many manufacturers specializing in machinery and engineering who offered their support to the growth of clothing production. For example, in the 1880s, it had fifteen sewing-machine makers.[19]

The presence of the US sewing machine manufacturer Singer in Glasgow was, of course, a big incentive to launch into such activity; however, local machine producers were better able to answer the special needs of Leeds apparel manufacturers and were hence able to keep competitive against the giant US multinational.[20] John Barran was one of the first companies to make large-scale use of industrial sewing machines to produce clothes in Leeds.[21] The firm was founded in the 1850s and operated a small factory before opening large production units successively in 1878 and 1887. It became one of the biggest employers in the Leeds clothing industry, with more than 2,000 workers in the 1900s.[22] The mechanization of clothing and a huge expansion in production went hand in hand with extensive use of cheaper female workers. In Leeds, the share of women among tailoring workers grew from 3 percent in 1851 to 56 percent in 1881 and 68 percent in 1911.[23]

Table 3.1 Tailoring Workers in England and Wales, 1851–1911

	1851	1861	1871	1881	1891	1901	1911
Bristol	1,151	1,402	2,732	3,715	4,776	6,572	6,930
Essex	1,998	2,314	2,686	3,404	5,172	6,684	5,961
Leeds	964	1,038	2,006	4,888	15,629	198,13	23,542
London	30,773	34,678	38,296	41,221	52,346	64,503	64,993
Manchester	2,324	2,297	4,210	4,575	7,347	9,598	10,261
Others	95,708	94,661	99,934	102,845	123,450	130,015	137,780
England and Wales, total	132,918	136,390	149,864	160,648	208,720	237,185	249,467
Leeds as %	0.7	0.8	1.3	3.0	7.5	8.4	9.4
London as %	23.2	25.4	25.6	25.7	25.1	27.2	26.1

Source: Honeyman, *Well Suited*, 12.

The clothing industry in Leeds was dominated by Jewish tailors, mostly immigrants from Eastern Europe who moved to Leeds during the second half of the nineteenth century. At first, they controlled a network of workshops that produced cheap ready-to-wear suits. There were also factories owned by non-Jewish entrepreneurs, mostly businessmen from the textile industry who had reallocated their investments into clothing. For example, Joseph Hepworth & Sons employed 2,000 people in its new factory built in 1891, which started as a woolen draper in the 1860s. As for Joseph May & Sons, a prominent menswear manufacturer, its roots go back to a woolen trade business opened in 1859.[24] Hence, during the second half of the nineteenth century, the Leeds clothing industry relied on a twofold production system, based on the mass-production of ready-to-wear menswear and specialized production by networks of workshops. Clothing sales occurred usually through contracts with department stores, although around the end of the nineteenth century some manufacturers, established their own retail system. One of the most successful examples was Joseph Hepworth & Sons. In the 1890s, the company had more than one hundred stores.[25] During this decade, many clothing firms in Leeds integrated retailing and manufacturing to better fulfill consumers' needs. It was an answer to the competition from London-based firms, which were closer to the market.

The industrialization of production made Leeds the uncontested center of British menswear manufacturing during the interwar years. In June 1931, the city employed more than 40,000 workers, of whom 73 percent were women and girls. Its share of the national menswear industry amounted that year to 19 percent.[26] Moreover, in the 1930s, more than 60 percent of suits sold in Britain were made in Leeds.[27] This success relied on multiple tailors—that is, clothing manufacturing firms that had integrated distribution. They were the largest employers in the city and dominated the national market. Most were Jewish entrepreneurs, and their success led to antisemitic sentiments by independent tailors and store owners. For example, in June 1917, there was an outbreak of antisemitic violence in Leeds because young Jews were accused of being reluctant to participate in the war effort.[28]

Montague Burton was one of the most successful Jewish entrepreneurs. He was born in Lithuania and emigrated to the UK in 1900. He started by opening menswear stores in Chesterfield and Sheffield before investing in manufacturing in Leeds in 1909. After the First World War, he had production units throughout the city and opened factories in Dublin, Walkden, Bolton, and Glasgow. At the same time, he diversified into retailing. The number of stores owned by Burton in the UK grew from 40 in 1919 to nearly 600 in 1939. That year, he employed around 10,000 workers.[29] The integration of production and marketing was a competitive advantage for Leeds garment producers. However, the scope of their business was largely limited to the domestic market. They expanded only a little abroad, mostly in the British Empire, though in the 1930s, to Continental Europe and the United States.

The mass production of clothing by large industrial firms was not only a British model, however. It could be observed in other Western countries. In France, for example, textile entrepreneurs invested also in garment manufacturing in the late nineteenth century.[30] Marcel Boussac (1889–1980) is the best embodiment of this model. He was the son of a garment maker and started his own business as a trader of fabrics in Paris before the First World War. He was successful with his colorful collections of new clothes and moved to the district of Le Sentier. In 1917, he founded a new company, the *Comptoir de l'industrie cotonnière* (CIC), and purchased his first factory, which he completely refurbished. He developed his production capacity during the interwar years through acquisitions of rival firms. This allowed his production capacity to grow from 7 million meters of fabric in 1922 to 88 million in 1936 and 132 million in 1952. At the same time, he invested in retail with the purchase of his first chain of stores in 1919. He was the king of cotton in France, controlling a huge and modern-equipped production system and having integrated all the operations in a single organization, from the purchase of raw materials to processing, manufacturing, and retail.[31] He became one of the most renowned businessmen in interwar France. In 1946, he partnered with Christian Dior to give a new start to French haute couture (see Chapter 6).

Beyond these two main organizational models, the growth of apparel manufacturing companies was a driving force for the development of fashion for the masses. It enabled the supply of cheap goods to the middle and working classes. Manufacturers, however, were not the only major actors. Retail was just as important as production. Yet, although a few apparel manufacturers invested in retailing, like the manufacturers of Leeds and Boussac in France, they only controlled a tiny share of this business. In the case of France, Didier Grumbach argues that "independent manufacturers only acquired real power after 1960."[32] Since the last part of the nineteenth century, retailers had established themselves as leading firms in making fashion accessible to the masses.

Figure 3.7 Au Pauvre Jacques Clothing Fashions Poster, circa 1900.
Photo by Swim Ink 2, LLC/CORBIS/Corbis via Getty Images.

Producing fabrics for the European colonies

The effects of the industrial production of fabrics and apparel were not limited to Europe and the United States. National markets soon became saturated, and Western enterprises had to find new markets for their manufactured goods. The colonies soon became a major outlet for European textile manufacturers. The latter had a competitive advantage in terms of price, reinforced by the institutional context of imperialism, which prevented the colonies from adopting protectionist measures. Generally, the colonies were there to deliver raw materials, like cotton, to the motherland, receiving in return the final products manufactured in Europe. The impact of British cotton fabrics on the decline of the Indian textile industry in the second half of the eighteenth century is one of the best-known illustrations of this phenomenon.

Indian cloth was exported globally in the early modern period and led some countries, such as France (1686), England (1702), and Spain (1717), to adopt protectionist measures because Indian manufacturers, who had mastered resistant dyes, excelled in finishing cotton textiles with colors and designs that attracted Europeans.[33] Between 1700 and 1750, cotton textiles constituted 60 percent of all commodities traded to Europe by the English EIC.[34] However, the flourishing Indian cotton industry entered a phase of decline in the eighteenth century after the industrialization of cotton spinning and weaving in the UK (see Chapter 4).

When the United States and Western European countries began in the 1870s to protect their infant textile and apparel industries with high tariffs, British textile producers had to find new outlets and refocus on their empire. Before the First World War, their two largest markets were India and China, the first absorbing 45 percent of British cloth exports.[35] Apparel manufacturers were mostly domestic-oriented, but the shift to mass production in industrial factories led some of them to export their surplus to colonies and dominions. For example, in Leeds, apparel manufacturers focused on Australia, Canada, and South Africa in the 1870s and 1880s. It was the empire, of course, but the targets were White settlers.[36] This suggests that apparel producers did not adapt most of their production to non-Western cultures. British companies provided Asian and African populations with fabrics to make clothing locally. They depended on British-made materials to manufacture their apparel.

The situation was similar in France. Between 1890 and 1929, the share of colonies in French exports of cotton fabrics grew from 34.8 percent to 49.9 percent. It was much larger than apparel, which declined slightly from 13.7 percent to 10.4 percent over the same period. The economic crisis and the rise of protectionism in the world during the 1930s strengthened the importance of colonial markets for French exporters. By 1938, they had grown to 84.6 percent of exports for cotton fabrics and 34.5 percent for apparel. The focus of textile and clothing companies on colonial markets accelerated between 1945 and decolonization.[37] The companies behind these numbers are not identified—historian Jacques Marseille argued they were uncompetitive firms that escaped the modernization of their business model—but the domination of fabrics over apparel suggests that, as in the British Empire, local populations had kept control over the production of their clothing but used fabrics manufactured in France.

The internalization model in apparel retail: C&A

The two organizational models in apparel retail that could be distinguished were retail companies that invested in production and those that outsourced production. Although apparel retailers specialized at first in the sales of garments produced by others, at the beginning of the twentieth century some of them began investing gradually in manufacturing, design, and advertising. This process of verticalization, or internalization, aimed to increase profits by making products that answered the tastes and needs of consumers—which retailers identified from their presence in the stores. It occurred both through the takeover of existing manufacturing companies and the investment in new factories. Developing a retail network through opening shops in major cities was not considered enough to control the development of the firm. The opening of their own workshops and factories enabled some retailers to control their supply directly and design their own garments.

The Dutch–German company C&A is a case in point. The roots of this company go back to the activities of a family of peddlers in the seventeenth century in Westphalia, northwest

Germany, the Brenninkmeijer family.[38] Three brothers created a company in 1790, H. Brenninkmeijer & Co., which was split in 1828 into two firms active in the sales of clothes. In 1841, the two sons of the owner of one of them, Clemens and August, founded the firm C.&A. Brenninkmeijer in Sneek in the north of the Netherlands. It essentially consisted of a warehouse, and they continued to sell womenswear in various markets in the Netherlands and northwest Germany. They already had a strong interest in fashion and trends, and, after 1863, the two brothers regularly attended the Leipzig Fair to observe which styles were popular with women and to learn about new fabrics and designs.[39] Later, they went to textile fairs in Berlin and Amsterdam for the same reason. These were places to meet wholesalers and retailers and understand changing fashion trends.

The Brenninkmeijer brothers opened their own stores in small towns in Germany and the Netherlands at the end of the nineteenth century. The first C&A shop was opened in Leeuwarden in 1881. Another followed in Amsterdam in 1893, then a second in Amsterdam in 1896, and two more, one in Groningen (1902) and one in Rotterdam (1908). A new marketing strategy was adopted in the 1900s. Observing that most of the apparel companies focused on middle- and high-income customers, the second generation of C&A managers decided to choose another target group that was less wealthy but growing fast and much larger: the working class. Hence, from 1906, C&A started to design and sell cheap clothes for women. Their suppliers were mostly clothing workshops based in Berlin so C&A could also expand its sales network in Germany. In 1912, a store and a sales subsidiary were founded in Berlin, one of the largest working-class cities in the world. It met with great success, and C&A opened a second store in Berlin the following year, as well as new outlets in Hamburg (1913), Cologne (1913), and Essen (1914). Their target was also the mass market of workers. The Berlin subsidiary adopted modern marketing techniques. It employed Kurt Lisser, a professional advertising agent trained in the United States, who introduced in 1913 a new C&A logo and made up the slogan *C&A ist doch vorteilhafter* ("C&A is more advantageous").[40] Large advertising campaigns also started during the interwar years. At the same time, C&A adopted a new marketing strategy—the integration of womenswear and menswear—while other entrepreneurs were usually focused only on one or the other.

The First World War was an opportunity to invest directly in manufacturing and to verticalize design, production, and distribution. C&A took over a small clothing company in the Netherlands and transformed it into a subsidiary in 1918 under the name N.V. Nationale Confectie Industrie (NCI). Then, in the 1920s, it opened production units in Germany to secure its supply of garments. The sustainability of growth made it necessary to control production. At first, internal production focused on womenswear, but C&A also started to manufacture menswear in Germany in 1930.

Meanwhile, the sales network continued to expand. The financial crisis was an opportunity to attract more consumers interested in the low prices offered by ready-to-wear firms. Hence, the C&A Dutch subsidiary experienced only a slight decline in 1931–1934, but it was still a highly profitable company throughout the crisis years, with gross profit consistently above 20 percent of sales from 1921 to 1939.[41] Between 1920 and 1939, C&A opened twelve new stores in the Netherlands and twelve in Germany.[42]

Moreover, C&A started its international expansion into the British market, with stores opening in London (1922) and Liverpool (1924). In 1940, C&A had a total of eighteen stores throughout the country.[43] The British market was highly competitive, with large retailers like Marks & Spencer or the American company Woolworths already present. C&A used its business model of vertical integration, which had proven successful in Continental Europe. In 1925, it took over the menswear company Hyam & Co., and manufacturing facilities were renamed Canda Manufacturing. It became C&A's production facility in the UK for womenswear. Production in this British unit was streamlined in the 1930s after some managers came back from a trip to the United States.[44] The rationalization of production was necessary to offer fashion to the masses for affordable prices.

The business model implemented by C&A during the first decades of the twentieth century is nonetheless far from unique. In many countries, retailers owned manufacturing facilities and even frequently outsourced orders to independent workshops for special goods or to answer a growing demand. In France, most department stores had their own production subsidiaries in the interwar years. Galeries Lafayette was a pioneer. In 1917, it turned its confection workshop into an autonomous subsidiary, under the name Société Parisienne de Confection (SPC) and in 1921 opened a garment factory in Paris inspired by scientific management.[45] In the early 1930s, SPC employed 500 workers, and the production of a man's suit was divided into some 300 discrete operations.[46] In 1935, Max Heilbronn, son-in-law of the director of Galeries Lafayette, adopted mass production within SPC, with a series of more than 100,000 pieces of dresses and shirts.[47] Meanwhile, Galeries Lafayette had founded a new subsidiary, Monoprix, to offer cheap, fixed-price goods, including clothing, to customers impoverished by the crisis. Other Parisian department stores also verticalized production and opened second-line stores during the interwar years.[48] The negative effect of this strategy was to reduce the range of fashion goods offered to customers, resulting in French department stores after the Second World War starting to reduce their in-house supply and work again with a growing range of independent suppliers.[49] Outside France, the internalization model can be observed in various places, such as the United States, where the department store Bergdorf Goodman had its own workshop since its beginnings, and in London, where some tailors like Thomas Burberry & Son built their successful growth on the integration of manufacturing and sales.[50]

The outsourcing model: M&S

Despite the growth in demand, the need to follow customers' changing tastes, and the tough competition in fashion retailing, some companies chose not to invest in manufacturing and to stay focused on marketing and sales. One of the best examples of this model is undoubtedly the British company Marks & Spencer (M&S).[51] It outsourced the production of garments to independent firms from its beginnings and still follows this path today.

The company's roots go back to the city of Leeds, in Britain, where Michael Marks (1859–1907), a Jewish immigrant of Polish origin, was selling various goods as a peddler. He moved his business to Manchester in 1891 and became associated three years later with Tom Spencer (1851–1905), a bookkeeper from Yorkshire who worked in a wholesale company in Leeds. They started to extend their network of bazaars throughout Britain during the 1890s, continuing into the twentieth century, notably through the takeover of competitors such as the London-based Arcadia Bazaar Company in 1911. The total number of M&S stores went from 34 in 1900 to 143 in 1914 and 234 in 1939.[52] The expansion required more capital, so the two partners established a limited liability company in 1903. It remained a family-controlled business, going public on the London Stock Exchange in 1926 to attract more capital.

From the beginning through the 1930s, M&S sold a broad variety of goods purchased directly from manufacturers without going through wholesalers. It was a way to cut prices and offer cheap goods to the British working class. Among household goods, leather goods, gramophones, etc., M&S sold clothes. Unlike many small independent shops, M&S was able to resist the rise of department stores and the competition of Woolworths, the American retailer that had entered the UK market in 1909. It could offer a broad range of products for low prices because they were mass-produced. The two most important products in the interwar years, however, were food and textiles, particularly the latter, which represented more than 80 percent of gross sales in the 1930s.[53] Simon Marks (1888–1964), the owner and director of the firm after the death of his father in 1907, explained to his shareholders in 1934: "We have to strike the right balance between variety and uniformity, for if uniformity makes for economy in production, it is variety which makes the appeal to the purchaser. We aim at standardisation of basic fabrics, but we avoid standardised uniformity in the finished article."[54]

M&S never invested in manufacturing facilities. It built rather strong business relations with British apparel makers—for example, I.J. Dewhirst, a clothing manufacturer from Leeds that supplied M&S with menswear.[55] However, that does not mean M&S was a passive partner. On the contrary, it organized some facilities to coordinate the design and production of garments. In 1928, it launched its own brand, St Michael, for garments made according to its own specifications.[56] It guaranteed the quality of the goods it sold. In 1933, M&S set up a merchandising committee to coordinate the activities of the different buying departments. During the Depression, reducing costs and waste was a major objective. In the following years, the company engaged more actively in the co-development of fashion, with the opening of a textile laboratory to control the quality of the goods supplied by different manufacturers (1935) and the organization of a design department, which incorporated a merchandising department (1936).[57] The design department employed Parisian designers.[58] Two years later, M&S began to purchase printed fabric designs from Paris.[59] The company kept close relations with its suppliers through cooperation with textile trade associations, such as the Wool Industries Research Association (WIRA), whose services it subscribed to in 1936.[60]

Most of the goods sold in M&S stores were made in Britain, although the company did source specific goods from foreign partners, such as artificial silk hosiery from Germany, during the interwar years. In 1939, 94 percent of goods sold by M&S were made in domestic factories and workshops.[61] The absence of investment in manufacturing by large fashion retailers before the Second World War, as in the case of M&S, was rare but not unique. It could be observed also in regional small department stores in Continental Europe. For example, in Switzerland in 1924, the company A. Girard & Cie, founded in the city of La Chaux-de-Fonds in 1905 as a mail-order business, introduced a confection department. It outsourced production to various independent manufacturers—for example, Jakob Weil in Zurich—and invested in a large new store in 1935, engaging in direct sales. Until the opening of its own factory in 1943, it outsourced production for nearly two decades.[62] In the United States, numerous specialized retailers of East Coast cities did not verticalize manufacturing, relying instead on the apparel industry, which had expanded rapidly since the late nineteenth century, particularly in New York. Subcontracting production to a network of independent small firms enabled them to offer a variety of garments at low prices.[63] Finally, Japanese department stores adopted this outsourcing model during the 1950s and 1960s, when they started the mass distribution of Western fashion. They cooperated closely with apparel manufacturers through a dense network of intermediaries to offer a broad variety of clothing to their customers.[64]

Conclusion

Fashion for the masses emerged in Western Europe and the United States at the end of the nineteenth century and was a phenomenon based on the growth of the urban working and middle classes. People stopped making their own clothes or buying them second hand, preferring to acquire them from the market. This fast-increasing demand was the driving force for the development of an apparel industry, divided between large firms and small independent workshops and new modes of distribution, essentially chains or retailers. The fashion industry also relied on the birth and growth of new kinds of services, such as the fashion press.

This model of fashion for the masses was still strongly rooted in Western culture. Important parts of the world, particularly in Asia and Africa, were outside this mode of consumption and social representation of what "fashion" was. Populations in these places were not "unfashionable" but had their own cultural values attached to this concept. Western dress and suits were not a globalized phenomenon yet. In the colonial world, outside the West, they embodied deeply imperialist values. Moreover, production remained primarily in the metropole, and colonies were used as mass markets. This does not mean that fashion systems in and out of the West had no connections to the rest of the world. Although they were different, there were numerous business and cultural exchanges between various parts of the globe, as the next chapter will discuss.

Chapter 4

West meets East and the Rest

> [The] clothing system differentiates our country from others and clarifies the differences between the high and low classes. It should not be overlooked as a pressing matter in the country's governance within the emperor system . . . We should establish a new system that follows the old laws, so to thoroughly demonstrate the original character of our country from the imperial court to the general public by abolishing yōfuku.[1]

In 1872, after the beginning of the Meiji Restoration, the Japanese emperor began wearing a Western-style uniform, marking the beginning of the modernization of Japanese society and the introduction of Western-style clothing for government officials, called *yōfuku*. The Japanese government in the Meiji era (1868–1912) used Western-style clothing to promote class equality, but the traditional elites opposed it, as the quote above shows.[2] In 1876, Monet painted a picture, *La Japonaise*, of a French woman wearing a kimono, reflecting excitement in France for Japanese culture. These events are embodiments of the circulation of fashion around the world. The cultural and material exchanges included not only textiles and fabrics but also values and styles. Moreover, these examples show that transfers were not only from the West to the rest of the world but were multidirectional—the West was also influenced by other parts of the world.

During the second half of the nineteenth century, fashion and textile relations between the East (Asia), the West (Europe and North America), and the South (Africa) developed in all directions. First, cotton connected the whole world, metaphorically. The Industrial Revolution, which began in Britain, was largely based on the production of cotton fabrics, which were then sold around the world. Raw cotton came mostly from the United States. The importation of silk and cotton fabrics from Japan increased steadily until the Second World War, and some Western entrepreneurs engaged in this business, also transferring their production technology to Japan to improve the quality and productivity of the textile industry. Japan would become the largest exporter of cotton fabrics in the world in the 1930s. To outperform the British Empire, however, Japanese manufacturers required state-of-the-art power looms, which were provided by British textile machine manufacturers, who dominated the world market, but also by a local family firm: Toyoda.

Second, the examples of China and Japan during the interwar years demonstrate the diffusion of Western fashions (accessories, clothes, styles, designs, etc.) in big cities (particularly Shanghai and Tokyo). This cultural transfer was an opportunity for European manufacturers to expand their commerce to this part of the world. It also allowed domestic entrepreneurs to launch their own production, promotion, and sales of Western fashion. The manufacture of military and school uniforms, which were the first mass-produced Western clothes in Asia, was extremely important for the diffusion of Western fashion. In Japan, for example, several textile companies specializing in the production of uniforms were engaged in the civil apparel business after the Second World War and became key players in this industry.

Third, printed cotton from India helped create demand for these fabrics in the West. This story goes back to the seventeenth and eighteenth centuries. Moreover, the exchange and imitation of wax fabrics from the East Indies to Europe, particularly the Netherlands, and the export to Africa shows how the fashion business had become global and simultaneously adaptive to local tastes during the nineteenth century.

This chapter addresses the following questions: How was fashion transferred between Western countries and Asia from the mid-nineteenth century to the mid-twentieth century? How did entrepreneurs adapt garments to local cultures? What were the business models behind these transfers? The chapter focuses mostly on the relations between China, India, and Japan, on the one hand, and Western Europe and the United States, on the other. However, the emergence of a market for wax fabrics in West Africa also shows how this continent was involved in the cultural and business exchange of a fashion industry that had, by now, become truly global.

How British cotton conquered the world and deindustrialized India

The first European traders to arrive in Southeast Asia after the discovery of the Cape route in 1497–1499 were the Portuguese. Their fleets (*Carreira da Índia*) were financed by the Crown. Only after the monopolistic spice trade declined at the end of the sixteenth century did the *Carreira da Índia* begin to trade in Indian cotton in Lisbon, as well as in East Africa, West Africa, and Brazil.[3] Around this time, the two most important East India companies were established in England (EIC) in 1600 and the Netherlands (VOC) in 1602, which broke the Portuguese monopoly. They were the first joint-stock companies in the world and could raise so much capital that they became dominant traders in commodities from the East, including spices, silk, cotton, tea, porcelain, and opium. Both chartered companies were granted monopolies to carry out trade with East Asia. They could be compared with the economic power of large multinationals nowadays, with settlements all over Asia that would eventually become the basis of the British and Dutch empires in the nineteenth century. However, their power was much greater than that of their modern counterparts—they had massive armies, could start wars, sign peace treaties, and conquer land.[4] In other words, the boundaries between early modern states and these companies were blurred.[5]

Although their governments had granted them monopolies, these two companies were constantly in competition. In India, the VOC and the EIC heavily competed for territories, trade posts, production centers, and port cities.[6] However, in the case of textiles, their interests differed. The VOC was much more interested in inter-Asian trade; Indian cotton was used to trade between Southeast Asia, India, and East Africa.[7] For example, to obtain Indonesian spices, it bought cloth at the Coromandel Coast, Gujarat, and Bengal, which was then used to trade on the market in Banda.[8] The EIC, on the other hand, aimed to bring back Indian cottons to Britain, the Americas, and West Africa. It became the dominant trader in the Indian cotton trade in the seventeenth and eighteenth centuries.[9] The EIC imported three types of cotton to Britain: muslin, white calico, and colored calico. Colored calico had become so popular in the home market that it was banned in 1721 under pressure from the woolen industry. White calico, which was more and more printed in England, and muslin, the finest expensive cotton, however, were not banned. Moreover, re-exports to West Africa and the British colonies in the Americas were not forbidden. It was also difficult to prevent the smuggling of colored calico via the ports of the Dutch Republic.[10] The trade of these chartered companies, despite the ban, created a taste for cotton and a market in Europe for a fabric that had previously had little value. It also laid the foundation for a worldwide trade in what would become the most important fabric of the nineteenth century. Cotton would connect the world as no other commodity had ever done before.[11]

The British Industrial Revolution, discussed in Chapter 1, changed the global production networks fundamentally. It was technology, capital, and ideas that created the machines for spinning and weaving in England, thus increasing productivity to unprecedented levels. The new factories soon outcompeted the Indian production technology, which was still based on hand spinning and handloom weaving. Moreover, the quality of British products improved to such an extent that they could compete with the Indian calico and muslin that had dominated the world market for two centuries. These large, new factories in Lancashire needed a constant flow of high-quality, cheap cotton, which came increasingly from the United States from the end of the eighteenth century. In the nineteenth century, American cotton became the main raw material for English factories, which depended on the abundant cheap labor in the United States because of the cotton fields worked by African slaves.[12] Furthermore, it was the British Empire, which emerged from the EIC's connections and possessions, that made it all possible. Markets all over the world, including India, absorbed stunning quantities of cotton fabrics from the Lancashire mills.

It is an ongoing debate whether the British Industrial Revolution and the expanding commercial empire destroyed the Indian cotton industry. We will not reproduce the debate here, but roughly, there were two phases of deindustrialization in India. First, weaving activity in India decreased when the British market was lost after the 1790s. Around 1850, a second phase began when cheap British cloth and yarn entered the Indian market, outcompeting Indian manufacturers.[13] Imports of yarn and textiles to South India increased by a factor of 6.5 and 7, respectively, during the period 1852–1882. In response, Indian manufacturers began to produce lower-quality cloth, which reduced the incomes of weavers and spinners. Hand spinning, often done by women as a side job in addition to agricultural work, vanished. As a result, many rural Indian families lost additional income.[14] In summary, a particularly negative picture can be drawn. However, this ignores the historical dynamics of the textile industry and the changes that occur constantly because of market disruptions. The West experienced this in the 1960s, India a hundred years earlier. It was inextricably linked to capitalism, a development Schumpeter called *creative destruction*: "the process of industrial mutation that incessantly revolutionizes the economic structure from within, incessantly destroying the old one, incessantly creating a new one."[15] The structure of the Indian cotton industry also changed in the second half of the nineteenth century. Cheaper yarns, increasingly imported from Britain, made Indian woven fabric cheaper and more competitive. In addition, from the 1870s onward, local capitalists in Bombay began to import spinning machines and power looms from Britain and produced cotton fabrics for global markets.[16]

Japan's Meiji Restoration, selective Westernization, and uniforms

After more than two hundred years of seclusion, Japan was forced to open to international trade in 1853 by the United States. The only exceptions had been the Dutch VOC, which was allowed to trade with Japan for more than two hundred years on the small artificial island of Deshima, near the port of Nagasaki, and Chinese merchants, also established in Nagasaki.[17] Between the late 1850s and the mid-1860s, Japan signed treaties with Western powers that allowed foreign merchants to settle in a handful of treaty ports, including Yokohama and Kobe. The Western impact led to a dramatic

Figure 4.1 Emperor Meiji and his Consort in the Plum Garden, by Kobayashi Kiyochika, Japan, 1887.
Source: Harvard Art Museums/Arthur M. Sackler Museum, Gift of Langdon Warner.

transformation of Japanese society and economy, characterized by the formation of a new state during the Meiji Restoration (1868). Clans of samurais from the southern island of Kyushu fought against the Tokugawa family, who had ruled Japan militarily since the early seventeenth century. They established the emperor as the head of state and initiated a policy of economic transformation. Technology and organizations transferred from Europe, and the United States contributed to the birth of modern Japan. However, despite the spread and growth of modern industries, change did not affect all aspects of society simultaneously. At first, the transformation of Japan relied on infrastructure, with the building of railways, electric power plants, banks, shipyards, etc. However, daily life and personal consumption remained less affected for several decades. Hence, some historians qualify the Meiji period (1868–1912) as an era of selective Westernization, to emphasize this difference.[18]

The slow Westernization of clothing and fashion must be understood within this context. On the one hand, the Japanese textile industry underwent deep and fast industrialization, especially in the field of cotton spinning. Modern factories modeled on British examples emerged in the 1880s. At the beginning of the twentieth century, these textile firms were internationalized. They invested in China and became established as competitive firms on the global market.[19] However, the Japanese people were still wearing traditional clothes. The first Western garments made in Japan were produced in the foreign settlements of Yokohama. Although these goods were mostly destined for Westerners living there, not for the Japanese, this contributed to the diffusion of a new material culture in Japan. Moreover, some tailors taught their sewing techniques to Japanese people as early as the late 1870s.[20] This was still exceptional; the shift toward Western-style apparel took several decades. The transformation of material culture for clothing was a three-stage process.

First, during the 1870s and 1880s, the Westernization of clothing was limited to military uniforms and tailored suits for men of the upper class. From 1872, the emperor and the imperial court began wearing Western clothes for official ceremonies. This expressed the will to be recognized as a modern developed country by Western powers. However, these aristocrats often continued to dress in traditional clothes at home.[21] Upper-class men and business executives followed this example. They wore Western suits at work and changed into kimonos when they returned home. Western suits were considered working uniforms. Department stores carried out several activities to offer male consumers new Western apparel. For example, Mitsukoshi appointed a British tailor as a cutter in 1906 and opened a sewing factory for menswear in Tokyo the following year.[22] As for tailored dresses for women, they emerged in the 1880s and spread slowly, starting in the upper class, where women imitated men. Production was mostly by hand by artisan tailors who had learned Western techniques abroad. Department stores also proposed Western clothing to their female customers. Between 1926 and 1930, Mitsukoshi appointed several Western women as designers and modelists for womenswear.[23] However, Western clothes for the upper class remained largely a niche market until the Second World War.

Second, the formation of a modern army based on conscription, as in Europe and the United States, not only led to the acquisition of new weapons but also the introduction of Western-style military uniforms. They were the first Western clothes mass-produced in Japan. This production stimulated the mastering of Western production techniques and the introduction of ready-to-wear. Several companies that acquired this knowledge shifted to civilian Western apparel production after the Second World War. This was also the case for Sanyo Shokai, which manufactured coats for the army and signed licensing agreements with Yves Saint Laurent and Burberry in the 1960s (see Chapter 7).

Third, and finally, home sewing for women and children appeared in 1920. Sewing schools had existed since the 1900s, especially under the influence of the Singer sewing machine, and dressmaking schools opened throughout the country in increasing numbers from the 1920s, diffusing sewing techniques to a young generation of women who became able to manufacture Western clothes at home for their families (see Box 4.1).[24]

The 1920s was a decade of social change during which the consumption of Western fashion spread outside the upper class thanks to the actions of department stores and sewing schools. One must also stress here the impact of the first fashion magazines. Their emergence in Japan needs to be understood in the context of a cultural change. For

Figure 4.2 Young *moga* (modern girls) walk down a Ginza street in 1928 dressed in "Beach Pyjama Style." Kageyama Kōyō.
Source: Public Domain via Wikimedia Commons.

Japanese people, particularly women, it was necessary not only to learn about and understand taste and style but also techniques related to producing Western clothes at home. During the interwar years, women's magazines helped diffuse such knowledge. According to Andrew Gordon, the monthly sales of women's magazines in the 1920s exceeded one million copies.[25] Most popular were *Fujokai* ("Women's World," launched in 1910), *Shufu no tomo* ("The Housewife's Friend," 1917), and *Fujin kurabu* ("Women's Club," 1920). These magazines did not specialize in clothing and fashion but were generally dedicated to the proper education of young women in a traditional way. The first magazine specialized in clothing and fashion was the monthly *Soen*, launched in 1936 by the designer school Bunka Gakuin, which played a key role in training young women to make Western clothes at home. Hence, the magazine of this school pursued the same objective. The goal of all these magazines was to raise and educate a new generation of girls suited to the modern, urban society but with respect for the traditional social order.[26] Indeed, during the 1920s, a new generation of young women, influenced by Hollywood actresses, used Western garments to express a new type of femininity—independent and free from traditional society. These "modern girls," or *moga,* as abbreviated in the Japanese language, gathered especially in the trendy district of Ginza in Tokyo. They were roundly criticized by the conservative bourgeoisie and disappeared in the mid-1930s during the Japanese militarist dictatorship when women were forced to be "good wife, wise mother" (see Chapter 5).

Box 4.1 The birth of designer schools in Japan

Designer schools played an important role, not only as places where young women could learn cutting and sewing techniques to make Western clothes but also as organizations that linked the various actors in the fashion business. The Bunka Fashion College (*Bunka Fukuso Gakuin*, BFC) was the leading institution for the dissemination of clothing knowledge and the training of designers. The institution traces its roots back to a small workshop in a clothing store. In 1919, the workshop began training young women to make Western-style clothes using sewing machines. It had close links with the manufacturer Singer and established itself as a pioneer in the creation of Western fashion in Japan during the interwar period, launching the country's first fashion magazine, *Soen*, in 1936. It aimed to promote the use and manufacture of Western clothing among the masses.

After the Second World War, the reopened BFC grew rapidly as the Westernization of fashion took off. Many young women and housewives entered schools like BFC to learn how to make Western-style clothes (see Chapter 7). At the same time, BFC expanded its activities from clothing to fashion. From the early 1950s, for example, it organized fashion shows in Tokyo and other major cities such as Nagoya, Osaka, and Kyoto. The college was also active in the fashion media. It relaunched *Soen* in 1946 and launched many of the first fashion magazines in postwar Japan for a more segmented market, notably *High Fashion* for the wealthy (1960) and *Mrs.* for young housewives (1961). The BFC also invited famous Western designers to give lectures and organize fashion shows, such as Christian Dior (1953), Howard Greer (1954), and Pierre Cardin (1958). Another way the institution promoted fashion in Japan was by creating several prizes for commendable design, including the Soen Prize (1957) and the Cardin High Fashion Prize; the latter was created when Pierre Cardin was appointed emeritus professor at the school (1961). Finally, in 1953, there was the creation of a department to train models.

Figure 4.3 Fabric selection for Christian Dior's new designs, in Tokyo, Japan on December 7, 1964.
Source: Photo by KEYSTONE-FRANCE/Gamma-Rapho via Getty Images.

Among other schools, Dressmaker Gakuin followed a similar model to BFC. Founded in 1926 in Tokyo by Yoshiko Sugino, a fashion stylist and businesswoman, it introduced the idea during the interwar period of ready-made women's clothing based on standardized sizes. Sugino and her students sewed and remade clothes for GIs (privates in the US army) in the postwar years, providing students with a good opportunity to study Western clothing patterns, materials such as buttons and fabrics, and style books. The school reopened in 1946 and expanded to include some 700 affiliated schools to teach sewing skills and dress patterns. Later, Sugino also founded a publishing company, Kamakura Shobo, which launched fashion magazines such as *Dressmaking* (1949) and *Madam* (1967), offering dress patterns that housewives could use for home sewing. In this way, Dressmaker Gakuin helped to spread the sewing of Western-style clothes in Japan; however, it focused on the upmarket, made-to-measure rather than the ready-made clothes that became popular in the 1960s. Another institution worth mentioning is the Kuwasawa Design School (*Kuwasawa dezain kenkyujo*), opened in Tokyo in 1954 by fashion and design journalist Yoko Kuwasawa. However, the size of its organization and

> the extent of its involvement in the fashion system were far less than those of the BFC and Dressmaker Gakuin.
>
> Sources: *Bunka Fukuso Gakuin: 40 nen no ayumi* ["Bunka Fashion College: 40th Anniversary"] (Tokyo: Bunka Fukuso Gakuin, 1963); Shigeichi Sugino, *Shigaku keiei no ikiru: watashino seikatsu to kangae [The Management of Private School]* (Tokyo: Nihon shobo, 1958); Yoko Yoshimoto, "Hana Hiraku Yosai Gakkou" [Developing Dressmaking School], In *Yosai no Jidai [The Era of Dressmaking]*, ed., Kazuko Koizumi (Tokyo: OM Shuppan), 21–46; Mikiko Tsunemi, *Kuwasawa Yoko to modan dezain undo* [Kuwasawa Yoko and Modern Design] (Tokyo: Kuwasawa gakuen, 2007).

Forced opening of China, the Opium Wars, and the Westernization of Chinese culture

Unlike Japan, China did not embark on a gradual Westernization of its clothing culture until the interwar years. After the end of the First Opium War in 1842, China had to open four new treaty ports to foreigners (Guangzhou had been accessible since the second half of the eighteenth century). Throughout the nineteenth century, Western power made a growing number of cities open to the settlement of foreigners. Their number amounted to forty-eight in 1913 and about eighty in 1930.[27] Shanghai was, however, the most

Figure 4.4 A studio photograph of a group of young society women in 1930s Shanghai proudly and confidently showing off their unbound feet and modern, Western footwear.

Photo by Pictures from History/Universal Images Group via Getty Images.

important of them, with a foreign community of about 65,000 people in 1937.[28] Foreigners established in these treaty ports gathered in special areas of the city, where they benefitted from their own political and administrative autonomy. They replicated their lifestyle in foreign settlements, eating Western food, living in Western houses, and wearing Western clothes. Their presence would have helped diffuse the new material culture to the Chinese population; however, the process was slow and limited in scope.

Chinese elites were much less keen to adopt Western fashion than the Japanese were. Although the imperial government decided to reform its army after its defeat in the First Sino–Japanese War, adopting a German-style uniform for its conscripts in 1903, this transformation of clothing culture was mainly limited to the military.[29] While dress culture was largely marked by tensions between various ethnic groups in the nineteenth century, the unification of China in the context of the struggle against semi-colonialism and Japanese expansionism led to the emergence of a cultural unification that had an impact on clothing.[30] The driver for this change was a shared feeling that China needed to enter an era of social change and economic growth to cast off the imperialist presence and take its destiny into its own hands. We can observe two main trends.

First, some modernist intellectuals and politicians advocated a drastic transformation of the country based on Westernization. After the establishment of the Republic of China under Sun Yat-sen in 1912, Shanghai and other large cities experienced social change characterized by a gradual Westernization of lifestyle. As in Japan at the end of the

Figure 4.5 Chinese-style garments in 1913, US. Abby E. Underwood / Meredith Corporation / Serials in Microfilm Collection (SIM).

Source: Public domain via Internet Archive and Wikimedia Commons.

nineteenth century, civil servants, male office workers in large corporations, and the young urban generation started to wear suits and Western clothes. In the 1920s, Chinese women in these large cities wore both Western and domestic garments, giving birth to a new fashion that expressed modernity.[31] The business of Western suits and dresses in Shanghai had a similar form to what was at that time worn in Paris and New York. Numerous tailors and small independent workshops manufactured these garments using sewing machines. The beginning of this industry was slow. Singer was hence unable to develop its sales satisfactorily in China before 1913.[32] However, in the 1920s, thousands of tailors, many of them migrants from Ningbo, were working in Shanghai. Some of them made Western clothing, while others produced Chinese garments inspired by the British and Russian material cultures. A Shanghai Cutting and Tailoring College was even opened in 1941.[33] These garments were notably sold through department stores.[34] Ningbo tailors emigrated to Hong Kong after the establishment of the People's Republic of China in 1949 and played a role in the development of the textile industry in that city.

Second, as early as 1912, the Republican government promoted the adoption of a new Chinese style, particularly for women, which would embody the specificity of Chinese culture in contrast to the West and Japan. The government issued guidelines about what the *ao qun* ensemble, consisting of a jacket and skirt, should look like to follow tradition. Then, in 1927, it engaged in the promotion of a new garment, the *qipao*, as the expression of a national dress.[35]

In the Western imagination, the *qipao*, seen as a Chinese dress, became the symbol of a new generation of Chinese women: free, modern, and sexualized. It lost its popularity after 1949 with the advent of Maoism but was resurrected in Hong Kong in the 1950s, where it enjoyed a second golden age.[36] *Qipao* dresses were mostly made at home by women themselves, although also individual tailors, inspired by some Western cutting techniques, manufactured some and sold them through department stores.[37] However, this new style, while promoted by the government, did not lead to the emergence of a new industry.

Chinese and Japanese influences on Western fashion

Although one can observe a slow Westernization of the clothing culture in Japanese and Chinese urban upper classes from the end of the nineteenth century, cultural exchanges between East and West were not unidirectional. Europeans had been fascinated by East Asia since the Middle Ages. The British and Dutch EICs brought back to Europe in their ships not only tea, raw silk, and spices but also fabrics and kimonos. Wearing Japanese-style garments in the seventeenth-century Netherlands became popular among the bourgeoisie.[38] However, the growing demand for Japanese-style silk gowns led the Dutch VOC to start manufacturing such products in India for the European market in the 1690s.[39] Similarly, the import of Chinese textiles and the imitation of Chinese designs by European designers goes back to the seventeenth century.

The development of trade relations after the opening of China and Japan in the mid-nineteenth century led to the growing influence of Asian culture on European fashion.

In the case of China, the import of silk, porcelain, umbrellas, and other manufactured goods popularized items identified with Chinese culture, such as lotus flowers and dragons. During the second half of the nineteenth century, these designs were used by some British, French, and American couturiers in their dresses, giving birth to a style called *chinoiserie*. Some elements of the style of Chinese clothing were also adopted, like long sleeves. Most of these dresses were luxury goods made from high-quality silk and often had embroidery.[40] Jeanne Paquin and Callot Soeurs are examples of French couturiers who made dresses inspired by Chinese culture at the beginning of the twentieth century. China was hence considered an exotic source of inspiration for Western designers. A study based on the American fashion magazine *Vogue* has shown that, until the 1920s, Chinese fashion was perceived as unaffected by outside influences such as Westerners. The study is based on the idea that Chinese civilization remained static because it had not undergone a process of modernization. This was the basis of the exoticism of Chinese fashion. However, after the 1920s, the social and economic development of China's major cities, particularly Shanghai, transformed how Chinese fashion was perceived in the West. The editorial writers at *Vogue* saw an evolving fashion system, shaped by Western influences but distinct. Stripped of imperial tradition, Chinese fashion

Figure 4.6 Silk dress with silk embroidery, 1933, attributed to Callot Soeurs. Tim Evansion via Flickr. Source: Reproduced under a CC BY-SA 2.0 license.

had its own modernity. This recognition went hand in hand with a certain loss of influence on Western designers.[41]

As for the Japanese material culture, it enjoyed enormous success in Europe and the United States between the 1870s and the beginning of the twentieth century, as part of what is commonly known as *Japonisme*. Artists, particularly Impressionist painters such as Monet, Manet, Renoir, and Van Gogh, were influenced by Japanese visual arts. Art collectors also played a significant role in this movement, purchasing numerous Japanese paintings, ceramics, and sculptures, which gave rise to the private collections that can be seen in Western museums.[42] Fashion was not an exception. European couturiers were largely influenced by fabrics, styles, and designs from Japan. For example, in the 1880s, Charles Frederick Worth used motifs and techniques inspired by Japanese *obi*, the belt of kimonos, in some of his creations. The material was French silk purchased in Lyon, but the style was influenced by Japan. This led Lyon manufacturers of silk fabrics to answer this new demand and propose some textiles with typical Japanese designs, such as chrysanthemums, flowing water, flowers, and birds.[43] After 1900, Paul Poiret created kimono-style coats, while from 1918 to 1920, Madeleine Vionnet made dresses based on Japanese techniques for making kimonos, such as cuts along straight lines and construction of clothes from rectangular pieces.[44] In the 1900s, some Parisian stores offered Japanese dresses to their customers, and some even advertised them in newspapers. This popularity was also supported by the activities of some Japanese personalities who had settled in Paris. One of the most famous was the actress Sada Yacco, a former geisha who performed (with her husband) kabuki theatre, wearing a kimono. She toured the United States and the UK in 1899 before making a career in Paris the following year, becoming a star among Parisian artists and the intelligentsia. Although she returned to Japan in 1902, her influence remained vivid in Paris—where she made a second visit in 1907. A boutique called *Au Mikado* sold Sada Yacco kimonos throughout the 1900s.[45]

Japonism reached its apogee at the beginning of the twentieth century. After the 1920s, however, Japanese cultural influence went into decline. The rise of a competitive Japanese industry, which challenged Western dominance in many markets, and imperial expansion in Asia, marked by the colonization of Taiwan (1895) and the Korean Peninsula (1910), as well as expansionism in China, made Japan less popular in the Western imagination. It lost its exotic and attractive character and became the expression of the Yellow Peril.[46] It was not until the 1970s that Japanese influence on Western fashion reemerged, thanks to the arrival of a new generation of Japanese designers in Paris and New York (see Chapter 7).

Wax fabrics connected Asia, Europe, and Africa

The production of wax fabrics in Asia and later in Europe and their consumption in Africa exemplifies how fashion, sometimes unintentionally, connects different parts of the world. The story of Indonesian batik, which was copied by Dutch, Swiss, and British industrialists and eventually became a great success in West and Central Africa from the late nineteenth century, is an example of how a fashion was copied, reproduced by other means, and eventually marketed on other continents.[47] Batik is a printed fabric based on wax resist. Its printing technique, which goes back to the Egyptian, Byzantine, and Indian cultures, became highly developed on Java.

During the Napoleonic Wars, the British took over the Dutch East Indies from the French for a few years (1811–1816) and began to export cotton to the archipelago. After they returned the Dutch East Indies to the Dutch, the new King William I saw ample trade opportunities in the nationalized colony. In 1799, the VOC had been declared bankrupt under the French occupation of the Republic of the Seven United Netherlands. Its possessions and conquered territories were taken over by the Dutch state, and the archipelago officially became a Dutch colony. The Dutch state immediately began to expand its territory and conquered other islands. At the same time, it expanded trade with the East Indies and exploited the islands. In 1824, the Dutch king established the Nederlandsche Handel-Maatschappij N.V. (NHM) to stimulate industry and trade, particularly with the Dutch colony. The aim of the NHM was, on the one hand, to trade in raw materials from the East Indies, such as coffee, tea, and sugar, and, on the other, to export textiles, particularly cotton, from the emerging Dutch textile industry to the colony. Dutch textile manufacturers were favored over foreign competitors because they paid much lower import duties. In addition, in 1830, the Dutch introduced a *Kultuurstelsel* (Cultivation System), which came down to a forced cultivation of export crops. Local peasants had to use 20 percent of their land for these colonial crops.[48]

Figure 4.7 Image of three cotton factories in Haarlem, Prévinaire & Co, in the 1840s. The top two factories are placed opposite each other in the image, while they were located at the extreme edges of the city. In 1875 the company was renamed Haarlemsche Katoen Maatschappij (HKM).

Source: North Holland Archives, 1100—image collection of the municipality of Haarlem, 45124.

In 1834, Belgium cotton manufacturer Jean Baptiste Theodore Prévinaire was attracted by the favorable contracts with the NHM and moved to Haarlem, where he opened the largest cotton-printing factory in the country, named *Prévinaire & Co* (from 1875 *Haarlemsche Katoen Maatschappij*, HKM). The company produced imitation batik for the Dutch East Indies market using a machine called the *javanaise*. In 1844, a competitor in Helmond in the south of the Netherlands, Pieter Fentener van Vlissingen, took over his father's cotton-printing factory. With a new printing machine, the factory began to compete on the international market for cotton and was renamed P.F. van Vlissingen & Co. Pieter's uncle, who owned plantations in Java, visited a small local batik factory and sent samples to Helmond, where they began to experiment with batik.[49] At the end of the 1850s, Van Vlissingen & Co. began to export its imitation batik to the Dutch colony and for some years the business flourished, although its main competitor in Haarlem was still bigger at the time. In the early 1870s, batik exports to the East Indies collapsed. The preferential treatment of Dutch imports ended in 1872, and the local producers introduced new competitive printing techniques with copper stamps (cap batik). Moreover, the Dutch imitation batik eventually did not meet the taste of the local population, who preferred locally made batik.[50]

It was a Scottish merchant, Ebenezer Brown Fleming, who found new market opportunities for the Dutch wax fabrics in Gold Coast (nowadays Ghana) in the 1890s. During the nineteenth century, Britain had incrementally conquered the land after several bloody wars and finally established a Crown colony in 1901. As the sole agent of HKM and through his connections to missionaries, Fleming learned that the rich local business elites, where wealth was based on the goldmines, palm oil, ivory, diamonds, and cacao, wanted to show off their fortunes with expensive wax fabrics. Fleming proposed that HKM adapt the patterns and prints on the fabrics to local tastes. Some of these prints became classics and are still popular today.[51] The initiative was a great success, which attracted other Dutch, Swiss, and British manufacturers of imitation batik. The Basel Mission Trading Company (BMTC) began to sell imitation batik, which was produced by Swiss manufacturers in Glarus. In 1910, another Dutch firm, Ankersmit & Co. (from 1902 NV Deventer Katoenmaatschappij, DKM), which originally produced indigo-dyed cotton (Blue Baft), also began to make wax fabrics. DKM had already worked with BMTC in Basel to sell its Blue Baft on the Gold Coast market, and now the Swiss traders started selling their batiks there too.[52] Van Vlissingen & Co., which had seen the lucrative East Indies batik market collapse, had entered East Africa with other printed cotton fabrics. However, it also noted the success of HKM in Gold Coast and aimed to follow its example. In 1910, it started collaborating closely with the British trading house F. & A. Swanzy for the sale of wax fabrics on the West African market. The fabrics were sold to local traders, mainly women, who also became wholesalers of wax fabrics outside Gold Coast into other countries in West and Central Africa.

The First World War brought an abrupt end to the wax fabrics boom in West Africa and the bankruptcy of HKM, the largest supplier of those fabrics, which had focused too much on one market and one product. Van Vlissingen & Co. and DKM survived the war by focusing on the domestic market with other fabrics. After the First World War, the West

African market recovered, and in 1930 F. & A. Swanzy was taken over by the United Africa Company, which, as part of Unilever, had become the leading trader in imitation batik in West and Central Africa. The two remaining Dutch companies, Van Vlissingen and DKM, were able to benefit from HKM's established position and know-how. They were given the exclusive rights to sell their wax fabrics through the UAC and became the undisputed market leaders during the interbellum.[53] After the Second World War, Unilever's UAC asked the Dutch manufacturers to expand their production capacity. DKM could not meet the demand of the Anglo-Dutch multinational, but Van Vlissingen & Co could. The company in Helmond grew to become the absolute market leader in West and Central Africa, both in quality and quantity, and was renamed Vlisco in 1970.

Conclusion

Fashion production and fashion styles moved in two directions, particularly during the period of modern imperialism. On the one hand, the manufacture of textiles and garments developed in Asia, leading, for example, to large and competitive firms in Japan. Department stores also became new actors in Asian cities and contributed to the diffusion of Western fashion. On the other hand, the transfers of styles and culture exchanges developed in both directions at the same time. Japanese and Chinese traditional designs influenced Western designers as much as Western clothing culture was diffused in Tokyo and Shanghai during the interwar years. The West African market became the most important destination for Indonesian wax fabrics, which were produced in Europe, particularly the Netherlands.

These fashion transfers, however, were not permanent but closely linked to national-identity policies. For example, in Japan, the Westernization of clothes came to a halt when the militaristic nationalist government came to power (see Chapter 6). Similarly, China's nationalist movement during the 1920s and 1930s created a stronger emphasis on China's cultural heritage and fashion style. The *qipao* dress was created in the 1920s and was turned into high-style evening wear.

The actors engaged in this process of transfers around the globe included large companies, individual businessmen, designers, and governments. However, it was not only a top-down process. Consumers played an active role as well, imitating the trends set by the upper class—as in Japan, for example, where urban white-collar workers started to dress like aristocrats and executives of large companies. Similarly, young women in Tokyo and Shanghai during the 1920s used Western dress to stress their female identity and independence. This chapter also clearly shows that private companies, often supported by local governments, be they colonial or independent, organized the exchange of products, cotton, or silk and the dissemination of styles. In addition, because of the industrialization of fabrics and clothes production, Western colonial companies could outcompete local artisanal firms in, for example, India. However, in independent countries like Japan, local manufacturers were able to increase productivity and industrialize fabric and clothing production, which were also supported by protectionist policies.

Box 4.2 Chinese and Japanese raw silk and the European and US silk industry before the Second World War

The revival of the silk route in the middle of the nineteenth century fits perfectly into the general story of this book on global fashion. The East was linked to the West and the other way around. Silk was the finest and most desired fabric in fashion industries worldwide because of its durability, luxurious feel, and shimmering appearance. Before the 1850s, Europe's silk industry depended largely on local production of raw silk. The silk industry in France was technologically more advanced and was, for the greater part, sourced with raw silk from Italy and France. Innovations in sericulture (the raising of silkworms and silk cocoons), the introduction of steam filatures (mechanized silk reeling), and the Jacquard power loom for silk weaving made France the most advanced silk nation in the world. However, a major silkworm disease destroyed French and Italian raw silk production in 1855. French silk manufacturers needed import substitution, which they found in China.

After the two Opium Wars in the 1840s and 1850s, China was forced to open treaty ports, including Shanghai, to Western traders. Although Britain had failed to set up its own sericulture, it gained a dominant position in the raw silk trade with China, particularly after the end of the Second Opium War in 1860. As a result, French silk manufacturers increasingly bought Chinese raw silk from London merchants. With the opening of the Suez Canal in 1869, the sailing distance to France became shorter, and French merchants became more independent from Britain. Japan also entered the international silk market after the opening of the country. The production and international trade of raw silk, also stimulated by the Japanese government, increased rapidly. Between 1880 and 1930, around half of French raw silk imports came from China and Japan. While the raw silk floated to Europe, technology and investments moved in the other direction. European manufacturers invested, for example, in steam filatures in Shanghai to boil the cocoons mechanically and reel the threats of silk. Western technology was also rapidly adopted in Japan, which increased productivity and lowered export prices.

Meanwhile, the United States was also developing its own textile industry based on cotton, wool, and silk. The infant industry was protected behind tariff walls against European, particularly British and French, imports. The know-how was, however, copied from the European textile industry. Many European immigrants in Paterson, New Jersey, the center of the American silk industry, had been trained in the industry in Europe. Beginning in the late 1860s, Chinese and Japanese raw silk entered the United States via the West Coast and was transported to the East Coast via the transcontinental railroad. Around 1900, the American silk industry flourished due to the increasing demand for luxury clothing, including lingerie, socks, and hosiery. Moreover, it was using the most advanced and largest machines in the world. By the 1910s, the United States surpassed French silk production, perhaps not in exclusivity but certainly in volume and value. Meanwhile, Japan had outcompeted China in exports of raw silk, particularly to the United States. The American mechanized industry preferred the more regular structure of Japanese raw silk because the large mechanical looms could process these fibers better. The Japanese were better able than the Chinese to apply Western technology and science to their production methods, including genetics. This allowed them to offer a more consistent product at competitive prices. In addition, the exportation of raw silk and fabrics from Japan was supported by design centers founded throughout the country by the government and trade associations to adapt Japanese-manufactured fabrics to Western tastes and markets. Around 1900, the United States became the largest importer of silk in the world, and by the 1910s, almost half of US imports came from Japan, which would even expand to 90 percent in the 1930s. However, in that decade, the silk industry entered an existential crisis because of the economic downturn following the Wall Street crash of 1929 and the spectacular increase in the use of rayon (artificial silk) in the fashion industry. The consequences for Japan were dramatic. Raw silk had been the most important export product and thus for decades the main source of foreign exchange and the driver of investment in the Japanese industry. As a result, significant parts of the Japanese population, especially in rural areas where people were heavily dependent on sericulture, became severely impoverished during the 1930s.

Figure 4.8 "Materials Our Grandmothers Never Knew." Advertisement for pine oil products manufactured and sold by the Hercules Powder Company for use in the production of textiles. Hercules Incorporated.
Source: Courtesy of Science History Institute.

Sources: William W. Lockwood, "Japanese Silk and the American Market," *Far Eastern Survey* 5.4 (1936): 31–36; John R. Stewart, "The Position of Silk in Japanese Exports," *Pacific Affairs* (1948): 46–51; Elson E. Boles, "Critiques of World-Systems Analysis and Alternatives: Unequal Exchange and Three Forms of Class and Struggle in the Japan? US Silk Network, 1880? 1890," *Journal of World-Systems Research* (2002): 150–212; Debin Ma, "The Modern Silk Road: The Global Raw-Silk Market, 1850–1930," *The Journal of Economic History* 56.2 (1996): 330–355; Lillian M. Li, "Silks by Sea: Trade, Technology, and Enterprise in China and Japan," *The Business History Review*, Vol. 56, No. 2 (Summer, 1982): 192–217.

Chapter 5

American fashion

These American designs differ from the Paris designs in this way: The Paris idea is to make extreme changes in designs and to make those changes as often as possible, so that a woman must change her dress or look out of style. The Paris modistes must do this because fashions with them are no longer an art as they once were—they have commercialized them. Their establishments have grown to be gilded salons, with enormous salary lists, and to keep their workrooms busy they must make a woman change her style often. Their life depends on this. I claim that this is wrong.[1]

This was part of an article, published in the *New York Times* in 1912, written by Edward Bok, one of the most avid promoters of American fashion at the expense of Parisian fashion houses.[2]

After the War of Independence, US patriots encouraged women to adopt a more simple, less extravagant style of dress; however, American middle-class women in the expanding cities of the nineteenth century mostly preferred the Parisian style. In the early twentieth century, fashion nationalists aimed to transform fashion consumption habits in the United States, in line with the general protectionist economic policies of the US administration. Tariffs on fashion and textile imports were very high to defend the country's textile and clothing industry, which had come to full development at the end of the nineteenth century. Some businessmen endeavored to develop American fashion for American women. These campaigns were not only driven by American business interests but were also intended to create a more sober, less extravagant domestic style. Fashion nationalists briefly appeared to have some success, particularly in the first year of the First World War when Parisian salons and couture houses were closed. However, it was clear that department stores, garment manufacturers, and fashion magazines like *Vogue* still looked to Paris for style direction.

Despite this failing nationalistic campaign, the influence of the United States on global fashion in the nineteenth and twentieth centuries was staggering. American cotton was feeding the European textile mills, and the market for cheap clothes for slaves in the cotton fields and uniforms during the War of 1812 (against Britain, Spain, and several indigenous tribes) and the American Civil War between North and South (1861–1865) would change how clothes were produced for and worn by the masses. Ready-to-wear manufacturing with uniform sizes and the use of sewing machines would revolutionize the fashion industry globally. This chapter explores how the American fashion industry changed after the middle of the nineteenth century and how the American industry aimed to create its own fashion. The American way of making simpler fashions with less refined fabrics and relaxed styles would first conquer the American market after the First World War and ultimately change how people dressed around the world in the twentieth century. People would dress in ways fashion nationalists had never imagined.

Fur, cotton, and slavery

From the beginning of the colonization of North America, fur—especially beaver fur—played a critical role in the development of internal and external trade. French, British, and Dutch chartered companies, including the French West India Company, the Hudson's Bay Company, and the Dutch West India Company (WIC), set up trading posts and forts for fur trade with the indigenous people during the seventeenth and eighteenth centuries. In Europe, fur was mainly used for the manufacturing of felt hats and the trimming of garments. However, during the nineteenth century, fur went out of fashion, which resulted in collapsing prices, bankruptcies of fur companies, and poverty for indigenous peoples in the Americas.[3]

In the early nineteenth century, a new raw material for the European fashion industry began to play a key role in US economic development: cotton. Since the Industrial

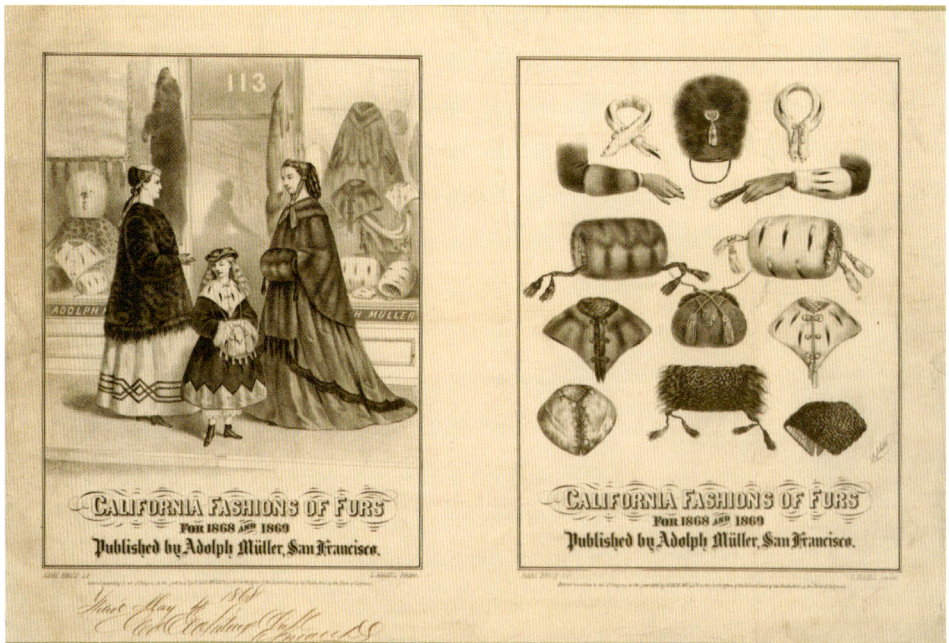

Figure 5.1 California fashions of furs for 1868 and 1869.
Source: Louis Nagel / Library of Congress Prints and Photographs Division.

Revolution, which began in England at the end of the eighteenth century, the hunger for "white gold" needed to be satisfied.[4] English manufacturers had begun to spin and weave cotton. Raw cotton, however, needed to be imported from the South, the Ottoman Empire, the Caribbean, India, and West Africa. With mechanization and the tremendous rise in productivity in the British spinning and weaving of cotton, demand for, as well as the price of, raw cotton skyrocketed. The rising demand could not be met by planters in the Ottoman Empire and India because of a lack of land and labor. Planters in the British and French Caribbean, and a little later, Brazil, however, had abundant land, European capital, and African unfree labor to increase the production of raw cotton massively. The rise of the mechanized cotton industry in England, and at a slower pace in France, went hand in hand with a tremendous increase in slavery in the Americas. However, a large slave revolt in Saint Dominque stopped production and exports to France in 1791. An alternative production location for slave-based cotton cultivation became the newborn nation of the United States of America (1776).[5] Climatic conditions in the South were perfect for cotton cultivation; land could be taken easily from the native people, and slaves could be imported from West Africa or the Caribbean. From the 1790s till the Civil War (1861–1865), the United States expanded its cotton production till it became the biggest supplier of raw cotton to the British and French textile mills.[6] Just before the Civil War, the value of cotton was 61 percent of the value of all goods exported from the United States.[7] During the Civil War, it became crystal clear how interconnected and dependent the world of textiles and fashion had become. In 1862, one year after the beginning of this bloody war, half of the British textile workers were pushed out of work as many mills were closed. In France, which had completely run out of cotton, the situation was even worse. Agitated British manufacturers lobbied the government to intervene in this war that was far from home but had tremendous repercussions for the European economy.[8]

Industrialization and textiles

At the beginning of the American Civil War, only 16 percent of the population lived in urban environments, and only one-third of national income was earned in an industry located in the northeast. The war between North and South was not only a war about the abolition of slavery but also a conflict between an economy based on agriculture and unfree labor and a modern industrialized economy based on free labor, mainly immigrants from the old continent.[9] The North and South also had different views on import tariffs. The industrial North wanted high tariffs to defend its infant industries against cheap products from more advanced nations like Britain. The South, on the contrary, wanted low tariffs because they had to import nearly everything, including fabrics and cloth, from the English factories.[10] During the war, the United States increased tariffs to finance the war, but at the end of the war, tariffs remained high, and its industry expanded at an unprecedented scale and speed.[11]

On the eve of the First World War, the United States was the most important industrial nation in the world. By 1913, its industry produced 36 percent of the global industrial output, two and a half times more than Germany and Britain and six times more than France.[12] The share of the population living in cities in the United States would soon increase to 41 percent. America's successful and rapid industrialization can be explained by three main factors. First, it had the largest and fastest-growing domestic market in the world: its population had increased rapidly in an unlimited space. Second, the US market was more homogenous—class distinctions mattered much less than in the old European Continent. Third, the large, open internal market stimulated mass marketing and manufacturing, supported by an openness to new technologies. As a result, the United States rapidly developed the machinery for mass production.[13]

The beginning of the Industrial Revolution in America can be traced back to the early nineteenth century when the textile industry started in the northeast. These new factories, built along the rivers in New England and New York, were powered by waterfalls. Steam engines were only introduced decades later. In the eighteenth century, spinning and weaving happened in households, and the making of clothes was mainly done at home by housewives or tailors. However, during the war years, from 1793 until 1815, the United States was cut off from cheap British imports of cotton fabrics; as a result, local production was stimulated. Manufacturers set up spinning mills with stolen British technology. British immigrant Samuel Slater is often called the father of the American Industrial

Figure 5.2 Young Spinner—Indian Orchard Cotton Mill. Photograph from the records of the National Child Labor Committee (U.S.), 1916.

Source: Lewis Wickes Hine / National Child Labor Committee Collection, Library of Congress Prints and Photographs Division.

Revolution because he introduced water-powered spinning technology to the United States. Weaving, however, was still done at home via the putting-out system.[14] This rather inefficient system was replaced by Francis Cabot Lowell and his associates, who built the first integrated spinning and weaving factory in Waltham, Massachusetts. Lowell (1775–1817) had visited several factories in England and smuggled plans for a power loom out of Britain, which he copied in his new factory. The initial capital of $100,000 (later raised to $600,000) for the Boston Manufacturing Company was gathered via stocks sold to the Boston mercantile families.[15] The method was later used for trading companies but not for industrial enterprises. Financing an enterprise in this innovative way made it possible to build the largest mill in the United States with a relatively cheap labor force of 300 mainly unmarried country girls from nearby farms, who mostly had experience with spinning and weaving at home. The girls lived in boarding houses near the mill under strict moral rules and worked an eighty-hour week. The Waltham mill had the lowest unit costs, was efficient, and highly profitable. After the introduction of tariffs on foreign textiles in 1816, it even became competitive with cheaper British cloth.[16]

By the early 1820s, river water did not deliver enough power for expansion; therefore, the associates looked for a new site, which they found at the Merrimack River. They built new mills, still based on waterpower, and founded a new city, Lowell, named in memory of the founding father of the first integrated textile mill, who had died five years earlier. While the city of Lowell would become renowned as the cradle of the American Industrial Revolution, the city of Waltham was at this time more significant.[17] Only during the 1830s, after coal had become available in the United States to feed the steam engines, were integrated steam mills built that could compete with British textiles. The cotton textile industry was not only the first industrial sector but would become the largest sector with the biggest firms in the United States (see Table 5.1).[18]

By 1860, the cotton goods industry was in the lead with a total value added of $59 million. Even though, because of mechanization, machinery and iron and steel would take over the leading position, the cotton textile industry remained one of the key industries for the next sixty years. The textile industry also became more diverse, incorporating in due course clothing, shoes, and woolen goods. However, if you add cotton goods and cotton clothing together ($458 million in 1900), the textile industry was still the largest industry measured in added value.

Ready-to-wear

Mechanization and industrialization in the United States thus started in the textile industry, first cotton and later wool as well. However, as labor was in short supply in this fast-growing country, causing wages to rise, the drive for mechanization was strong.[19] Slave labor and immigration had to solve the labor shortages; mechanization of production processes was another solution. A major prerequisite for the mechanization of cloth making was a change of fashion around the beginning of the nineteenth century toward

Table 5.1 Ten Leading Industries in America 1860–1920, by Value Added, 1914 Prices (Millions of 1914 American Dollars)

1860 Industry	Value Added	1880 Industry	Value Added	1900 Industry	Value Added	1920 Industry	Value Added
Cotton goods	59	Machinery	111	Machinery	432	Machinery	576
Lumber	54	Iron and steel	105	Iron and steel	339	Iron and steel	493
Boots and shoes	53	Cotton goods	97	Printing and publishing	313	Lumber	393
Flour and meal	43	Lumber	87	Lumber	300	Cotton goods	364
Men's clothing	39	Boots and shoes	82	Clothing	262	Shipbuilding	349
Machinery	31	Men's clothing	78	Liquor	224	Automotive	347
Woolen goods	27	Flour and meal	64	Cotton Goods	196	General Shop construction	328
Leather goods	24	Woolen goods	60	Masonry and brick	140	Printing and publishing	268
Cast iron	23	Printing	58	General shop construction	131	Electrical machinery	246
Printing	20	Liquor	44	Meatpacking	124	Clothing	239

Source: Joël Mokyr. *Economic History of the United States Since 1865*. Lecture Notes Economics Northwestern University, https://faculty.wcas.northwestern.edu/~jmokyr/Graphs-and-Tables.PDF (accessed December 15, 2021).

a simpler, natural look for men in line with the neoclassical interpretation of the natural forms of the body. While female fashion would take longer to move toward more simple dresses, men's fashion in England and the United States had already changed. These simpler and easier forms could be measured proportionally, and their production multiplied.[20] This principle was used for the first time to produce uniforms during the War of 1812, an unpopular war that ended in a stalemate. However, the Peace of Ghent[21] brought more unity to the new state, the final removal of indigenous people from their territories, and the expansion of the United States to the Pacific. Moreover, it created innovation in the textile and fashion industry—that is, ready-to-wear. After the war, ready-to-wear or readymade clothes made in different uniform sizes (contrary to made-to-measure or bespoke) were used more and more in the American men's clothing industry.[22]

The invention and introduction of the sewing machine was the next step in the mechanization of shoe production and clothing in the United States during the 1850s. The sewing machine revolutionized the clothing industry in the United States by increasing labor productivity, making apparel cheaper, and creating many new jobs in the clothing industry. At first, the simpler ready-to-wear clothes were produced for seamen, workers, and slaves on the cotton fields, but as sewing machines improved, clothes-making became more sophisticated. Sewing machines were also used more and more to make coats and suits.

The Civil War (1861–1865) created a huge demand for military uniforms, and this stimulated the development of the American made-to-measure clothing industry. The government also standardized sizes for uniform production, and these standards were later applied to civilian production. After the war, children's and women's ready-to-wear developed, and the machines used for uniforms began producing civilian clothes. The Panic of 1873 triggered an economic depression that forced many consumers to buy cheaper clothing and stimulated a further rise in the American readymade clothing industry.[23]

The rise of New York fashion

The advent of department stores in the growing cities of the East and mail-order catalogs created a demand for made-to-measure fashion. With the introduction of the sewing machine in larger production units in Philadelphia, Boston, and New York, a constant flow of clothing was guaranteed. New York, however, began to control the industry during the 1880s because it had significant competitive advantages over Philadelphia and Boston. First, it could use the Hudson Seaway Valley to bring in raw materials via steamships. Secondly, New York's seaport received a constant flow of immigrants, mainly Italians and Jews from Germany, Eastern Europe, and Russia. Thirdly, many Jewish immigrants had a traditional tailoring background and could be hired cheaply in the sweatshops, as they would later be called. The number of clothing manufacturing firms more than tripled from 562 in 1880 to 1,823 in 1900, mainly located in Manhattan's Lower East Side, where many immigrant communities from the other side of the Atlantic had settled.[24] Labor conditions in these sweatshops were so appalling that the workers often went on strike, which eventually led to the formation of the International Ladies Garment Workers Union (ILGWU) in 1900. Labor conditions remained poor, and salaries were very low. In 1909, 20,000 women went on strike in New York, making it the then-largest female strike in US history. It was not until the First World War that labor conditions in the American fashion industry would improve.[25]

While haute couture flourished in Paris, and fashion for the masses boomed in Berlin and Leeds, on the other side of the Atlantic, on the East Coast, the textile and fashion industries were developing rapidly as well. In the fast-growing cities of the United States, demand for both high fashion and cheaper clothes was growing tremendously. Before the First World War, however, French fashion still dominated the minds of American women, confirmed by the images in the department stores, where French designer clothing, newspapers, and fashion magazines were on display. By 1911, the Chambre Syndicale de la Couture Parisienne was organizing regular fashion events for American buyers and the press to show the latest Parisian styles.[26] There was constant communication with Paris about the latest design ideas; however, a lot of the Parisian styles distributed in newspapers were sketches made at home, and thus interpretations of Parisian style were sold as French. As Marlis Schweitzer states: "Ironically, the American cultural institutions, publications, and dressmakers—perhaps more than the Paris couturiers—shaped American perceptions of Paris fashion."[27]

New York not only became an important production location for clothing. Fashion distribution and marketing began to play a big role through the newly founded department stores via the local market and mail-order catalogs for more distant customers. The rise of New York as a fashion city is demonstrated by the publication of two fashion journals, *Harper's Bazaar*, launched by the Hearst Corporation in 1867, and *Vogue*, produced by Harper's art director, Arthur B. Turnure, and launched in 1892 (later purchased by Condé Nast in 1909). Originally, these journals focused on the elite fashionistas, but in due course, they also served the reader interests of the female middle class all over the United States. In the same period, two fashion design schools were established in the city: the Pratt Institute's fashion design program (1888) and the Parsons School of Design (1897).[28] However, fashion was still not designed in the United States—inspiration came from Paris.

Paris was leading; it was synonymous with fashion. Very conscious of their reputation in the United States, Parisian designers created a business model whereby they sold their sketches to companies in New York. The clothes were then made with local fabrics and local production methods and often sold in department stores or through mail-order catalogs. Department stores also opened buying offices in Paris and showcased original Parisian designs. *Harper's Bazaar* and *Vogue* would further arouse female lust for Paris extravaganza.[29] But the French couturiers themselves also directly advertised their designs in the US market. In 1910, Jeanne Paquin showed her creations at fashion exhibitions in the United States, and two years later, she opened a fur shop in New York. In 1911, Paul Poiret made a similar fashion tour in the United States, showing his collections.[30] However, in 1914, he set up a syndicate to defend French dressmakers and fight imitation and counterfeiting of French designs by American garment manufacturers. His initiative was short-lived because many French couturiers did not want to alienate the American buyers of French high-end fashion.[31]

In the interwar period, the ready-to-wear industry in New York reached its zenith. As a result of new techniques, like powered cutting machines and new materials like rayon, large-scale production became more efficient than homemade or tailormade clothing. Despite the rise of several large garment companies in New York, like the shirtwaist and dressmaker Gill & Rentner, most of these companies remained rather small.[32] By 1923, New York produced 80 percent of all apparel in the United States. In the same period, the textile industry moved to the western half of Midtown Manhattan as the manufacturers followed the retailers, who wanted to be closer to Pennsylvania Railroad Station to serve outside buyers but also followed the workers who were leaving the boroughs. Hence, the "Garment District" or "Seventh Avenue" was born.[33]

The rise of denim

Levi Strauss, born in a Jewish family in Bavaria as Löb Strauß, emigrated to New York in 1847 to join his brothers' wholesale dry-goods company, J. Strauss Brother & Co. When he heard the news of the Gold Rush on the West Coast, he decided to try his luck on the other side of the United States, where he set up his own dry-goods business in San Francisco in 1853. There, he sold goods like clothing, underwear, textiles, and tents to small shops that outfitted gold diggers but also families who had recently moved to the West.[34] His company also represented the family business in New York and was named Levi Strauss & Co. In 1872, Strauss received a letter from one of his customers, Jacob Davis, a tailor. Davis proposed that Strauss patent his idea of using rivets at the points of strain in a pair of jeans. The tailor needed capital to patent his idea, and the merchant saw a business opportunity. The patent for riveted jeans was granted to Jacob Davis and Levi Strauss & Company in 1873.[35] Workers' trousers made from denim—previously called "waist overalls" or simply "overalls"—had been around for years, maybe centuries.[36] Nevertheless, riveted blue jeans became an instant fad and one of the icons of American fashion history.

Competitors followed suit to the extent that, before the patent expired in 1890, Levi Strauss sued several competitors for infringements.[37] Because the courts could not stop the many small imitators, Strauss began to brand his product with colored stitches, a small watch, or coin pocket, lot-numbering, and a two-horse leather patch logo. Some competitors were also successful and conquered part of the US market. Henry David

Figure 5.3 Advertising for Levi Strauss: "It's no use they can't be ripped." Included in the exhibit "Levi Strauss: A History of American Style," February 13, 2020–August 8, 2021 at the Contemporary Jewish Museum in San Francisco.

Source: Levi Strauss.

Lee, a Kansas-based merchant who sold working clothes first made by others, began to sell his own "coveralls" under the Lee brand. As Levi Strauss had almost monopolized the gold miners' and farmers' markets in the West, Lee targeted the workers in the rapidly expanding industry in the northeast of the United States. Another competitor that became big was Hudson Overall Company, set up in 1904 in Greensboro, North Carolina, which targeted cowboys, whose numbers had risen owing to the rapidly increasing population needing more meat. In 1919, it changed its name to the Bell Blue Overall Co. and became famous with a brand called Wrangler during the 1940s.[38]

During the First World War, more women took factory jobs to replace men, and the demand for denim overalls grew because skirts were too dangerous to wear in many war plants. This reality had two long-lasting effects. Wearing trousers became more acceptable for women, and denim overalls entered the leisure market. Jeans became a gender-neutral fashion item in the United States during the 1930s.[39] Changes in the production, distribution, and consumption levels created a massive shift from a working-class to a middle-class garment.

On the production side, Levi Strauss, for example, suffered tremendously from the economic crisis because expenditures on work clothing plummeted. The company began to target the middle-class market using Western and frontier advertising campaigns. This eventually led to an article in *Vogue* in 1935 on the Lady Levi, which led to new outlets for denim, including department stores. Meanwhile, the New Deal stimulated workers' activism and egalitarianism and inspired writers, singers, artists, and photographers, many of whom promoted jeans as the new symbol of the Empire of Liberty.[40]

Leisure and sportswear

The First World War destroyed empires, many traditional values, and economic and political systems; however, it also ushered in modern art, the motor vehicle, the airplane, new ideas, and a revolution in fashion. Before the war, Paul Poiret had innovated the modern silhouette, got rid of the repressive corset, and showed the natural female form. He traveled several times to the United States and enjoyed celebrity status there. After the war, new designers with revolutionary ideas entered the stage, one of whom was Gabrielle Chanel, better known as Coco Chanel. She introduced the idea of elegant simplicity to high fashion and used cheaper new synthetic textiles like rayon instead of natural silk, the most important fiber of high-end fashion. American buyers loved her ideas. In 1931, she was invited to design clothes for Hollywood movies, introducing her *garçonne* style—boyish silhouette, loose and comfortable clothes, sporty haircut, and very little make-up—popularizing her fashion ideas to audiences in the United States and the rest of the world.[41] Another Parisian star designer who promoted the new style of simplicity was Jean Patou (1887–1936). Before the First World War, he had already sold his collections to New York stores, but after the war, he wanted to connect to the US market directly and sailed to the United States. Patou wanted to study American women in their natural

Figure 5.4 Vogue 1928. Model, holding a pole and reaching for gymnastic rings, wearing a two-piece bathing suit with a belted striped sweater top and wool jersey shorts with a white bathing cap, by Jean Patou.
Source: Photo by George Hoyningen-Huene/Condé Nast via Getty Images.

environment and finally returned with six American models to showcase his next collection. Furthermore, he was inspired to open a sportswear boutique in his couture house in Paris.[42] These two cases reveal how globally connected the fashion world of that era had become. It was no longer a one-way street—France inspired America and the other way around.[43]

Although American fashion nationalists were not as successful as they would have liked, American styles and fashion production would continue to develop in their own directions in the 1920s and 1930s. This had a huge impact on the way Americans, and later Europeans, and eventually the rest of the world dressed. During the 1920s, American middle-class culture changed, and sportswear became a popular word to describe a less formal style and the wearing of interchangeable fashion items.[44] On the West Coast during the 1930s, sportswear would get another connotation, meaning informal, relaxed leisurewear not necessarily related to sports. The masculine California style was a mixture of Hollywood and Palm Springs, blending "the American Ranch and the French Riviera," as William Scott describes it.[45] Los Angeles would take the lead in developing the men's leisure and sportswear industry during the 1930s and 1940s. At the beginning of the 1930s, garment production in California was limited, and the market was quite regional compared to manufacturing clusters in New York and Chicago. However, within twenty years, Los Angeles manufacturers had become serious competitors in the national menswear market. California-style clothing, produced on the West Coast, was increasingly sold on the East Coast. As a journalist observed in 1943:

> Los Angeles is not by any means first as a garment production center in the United States, but its influence on styles is of the widest. It ranks second only to New York in the numbers of ready-to-wear buying offices through which leading American stores contact manufacturers of women's clothing.
>
> Southern California, and particularly Los Angeles, has won pre-eminence in the field of sports or leisure-time fashion for men and women, primarily because California provides a marketable romantic background for merchandise and also because Hollywood holds its unique leadership as dictator of styles.[46]

Some firms in Los Angeles had been established as early as the 1890s, like Cohn, Goldwater & Company (1896), making and selling branded (The Boss) overalls and shirts.[47] In 1898, Brownstein, Newmark & Louis also began manufacturing and selling branded overalls (Stronghold) in Los Angeles. Newark left the firm in 1910, and Brownstein-Louis Co. was incorporated a year later. The company also began to produce and sell other fashion items, including trousers, shirts, and jackets, under the brand name Hendan and became recognized as one of the pioneers of the California sportswear industry.[48] In 1907, Bentz Knitting Mills started as a small manufacturer of underwear and sweaters; it later changed its name to Pacific Knitting Mills in 1912 and finally to Catalina. The company became big and famous as a sportswear brand after its swimwear was worn by female Hollywood stars during the 1930s.[49]

Box 5.1 Hollywood and fashion: How the movies changed the way we dressed

During the 1920s and 1930s, Hollywood changed the way women and men in America and Europe dressed themselves. At the time, there existed no stronger fashion influencer in the world than Hollywood movies. Fashion magazines, of course, had an impact, particularly on the higher strata of society, but the moving images of fashionably dressed Hollywood stars inspired the masses more. In 1930, around 90 percent of the American population of 117 million people went to the movies every week. The Great Depression of the 1930s made these numbers drop to a "mere" 50 percent, but by 1940, the figures were again above 90 percent. Of all the movies made in the entire world, around 80 percent were made on the American West Coast, showing that not only American minds were influenced but the fashion tastes of millions around the globe.

Between 1928 and 1941, Adrian Adolph Greenburg, famously known as Adrian, designed the outfits of numerous movie stars, including Greta Garbo, Joan Crawford, Jean Harlow, and Katharine Hepburn, in hundreds of Metro-Goldwyn-Mayer (MGM) movies. He designed, for example, Garbo's slouch hats and coats, which became a popular trend worldwide. He left MGM in 1941 to start his own firm to create and sell his couture and ready-to-wear collection.

Figure 5.5 Actress Greta Garbo poses for a publicity photo for the MGM movie "A Woman Of Affairs" which was released in 1928.
Source: Photo by Donaldson Collection/Getty Images.

Not only American fashion designers but French couturiers worked for Hollywood and designed costumes for the movies. In 1931, Samuel Goldwyn invited Gabrielle Chanel to create some outfits for the musical comedy *Palmy Days*, which would become one of the year's blockbusters. A little later, Gloria Swanson visited Chanel's atelier in Paris to order her costumes for the comedy *Tonight or Never*. Although the movies popularized Chanel's boyish style, she didn't like the whims and demands of the Hollywood stars and preferred to follow her own creative ideas.

Another designer from Paris was the Italian Elsa Schiaparelli, who had opened a shop in Paris called *Pour le Sport* in 1927, following the sportswear trend during the 1920s. She would become one of the most famous fashion designers of the 1930s. Her new formal architectural style, which accentuated the female body, was heavily influenced by surrealist artists like Salvador Dali and fitted quite well with the illusory image of luxury that Hollywood created. She introduced the shoulder pads for Greta Garbo and Joan Crawford that were copied everywhere throughout the world.

Next to the glamorous world portrayed in the movies, which was mostly unreachable for the average American, let alone the European masses, Hollywood also showed many examples of a much more relaxed, less formal, sporty style of dress. In addition,

> it changed the items that people could wear; women wearing trousers became much more accepted through Marlene Dietrich and Katherine Hepburn. Copying the new styles and fashion items, however, was not a spontaneous process. It was partly orchestrated by the fashion industry. One example is Bernard Waldman's Modern Merchandising Bureau Inc. He set up this intermediary company to share information between the studios in Hollywood and big retailers in New York. The retailers received first-hand information about the costumes and accessories that would appear in the upcoming movies. By the time the movie was released, the fashion items would be ready in the department stores. Bernard received a commission on the pieces that were sold. Another example was the popular Hollywood Western, which romanticized the US expansion to the West but also introduced denim jeans to other consumers than workers and cowboys. During the 1930s, Levi's used Hollywood stars, male and female, to market its riveted jeans in advertising campaigns in California, wearing the symbol of the Western frontier in the movies.
>
> *Sources*: Elizabeth Ewing and Alice Mackrell, *History of Twentieth Century Fashion* (London: Crysalis Books Group, 2005); Véronique Pouillard, *Paris to New York: The Transatlantic Fashion Industry in the Twentieth Century* (Cambridge MA: Harvard University Press, 2021); Patricia Campbell Warner, "The Americanization of Fashion: Sportswear, the Movies and the 1930s," in *Twentieth-Century American Fashion*, eds Linda Welters and Patricia A. Cunningham (Oxford: Berg, 2008), 79–98.

Many apparel companies in Los Angeles were founded during the 1920s and 1930s.[50] By 1928, more than one hundred textile companies operated factories in Los Angeles with over 5,000 workers. Ten years earlier, there had been only 25 textile factories. By the mid-1930s, 13,000 workers were employed in the city in more than 250 textile and garment factories, making it the second-largest manufacturing center in the United States. Companies were attracted by the lower prices of raw materials and energy and the anti-union mentality of the city; workers were attracted by the lower cost of living and better climate.[51] Another reason for California's fast-growing textile sector was the formation, in 1934, of a new trade organization, Men's Wear Manufacturers of Los Angeles, and its active marketing strategy. During the war, it organized the first menswear fashion show in history, the Sportswear Round Up in Palm Springs in 1942.[52] In 1948, the organization changed its name to Men's Apparel Guild in California (MAGIC) and simultaneously incorporated a fashion fair. In due course, the fair would become one of the largest national and international fashion fairs for leisure and sportswear in the world.[53] It also reflected the success of California style and industry.

Conclusion

Since the colonial period, the United States has played a role in the development of Western fashion. The highly profitable fur trade was one of the main reasons French,

British, and Dutch merchants created settlements on the other side of the Atlantic in the seventeenth and eighteenth centuries. With the rise of King Cotton in the South, the United States became essential in the global production network of the cotton industry. Cotton mills in Europe were increasingly stocked with American raw cotton, and the British Industrial Revolution, based on the manufacturing of cotton textiles, relied more and more on African slave labor in the cotton fields in the South. The American Industrial Revolution, which took off much later than the British, started with cotton mills and companies in the northeast of the United States. During the first half of the nineteenth century, these cotton mills were the largest factories in the country in terms of employee numbers and size of buildings. In 1860, cotton was also the largest industry by value added compared to other sectors, and sixty years later, it was still among the top five industrial sectors in the United States.

In terms of the symbolic aspect of fashion, the United States relied heavily on Paris as the fashion capital of the world. During the 1880s, New York evolved into the leading cluster of the American clothing industry. Production of ready-to-wear clothing was organized in sweatshops, first in Manhattan's Lower East Side and later, during the 1920s, in the western half of Midtown Manhattan (known as Midtown West), the so-called Garment District.

Paris, however, was still seen as the Walhalla of fashion. Department stores were showcasing Parisian styles, and fashion magazines brought the latest news on Paris fashion to American women. Manufacturers bought the designs of French couturiers. Fashion nationalists aimed to turn the tide before the First World War, wanting to promote American fashion for American women. They were not so successful at introducing American designers for high-end fashion at that time. On the other side of the country, however, a completely different style of menswear developed: California Casual. Manufacturers of sports and leisurewear were extremely successful in marketing their colorful clothing, which fitted the relaxed lifestyle of the West Coast (covering California, Oregon, Washington, and Alaska). The introduction to the middle class of denim originally worn by workers coincided with this new wave. The new-style garments spread across the United States during the 1940s and 1950s to such an extent that they became emblematic of American fashion. The rest of the world would follow suit.

Box 5.2 The rise of synthetic fibers and foreign direct investment in the United States

Silk has been the favorite textile to produce luxury fashion for centuries. Being the most expensive fiber with superior qualities for dying and comfortable wearing, it stimulated scientists during the Second Industrial Revolution (1870–1914) to find artificial substitutes. The solution was found in cellulose mixed with chemical acids to produce artificial silk. In France, Germany, and Britain, different processes were developed and patented.

British natural silk manufacturer Samuel Courtauld & Co. saw the possibilities of these fibers and bought the viscose patent to start production in a new factory in Coventry in 1905. The new fiber was also exported to the fast-growing American textile market. When the US government increased import tariffs to 35 percent, Courtaulds decided to start viscose production in the United States behind the tariff wall.

Figure 5.6 Mid-twentieth-century postcard showing an aerial view of the American Viscose Corporation Plant in Front Royal, Virginia, USA.
Source: The Tichnor Brothers Collection, Boston Public Library.

The Viscose Company (later the American Viscose Corporation) was the first and only artificial silk manufacturer in the United States in the early 1920s. The US viscose market (officially called "rayon" after 1924) was highly profitable and thus attracted new entrants from within and outside the country. A domestic challenger was explosives manufacturer DuPont, which was diversifying at the time into other chemical products. DuPont, however, lacked the technology and instead set up a joint venture with a French rayon manufacturer *Comptoir des Textiles Artificiels* (CTA), based on French know-how. DuPont Fiber Silk Company started production in the state of New York in 1921. During the 1920s, other European companies, including the Dutch *Nederlandse Kunstzijdefabriek (ENKA)* and German *Vereinigte Glanzstoff-Fabriken (VGF)*, entered the attractive American rayon market and started production facilities.

Production increased rapidly in this new industry, particularly in autarkic countries like Germany, Italy, and Japan, often based on inward foreign direct investment (see also Chapter 6). The United States also showed staggering growth figures during these twenty years; by 1939, it had become the third-largest rayon producer in the world. American growth, for the large part, had been realized by foreign direct investment from

Britain, Belgium, France, Germany, Italy, and the Netherlands. With the investments came the technology transfers and patents. DuPont was one of the few domestic rayon producers, particularly after it bought out its French partner in 1929. Three years earlier, it had set up a research laboratory as part of its diversification strategy. DuPont's lab discovered a new polyamide fiber, which was marketed under the name "nylon" in 1938; at first, it was mainly used to produce women's stockings.

The innovation of the first fully synthetic fiber would bring DuPont into a leading position in the global man-made fibers market. On the eve of the Second World War, in 1939, DuPont signed a cross-license contract with the largest chemical firm in the world, IG Farben, which had developed a similar product, called Nylon 6. To avoid a conflict with the German giant, DuPont allowed IG to use its technology under the condition that it would stay out of the US market. Foreign technology had developed the American rayon market, but by the time the war broke out, an American company had taken the lead, also from a technological point of view. The introduction of man-made fibers would also change the global fashion industry forever. Suddenly, glamorous and shiny fabrics were also available for women on modest budgets all over the world.

Sources: Geoffrey Owen, *The Rise and Fall of Great Companies: Courtaulds and the Reshaping of the Man-made Fiber Industry* (Oxford: Oxford University Press, 2010); Mira Wilkins, *The History of Foreign Investment in the United States 1914–1945* (Cambridge MA: Harvard University Press, 2004).

Chapter 6

Fashion, fascism, and the Second World War

> The "noble" woman, the German woman, must know that she should clothe herself nobly, elegantly, purely . . . She does not want to win over with bright colors and banners, with "forced elegance." She leaves that to the whores, whose business requires it . . . We know . . . that the Parisian whores set the tone for the fashions offered to German women, yes that . . . Jewish Konfektion dealers and designers concoct "high" fashion in cahoots with the spinning and weaving industries, and with the help of the whore world that parades their wares . . . Shame and disgrace, degradation and debasement of German taste, of German self-reliance.[1]

Irene Guenther quotes an article written by Kurt Engelbrecht in 1933, which summarizes Nazi Germany's views on the direction the German fashion and textile industries should go in the Third Reich—clearly, away from degenerate Parisian elegance and toward German autarky. The Nazis endeavored to create a German fashion industry, from low to high fashion, based on "Aryan" taste and local supply chains, devoid of French and Jewish influences, which were almost synonymous in Nazi propaganda. In Italy, during the 1920s, Mussolini also aimed to create an Italian fashion industry based on fascist nationalist ideology and, during the 1930s, autarky policy. In Japan, Western clothes had become more popular in the 1920s, but most women were still wearing kimonos. War shortages and nationalist ideology put an end to this trend toward the Westernization of fashion. An apparel industry focused on military uniforms and stimulated by the domestic production of man-made fibers rapidly grew during the Pacific War (1941–1945).

Not only did the fascist and national-socialist states pursue a nationalist economic policy to support their national fashion industry, but also democratic states like Britain and the United States aimed to invigorate this sector during the Second World War. During the First World War, New York endeavored to take over Paris' leading position and create a genuine American fashion style. Similar plans were made in London, which always had to recognize Paris' reputation as the world's fashion capital. Both the British and American fashion industries sought to emancipate themselves from Paris, which had been leading the global fashion business for centuries, to create a stronger mechanized ready-to-wear industry that was less and less custom-based. This chapter addresses the following questions: What were the long-lasting effects of economic nationalism, autarky, and another world war on the national and global fashion industries, and what was the role of the respective governments?

Italian fascism, fashion, and fibers

The symbolic value of textiles and clothing has always played a significant role in fashion throughout history, but more so during the 1920s and 1930s in Europe, where the way people dressed themselves often revealed their political position. Generally, uniforms were still in vogue after the "Great War" (First World War) had ended and the Treaty of Versailles was signed. The far right in Italy and Germany showed their militaristic intentions and their total disagreement with a return to a peaceful and liberal worldview. The experience of brutal manslaughter in the world had revolutionized the masses and elites in the belligerent countries. In Russia, the war led to the Bolshevik or Russian Revolution of 1917 and, in 1922, to the formation of a communist state, the Union of Socialist Soviet Republics (USSR). The USSR created a uniform socialist fashion.[2] In Italy, however, political power was usurped by an extreme nationalist movement, which was the exact opposite in many ways to socialism, communism, and internationalism and which called itself fascism.

Benito Mussolini (1883–1945), the founder of the *Fasci di Combattimento* in 1919, was a young journalist who had been a member of the Italian Socialist Party (PSI) but was expelled in 1914 because he favored Italy's intervention in the First World War when the PSI was holding to a neutral position. Discontent mounted in Italy over the First World War peace settlement, especially among unemployed war veterans attracted by Mussolini's new but small political movement dubbed the "Blackshirts" because of the black shirts they wore. These black shirts became one of the symbols of Italian fascism. After disastrous elections for the fascists in November 1919, they began to apply a much more aggressive tactic that involved violently attacking political enemies, socialists, and trade unionists via armed gangs (*squadrismo*). The black-shirted *squadistri* were supported by big landowners from Italy's most important agricultural regions.[3] Other members of the Italian elite and ruling class also supported Mussolini's anti-socialist agenda. On October 31, 1922, he was appointed prime minister by King Victor Emmanuel III after the so-called march on Rome. Mussolini took the train to stop the violence of his Blackshirts in the capital and accepted the political leadership of the country, which he would turn within five years into a one-party fascist dictatorship with himself as the uncontested *Duce* until 1943 when he was dismissed by the same king that appointed him.[4]

Meanwhile, uniforms were everywhere in daily life in Italy. For members of the Republic Fascist Party, a fixed code existed: "a long jacket with a bandolier, under the jacket a [black] shirt and a tie, and then trousers tucked into leather boots, gloves and finally, an original item, a fez, headgear taken from the 'Arditi,' a special corps of shock troops."[5] The fixed code was meant to show the discipline and militaristic nature of the movement; however, it also emphasized that the wearer belonged to an elite group separate from the

Figure 6.1 Blackshirts taking part in a meeting in Naples. Naples, October 24, 1922.
Source: Photo by Mondadori via Getty Images.

masses—what Simmel has described as the differentiating nature of fashion.[6] The rise of fascism in Italy did not just mean more uniforms and black shirts—fashion itself became part of Mussolini's nationalistic ambitions. He wanted to create a genuine Italian national fashion style independent of Paris.

Fashion was meant to be one of the main tools to create a national Italian identity, which did not exist before, an identity based on the Italian Renaissance, Romanticism, and regional folklore.[7] The question, however, is to what extent the fascists were successful. According to many authors, the regime failed to push a national Italian style. Parisian haute couture was still the leader for fashionistas in the Italian elite, including the simpler, emancipating, and boyish style communicated through international fashion magazines. The fascists, on the contrary, promoted a feminine style based on the traditional Italian role model.[8]

When the fascists came to power in 1922, the Italian fashion industry consisted mainly of small artisanal production units. Most Italians preferred their clothes tailormade or bought them second-hand. Although the regime endeavored to develop an Italian ready-to-wear industry based on the standardization and rationalization of the industry, this was hard to accomplish. Apart from some larger clothing and textile firms in Turin and Milan, most Italian fashion was still custom-made and often copied Parisian designs.[9]

To improve the backward condition of Italian textile and clothing production and to promote Italian fashion, the government established *Ente Autonomo per la Mostra*

Permanente Nazionale della Moda ("Autonomous Body for the Permanent National Fashion Exhibition" or EAMPNM) in Turin in 1932. The promotion of Italian fashion was also inspired by economic factors and foreign currency shortages. The large amount of French fashion imports had become a pressing challenge for the Italian economy.[10] The first exhibition organized by the institution showed it had far too many shortcomings. As a result, in 1935, another institution was set up: *Ente Nazionale della Moda* (ENM). It aimed to create a distinctive Italian style and checked if the whole supply chain was Italian. ENM certified the Italian origin with its own label. It also created a network of manufacturers and media outlets. ENM published the *Commentary and Italian Dictionary on Fashion* in 1936 to replace French fashion terminology with Italian. In 1940, it published its own fashion magazine, *Bellezza,* to compete with foreign fashion magazines. Although

Figure 6.2 Italian menswear 1930s.
Source: Gift of Woodman Thompson, The Metropolitan Museum of Art.

the ENM may not have been as successful as the fascist regime had hoped during the 1930s, its postwar successor, EIM (*Ente Italiano Moda*), was vital for the national and international expansion of Italy's fashion industry during the 1950s and 1960s.[11]

The companies that profited the most from Italy's autarky policy were those that could substitute necessary imports of raw materials, which also meant a saving of scarce foreign currency. The most important example is Italy's largest artificial silk (rayon) manufacturer, Snia, which would also rapidly become Italy's largest company by capital during the interwar period.[12] Riccardo Gualino had made a fortune by shipping American coal to Italy during the First World War and had created the *Societa di Navigazione Italo-Americano* (Snia) in 1917.[13] In 1921, when the coal trade collapsed, he switched to rayon and changed the name to *Societa Nationale Industrie Applicazione Viscosa* (Snia Viscosa). The company, with plants around Turin and Milan, received technical know-how from the French conglomerate *Comptoir des Textiles Artificiels* (CTA), one of the key players in the world of this high-tech, capital-intensive, and fast-growing industry during the 1920s. In return, CTA took a minority shareholding position in the Italian company, which was licensed to use CTA's patents provided they would not export to the French market.[14] The Italian domestic market for rayon was non-existent in the early 1920s. As a result, Snia exported most of its low-quality and cheap rayon based on low labor costs. It was undercutting the biggest viscose manufacturers in the world: Courtaulds in Britain and Glanzstoff (VGF) in Germany.

Despite the initial success of Snia, particularly in the American, British, Chinese, Indian, and German markets, the company ended up in severe financial and technical difficulties. The technical difficulties were resolved by Glanzstoff, which provided additional technical know-how in 1926; the financial difficulties were resolved in 1927 when Courtaulds and VGF acquired three-quarters of Snia's capital in an attempt to limit Italian exports.[15] During the 1920s, the global rayon market was skyrocketing, and the competition was fierce, with many new entrants. Therefore, the largest companies sought to reduce the competition via cartel agreements and hostile takeovers. In 1929, the founder of the company, Gualino, was replaced by two textile industrialists, Senatore Borletti and Franco Marinotti.[16] During the 1930s, when Italy was moving toward autarky, Marinotti especially was very useful for his close contacts with the fascist regime. As a result of acute foreign currency shortages, economic self-sufficiency was the only logical step after 1934. Snia became, therefore, one of the favorite companies of the regime, although it was, for the greater part, in the hands of foreign multinationals. Through Snia's ample exports, it provided Italy with foreign currency.

Moreover, man-made fibers could replace imports of cotton and wool. Snia began to produce staple fibers, which could be mixed with cotton. In that way, Italy could reduce its cotton imports. Marinotti, who was also leading the textile guild, convinced the wool and cotton manufacturers to use staple fibers. The state fully supported domestic use by limiting cotton imports, making rayon and staple fibers mandatory, and establishing research institutes. As a result, domestic consumption of man-made fibers sky-rocketed after 1935—for example, domestic consumption of staple fibers by cotton spinners quadrupled until 1939.[17]

A challenge to increased output was the need for more raw materials. Rayon and staple fibers were based on cellulose, made of wood pulp imported from Scandinavia. In 1937, Snia invested heavily in transforming the basis of raw materials and set up the *Società Agricola Industriale Cellulosa Italiana* (Saici). The aim of the company was to make cellulose based on reeds instead of wood and thus limit wood pulp imports. It was one of the most ambitious projects of the fascist regime but should also not be exaggerated. From 1941, during Italy's occupation of part of Yugoslavia, Saici massively imported wood from Slovenia to produce domestic cellulose.

Two examples of now-famous luxury fashion companies that flourished during the fascist period were Ferragamo and Gucci. Salvatore Ferragamo (1898–1960) was an Italian shoemaker. He was born into a poor family in the south of Italy and immigrated to the United States in 1915, eventually making a career in California with made-to-measure shoes for several Hollywood divas. In 1927, however, he decided to return to Italy to start his own workshop in Florence, where he began to design shoes for rich, international celebrities.[18] He became most famous for using all kinds of non-rationed inferior materials in a period of great scarcity, including cork, rubber, fish skins, and cellophane.[19] He claimed many patents for his designs, also during the war.[20] After the war, the company would expand into an international luxury fashion company.

Guccio Gucci (1881–1953) was born in Florence as the son of a leather craftsman and went as a teenager to Paris and then to London to work at the elegant Savoy hotel. There, he became inspired by the luxury luggage of the upper-class guests. In 1921, he returned to Florence and started his own fashionable leather goods and equestrian shop.[21] He also started a workshop and hired the finest craftsmen to produce his luxury leather goods. Despite the autarky policy and scarcity of raw materials, he expanded the business, diversified into handbags, and opened a shop in one of the best neighborhoods in Rome. Due to the raw material shortages, Gucci switched to linen, jute, hemp, and horse bits and stirrups when leather was unavailable or was being used for war purposes.[22] After the war, the horse bit would become the symbol of Italy's most successful luxury fashion company.

Nazi autarky, Aryanization, and artificial fibers

In June 1933, within five months of the Nazi takeover, the Deutsches Modeamt, later renamed Deutsches Mode-Institut (German Fashion Institute), was founded after Hitler had stated in an interview with a fashion journalist: "The Berlin women must become the best-dressed women in Europe."[23] The foundation of the institute was fully supported by Joseph Goebbels, the Reichs Minister of Propaganda. The aim was to create German fashion, independent of Paris, based on German textiles and clothing manufacturing. Furthermore, this new national fashion should not just be for the happy few but for all

Figure 6.3 Frauen-Warte, the only official woman's nazi magazine, 1942.
Source: Anne Rüger / Universitätsbibliothek Heidelberg.

German women. (Fashion was also seen as a woman's affair in Nazi Germany.)[24] How this was to be realized was still a question. The fashion shows organized in Berlin in 1933 and 1934 showed the top designs of famous German fashion houses—not exactly fashion for everyone. In the first two years, Jewish fashion designers were still accepted as members; however, as of 1936, when the regime radicalized, they were abandoned. According to Irene Guenther, the fashion institute was not very successful in putting German fashion on the map. Paris remained the fashion capital also for Germany. Moreover, the institute was criticized by the German clothing industry for doing very little to support German fashion.[25]

The German fashion, textile, and clothing industries had formed the largest sector of the German economy. Before the global economic crisis, they had employed over 3 million people.[26] The industries consisted of textiles, clothing, ready-to-wear, high-fashion, shoes, and accessories but also man-made fibers—most importantly, rayon and, later, staple fibers. The Nazi takeover had a devastating impact on this sector, which consisted of a sizeable number of owners and workers of Jewish descent. According to the Nazis, the industry needed to be cleared of Jewish and foreign (French) influences. Jewish companies needed to be Aryanized, Jewish employees dismissed, and Jewish designers left without orders. During the 1930s, the core of the German fashion industry was destroyed because many with a Jewish background, wittingly or unwittingly, were pushed out of the industry. The companies were, in many cases, Aryanized, often by less-experienced entrepreneurs or artisans. The effects on German ready-to-wear exports were devastating—export figures dropped to almost zero. While this was also a result of protectionist policies all over the world, the destruction of the backbone of the German textile and clothing industries certainly had long-lasting effects.[27] Those Jewish people who had the opportunity and financial means to emigrate sought refuge in the Netherlands, France, Britain, or the United States, where they often started new fashion businesses (see Box 6.1). Those who didn't have the chance or the means to leave Germany were probably persecuted and killed.

The loss of Jewish artisans and foreign markets was partly compensated for by uniform manufacturing, which experienced a tremendous boost in the highly militarized German economy. Hugo Boss (1885–1948), often referred to as "Hitler's tailor," was the founder of a clothing company and an early member of the Nazi party; he would remain a Nazi until the end of the war. Hugo Boss AG produced different types of Nazi uniforms, including SA, SS, Hitlerjugend, and Wehrmacht, and benefited widely from Germany's militarization and later war campaigns. It was, however, one of many companies and not even specialized at the beginning in the manufacture of uniforms. Generally, uniform manufacturing was a profitable branch that expanded during the war and fitted well in the rationalization schemes of the Nazis. The sector was favored by the regime when it came to raw materials and labor. In the long run, it stimulated the ready-to-wear industry in Germany and the scale and scope of the German textile and clothing industries.[28]

When Germany ran into foreign currency shortages one year after the Nazis came to power, the regime was forced to adopt serious measures to improve the balance of payments. From 1934, Germany needed to restrict imports, particularly raw materials, or make better deals. The German textile industry had to import most raw materials, including cotton and wool. One exception was rayon, mostly used as a substitute for silk, which was, for the greater part, produced in Germany. The biggest rayon manufacturer was VGF, which was one of the largest players in the global market. Staple fiber was another local product made by IG Farben, the largest chemical company in Germany after the merger in 1925. Rayon had played an increasingly important role in the global fashion industry, particularly after the First World War. Staple fiber, which could be used as a cheap substitute for wool or cotton or mixed with those two natural fibers, was a rather new product in the 1920s and was seen as the most promising artificial fiber in the 1930s and 1940s.[29]

Hjalmar Schacht, the president of the Reichsbank and Minister of Economics since August 1934, presented his New Plan to restrict imports to save foreign currency

Table 6.1 Major Rayon-producing Countries 1921–1939 (in 000 Tons)

	1921	1930	1939
USA	6.8	57.9	172.3
Germany	3.5	29.3	278.3
Japan	0.1	16.8	244.9
Italy	1.5	30.5	138.3
UK	4.1	21.2	77.0
France	2.0	23.0	32.4

Source: Geoffrey Owen, *The Rise and Fall of Great Companies: Courtaulds and the Reshaping of the Man-made Fiber Industry* (Oxford: Oxford University Press, 2010), 25.

preserved for Hitler's ambitious rearmament programs. The plan proved disastrous for Germany's huge textile industry, which employed around 18 percent of the workforce, and national unemployment rates were still sky-high. The regime, therefore, launched a *Nationales Faserstoffprogramm* ("National Pulp Program") to expand the production of cellulose-based fibers. It proved extremely successful; artificial fiber consumption in the textile industry in Germany increased from a mere 5 percent in 1928 to 43 percent in 1943.[30] Table 6.1 shows the major rayon-producing countries in the world during the 1920s and 1930s.

Production increased rapidly in this new industry, particularly in autarkic countries like Germany, Italy, and Japan. The oldest and biggest rayon manufacturer in Germany was *Vereinigte Glanzstoff Fabriken* (VGF), which had started in Oberbruch, near Aachen, in 1899. Together with the British Courtaulds and the French CTA, it had dominated global rayon production until after the First World War with subsidiaries abroad, including in the rapidly expanding US market. During the 1920s, cut-throat competition arose due to the rise of cheap competitors like the Dutch Enka and Italian Snia, which exported most of their production. Within Germany, another gigantic competitor was IG Farben, which was a merger of the large German chemical firms Hoechst, Bayer, and BASF.[31] In 1929, VGF got into serious financial trouble. The smaller but financially stronger Dutch Enka, which lagged in technology, acquired almost all the shares of the dynamic but highly indebted German VGF. A joint Dutch–German holding company, *Algemene Kunstzijde Unie* (AKU), controlled both Enka and VGF, which was formed through an exchange of shares and located in the Netherlands. During the 1930s, however, the German side of the company became highly indebted to the Dutch side. As a result, an ever-greater part of the company came into Dutch hands.[32] Nevertheless, most of AKU's production took place in Germany. In 1930, its market share amounted to almost 64 percent of Germany's total rayon sales.[33] As a result of the Nazi autarkic policy, production in the Dutch plants was cut back and employment figures decreased dramatically. Total Enka staff in the Netherlands decreased

Figure 6.4 Milk wool manufacturing: stand of AKU, Arnhem (Algemene Kunstzijde Unie NV) at the Jaarbeurs in Utrecht, 1941.
Source: Wiel van der Randen / Spaarnestad Photo. Public Domain via Wikimedia Commons.

from 8,000 in 1929 to only 2,000 in 1936, while at the same time, employment in Germany increased spectacularly, from almost 12,000 in 1931 to 25,000 in 1938.[34]

As soon as the Nazis came to power, they began to ask questions about the multinational character of the company and the Dutch ownership construction. In 1937, Göring's Four Year Plan asked the German board members whether there were plans to nationalize the company. They answered that it would be tactically wrong to do so at the time. The firm had to appear as non-German-owned with majority Dutch participation to avoid retaliation from US subsidiaries. The company was not nationalized but a fervent Nazi was appointed chair of the board. During the occupation of the Netherlands, the majority of the AKU shares would fall into German hands.[35] However, as in the case of Snia in Italy, the VGF story shows that, despite the economic nationalism of the Nazi regime, the artificial fibers industry would remain a multinational business. Autarkic policies greatly stimulated the production of synthetic fibers. This trend would continue after the war under completely different conditions.

Japan's fashion during the military dictatorship

The 1920s in Japan was a decade of social change characterized by urbanization, the growth of the middle class, and the Westernization of consumer culture (see Chapter 4).

In the 1930s, Japan entered a new era characterized by the rising power of bureaucrats and the military.[36] No coup but a gradual transition from parliamentary democracy brought the military to power. Unfolding in the background of the military dictatorship was Japanese imperialist expansion into China and the increasing power of large financial and industrial business groups (zaibatsu).[37]

The Japanese textile industry experienced dramatic growth and became one of the world's largest exporters following the end of the gold standard and the devaluation of the yen in 1931. In 1933, Japan became the world's largest exporter of cotton fabric, ahead of the UK. The competitiveness of this good was based on the presence of large verticalized firms and the low cost of labor.[38] The following year, in 1934, cotton products became Japan's first export products, ahead of silk, which faced a crisis following the advent of artificial fibers (rayon). The decline of the silk industry was a trauma for many regions that specialized in this agricultural and industrial good. However, at the same time, Japanese companies engaged in the formation of a domestic rayon industry, following a classical pattern of import substitution. To avoid the mass import of cheap rayon from Italy, the government adopted a protectionist policy in 1926, while in 1927, the seven largest firms engaged in this business organized a cartel. Benefiting from technology transfer from Europe, notably through joint ventures set up with German enterprises, they expanded rapidly on the domestic market, supplying textile and apparel firms with artificial fibers. In the 1930s, Japan became one of the major exporters (see Table 6.1). By 1937, it had become the world's second-largest exporter, behind Germany but ahead of Italy.[39] The companies behind this success formed the core of the postwar chemical industry in Japan. Toyo Rayon (Toray), founded in 1926 and a member of the cartel since 1927, has continued its production of artificial fibers up to the present day. In 1999, it entered into a partnership with Uniqlo to develop new fibers for functional clothes (see Chapter 9).

War with China resulted in the increasing involvement of the government in the economy. State control became necessary to organize a war economy. In 1937, the government took its first measures to control the allocation of supplies and sales in many industries, including the apparel industry.[40] This control was strengthened throughout the war. After the outbreak of the Pacific War in 1941, the largest apparel manufacturers were put under the direct control of the Hiroshima Uniform Factory of the Army. They transformed into large verticalized firms, which became the basis for the postwar growth of this industry.[41] Manufacturers of cotton cloth and apparel were mostly small- and medium-sized enterprises clustered in several districts throughout Japan. They used to supply large apparel companies, which changed their business after 1941. Mass production of military uniforms was also a way to engage in the development of Western apparel after 1945. An excellent example is undoubtedly Renown, one of the largest apparel and fashion companies of postwar Japan (see Chapter 7). Its origins date back to a small clothing company founded in Osaka in 1902 under the name Suzuki Shokai, whose sewing factory merged in 1942 with other small companies.[42]

Nationalism and war had a major impact on the way Japanese people dressed. Austerity policies aimed at saving resources, and the increasing engagement of women in agriculture and industry while men were at the war front, led to the disappearance of the modern girl of the 1920s. Although the country had built a large and competitive textile industry, it was not used to develop varied fashion items for the masses but mostly military-style uniforms. In the 1930s, women started to wear headscarves and *mompe*, baggy trousers in traditional patterns, as the expression of the home front.[43] Austere, simple clothing was encouraged by nationalist campaigns, which claimed that "Luxury is the enemy" (*zeitaku ha teki da*).[44]

Paris fashion during the German occupation

During the Second World War and the German occupation of important parts of France, there was a certain continuity in Paris fashion and couture. Paris had been the leading fashion capital from the middle of the nineteenth century and had produced high-end fashion for the wealthy and powerful, royalty, and the haute bourgeoisie. Under the new conditions, most fashion houses, including Lelong, Balenciaga, Heim, Patou, and Piguet, endeavored to continue the business as much as possible, but Jewish-owned fashion houses were closed or Aryanized. Some couturiers went abroad. Schiaparelli and Mainbocher went to the United States; Molyneux and Delanghe set up businesses in London; and Balenciaga could travel freely, more or less, to his "neutral" home country of Spain.[45] Chanel closed her salon once the war began and stayed in the Ritz Hotel in Paris with her Nazi lover and even worked for the German secret service.[46]

Many couture houses and couturiers thus continued to make Paris fashion or, at least, spread information about the latest seasonal styles.[47] The Nazi occupier had plans to make Berlin and Vienna Europe's fashion centers at the expense of Paris but met opposition from couturier Lucien Lelong, director of the *Chambre Syndicale de la Couture Parisienne*. His strategy, which he also used to defend himself after the war, was to collaborate closely with the occupying power to ensure the survival of the French fashion industry.[48] In September 1940, he went to Berlin to discuss the German plans to relocate the French couture industry to the German Reich. Here he argued that Parisian couture was a complicated industry consisting of many small and different parts that could not just be transferred to another location.[49] The occupier immediately abandoned its centralizing plans and supported Parisian couture by becoming an important customer. Obviously, overseas markets had disappeared (although some contacts via neutral states remained)—but the domestic French market and foreign markets in Greater Germany functioned quite well despite raw material shortages. In fact, during the war, French couture recovered from the economic crisis years of the 1930s. According to Grumbach, sales figures increased fivefold between 1941 and 1943.[50]

During the first two years of the war, France was divided into two main parts: German-occupied France, including Paris, and a collaborationist Vichy France under Maréchal

Figure 6.5 Lucien Lelong at his desk in Paris, France, around 1940.
Source: Photo by KEYSTONE-FRANCE/Gamma-Rapho via Getty Images.

Pétain, which included Lyon. Under normal circumstances, the two cities worked closely together, Paris producing couture and Lyon delivering high-quality silk fabrics, one of the most important components of Parisian couture. Therefore, Lelong tried to keep the supply lines to Lyon open. However, the international silk trade was seriously disrupted by the war conditions. China was occupied by Japan, and the Japanese and Italians were not exporting any silk. The only solution was to increase the production of artificial silk (rayon). This is exactly what happened in the whole of France, not only in Lyon. All French textile manufacturing was now centralized under the direction of Hans Kehrl, Chief of the Textile Department of the Reich Economics Ministry. Before the war, Kehrl had been an industrialist who had promoted the use and further development of artificial fibers and organized industry in the *Kunstseide Ring*. He ordered the export of French stocks of wool, cotton, linen, and silk to Germany and replaced natural fibers with man-made fibers or mixed the two. As an interested party, he was not just defending the interests of the German occupier but also his industrial network, which could sell the raw materials (cellulose) to France.

In the end, the quality of the fabrics deteriorated sharply during the war as more and more synthetic fibers were mixed in.[51] For the ordinary French person, it became increasingly difficult to purchase rationed clothing or textiles, the quality of which deteriorated in due course. Meanwhile, the bourgeoisie, black marketeers, and German officers could still buy couture, partly exempted from raw material restrictions and still made in Paris.

British-controlled fashion

During the Second World War, the British government intervened much more in the economy than it had done during the First World War. The experience of war had taught the lesson that a free market would not be able to cope with a formidable opponent. In response to labor and raw material shortages, the British government introduced a Utility scheme, which had serious consequences for consumers and clothing and textile manufacturers—85 percent of all clothing was rationed and could only be bought with coupons, and production was also strictly regulated. The amount of cloth and the number of styles were limited. Leading designers, including Molyneux, who had come home from Paris, helped the Board of Trade to design some prototype models.[52] According to Bethan Bide, the Utility scheme had massive consequences for the British fashion business. Larger ready-to-wear firms were better able to adapt to the rationalization policies of the

Figure 6.6 Utility Clothes—Fashion Restrictions in Wartime Britain, 1943. Ministry of Information Second World War Official Collection.

government. The smaller, less-mechanized firms in London, which often still made high-end bespoke clothing, were at a disadvantage and could not adapt well to the new conditions. As a result, and because German bombs had destroyed many factories, production partly moved out of London. Other clusters of clothing manufacturers, like in Manchester and Leeds, were much better able to meet the increasing demand for clothes from the middle and lower segments.[53] Elizabeth Ewing concludes that the ready-to-wear industry improved a great deal because of government policies. The industry became more business-like and, through economies of scale, more efficient and therefore more competitive, particularly after the war. It had made a clear move to larger production units with higher productivity.[54]

Despite the Utility scheme and material shortages, London high-end fashion designers took the initiative to establish the Incorporated Society of London Fashion Designers (shortened Inc. Soc.). The aim was to defend the interests of London's top designers and stimulate exports of British high-end fashion, particularly to the United States, to earn the hard currency badly needed for the British war effort. It was modeled after the powerful Chambre Syndicale de la Couture Parisienne in the sense that the conditions for membership of Inc. Soc. were based on originally designed bespoke clothing. However, the London association was much smaller—in 1946, it counted only ten fashion design houses and Paris seventy—and less influential than the Chambre Syndicale, which was heavily supported financially by the French government. The Inc. Soc. received some financial support and materials from the British textile industry but hardly anything from the British government.[55] For the most part, the organization was financed by its members, including Molyneux and Creed, who had built their reputation in Paris before the war. The benefit for British high-end fashion, however, was not so much in wartime but after the war during the 1950s and 1960s, when it helped stimulate exports to the United States. The founding of this society during the war, nonetheless, shows that the London high-end fashion industry used the war to break Parisian dominance.

During the war, Britain also increased rayon production and its application in the textile industry, but less than on the Continent or in the United States and Japan. Courtaulds had been one of the first movers in this new industry when the British silk weaver Samuel Courtauld acquired the French patents to produce artificial silk in 1904. It had been a huge success, and rayon (first called viscose) proved to be much more profitable than textile weaving. Courtaulds opened new factories and joint ventures overseas, but it never became a chemical company, which was a disadvantage when new man-made fibers were developed.[56] During the 1920s, fierce competition came from all sides: the United States, Italy, Germany, the Netherlands, and Japan. Moreover, chemists were researching polymer technologies, particularly IG Farben in Germany, and, in the United States, DuPont. DuPont was the first to introduce a fully man-made fiber not based on cellulose but on coal or crude oil, which was called nylon. Women's stockings made from nylon became a huge success and conquered the market rapidly. Courtaulds eventually set up a joint venture with Imperial Chemical Industries (ICI) and British Nylon Spinners. ICI had a cross-licensing agreement with DuPont and was delivering the nylon that could be spun by Courtaulds, but the latter had to remain outside the chemical industry. Nylon was used on a very limited scale during the war in Britain. However, the next invention of a new fiber was done in Britain in the laboratory of a textile company, Calico Printers Association. The patent for polyester, as it was called, was filed in 1942 and shared with ICI, which began to develop this fiber and share the technology with DuPont. Courtaulds was left out completely. After the war, polyester would become the most important man-made fiber in the world.[57]

Box 6.1 Jewish fashion district in London during the war

Jewish migrants have played a highly significant role in the development of the fashion industry in Europe and the Americas since the late nineteenth and first half of the twentieth century. London was no exception, but because of pogroms in Russia and persecution by the Nazis in Germany, London became a refuge for many Jewish people, often as a destination but sometimes also as a stopover to New York.

The Jewish migrants that came in the seventeenth and eighteenth centuries were mostly Sephardic Jews coming from Spain, Portugal, or the Middle East after they were permitted to settle in Britain. Ashkenazi Jews came from Eastern Europe and Russia in the nineteenth century, with a sharp peak from 1881 to 1914 when the Jewish population in London tripled from 46,000 to 150,000. According to the 1901 census, Jewish men, women, and children worked disproportionately in London's garment industry and lived in the East End and West End. After the Aliens Acts of 1905 and the Aliens Restrictions Act of 1914, it became harder to migrate to Britain. A new wave of Jewish immigration started when the Nazis came to power and began to make life unbearable for Germans with Jewish backgrounds. Between 60,000 and 80,000 Jews migrated to Britain; many traveled on to America.

During the 1930s, the British government introduced stricter refugee laws, and anti-semitic sentiments were also expressed in the British press. The new migrants from Germany and Austria after the Anschluss often had a background in the fashion industry as designers, tailors, or company owners; therefore, they were able to start new businesses in the extensive London fashion market. It is important to note that these Jewish Londoners were difficult to define because they were never one group. Jewishness is based on religion, cultural and social background, and family ties, but it is also defined by antisemitic persecutors throughout history who blame Jews for all misfortunes. The overrepresentation of Jewish people in the fashion industry in Britain can be explained by the fact that they were not allowed to follow university training or work for the government. Therefore, many began a fashion business. In addition, migrants from Eastern Europe and Russia knew by experience that they needed a transferable skill that was in demand everywhere—like garment or shoe making. Moreover, work in the fashion

> industry was poorly paid and therefore attracted migrants who had few alternatives. One didn't need a lot of capital to start a tailor shop, and a sewing machine could be paid for on an installment plan.
>
> Around 1900, the East End developed into a manufacturing center for ready-to-wear men's clothing; however, in the interwar period, the making of womenswear also grew in significance. Individual tailors had become owners of larger businesses. The West End specialized more in high-end ready-to-wear, called "wholesale couture," with connections to other major fashion cities like New York, Paris, Berlin, and Vienna. After the Nazis came to power in Germany (1933) and after the Austrian Anschluss of 1938, many Jewish fashion business owners and designers fled to London, where they were sometimes viewed with suspicion by competitors. However, their high-end skills tended to be highly regarded, making them acceptable in the London fashion scene. Successful examples of Jewish refugees were Walter Loewinberg and Fritz Dannenbaum (Silhouette de Luxe), Leo and Greta Neumann (Rima), and Walter and Otto Marcus (Marcus Ltd), who would play a significant role in London's high-end fashion after the war.
>
> *Source*: Bethan Bide and Lucie Whitmore, *Fashion City: How Jewish Londoners Shaped Global Style* (London: Bloomsbury 2023); Irene Guenther, *Nazi Chic: Fashioning Women in the Third Reich* (Oxford: Berg Publishers, 2004); Liz Tregenza, *Wholesale Couture: London and beyond, 1930–70* (London: Bloomsbury, 2023); Uwe Westphal, *Fashion Metropolis Berlin 1836–1939: The Story of the Rise and Destruction of the Jewish Fashion Industry* (Leipzig: Seemann Henschel, 2019).

American independence from Paris

Threats to Paris' position as the global fashion capital not only came from Berlin, Vienna, and London but also from New York and other places in the United States. Despite fashion nationalism, the United States still depended on Parisian designers and fashion houses during the interwar period. The American fashion industry, strongly clustered in New York's Seventh Avenue, had become the second-largest sector of the national economy and was, for the greater part, sourced with American raw materials and made by American workers. In 1940, these manufacturers created a total value of $3.5 billion, a figure unthinkable for Parisian couture.[58] The outbreak of war in Europe and the German occupation of Paris in June 1940 stimulated the American industry to become even more independent and self-sufficient, particularly regarding style and design. Two months later, the American Council for Style and Design (ACSAD) was established in New York, supported by retailers, manufacturers, and designers. According to Veronique Pouillard, its first aim was "to establish New York as the fashion center of the world."[59] This private initiative was also supported by New York's mayor, Fiorello La Guardia, who set up a committee at the World Fashion Center in 1943, which led to the founding of the New York Fashion Institute of Technology (FIT) a year later.[60]

Box 6.2 Rosie the Riveter: How leisurewear and denim liberated American women

When the United States entered the Second World War after the Japanese attack on Pearl Harbor in December 1941, the country needed to employ millions of female workers and reallocate those who already had been working in major war industries. As labor shortages reached critical points, the federal government started using propaganda and engaged in massive recruitment drives to assimilate women into the workforce. Wartime propaganda idealized the image of the female war worker, portraying her as a strong, competent, and courageous national heroine of the home front. Rosie the Riveter, wearing denim overalls, was used by the American media as the symbol of feminine wartime patriotism. This was not for the first time.

Figure 6.7 Woman worker in the Douglas Aircraft Company plant (October 1942).
Source: Howard R. Hollem / Library of Congress Prints and Photographs Division.

During the First World War, women had also had factory jobs. At that time, female workers began wearing denim overalls because skirts were too dangerous in war plants. During the interwar period, wearing trousers became more acceptable for women, and denim overalls entered the leisure market. Throughout the Second World War, wearing jeans became even more of a symbol of patriotism, liberty, and democracy for American women. More college girls began wearing jeans, and women who worked in war factories became accustomed to wearing jeans. As these women were viewed in a positive light, their denim overalls ("womanalls") gained greater social acceptance. The Second World War was another milestone in female employment, changing women's roles and behavior in society and the way women dressed. Women were also better paid and entered new kinds of occupations, participating much more in the industrial workforce. But it should also be acknowledged that women did work prior to the war.

Collaboration between the War Advertising Council and the government began only in early 1944, about eighteen months before the end of the war. Until 1944, all the ads in women's magazines that used images of female defense workers also included commercial advertisements. Because there were different classes of war work and each had its own dress requirements, the magazines attempted to cover a range of outfits and addressed themselves to issues of safety and cleanliness, as well as attractiveness. For example, factory work required some kind of hair covering for safety reasons, and a persistent problem for employers was that women wouldn't wear their kerchiefs, caps, or snoods because they didn't want to cover up their hair. Magazines suggested ways to make hair coverings more stylish and proposed using other things like lipstick and nail polish for color and femininity. Trousers, of course, appeared prominently in magazine features. However, the magazines had been showing pants since the mid-1930s, so this was not as big a stretch as it would have been in previous conflicts. Many of the war jobs required uniforms, and though you would think that selling readers on uniforms would be anathema to a fashion magazine, the editors of the women's press stepped up to the challenge. The emphasis on beauty and womanliness was a prevalent theme in both propaganda and advertising discourse. Although they had distinct interests in promoting these values—maintaining traditional gender boundaries versus selling products—propaganda agencies and the advertising industry nevertheless conveyed the same message: beauty and femininity should not be compromised. Several new styles emerged during this period. Designers had to adapt to the limitations of materials and the restrictions enforced by the US government. Women covered their heads with turbans or snoods to keep from getting their hair caught in machines. Leather shoes were rationed, so shoes made of cloth with synthetic soles, like the espadrille, became popular. While women coped with the lack of frills and new American designs, they came up with ingenious ways to create fashion within these imposed restrictions.

Sources: Lauren Dalton, Pauline Sullivan, Jeanne Heitmeyer, and Ann DuPont, "Robertson's Model: A Framework for Exploration of the Second World War Conservation Consumption Policy Influence on Fashion in the US," *International Journal of Consumer Studies* 36, no. 6 (2012): 611–621; Rika Fujioka and Ben Wubs, "Competitiveness of the Japanese Denim and Jeans Industry: The Cases of Kaihara and Japan Blue, 1970–2015," in *European Fashion: The Creation of a Global Industry*, eds Regina Lee Blaszczyk and Véronique Pouillard (Manchester: Manchester University Press, 2018), 223–243; Bilge Yesil, "'Who Said This Is a Man's War?': Propaganda, Advertising Discourse and the Representation of War Worker Women during the Second World War," *Media History* 10, no. 2 (August 2004): 103–117.

As in Britain, the fashion and textile industries in the United States were also restricted due to raw material shortages and the prioritization of war production. The big difference with Britain was that the United States entered the war only in December 1941, after Pearl Harbor, and so the total period of price and production controls by the War Production Board was much shorter. The positive effect, however, was that the organization, as well as the scale and scope of the fashion industry in the United States, improved tremendously during the war. There were restrictions on styles and standardization of sizing was given a lot of attention, but these eventually boosted the American ready-to-wear industry.[61] Also, domestic man-made fiber production profited tremendously from war conditions. Before the war, rayon output had already increased from 6.8 tons in 1921 to 172.3 tons in 1939 (see Table 6.1). The most important producer was a Courtaulds subsidiary, American Viscose, but during the 1920s, DuPont entered this highly profitable market. It diversified from explosives production after the First World War and had even attempted (in vain) to acquire the British subsidiary. During the 1930s, DuPont entered a period of fierce competition with American Viscose on the technological front. Its introduction of nylon just before the war had been a major blow to Courtaulds. However, because of the forced sale of American Viscose in 1941 to American investors as part of the Lend-Lease Act (to finance British war loans), the British company lost the largest market in the world. From that moment on, the rapidly growing man-made fiber market was largely left to American producers, including DuPont.[62]

Not only did the industry on the East Coast benefit from war conditions, but the turnover of companies on the West Coast also increased spectacularly. A major leap in total sales

Figure 6.8 The worn-out nylon [and silk] stockings in this barrel full of salvaged stockings will be reprocessed and made into parachutes for army fliers, tow ropes for gilder planes and other war material.

Source: Office for Emergency Management / Office of War Information. Franklin D. Roosevelt Library Public Domain Photographs.

Figure 6.9 Lunchtime brings a few minutes of rest for these women workers of the assembly line at Douglas Aircraft Company's plant, Long Beach, California, October 1942. Sand bags for protection against air raid form the background.

Source: Alfred T. Palmer / Library of Congress Prints and Photographs Division.

of manufacturers in Los Angeles was realized during the Second World War. From 1940 to 1948, sales skyrocketed from $50 million to $400 million. While New York was still the largest production center for formal men's suits and women's dresses, Los Angeles had become the national cluster for informal leisure and sportswear manufacturing.[63] The rise and success of California Casual cannot be explained by innovative marketing methods alone—demographic changes were equally important. The population of Los Angeles, for example, almost quadrupled, from 576,673 in 1920 to 1,970,358 in 1950.[64] The fast-growing population had more leisure time, especially after the introduction of the 48-hour workweek in 1938. The rise of Hollywood in the interwar period augmented the Californian image of sun, beach, and leisure time. In addition, during the war, the city became the hub of US military operations in the Pacific and the most important location for military production. As a result, it was flooded with military men and workers in the armaments industry, who preferred wearing leisure and sportswear.[65] All in all, California Casual became so popular that it was copied all over the United States during the 1950s and almost became a synonym for American fashion, which would conquer the postwar world.

Conclusion

War was a disruption but also an opportunity for newcomers to emerge. Mostly independent of ideology, it stimulated national fashion and textile production. In most countries, ready-to-wear production was rationalized and transformed into larger production units. It remains debatable to what extent national fashion systems were created in the long run. There were strong efforts in Italy, Germany, the United States, and Britain to outcompete Paris as the global fashion capital. But after the war, Paris and France rapidly took back the number one position again, from a high-end fashion perspective. However, the seeds of change had been sown.

Although Dior's New Look seemed to be a return of Paris to the stage with a rather backward-looking style, several countries, such as the United States, Italy, Germany, and Britain, developed new institutions and new directions in the fashion industry, both high-end as well as fashion for the masses. This time, France had to follow.

Economic nationalism and protectionism during the 1930s and the war years had another long-lasting effect on the global fashion chain: the massive application of man-made fibers. In all major textile and clothing manufacturing countries, the basis for raw materials had changed. Synthetic fiber production started at the beginning of the twentieth century with artificial silk (rayon) and increased spectacularly during the 1920s, both in terms of production and number of companies. However, during the 1930s and 1940s, man-made fiber production (staple fibers, nylon, and polyester) showed explosive growth rates, often promoted by autarkic policies and wartime shortages of natural fibers. It would completely transform the global fashion industry in the second half of the twentieth century.

Chapter 7

Postwar fashion systems

In 1960, textile king Marcel Boussac was considered the richest man in Europe and was ranked by the *Sunday Times* among the six wealthiest in the world.[1] His textile empire was built during the interwar years (see Chapter 3), and after the war, he diversified his investments into newspapers, horseracing, and electric appliances.[2] An article published in *Life* magazine in 1954 summed up the scope of his activities:

> In France's tightly compartmented economy, Marcel Boussac is a one-man Texas, a free-wheeling operator who flits about in his own four-motored planes, raises race horses and owns two Rolls-Royces. He is so well integrated in the textile business that he grows the cotton, spins, weaves, naps, bleaches, dyes and prints it, sets the styles through his backing of Dior, sells the dresses and also the washing machines to launder them when they get dirty.[3]

Boussac's core business remained, however, textiles and fashion. In 1946, Boussac made a decisive step into haute couture. Being the owner of the House of Gaston since 1937, an haute couture company founded in 1922, he needed a new designer to relaunch it. He invited Christian Dior, who rejected the offer because he wanted his own company. Boussac agreed to invest in a new firm, Société Christian Dior.[4] It was about to rock the world of haute couture.

The three decades between the end of the Second World War and the first oil crisis in 1973 were a period of great expansion for Western fashion around the globe. Christian Dior in the 1950s, then Yves Saint Laurent in the 1960s and 1970s, made Paris the global center of fashion once more. The business model was, however, dramatically different from what it had been before the war. Fashion had become a business system that comprised a large variety of actors (fashion media, trade associations, designers, consultants, producers, etc.) who contributed to creating fashion as a cultural value through a broad range of events (international fairs, shows, awards, etc.). Simultaneously, different national business models emerged during this formative period of the postwar global fashion system. This chapter aims to answer the following questions: How did the new fashion industry emerge in France, Italy, the United States, and Japan after the Second World War? How were the actions of various actors coordinated to produce cultural and economic values?

A new business model for Parisian haute couture

Parisian haute couture faced a deep crisis in the immediate postwar years. The intrinsic instability of this business, which relied on many small houses with an unstable financial basis, led to serious difficulties after the war. In 1945, there were still 106 fashion houses in Paris—for many, the German occupation had been an opportunity to do business (see Chapter 6). However, their number dropped to fifty-one in 1955 and twenty-five in 1970.[5] Numerous renowned couturier houses closed, including Lelong (1948), Soeurs Callot (1950), Agnès, Decoll & Cie (1953), Paquin (1956) (two years after purchasing Worth), and Balenciaga (1968). A survey conducted by the French Ministry of Economy and Finances in 1954 gives a clear picture of the state of the industry (see Table 7.1). It was based on data from the forty-eight companies officially acknowledged as haute couture houses (*Couture-Création* in French) at the time. Statistics related to the average workforce by size of house show many very small businesses. Half of the couturiers employed an average of only forty-one people. While twelve houses were middle-sized, with an average of 181 workers, the five largest houses, all with more than 300 employees, gathered nearly half of the workforce of the industry, with an average of 500 employees. Christian Dior was the largest, with 969 employees (18.9 percent of the total workforce).

The structure of the Parisian haute couture industry thus resembled the structure before the war. However, the industry was faced with a new phenomenon that challenged the traditional business model: declining customer numbers. This was the biggest problem of the sector after 1945. Customers fell from some 20,000 in 1943 to 2,000 in 1970.[6] Making expensive handmade dresses for bourgeois women was not a profitable business anymore. Parisian couturiers had to invent a new business model.

In the early 1950s, the growing ambitions of Italian entrepreneurs to establish their country as a new leader in the global fashion industry, along with decreasing French exports of textiles, threatened the industry. Parisian haute couture had been a driving force for the national textile industry since the middle of the nineteenth century. Both were under pressure, and the French government started working on a plan to support them.[7] In 1952, it adopted a couture-aid plan, prepared by the Chambre Syndicale de Couture de Paris, which offered fashion houses 400 million francs to help them purchase national fabrics for

Table 7.1 Haute Couture Houses in Paris, 1954

	1–99 employees	100–299 employees	Over 300 employees	Unknown	Total
Number of firms	24	12	5	7	48
Percent of total	50.0	25.0	10.4	14.6	100
Number of employees	982	2,166	2,488	–	5,137
Average per firm	41	181	498	–	107
Percent of total	19.1	42.2	48.4	–	100

Source: Drafted by the authors based on Pouillard, "Recasting Paris Fashion," 42–46.

their haute couture creations—the plan limited the use of foreign fabrics to 10 percent. The decline of the textile industry in the 1950s led to some changes in this policy. The government decided to focus its support on promoting French products through haute couture houses by the end of the decade, making them the early promoters of French soft power through fashion. The interests of the textile and fashion industries were, therefore, separated in the early 1960s.[8] Fashion became a specific industry for the authorities.

However, it was not government action that saved the French fashion industry but new initiatives by entrepreneurs to make the business profitable. These included diversification into ready-to-wear and the proliferation of licenses. Haute couture creation in Paris was not profitable, but its continuity was necessary to build luxury brands and sell licensed goods and industrially manufactured garments. Christian Dior was a pioneer of this new business model.[9]

Since the foundation of Christian Dior SA in 1946, the management of the firm had been divided between creative activities, carried out under the direction of Christian Dior himself, and finance, under the responsibility of a team of professional managers appointed by Boussac and led by Jacques Rouët. In 1947, the presentation of Dior's first collection was a stunning success. The generous use of fabrics and a particular silhouette characterized

Figure 7.1 A woman holding a bottle of Miss Dior perfume by Christian Dior, December 1954.

Source: Photo by Housewife/Getty Images.

by the bar suit marked a stylistic break with simple fashion aimed at liberating the female body, symbolized by the creations of Coco Chanel during the interwar years, as well as by wartime restrictions. The return to classic fashion was described as the "New Look" by the American fashion journalist Carmel Snow.[10] Yet Christian Dior was not a revolutionary. He was a conservative, even reactionary, and was criticized by feminists such as French journalist Françoise Giroud. However, his traditionally styled creations catered to the tastes of his clientele: women from the bourgeoisie. After the death of Christian Dior in 1957, haute couture was entrusted to Yves Saint Laurent, a young and promising couturier who had entered the House of Dior in 1955. His creations were, however, too modern for the clientele, so he left the house in 1960 to set up his own business. He was succeeded at Dior by Marcel Bohan, a more traditional designer who pursued the haute couture activities of the company until his retirement in 1989.[11]

Producing haute couture in Paris was, however, not enough to ensure the profitability and growth of the company. Dior and Rouët had worked to expand and diversify their business. A big step was opening a subsidiary in the United States in 1948, Christian Dior New York, to manufacture ready-to-wear garments for American department stores.[12] Based on this experience, Dior expanded the geographic scope of its presence and opened subsidiaries in Mexico (1950), Cuba (1950), Canada (1951), Australia (1951), and the UK (1952). At the same time, it diversified to accessories, signing licensing agreements in France and abroad for perfumes (1947), furs (1947), ties (1950), shoes (1950), hosiery (1951), and menswear (1954).[13] The international expansion based on the exploitation of licenses continued to expand dramatically during the 1960s and 1970s. In 1975, more than 130 licensed goods were sold in 80 countries.[14] Royalties from licenses grew from less than 10 million French francs in 1965 to more than 30 million in 1975 and more than 90 million in 1980.[15] A look at the sales and profitability of the various divisions of Christian Dior SA in 1977 perfectly illustrates how the business model worked (see Table 7.2). Haute couture was a highly loss-making activity. As for ready-to-wear and fur, they were also negative, but their rate of loss was much lower, and they were profitable in some

Table 7.2 Gross Sales (FF), Profit (FF) and Profitability (%) of Maison Christian Dior, 1977

Line	Sales (FF)	Sales (%)	Profit (FF)	Profit (%)	Profitability
Haute couture	10,000,776	5.9	-3,998,867	-17.0	-40.0
Ready-to-wear	12,561,240	7.4	-2,159,352	-9.2	-17.2
Fur	15,550,363	9.2	-933,728	-4.0	-6.0
Accessories	69,359,682	41.0	16,541,583	70.4	23.8
Licenses	22,249,850	13.2	10,634,614	45.3	47.8
Boutiques	39,253,970	23.2	3,110,507	13.2	7.9
Headquarters	0	0.0	304,129	1.3	–
Total	169,065,818	100	23,498,886	100	13.9

Source: Drafted by the authors based on Okawa, "Licensing Practices at Maison Christian Dior," 103.

other years.[16] It contributed, however, to building the brand Dior and must be understood as a form of investment and early luxury marketing. The large sales of accessories and licenses were highly profitable, making the firm generate an overall 13 percent profit.

Haute couture, ready-to-wear, and licensing were interconnected activities that contributed to making fashion a profitable business. Although a few couturiers decided not to follow Dior—Balenciaga, for example, declared, "I will not prostitute myself"—many fashion designers were inspired by this new business model.[17] One of the most famous cases is undoubtedly Pierre Cardin. According to fashion journalist Teri Agins, Cardin had about 800 licenses for anything that could be considered an accessory.[18]

Some couturiers took collective initiatives in the 1950s and 1960s to manufacture ready-to-wear, but these joint initiatives did not last.[19] In the mid-1960s, the apparel manufacturer C. Mendès, a family firm founded in 1902 that worked for Parisian couture houses in the 1950s, established a subsidiary in the United States called Paris Collection Inc. for the production and sale of ready-to-wear on the American market for several fashion designers, including Ungaro, Yves Saint Laurent, Givenchy, Chanel, and Valentino.[20] Karl Lagerfeld became famous during the 1960s as the designer of luxury ready-to-wear collections for Chloé.[21] The promotion of French garments in the US market was also supported by the activities of a fashion forecasting organization, *Comité de coordination des industries de la mode* ("Committee for the Coordination of Fashion Industries" or, CIM). Founded in the mid-1950s, CIM aimed to provide information to textile and apparel producers about the evolution of trends from the United States. It was followed by the opening of various agencies in Paris, such as Promostyl (1966) and Mafia (1968). Connecting designers, manufacturers, and fashion medias, they contributed to forecasting trends and supported the growth of the French apparel industry.[22] The importance of ready-to-wear is embodied by a specific association in France, the *Chambre Syndicale du Prêt-à-Porter des Couturiers et des Créateurs de Mode* (1973). Moreover, together with ready-to-wear, some innovative couturiers started opening their own boutiques. Courrèges was one of the first when he opened his first store in Paris in 1966, followed by Houston and New York the next year.[23]

Yves Saint Laurent was the couturier who had the deepest influence on the development of French fashion in the 1960s and 1970s. He became the new star of global couture after the death of Christian Dior in the context of social change and the sexual revolution. Having left the House of Dior, he opened his own couture company in Paris in 1961, with the financial support of his partner Pierre Bergé (born in 1930), a manager and financier involved in arts and culture, and an American investor. The new driving force of Parisian haute couture was no longer elegance, as it was until the 1950s, but seduction. The sexualization of fashion had become a major trend—Courrèges introduced the miniskirt in haute couture in 1965—and Saint Laurent was an icon of this new movement. He was influenced by art, as he showed by creating a dress inspired by Mondrian's painting (1965) and pop art (1966). Ready-to-wear was an important part of Yves Saint Laurent's business. In 1966, he cofounded the subsidiary Saint Laurent Rive Gauche for the production and sale of luxury garments, together with C. Mendès.[24] Nor did Saint Laurent hesitate

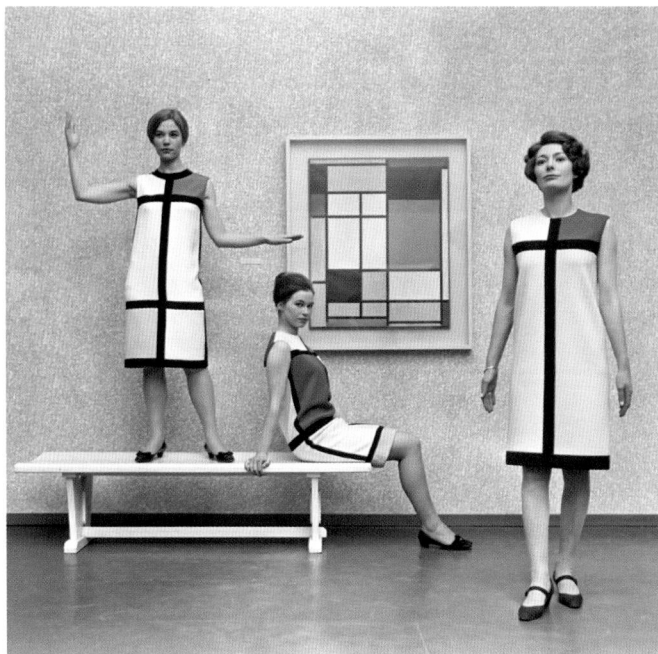

Figure 7.2 Mondriaan Fashion from Paris, dresses made by Yves Saint. Laurent, the models in The Hague Municipal Museum, 1966.v

Source: Eric Koch for Anefo.

to stage his homosexuality in advertising campaigns, as in 1971, when he posed nude in magazines for the launch of a perfume for men.[25] Yves Saint Laurent had himself become a product. The fashion show organized in 1976 was a peak and a turning point. For the first time, it was not held in the house itself but in a salon of the Inter-Continental Hotel. About 1,000 guests, including journalists, photographs, buyers, and the global jet-set, "moved to tears by emotion,"[26] had assisted a sumptuous event, which cost some $500,000. Such expenses were still low if one considers that sales had reached $200 million the previous year, thanks to 128 accessories under license and 111 Rive Gauche boutiques.[27] The *New York Times* lauded "the abstract beauty of the collection," although "it doubted its relevance to today's life."[28] Yves Saint Laurent was no longer a designer of dresses for wealthy women but an iconic artist dedicated to art creation in fashion. Meanwhile, Balenciaga closed his house in 1968 under the assumption that luxury dressmaking had come to an end. Three years later, Coco Chanel died.[29] Traditional fashion had seen its day. Shows, brands, art, and sex were the new values of haute couture. Saint Laurent had paved the way for a new generation of couturiers (see Chapter 8).

US fashion industry—mass production, creativity, and imitation

Many French designers returned to the US market after 1945, making the United States the world's largest fashion market after the war. Christian Dior and his subsidiary, but also

Figure 7.3 Men pulling racks of clothing on busy sidewalk in Garment District, New York City, 1955.
Source: World Telegram & Sun photo by Al Ravenna / Library of Congress Prints and Photographs Division.

Pierre Balmain, a young designer trained by Dior and a promotor of ready-to-wear, launched collections in the United States during the 1950s in collaboration with an American apparel manufacturer, Maria Krum.[30] Others followed his example. The United States not only attracted French and then Italian couturiers (see below) but formed the basis for the rapid expansion of the American fashion industry after 1945. Centered in New York, the industry benefited from the presence of new institutions, such as the Fashion Institute of Technology (created in 1944), which helped to set up a business system comprising numerous players, including the chemical industry (DuPont de Nemours, which had invented nylon in 1938; see Box 7.2), the fashion consultant Tobé Coller Davis, the media industry, notably with the publisher Condé Nast, which owned *Vogue* and *Vanity Fair*, as well as, of course, dressmakers and numerous garment workshops. A new fashion system crystallized in New York after the Second World War.[31] Designers included Bill Blass, Oleg Cassini, Rudi Gernreich, and Anne Klein. Their style was mainly inspired by French couturiers, and their houses were independent companies of modest size.[32]

While fashion in New York and the East Coast focused on womenswear, designers specializing in menswear grew on the West Coast, following their early development during the interwar years (see Chapter 6). In 1945, Los Angeles became the country's third-largest clothing center.[33] It continued to grow fast in the following decade thanks to its ability to address changes in consumption habits for menswear characterized by a "cultural shift toward informality."[34] Leisurewear, instead of the traditional three-piece suit, had become the new trend in the United States. Apparel makers in California had gathered within a trade association since 1934, an association that would become known as MAGIC (Men's Apparel Guild in California) after the war. These apparel makers launched fashion shows and merchandising events featuring the Californian lifestyle. They offered retailers lifestyle wear associated with the new values in the fashion industry, such as "youth, celebrity, leisure, and heterosexuality."[35] The West Coast apparel industry was based on many small manufacturers, which enabled retailers to offer a broad range of products and lifestyle marketing. The rise of Hollywood and the development of California as a holiday destination made this industry famous. For example, in the 1950s, Catalina Knitting Mills, one of the largest apparel producers on the West Coast (founded in 1907), launched advertising campaigns, shot in Palm Springs, that staged "beach boys" and "California girls."[36]

However, the creativity of fashion designers and the formation of a US fashion system did not prevent the national apparel industry from experiencing an early decline due to the rapid growth of the internationalization of sourcing. US apparel manufacturers started to outsource production to Asia as early as the 1950s. American retailers started to import cheap cotton blouses made in Japan in 1947. Their number peaked at several million items in 1955, surpassing domestic production.[37] Although the US government negotiated voluntary export restraints with Japan, these were only temporary measures. Apparel imports from Japan increased twelvefold between 1947 and 1960.[38] In the 1960s, US importers shifted their attention to Hong Kong and Taiwan, where apparel-making firms, sometimes controlled by Japanese companies, produced clothing for the US market. It was a way for the Japanese to overcome the voluntary export restrictions of 1956. For example, the discount store J.C. Penney opened a buying office in Hong Kong in 1970.[39] Hence, there was strong pressure on US apparel manufacturers. In 1961, Jerome Asher, president of the Trouser Institute of America, wrote a letter to Lawrence Phillips, the Vice-president of Phillips-Van Heusen (PHV), one of the largest apparel manufacturers in the United States and a promoter of protectionist policy. He shared his worries about the future of the industry: "You can imagine what would happen if we were to open a warehouse in New York City or other key cities, offering this type of merchandise. In short order, little would be left of the American pants industry."[40]

This is exactly what happened: PHV would soon begin producing outside the United States. This company had based its growth on the merger of numerous specialized garment manufacturers and reached gross sales of $143 million in 1966 and $254 million in 1971. However, in the 1970s, it started to disinvest and close factories, relocating production to the Caribbean.[41] Low-wage countries in Central America, the Caribbean, and Mexico were among the first destinations where US apparel manufacturers moved their operations. Sears, McGregor, PVH, Wrangler, and many others had production sites in these countries in the early 1970s.[42]

A new generation of designers took the opportunities offered by the internationalization of the US apparel business. Focusing on design and concepts, they developed strong brands and outsourced their production, first to American manufacturers and then to foreign suppliers. Ralph Lauren was one of the first examples. Born in 1939, he launched a tie line in New York under the Polo brand in 1967, followed by a full menswear collection the next year. Calvin Klein and Liz Claiborne founded their own companies soon after, in 1968 and 1976, respectively.[43] Unlike French couturiers, their designs were based on leisure and sportswear, and they targeted the mass market with aggressive marketing methods.

The emergence of Italian fashion

During the 1930s, Italy's fascist government tried to set up a fashion industry centered in Turin and linked to the boom in the textile industry and the activities of a few couturiers (see Chapter 6). However, after the war, it was in a different context that a fashion system emerged that made Italy one of the giants of the industry and a direct competitor to French supremacy. The US market played a major role in the formation of the postwar Italian fashion business. Collaboration between long-lasting textile industrial districts and designers, as well as strong cooperation with American buyers, was the driving force of this growth. In the context of the Cold War and the Marshall Plan, the United States supported Italian exports of textiles and garments to their domestic market. American aid programs supported the transfer of technology and knowledge to some Italian textile and apparel companies, which were consequently able to improve their productivity and engage in mass production.[44] Hence, in 1960, American silk imports from Italy exceeded those from France.[45] In this context, and with the objective of selling garments in the United States, the producers of textiles started to finance fashion.

The postwar formation of Italian fashion started in Florence. In 1951, Giovanni Battista Giorgini (1899–1971), a buyer of Italian goods for American department stores, organized a fashion show in Villa Torregiani in Florence, inviting international fashion journalists and representatives of US department stores. A year later, Giorgini moved to the Sala Bianca of Pitti Palace to start a series of spectacular fashion shows. His approach to fashion, however, was rather traditional. The creations presented in his show were handmade by artisan designers who lacked the necessary connections with the textile industry to expect to enter a phase of lasting growth.[46] Giorgini stopped his fashion shows in Florence in 1965.

Meanwhile, some other shows had taken place in Rome and Milan. The latter was the industrial center of Italy, with a strong textile industry. In 1951, the province of Milan had 3,551 firms employing more than 100,000 persons in this sector, while the province of Florence had only 1,226 firms employing less than 25,000 people.[47] Moreover, Milan was a large market, with a local aristocracy and industrial bourgeoisie attracted by high-quality and relatively simple clothing. Elisabetta Merlo and Francesca Polese emphasize that "sobriety and severity emerged as the hallmarks of Milanese fashion."[48]

One must stress the presence of numerous national media in Milan, particularly the Italian version of *Vogue*, launched in 1966, four years after Condé Nast purchased the lifestyle and fashion magazine *Novità*, founded in 1950 by architect Emilia Kuster Rosselli. *Vogue Italia* became a major platform for the new generation of Italian designers, and other fashion magazines soon imitated its approach to fashion.[49] Finally, Milan was the home of several institutions that enabled various actors to meet, exchange, and organize the fashion business together. The Milan Sample Fair (*Fiera Campionaria*), one of the most important industrial fairs in Europe, organized the first exhibition dedicated to fashion in 1951.[50] It was set up by the *Centro Italiano della Moda*, the trade organization of fashion houses in Milan, which founded the Italian Fashion Service in partnership with industrialists from the clothing industry in 1952. Six years later, the *Camera Sindacale della Moda Italiana* organized the first fashion show in Milan.

The presence of a highly varied textile industry, based on thousands of independent enterprises, supported the growth of Italian fashion. Designers had the opportunity to outsource production to these specialized firms and to market a broad variety of clothing. For example, Ermenegildo Zegna was at first a wool-weaving workshop that opened in 1889 and focused on manufacturing fabrics for professional tailors. In 1968, it opened a factory for ready-to-wear and a first production facility abroad, in Spain, five years later. It remained, however, an important provider of fabrics and garments for luxury brands, signing, for example, a license contract with Versace in 1978. It went on to launch its own branded garments in 1980.[51]

The most important apparel company supporting the development of Italian fashion was *Gruppo Finanziario Tessile* (GFT), one of the largest ready-to-wear manufacturers in Italy, based in Turin. GFT was founded in 1930 by the Rivetti brothers, who came from a family of wool entrepreneurs. It became famous for its partnerships with independent designers. Unlike Boussac or C. Mendès in France, who had direct financial control over couturier houses, GFT developed a broad range of partnerships based on licensing contracts and joint ventures. One of the first cooperations started in 1957 when GFT asked Elvira Leonardi Broyure (or Biki, as she was personally and professionally known) to design a womenswear collection.[52] As she was a female designer known for the simplicity of her creations, it would be suitable for serial production.[53] The idea of GFT was to escape the pure mass production of standardized clothes and add creativity to its garments. However, the GFT–Biki

Figure 7.4 Italian fashion designer Biki (Elvira Leonardi Bouyeure) in the fashion show room at her atelier with two models. Beside her, her son-in-law Alain Renaud. Milan, 1968.

Source: Mondadori PortfolioPhoto by Mondadori Portfolio via Getty Images.

partnership did not result in satisfying financial results, as these creations did not meet the new tastes of Italian women. The products looked too much like classical haute couture for bourgeois women—Biki was in her sixties—and so they stopped in 1972. This failure was the opportunity to engage in business with younger and more casual designers, like Emanuel Ungaro, a designer in his late thirties engaged by GFT in 1971. He designed more audacious and provocative fashion for women.[54] Other designers, like Valentino, followed, but it would be a promising young couturier from Milan who would turn the partnership between GFT and designers into big business: Giorgio Armani (see Chapter 8).

Western fashion and garments in Japan

The formation of fashion systems around the world between 1945 and the early 1970s was not limited to Europe and the United States. Japan offers an excellent example of a non-Western country that experienced a similar process. It occurred, however, in a particular context characterized by the transfer of foreign knowledge. As we have discussed previously, although Western dresses were introduced to Japan at the end of the nineteenth century, traditional Japanese products like kimonos continued to dominate clothing until the Second World War (see Chapters 5 and 7). However, during the postwar high-growth years, Japanese society experienced a deep Westernization of lifestyle and material culture that affected clothing. By 1967, the share of Western garments in clothing expenses by households already amounted to 76 percent. It had grown to 82 percent by 1980.[55]

The shift from Japanese to Western garments needs to be understood within the context of a transfer of technology and knowledge regarding the making and wearing of clothes. This change occurred in two stages. First, between 1945 and the 1960s, dressmaking was still an activity largely conducted by women at home. Hence, they had to learn the techniques to cut and sew skirts, dresses, shirts, etc. This period was the heyday of designer schools. An increasing number of such organizations, which included the famous Bunka Fashion College, where famous designers like Kenzo Takada started their education, and Dressmaker Gakuin, both in Tokyo, taught young women and housewives how to make Western-style garments.[56] This learning process went together with the fast diffusion of sewing machines (owned by 75.5 percent of all households in 1960).[57] Moreover, the first generation of fashion magazines, usually published by designer schools (like *Soen*), aimed precisely at giving technical advice to young women. They were not focused on lifestyle, brands, and celebrities but offered patterns to cut and sew at home a variety of Western-style dresses. Fashion was not related to the creation of cultural value but to the ability to manufacture a foreign product.

Second, during the 1960s, apparel companies started to mass-produce and mass-distribute Western-style garments. Working closely with department stores and many manufacturers throughout Japan, they were able to offer large amounts of industrial-made garments. These firms, notably Renown, Kashiyama, and Sanyo Shokai, employed thousands of employees and became industrial giants. The number of workers in the

Japanese clothing industry increased from nearly 95,000 people in 1948 to more than 210,000 in 1960 and more than 580,000 in 1985.[58] As a result, household production of garments started to decline, and designer schools experienced a sharp decline in the number of students—from a peak of nearly 10,000 in 1967 at Bunka Fashion College to 5,120 in 1980.[59] Western garments became a consumer good, and apparel companies started to develop branding strategies in the early 1970s. However, brands were not developed based on creativity and concepts, as in Western countries, but on a scientific analysis of market characteristics. Managers in textile and apparel firms worked together to identify many niches (by sex, age, size, purchasing power, cultural preferences, etc.) for which specific products were developed. This led to an over-segmentation of the market and the development of many brands, none of which had the potential to establish itself in major markets.[60] Consequently, the role of fashion magazines changed in this context. Their role was not to offer technical education anymore but to communicate to consumers. The overwhelmingly segmented market led to a massive number of new fashion magazines aimed at specific audiences. More than twenty new titles appeared on the market during the 1970s and 1980s.[61] Finally, because clothing companies had little interest in creativity, the role of fashion designers in these companies was limited to drawing garments according to the schedule drawn up by engineers.

Designers unable to express their creativity often left Japan and settled in Paris, where they participated in fashion shows and enjoyed great success in the 1970s.[62] Kenzo Takada, Issey Miyake, Yohji Yamamoto, Rei Kawakubo, and Hanae Mori became famous fashion designers in Paris. Except for Kenzo, who continued his life and career in Paris—his house, established in 1970, was purchased by LVMH in 1993—other designers returned to Japan.

Figure 7.5 Designers Sonia Rykiel, Karl Lagerfeld and Kenzo Takada seated in Rykiel's Paris apartment to discuss fashion in the 1970s for WWD (Nathalie Rykiel stands in the background leaning forward). Article title: "French Fashion Talk."

Source: Photo by Fairchild Archive/Penske Media via Getty Images.

In 1974, some formed a group to present their collections twice a year, evolving into Tokyo Fashion Week in 1975. These fashion designers sold their products in department stores and their own boutiques. Their houses have, however, never become big businesses, as in France or Italy, mainly due to a lack of cooperation with the apparel industry.[63]

Despite the difficulties faced by independent designers, Western fashion brands such as Armani, Burberry, Chanel, and Dior have been very successful in Japan since the 1950s. For the most part, these brands entered the Japanese market through business relationships with local companies, both for licensed production (textile companies) and distribution (department stores).[64] Christian Dior is a case in point. In 1953, this company signed a contract with the department store *Daimaru* for the production under license of dresses designed in France and adapted by Japanese couturiers. Ten years later, in 1963, a second license was signed by Dior with the textile and cosmetic firm *Kanebo* for the production under license of a great variety of products from designs approved by Paris. This helped make the brand very popular in Japan and led to massive profits (from 100 million Yen in 1972 to 800 million in 1982).[65] This business model largely remained in force until the 1990s, when the luxury conglomerates, which now owned most of the major fashion brands, decided to end licensing contracts and take control of their brands on a global scale (see Chapter 9).

Box 7.1 Licensing strategies of Western fashion companies in Japan

After the Second World War, Japan was the first non-Western market to gain significance for European brands. It was, however, a market difficult to enter due to strict regulations against foreign investment and the presence of a complex distribution system. Hence, Western fashion companies had to partner with Japanese companies. They signed licenses that allowed the production and sale of clothes and accessories with foreign brands against royalties. Various kinds of Japanese companies were engaged in this business: department stores, general trading companies (*sogo sosha*), and textile firms.

Department stores were the first partners of French couturiers. Daimaru was the first to sign an agreement for the production under license by its own manufacturers with Christian Dior in 1953. This example was soon followed by Takashimaya with Pierre Cardin (1959), Matsuzakaya with Nina Ricci (1961), Mitsukoshi with Guy Laroche (1963), and Isetan with Pierre Balmain (1963). These stores became the most reputable places to sell fashion and luxury goods in Japan since the interwar years. Hence, they were the natural partners of European couturiers.

As each department store produced only for its own outlets, the scope of the business was rather limited for European fashion companies. From the 1960s, to extend the scope of their business with a broad variety of accessories for the mass market, they started shifting partnerships to different companies: textile manufacturers. This prevented limiting the business to the adaptation of haute couture for the Japanese market. Dior was again a pioneer. In 1964, it signed a new licensing agreement with Kanebo, a textile company with a large production capacity and huge financial resources. The following year, Itokin, another textile company, signed an agreement with the American sportswear brand Aspen, while Sanyo Shokai signed with Burberry in 1969 and Kawabe with Yves Saint Laurent in 1970. In some cases, the Japanese manufacturers received training and technical assistance from their Western partners. For example, technicians from Sanyo Shokai went to London to learn cutting, dying, and sewing techniques from Burberry.

Moreover, while these firms were producing garments, the European fashion companies extended the scope of their business to include the production of numerous accessories through additional licenses. For example, in 1984, Pierre Cardin had license and sublicense contracts with forty-six Japanese firms, Pierre Balmain with thirty-six, Yves Saint Laurent with thirty-three, Christian Dior with nine, Thierry Mugler with eight, and Jean-Paul Gaultier with eight.

European luxury fashion companies learned in Japan to expand rapidly into distant markets by exploiting licenses. However, most of them had only weak and indirect control over the design of the goods produced and sold locally under their brand names. Taking back control over accessories would become a challenge during the 1990s with the formation of luxury conglomerates (see Chapter 9).

Sources: *Kaigai raisensu burando no genkai to kongo no kadai* (Osaka: Yano Institute, 1984), 13–89; Tomoko Okawa, "Licensing and the Mass Production of Luxury Goods," in *Oxford Handbook of Luxury Business* ed. Pierre-Yves Donzé, Véronique Pouillard and Joanne Roberts (Oxford: Oxford University Press, 2022), 173–193; Simon James Bytheway, *Investing Japan: Foreign Capital, Monetary Standards, and Economic Development, 1859–2011* (Cambridge University Press, 2014); Rika Fujioka, Zhen Li, and Yuta Kaneko, "The Democratization of Luxury and the Expansion of the Japanese Market, 1960–2010," in *Global Luxury: Organizational Change and Emerging Markets since the 1970s*, ed. Pierre-Yves Donzé and Rika Fujioka (Basingstoke: Palgrave Macmillan, 2018), 133–156.

Growth of global apparel industry

The fast growth experienced by couturiers in Western Europe and the United States through their collaboration with the apparel industry does not mean that all garment manufacturers were directly related to these designers. Many companies pursued their development of fashion for the masses in the continuity of the models implemented during the interwar years, embodied by C&A (vertical integration of retail and production) and M&S (outsourcing of production by a retailer). After the Second World War, C&A entered a phase of fast internationalization based on the opening of local subsidiaries and the expansion of its retail network. Production was, however, concentrated in the Netherlands and Germany.[66] In 1946, it founded a subsidiary in New York and entered the United States, with a first store in Brooklyn (1948), followed by a second one on Fifth Avenue (1950). The US market was nonetheless too competitive, and so C&A was unable to secure enough sales to be profitable. In 1954, it sold the store on Fifth Avenue with a loss of $700,000. During the 1960s and 1970s, it purchased the department store *Ohrbach*, which had subsidiaries in California, and five other chains. In 1983, it owned more than 400 points of sale in North America.[67] Meanwhile, growth in Europe depended on Germany. Between 1950 and 1960, C&A opened twenty-one new stores in this country, while the number of employees went from 1,792 to 7,580.[68] It also entered Belgium in 1963, then several Western European countries—France in 1972, Switzerland in 1977, Luxembourg in 1982, Spain in 1983, and Austria in 1984. It entered Brazil in 1977.[69] In terms of production, although C&A started signing contracts with external suppliers, it continued to expand its production capacity, especially in the Netherlands. The Dutch subsidiary NCI opened or took over eight factories during the 1950s.[70] In Germany, C&A owned eleven factories in 1961.[71]

The vertical integration model was also adopted by some of the garment manufacturers who diversified into retail after 1945. The Italian company Benetton is a case in point.[72] The roots of this firm go back to 1955 when the siblings Luciano and Giuliana Benetton purchased a knitting machine and started to manufacture woolen sweaters. Two brothers joined them in the following years, and they founded a company, *Maglificio di Ponzano Veneto dei Fratelli Benetton*, in 1965. To distinguish themselves from their competitors, the brothers decided to sell their sweaters themselves rather than supplying wholesalers. They opened their first store in the north of Italy in 1968 and a second one in Paris in 1969. During the early 1970s, Benetton adopted innovative management practices to achieve growth, high quality, and remain independent. It started to outsource production massively to hundreds of independent small firms. At the same time, it decided to dye assembled clothes rather than the yarn before knitting to reduce manufacturing time. A broad range of colorful sweaters soon became a characteristic of the brand—it would adopt the United Colors of Benetton trademark later (1989).

M&S followed its business model of an apparel retailer that completely outsourced production to British manufacturers that were mostly based in Leeds. It strengthened its design capabilities to better control the garments it would offer to consumers. In 1946, M&S opened a textile-testing laboratory, and the following year, it set up a factory section that offered technical assistance to its suppliers to modernize their equipment. By 1964, a total of 140 firms had transformed their equipment through such cooperation.[73] Dewhirst was one of the major partners. This company specialized in the production of workwear and shirts mainly supplied to M&S. Its gross sales grew from less than £700,000 in 1955 to £23 million in 1982.[74] M&S operated the St. Michael brand for its clothing and began expanding its store network internationally in the early 1970s. It opened a store in Canada in 1972 and one in Paris in 1975 before expanding into all the European Economic Community member states.[75]

After the Second World War, several other garment retailers implemented a business model like that of M&S—for example, Hennes & Mauritz (H&M) (see Chapter 9). On the other side of the Atlantic, The Gap focused first on the retail of a single product: denim jeans. The roots of this company go back to Sacramento, California, in 1969, when Donald Fischer, a real estate developer, was shopping for a pair of Levi jeans and could not find the right size. He understood jeans had become a new popular item for young people and decided to open his own store specializing in this product. By 1974, he had opened 186

Figure 7.6 The gift display in a ladies fashion shop on Saville Row, Newcastle upon Tyne, 1966. Source: Tyne & Wear Archives & Museums.

stores throughout 21 states, and sales had nearly reached $100 million. The firm was still focused on the United States and would internationalize over the following decades.[76]

Conclusion

After the Second World War, the global fashion industry underwent a profound transformation. While the old Parisian fashion houses faced great difficulties and eventually disappeared, new business models based on cooperation between designers and the clothing industry emerged. The nature of this cooperation took different forms in different countries. In France, some large textile companies invested directly in fashion houses, such as Boussac in Christian Dior and C. Mendès in Yves Saint Laurent. This led to strong business growth and supported the international expansion of these brands. Italy had a significantly different model, characterized by more flexible relationships between partners, mainly in the form of license agreements or joint ventures. Textile giant GFT, for example, teamed up with several Italian designers, such as Emanuel Ungaro and Valentino Garavano. The American fashion business model was more like the Italian model. New York designers had their creations produced by a wide range of garment companies. These multiple cooperative ventures between designers, the clothing industry, consultants, fashion shows, retailers, and fashion magazines gave rise to veritable fashion systems.

Finally, outside Western countries, Japan experienced a dramatic expansion of its clothing industry in response to the new consumer habits of its population, characterized by the Westernization of lifestyles. In this context, clothing companies showed little interest in fashion

Figure 7.7 Pierre Balmain Show in Victoria Hotel, Amsterdam, 1951.
Source: Noske, J.D. / Anefo / Nationaal Archief.

design. Clothing production was seen primarily as an industrial affair. Couturiers wishing to express their creativity moved to Paris, where they took part in the haute couture shows.

Despite the undeniable success of these new fashion brands, the first signs of challenges to these new business models appeared in the United States. From the 1950s onward, American apparel companies began outsourcing their production and buying from Asian producers. They soon relocated production units to the Caribbean, Central America, and Mexico. The internationalization of sourcing was not yet very visible in Europe, but it was to become a major trend after the first oil crisis (Chapter 8). In addition, certain players, such as The Gap in the United States and Benetton in Italy, rapidly understood the importance of controlling a retail network to establish fashion brands, even in the absence of cooperation with recognized couturiers. They contributed to the gradual blurring of the distinction between fashion brands and clothing for the masses.

Box 7.2 The nylon revolution and the emergence of synthetic fibers

In 1938, after eleven years of research and $27 million invested, the American chemical company DuPont de Nemours launched a new material: nylon. While the production of rayon had increased sharply since the late 1920s, leading to the wide use of this material by ordinary women and making it a cheaper product, nylon offered new prospects to the fashion industry. This fully synthetic fiber—used by the Allied armies during the Second

World War for parachutes—was fine, shiny, and strong. Stockings were one of the first apparel accessories developed with nylon, and its use became widespread in the 1960s when designers were looking for new materials to break with traditional couture. For example, Saint Laurent Rive Gauche launched several collections using nylon in the 1970s.

Following nylon, new synthetic fibers were developed, the most prominent being polyester, a material made from oil. It developed in the early 1940s and has been used by fashion companies since the 1950s—at first, especially for men's suits. These artificial fibers were mostly used in blends with cotton and with other synthetic fibers. This made it possible to increase the possibilities and new ideas for fashion. The share of cotton among world fibers dropped from 75 percent in 1945 to 49 percent in 1976. This also marks the arrival of the petrochemical industry as a supplier of materials for the fashion industry. It has also made fashion a contributor to the destruction of the environment and the presence of plastic pollution in the oceans. Moreover, synthetics have become the agents behind the obsolescence that lies at the heart of the modern fashion industry—mass-produced garments made from artificial substances can be discarded as casually and easily as they are purchased (see Chapter 9).

Source: Susannah Handley, *Nylon: The Story of a Fashion Revolution: A Celebration of Design from Art Silk to Nylon and Thinking Fibers* (Baltimore: Johns Hopkins University Press, 1999).

Figure 7.8 Magazine advertisement for DuPont Lycra, the brand name for the polyester-polyurethane copolymer invented by Joseph Shivers in 1958 at the DuPont laboratory in Waynesboro, Virginia. The advertisement was published in the September 22, 1961 edition of *Life* magazine.
Source: Courtesy of Science History Institute.

Chapter 8

Global fashion: Outsourcing and the end of the production paradigm

In 1970, during a meeting with trade unions of the textile and apparel industries, the German Federal Minister of Economic Affairs, Karl Schiller, a member of the Social Democratic Party, declared that "the force for further liberalization of imports cannot be denied," and he let the trade union know that the restrictive trade policies of other industrialized countries "has led to backward textile industries in the end, while in contrast the liberal German attitude has forced the German industry to modernize early."[1] The German apparel industry had to face competition from Eastern Europe and Asia and find ways to survive in the global market without protection from the government. This sector lost more than half of its jobs; it went from nearly 400,000 workers in 1970 to less than 200,000 in 1990. Meanwhile, the average revenue per employee increased from 40,000 Deutschmark (DM) to 160,000 DM.[2] Famous German household brands like C&A, Triumpf, Seidensticker, and adidas (see Chapter 10) outsourced manufacturing to focus more and more on design, marketing, and branding in Germany, keeping high added-value activities in their home country.

As illustrated by the example of Germany, the 1970s and 1980s were a turning point in the long-term evolution of the fashion business. The industry became global during this period and experienced three fundamental changes: 1) the reorganization of global supply chains; 2) the growing impact of marketing and branding; and 3) the increasing importance of retailers. As a result of growing competition from low-wage economies, most of the textile industry disappeared from Northwestern Europe and North America. Fashion enterprises, which used to work closely with local textile producers, reorganized their businesses and started to outsource production to low-wage countries, first to Eastern Europe, then to Asia and North Africa. The 1984 takeover by the French financier Bernard Arnault of the Boussac Group, which had been the largest French textile company and the owner of Christian Dior and the department store Le Bon Marché, is an illustration of this decline.[3] Western fashion companies had to reinvent themselves and build a competitive advantage based on different capabilities, mostly focused on brand management and expanding their licensing strategies, and on diversification toward accessories. The influence of the fashion media increased dramatically during this period because they offered legitimacy to fashion companies that had refocused their narrative on the genius creativity of their designers.

At the same time, modern fashion businesses took various forms outside Western countries. Japan experienced rapid growth in foreign brands during this period, and some Japanese apparel companies invested in Western design firms, with an example being Takihyo's control of half of the capital of Donna Karan New York (DKNY) after it was founded in 1984. In Europe, the increasing importance of brands led Bernard Arnault to take control of Moët Hennessy Louis Vuitton (LVMH) a few years after he had purchased Boussac (1987). The investment in retailing was another strategy adopted by American (The Gap) and European (Benetton, Marks & Spencer) manufacturers of garments. Controlling a network of stores was not only a way to internalize profits but also to build strong brands and enter foreign markets. In Japan, the apparel industry continued to work with department stores and was late to invest in retail. Finally, emerging economies like China and India engaged in the organization of fashion systems inspired by the Western example, aiming to increase the competitiveness of their national brands.

This chapter explores the transformation of the fashion business throughout the world during an era of globalization. It addresses the following questions: What were the dynamics of the global shift in the textile and apparel industry? How did they impact existing fashion systems, and how did fashion companies react to these new conditions?

Global shifts in the textile and apparel industries

The clothing industry was one of the first to take on a global dimension during the 1970s, with a sharp global shift from industrialized countries toward low-wage economies.[4] As we have seen in Chapter 7, some American apparel retailers started to outsource part of their production in the 1950s. This practice, adopted in other developed economies, increased over the next decade and became dominant in the 1970s. This was indeed not limited to the United States or Western countries, as embodied by the example of Germany tackled above. Japan's textile industry also experienced a dramatic decline in the second half of the 1960s, although apparel manufacturers were able to maintain employment until the early 1990s due to the fast growth of domestic demand at that time.[5]

Relative labor costs were the most significant factor that led to this transformation. However, one must also stress institutional change after adopting the Long-Term Arrangement for Cotton Textiles (LTA) in 1962, extended to all textiles in 1973 with the adoption of the Multi-Fiber Arrangement (MFA). It regulated most trade in textiles and fibers around the world until 2005. MFA was an arrangement whose objective was to smooth the production shift from developed to developing countries. It imposed export quotas on textiles and garments from Asian countries to the United States and Western Europe to offer some protection to firms and employment. Import quotas were negotiated on a bilateral basis to protect disrupted markets. The MFA, which was renegotiated and extended several times, restricted the growth of exports by developing countries. In 1995, the MFA was included in the World Trade Organization, but a gradual demise occurred within ten years. The MFA was abolished in 2005.[6] Other international agreements, like the North American Free Trade Agreement (NAFTA), enforced in 1995, contributed to the relocation of apparel production in developing economies.

The global shift in the world production of synthetic fibers is an excellent illustration of the global dynamics of the textile and apparel industries since the 1970s (see Figure 8.1). In 1975, developed economies, as a group, still dominated the market. Collectively, the United States, Western Europe, and Japan had a 66 percent share. However, the share of production of these three regions declined steadily over the years, while other regions, including China, grew from 34 percent in 1975 to 50 percent in 1990 and 91 percent in 2015. These numbers express the global shift in the production of textiles and garments.

East Asia, particularly Hong Kong, Taiwan, and South Korea, emerged as the new production centers for the international apparel industry. Hong Kong was a major hub within globalized production networks. Its clothing industry developed rapidly during the 1970s and peaked at about 300,000 employees in 1980. It started to decline at the end of the decade with the relocation of factories to mainland China and other Asian countries. Since 1995, it has had less than 100,000 workers. That year, the Hong Kong export of garments included only 19.5 percent of goods made in the British colony, against 50.5 percent in 1988.[7] Following the reforms adopted in 1978, China's clothing production experienced fast growth mainly focused on exports for the global market. Entrepreneurs based in Hong Kong played a major role in moving their factories to the special economic zones created by the Chinese government, founding joint ventures with state-owned enterprises and nurturing the development of hundreds of private companies in China. While the Chinese

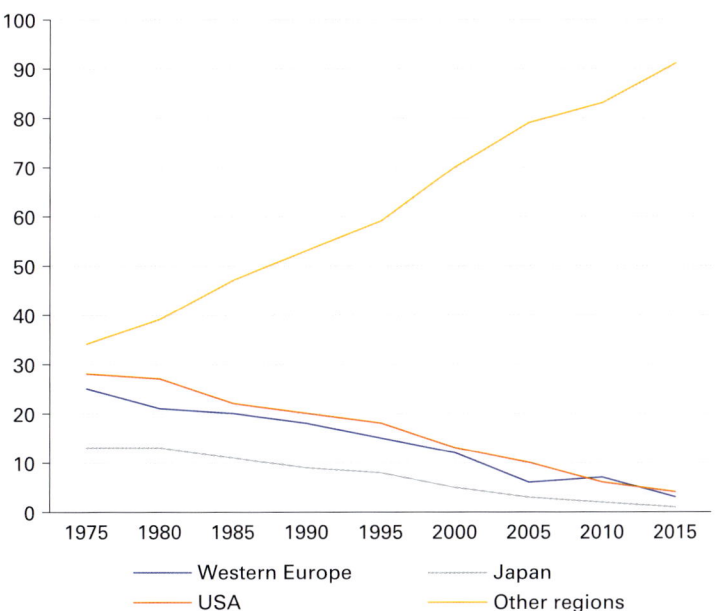

Figure 8.1 Share in World Production of Man-made Fibers, by Region, as a Percentage (1975–2015)

Source: Industrievereinigung Chemiefaser e.V., *"Production since 1975, World production Man-made fibers Wool, and Cotton,"* https://www.ivc-ev.de/live/index.php?page_id=87 (accessed October 28, 2018).

Figure 8.2 A Chinese female worker in a textile factory in Huaibei, Anhui province, 2015.
Source: Photo by Jie Zhao/Corbis via Getty Images.

apparel industry exported only 17 percent of its production in 1981, this share increased to 90 percent in 1994, making China the world's largest exporter of clothing.[8] After the handover of Hong Kong to China in 1997, the "one country, two systems" policy implemented by the Chinese government offered autonomy to enterprises headquartered in Hong Kong so that we must still discuss them separately from firms based in mainland China.

Many companies based in Hong Kong were intermediaries between factories established in China and other Asian countries, usually legally independent, and customers in developed countries. For example, the trading company Li & Fung, founded in Guangzhou in 1906 and whose headquarters were moved to Hong Kong after the establishment of the People's Republic of China, became a major intermediary between factories based in mainland China and Western retailers. It was one of The Gap's main suppliers until this company opened its own buying office in Hong Kong in 1987.[9] Similarly, the fashion company Esprit was founded in 1968 by a couple of American entrepreneurs who wanted to sell clothing and apparel in their home market. They moved headquarters and manufacturing to Hong Kong in 1972, from where they could easily purchase garments made in China after the opening of this country. Design and retail were kept in America. This transnational business model increased sales from $1 million in 1970 to $700 million in 1985.[10]

Beyond China, Asian subcontractors played a major role in disseminating apparel manufacturing in developing countries, looking for low wages and avoiding restrictions made by MFA. In Taiwan and South Korea, vertically integrated firms invested abroad and

Figure 8.3 Bangladeshi women sewing clothes, 2013. Fahad Faisal.
Source: Public Domain via Wikimedia Commons.

globalized their production network essentially through mergers and acquisitions. They controlled the production of clothing for global brands. For example, the Taiwanese company Nien Hsing Textile Co., founded in 1988, produced denim and jeans for American brands like Calvin Klein, Tommy Hilfiger, The GAP, and DKNY. It opened and acquired production units in Nicaragua (1993 and 2000), Mexico (1997), Cambodia (2000), Vietnam (2000), and Lesotho (2002).[11] As for the Korean giant conglomerate Daewoo, its textile subsidiary was an important actor in developing the clothing industry in Bangladesh. In 1979, in cooperation with the Bangladeshi company Desh Garments, it opened its first sewing facility in the country. The objectives were to benefit from the cheap labor force and to overcome the restrictions of MFA that limited Korean textile exports. The Daewoo plant benefited from the training and know-how of the Korean headquarters, a classical pattern of technology transfer. It started production for export markets and experienced very fast growth during the 1980s, finally becoming an example for the whole garment industry in Bangladesh. This firm led many other private entrepreneurs, a few in cooperation with foreign companies but mostly independent second-tier subcontractors, to engage in apparel manufacturing. Among the 130 middle managers of Desh who were sent to Daewoo's Korean plant, a total of 115 later opened their own garment factory.[12] A trade association was founded in 1982—the Bangladesh Garment

Manufacturers and Exporters Association (BGMEA)—and the number of apparel factories throughout the country rose from only nine in 1977 to about 5,600 in 2012.[13] In 2005, this industry employed more than 3 million workers throughout the country, and within five years, Bangladesh had become the third-largest exporter of garments.[14]

The shift in production led to a crisis for the European and American textile industries. Nearly all the manufacturers of fabrics disappeared or relocated their production facilities outside; for example, in Germany, the total number of employees in the apparel industry peaked at about 400,000 in the second half of the 1960s and then declined to less than 50,000 after the mid-2000s.[15] This shift led to the bankruptcy and closure of many large companies, such as Van Delden Group (1981), Ravensburger (1989), and Adolff (1991) in Germany.[16] In France, this was, for example, the case for the Boussac Group. While it largely depended on protected colonial markets, the end of the French Empire was a first shock for this group. The conservative management of Marcel Boussac, the founder and owner of the group, who decided not to invest abroad nor use synthetic fibers, led to a decline in its competitiveness. Despite aid from the French government, which was keen to maintain employment in the north of France, the Boussac Group went bankrupt in 1978. The textile business was taken over by another textile conglomerate, Willot Frères, which was unable to implement a profitable business and was eventually purchased by Bernard Arnault in 1984 (see Chapter 9).[17] Similar examples of apparel and textile firms unable to understand the opportunities offered by global production networks can be found throughout Western Europe, the United States, and Japan.[18]

For the apparel manufacturers, there were two ways to survive in this environment. First, they could follow the example of Esprit and outsource their manufacturing operations while refocusing on design, branding, and retail, which is what the US jeans company Levi Strauss did. In the 1980s, this company employed a total of 40,000 workers, of which 70 percent were in the United States. It started moving its operations to low-wage countries at the end of the decade and closed most of its American plants in 1998 and 1999, eliminating almost 6,000 jobs in the United States. In 2002 and 2003, the company closed all its remaining factories in America, cutting again some 5,000 jobs. It had not only transferred production abroad but mostly outsourced it to independent companies. It refocused on branding (making Levi's 501 an iconic product) and expanding its retail activities. The share of in-house production declined from 90 percent in 1980 to 30 percent in 1999.[19] Meanwhile, earnings grew from $155 million, on average, in the 1980s to over $700 million in 1995.[20]

Second, moving up in the market was another way to maintain high value-added activities in Western countries. The luxury strategy can be found in nearly all European countries. Numerous Italian firms chose to manufacture high-quality fabrics and clothing addressed to specific niches. The wool fabric manufacturer Ermenegildo Zegna, whose roots go back to 1889, opened mono-brand stores in Paris (1980) and Milan (1985) to sell menswear made in Italy directly to customers. In the 1990s, it took over several producers of wool and fabrics to have better control over quality and production. These operations were necessary to build a global luxury brand based on the excellence of wool manufacturing.[21]

In the UK, Abraham Moon & Sons represents a similar case.[22] This company refocused on developing luxury wool fabrics for European high-end fashion brands and developed a concept of heritage based on their tradition of wool making; for example, it started collaborating with the Italian luxury fashion brand Dolce & Gabbana in 2011.[23] Moon strengthened its production capabilities with takeovers of financially troubled companies like Wallas & Co., a Yorkshire worsted yarn manufacturer (2007), and J. D. Matthewman (Textile) Ltd., a manufacturer and supplier of specialist woolen cloths and fabrics (2009).[24]

The rise of global fashion companies

Fashion houses underwent a profound transformation in the context of the globalization of textile and clothing production. Although designers since Worth have always embodied brands, found on clothing labels since the mid-nineteenth century, the function of branding changed profoundly in the 1970s and 1980s. Building on the model gradually put in place by Yves Saint Laurent in the 1960s (see Chapter 7), couturiers focused more and more on the symbolic value of fashion, which was used largely to target the mass market through accessories. The business model of fashion that became dominant during this period was based on a new relationship between creativity and profit. The dresses made by couturiers were no longer classically elegant goods to dress a few women of the wealthy classes but rather art creations destined to build attractive brands.

Figure 8.4 Launch of "Opium" Perfume, Yves Saint Laurent and models, 1978.
Source: Photo by Ron Galella/Ron Galella Collection via Getty Images.

As a result, the nature of fashion changed profoundly. The goal was no longer to sell dresses but to express the brilliant creativity of couturiers for fashion media. The role of fashion fairs also evolved in this context. For example, Interstoff in Frankfurt changed from a fabric fair in the 1960s to a fashion event in the 1980s, where companies and intermediaries, like fashion forecasters and fashion media, could meet.[25]

However, creativity was only one side of the new fashion business. Accessories, including leather goods, scarves, perfumes, and (sun)glasses, started to be mass-produced to provide high profits to fashion houses. Their production costs were low, and the brand names they carried allowed them to be sold for high prices. Couturiers had launched perfumes since the interwar years to improve their financial stability. In the 1970s, they became a major source of profits. In 1975, Karl Lagerfeld, the chief designer of the Chloé fashion brand since 1973, signed a contract to launch a perfume in the United States.[26] Yves Saint Laurent went further two years later. His new perfume was released under the provocative name Opium. It was launched at a fashion show organized in July 1977, during which Saint Laurent presented a new collection inspired by imperial China. The new perfume had become the core of fashion creativity that year, and all communication was based on it. The famous photographer Helmut Newton took pictures of the couturier in his apartment in Paris, in a fantasy setting inspired by Buddhism. In New York, a launch party was organized on the sailing boat *Peking*. Opium became a huge success. Sales, which amounted to approximately $100 million, exceeded those of Chanel No. 5.[27]

Figure 8.5 Karl Lagerfeld fits one of his designs on top model Ines de la Fressange at Chloe's Paris studio, 1983.

Source: Photo by Pierre Vauthey/Sygma/Sygma via Getty Images.

Hence, companies capable of making some goods, such as cosmetics or glasses, became important partners of couturiers as suppliers of accessories. L'Oréal, for example, signed contracts for making perfume for French couturiers like Guy Laroche (1965) and Courrèges (1970), followed by international licenses with Ralph Lauren (1985) and Giorgio Armani (1988). As for Luxottica, the Italian manufacturer of glasses, it experienced fast growth from the 1980s through contracts with global fashion companies.[28]

Consequently, the role of designers changed substantially. Their ability to develop concepts and to embody the genius of the brand—as Yves Saint Laurent already had in the 1960s— became extremely important. This is why Alain Wertheimer, the owner of the haute couture house Chanel since 1974, appointed Karl Lagerfeld as the chief designer. At that time, Chanel was a small company struggling to grow. It owned only one boutique, located in Paris, and perfume sales had stagnated. In 1980, the company decided to give up its license for ready-to-wear, signed in 1977 with Mendès, and to control this activity directly. Lagerfeld had to develop ready-to-wear and the accessory business by adapting Chanel's style to suit the times. This made Lagerfeld and Chanel the new rising stars of French fashion in the 1980s.[29]

The new paradigm of the fashion industry also saw the emergence of a new generation of designers in New York. Following the example of Ralph Lauren and Calvin Klein, who started in 1967 and 1968, respectively, numerous other designers engaged in fashion, including Tommy Hilfiger, Donna Karan, and Micheal Kors. Their fame was not only based on their ability to create dresses but also—or mostly—because they had become celebrities who exposed their fancy lifestyles in fashion magazines. The American fashion journalist Teri Agins gave a harsh assessment of their work, arguing that they were "designers without portfolios, [who] neither had apprenticed in Paris, nor studied fashion in school or anywhere else. They didn't sketch; they didn't sew; they hardly designed, so to speak."[30]

However, even if designers focused more and more on creating symbolic value, the production of clothing remained a major activity in the fashion industry. This raises the question of how the relationship between designers and the garment industry evolved in the context of the latter's globalization. The new global supply chains obviously made it possible to offer a wide range of products at low prices; however, it was important, particularly for luxury brands, to keep some production in Europe. The Italian fashion designer Giorgio Armani is an excellent example. The story of Armani highlights how the various challenges of creating symbolic value, the relationship with a globalized clothing industry, and the need to guarantee that certain products were made in Italy all came together.[31]

Born in 1934, Giorgio Armani began his career in Milan as an interior decorator and then as a menswear salesman in the department store La Rinascente (1957). In 1964, he joined the Nina Cerruti fashion house, where he worked as a designer before establishing himself as a freelancer in 1975 with the financial backing of his partner, businessman Sergio Galeotti. He launched his first men's fashion collection in 1976 and gradually established himself as a designer who developed both men's and women's clothing. The company rapidly experienced tremendous growth thanks to its entry into the American market and its cooperation with Hollywood. In 1980, the film *American Gigolo* was released and made actor Richard Gere the sex symbol of a whole generation. Dressed by Armani, he made the Italian designer the representative of a new elegance that was less classic and more casual. Aware of the media impact of his ambassadors, Armani hired Lee Radziwill in 1986, sister of Jacqueline Kennedy Onassis and a key figure in the American jet set, as the fashion house's social events manager.[32]

The success of Armani, however, was not the only result of his links to Hollywood. He cooperated with the Italian apparel producer GFT, who had founded a joint venture for the distribution of luxury ready-to-wear in North America (1979). GFT was the producer of Armani clothes, among other Italian designers. To cut production costs, it invested in manufacturing in China in 1988. GFT was one of the world's largest apparel producers at that time, with sales close to $700 million.[33]

Meanwhile, Armani started to diversify his business. He opened a jeans boutique in Milan in 1981, which became the basis of Emporio Armani, and signed licenses to manufacture various accessories—for example, with Luxottica for glasses (1988). Keeping the "Made in Italy" image for the couture collection was, however, necessary. Hence, Armani reinvested profits in various textile companies in Italy. In 1999, he owned seven factories in Italy, and the following year, he signed a cooperation agreement with his rival Ermenegildo Zegna Group for the joint management of a former GFT production center in Milan. Finally, in 1991, he verticalized fashion distribution with the creation of the A/X chain store in the United States as a response to the meteoric rise of The Gap.[34] The concentration on jeans alone, however, was a financial failure, and the A/X Armani Exchange chain was repositioned as a general fast-fashion brand after 2000. Horizontal (various Armani lines) and vertical (design, production, marketing, sales) concentrations in the 1980s and 1990s, respectively, gave rise to a highly internalized group, which continues to grow strongly. The company's revenues rose from $306 million in 1990 to about $2 billion in 2004.[35] The composition of turnover in 2004 (Table 8.1) highlights the balanced position in various business segments, from high-end (Giorgio Armani) and luxury ready-to-wear (Armani Collezioni) to consumer fashion (Emporio Armani) and fast fashion and accessories (Armani Jeans and A/X Armani Exchange). Its presence in all fashion segments was accompanied by strong product diversification, as clothing accounted for just over half of the group's sales in all segments.

Table 8.1 Armani Group Turnover, in Millions of Euros, 2004

Brand	€	%	Products	€	%
Giorgio Armani	531,1	32	Clothing	892,2	53
Emporio Armani	428,8	26	Perfumes and cosmetics	450,5	27
Armani Collezioni	305,1	18	Glasses	130,2	8
Armani Jeans	263,2	16	Watches and jewelry	104,5	6
A/X Armani Exchange	118,6	7	Other	93,9	6
Other	24,5	1			
Total	1 671,3	100	Total	1 671,3	100

Source: Merlo, Elisabetta, "Italian Fashion Business: Achievements and Challenges (1970s–2000s)," *Business History* 53, no. 3 (2011): 353.

Global fashion: Outsourcing and the end of the production paradigm 151

Figure 8.6 Giorgio Armani with Models, 1982.
Source: Photo by Vittoriano Rastelli/CORBIS/Corbis via Getty Images.

Box 8.1 From trench coats to fashion: Burberry

Today, Burberry is the most important British fashion brand. Although its origins date back to the mid-nineteenth century, it was during the 1970s and 1980s that it established itself as a global fashion brand. The company was originally founded by Thomas Burberry in 1856 in Basingstoke, Great Britain, as a drapery and fabrics business. It soon specialized in the development and sale of water-resistant products, notably for the manufacture of uniforms for British officers. During the First World War, its raincoats became known as "trench coats." Burberry remained focused on the sale of military and work uniforms until the 1950s. Its takeover by the Great Universal Stores (GUS) retail group in 1955 gave it the means to internationalize its sales network more intensively and develop new products. During the 1960s, this expansion was underpinned by many licensing agreements signed with numerous partners in Europe, the United States, and Asia. Using the Burberry check as an easily identifiable design element (in use since the 1920s), these partners launched a whole range of fashion accessories.

Japan is the main country behind this diversification into fashion accessories. In 1964, a major Japanese clothing manufacturer, Sanyo Shokai, began importing and selling trench coats. Following the success of these products, the two partners signed a licensing agreement in 1970 to produce raincoats in Japan, with technical assistance from Burberry, as well as the licensed manufacture of a wide range of products. The challenge was to adapt to the climate of a country less cold than Great Britain and to offer cheaper products, particularly scarves and skirts, to target the mass market. It became one of the most popular brands among young Japanese women in the 1980s.

> The collapse of Burberry's sales in Japan in the second half of the 1990s due to the financial crisis affecting that country led to serious difficulties for the British company. Sanyo introduced new sub-brands, which were very successful in Asia, such as Burberry Blue Label (1996) and Burberry Black Label (1998). However, in Britain, Burberry adopted an important strategic change at the beginning of the twenty-first century. In 2001, GUS took the company public and appointed Christopher Bailey, an English designer who had worked for Donna Karan and Gucci, as creative director. Adopting the new principles of global luxury fashion (see Chapter 9), Burberry decided to regain control of its brand management and exercise centralized control over its creative management. In 2009, it announced the end of its licensing contract with Sanyo Shokai for 2015.
>
> *Sources*: Christopher M. Moore and Grete Birtwistle, "The Burberry Business Model: Creating an International Luxury Fashion Brand," *International Journal of Retail & Distribution Management* 32, no. 8 (2004): 412–422; Kenichi Ohkita, "Coopetition through International Luxury Brand Licensing: Burberry in Japan," in *Global Opportunities for Entrepreneurial Growth: Coopetition and Knowledge Dynamics within and across Firms* (Bingley: Emerald Publishing Limited, 2017) 143–161.

Mediatization of fashion

Designers and fashion companies needed media to build a successful new business model based on the exploitation of brands and emotional value. Fashion historians and social scientists have argued that fashion magazines played a major role in connecting producers and consumers, consequently contributing to the production of fashion as a symbolic value.[36] However, from the late 1960s, fashion magazines started to play a new role in the context of the shift of haute couture houses toward the mass market. Media began to diffuse a new image of women and men, linked to something more sexual, younger, and more glamorous, which Christopher Breward has called "a sexual objectification of the body."[37] Young girls replaced mature and often married women. Fashion media became oriented to mass consumption. They fulfilled three main functions in the fashion system. First, they gave information to the public. This was the oldest objective of fashion media, either newspapers and magazines, on the one hand, or television, cinema, and the internet on the other. In the postwar years, Christian Dior, although he did not allow journalists to attend the shows he organized for his private customers, was very conscious of the power of the mass media to transmit information about his work, his creations, and himself. He appeared frequently in *Paris Match* magazine and, after his death in 1957, was on the cover of *Time* magazine. He had a large public relations department and wrote in his autobiography that "the relationship of a couturier with the press is like a love affair—a never-ending love affair, renewed each season, involving endless intrigues and reconciliations."[38]

Information to the public was integrated into a communication strategy that contributed to the construction of fashion as a cultural value. The advent of the communication society and the development of the presence of media had a strong impact on the relations between couturiers and apparel companies, on the one hand, and fashion media, on the other. The "public relations manager" was a new profession invented in the United States and introduced into European fashion companies. These new professionals adopted new marketing techniques, like using Hollywood actors and actresses, First Ladies, and princesses as ambassadors. They became considered as "cultural capital" for fashion brands.[39] In 1961, Sophia Loren was one of the first actresses to be on the cover of *Vogue*. She was followed by several stars, including the British actress and singer Jane Birkin (1970), French actress Catherine Deneuve (1971), and Hollywood star Elizabeth Taylor (1971).[40] The use of celebrities made it possible to stage glamorous people wearing cool clothes.[41] US apparel companies already had a similar strategy during the interwar years, and it was done systematically by European brands in the 1970s.

A second important role played by fashion media was to legitimize brands as representatives of "fashion" and designers as "creators."[42] The sociologist Yuniya Kawamura argues that, as magazines and newspapers are financed by advertisers rather than subscribers, they just repeat the narratives developed by advertising departments and then support the diffusion of their ideas about creation and fashion. However, some fashion editors play a more active role, promoting various styles, colors, and designers and contributing to the creation of fashion. The final role of all the fashion press is "maintaining and continuing the belief in fashion."[43]

The legitimacy of brands and designers became particularly important within the context of the transformation of fashion into big business for the masses based on ready-to-wear and accessories. In the United States, for example, magazines founded as publications for families, like *Cosmopolitan* (1886), or for the upper class, like *Vogue* (1892), repositioned toward fashion for the masses. A new generation of editors, mostly female, changed the focus of these media to modern lifestyle, shopping, and sexuality. In France, the magazine *Elle* was launched in 1945 by Hélène Lazareff, an editor who got her inspiration from the United States. The magazine promoted sportswear and ready-to-wear instead of only high-fashion creations and contributed in the 1960s to the growth of this industry.[44] In this context, couturiers, chief designers, and artistic directors started to be introduced to the public as celebrities themselves.

Finally, the third major function of fashion media was to support the global expansion of fashion companies. They introduced designers and brands to new markets through their international extension based on license agreements with local publishers. It started with local versions in Western countries in the postwar economic fast-growth period. Japan followed between the 1960s and 1980s. Then, from the 1990s, one can observe a strengthening of this trend in the context of the transformation of fashion companies into large multinational enterprises. Fashion brands were important financial contributors to global media. Consequently, they supported the internationalization of magazines that introduced them as legitimate representatives of fashion to new audiences.

Vogue was the first major fashion magazine to expand abroad. Its internationalization started before it shifted its focus toward the mass promotion of ready-to-wear. Before the Second World War, foreign editions were launched in the UK (1916) and France (1920). New Zealand and Australia followed during the 1950s. When *Vogue* became a fashion magazine addressed to a larger and younger target, it put four new editions on the global market (Italy, 1964; Brazil, 1975; Germany, 1979; Spain, 1988). After 1990, *Vogue* expanded beyond the West and became a pillar for the globalization of Western fashion brands. Asia was a major target, with editions in South Korea (1996), Taiwan (1996), Japan (1999), and China (2005).[45]

The international editions of fashion magazines also contributed to making Western taste and culture the global standard for fashion and beauty.[46] Although there are some differences between host countries, the beauty business became essentially a Western business. For example, the covers of the international editions of fashion magazines were a good indication of the degree of localization of fashion standards. Between 2000 and 2015, for all covers of the Japanese edition of *Vogue*, there were only eight covers with a Japanese model in a total of 172 covers.[47] This rate was far higher in countries such as China and Russia, where nationalism was stronger than in Japan.

The Japanese way

Clothing consumption increased dramatically in Japan during the 1970s and 1980s, but this development was not used as an opportunity by apparel companies to build fashion brands, as European and American competitors did at the time.[48] They pursued a model established in the 1960s characterized by the mass production of Western clothing, the absence of cooperation with independent designers, and an extreme segmentation of the market. This led to the multiplication of brands without creating emotional value. Garments were, above all, considered as manufactured goods. Such a strategic positioning had three major consequences.

First, the lack of emotional value or brands with a strong identity made it difficult for them to expand internationally. While Western companies offered fashion products identified by strong brand images, Japanese apparel firms had only material goods to offer. A good example of the difficulty internationalizing sales was Renown, one of the major apparel producers in Japan.[49] This company, whose roots go back to a textile trading company founded in Osaka in 1906, engaged in the mass production of Western clothing sold in department stores under various brands after the Second World War. In 1970, it launched D'URBAN, a new brand of suits for male employees, the so-called salarymen, with an image of casual elegance. This new business line was ambitious. Renown cooperated with the chemical company Mitsubishi Rayon to develop new fabrics and with the trading company Itochu to distribute these suits throughout the country. Moreover,

Renown contracted the French actor Alain Delon, who became the face of D'URBAN. It achieved great success in the Japanese market. In 1976, the subsidiary in charge of producing and selling D'URBAN was ranked the third-largest apparel company in Japan in terms of sales.[50] Hence, the same year, Renown decided to expand overseas. It founded a subsidiary in Lichtenstein, the International Division of D'URBAN and started to export to Hong Kong, Germany, Belgium, and the UK. However, this brand has never been able to carve a place in world markets. Italian casual fashion, which was obviously D'URBAN's inspiration, had established a much more competitive business model. As a result, Renown remained focused on the domestic market and started to decline in the late 1990s amid the rise of fast fashion.

Second, foreign brands, mostly Italian and French, experienced rapid growth in the Japanese market, particularly when the yen became extremely strong after the end of the Bretton Woods system of fixed exchange rates in 1971. While a few companies opened wholly owned subsidiaries in Japan to control brand identity and sales, like Zegna (1977), Chanel (1981), Louis Vuitton (1981), Bottega Veneta (1986), and Gucci (1990), most European brands cooperated with trading companies and department stores. They founded joint ventures to import, distribute, and manufacture under license some products in Japan; for example, in 1987, Giorgio Armani created two joint ventures in Japan. It had entered Japan two years before through an exclusive distribution contract with the department store Seibu and wanted to expand on this promising market. Giorgio Armani Japan was a joint venture with 34 percent of capital owned by the Italian headquarters, while the trading company Itochu and Seibu Department Stores both had 33 percent. This company oversaw importing and selling Armani's high-end ready-to-wear in Japan. The second joint venture, Emporio Armani Japan, also with 34 percent of Italian capital, was a partnership with Itochu (33 percent) and an apparel manufacturer, Raika Co. (33 percent). It produced fashion under license for the mass market in Japan. This twofold strategy made it possible to keep the Made in Italy brand image intact and adapt to the local mass market.[51]

The import of foreign brands was only realized by large Japanese trading companies. Many individuals and small firms, particularly clustered in Harajuku, Tokyo's fashion district, went to the United States and Western Europe to discover smaller brands and introduce them to the Japanese market.[52] Finally, the absence of strong domestic brands led some Japanese apparel companies to invest in Western design firms. For example, Takihyo Inc. acquired half of the capital of Donna Karan New York (DKNY) after its founding in 1984 (see Box 8.2).

Third, Japanese independent designers who did not cooperate with large apparel companies encountered great success in Western countries during the 1980s. Kenzo was the first to present a collection of haute couture in Paris (1970). He was followed by Issey Miyake (1973), Kansai Yamamoto (1974), Hanae Mori (1977), and Rei Kawakubo (1981), among others.[53] They represented the first wave of Asian designers in Paris and contributed to the renewal of haute couture. However, their success was based on cultural

Figure 8.7 Issey Miyake, spring/summer 1995.
Source: Niall McInerney, Photographer © Bloomsbury Publishing Plc.

differences. They had to stress their foreignness to be acknowledged. Japanese fashion was an ethnic business. Lise Skov argued that Kenzo and Hanae Mori adopted a "self-exoticizing strategy."[54] She also demonstrated that the success of Yohji Yamamoto, Rei Kawakubo (Comme des Garçons), and Issey Miyake in Western countries during the 1980s relied on their style embodying the stereotype of Japanese culture that had become popular in the West at that time, with many eclectic references from Japanese culture, such as the use of Zen Buddhism by Yamamoto.[55]

Box 8.2 Japanese capital and American designers: Donna Karan New York (DNKY)

The company DKNY was launched in 1985 with 50 percent of capital owned by a Japanese trading company specializing in textiles, Takihyo Inc., owned by Tomio Taki. Takihyo was a family firm based in Nagoya, with roots going back to a kimono business in the eighteenth century. In the 1960s, this company distributed cotton raincoats in Japan and started to export them to the United States. In 1973, it purchased half of the capital of the designer sportswear brand Anne Klein & Co., and the following year, when

> Anne Klein passed away, Taki appointed her top assistant, Donna Karan, as the new designer of the firm. He also hired Frank Mori to manage the firm. The relaunch of the brand Anne Klein was a big success, with gross sales peaking at more than $400 million in the late 1980s.
>
> Donna Karan wanted to have her own business and cofounded her own company with the financial support of Takihyo in 1985. The brand DKNY was launched in 1989 for casual sportswear. Donna Karan herself was engaged in worldwide fashion circles. She became a regular visitor of *Premier Vision*, the annual trade fair of fabrics and colors organized in Paris. She also launched a range of brand products (children's wear, menswear, perfume) to enlarge her profits. While this diversification was based on licenses for specific products like lingerie, supplied by the Japanese firm Wacoal since 1991, Donna Karan invested large amounts of capital in developing in-house production facilities for various other accessories. However, it made the company so unprofitable that it was nearly declared bankrupt. Thereupon, it went public in 1996. The firm pursued a growth strategy based on casual wear and accessories under license.
>
> In 2001, DKNY was acquired by LVMH. The French luxury conglomerate sold it again in 2016 to the American apparel group G-III Apparel, which owned numerous brands, including Tommy Hilfiger, Calvin Klein, and Ivanka Trump.
>
> *Source*: Teri Agins, *The End of Fashion: How Marketing Changed the Clothing Business Forever* (New York: Harper Collins, 1999), chapter 6.

Fashion in developing economies

Of course, Japan was not the only non-Western country where a fashion industry developed within a specific cultural and social context in the 1970s and 1980s. China became a major player in the global apparel industry during this period.

Fashion had been strongly attacked during the Maoist era as a bourgeois and Western value.[56] For example, the *qipao* dress, which had been developed in Shanghai during the 1920s by young girls who enjoyed urban nightlife, was banned after 1949 when standardized jackets and uniforms were introduced for the entire population. There was essentially no fashion and no ready-to-wear industry until the end of the 1970s. When Deng Xiaoping implemented his reforms in 1978, the shortage of fabrics was the biggest obstacle to the growth of the garment industry. In 1958, the Central Academy of Art and Design introduced design programs, but it was only in 1980 that the first graduates in clothing design left the school.[57] In the early 1980s, the modern Chinese textile industry started to develop as an export-oriented sector dominated by state-owned firms. Between 1981 and 1990, the share of the national production of clothing exported grew from 17 percent to 66 percent. It reached nearly 100 percent of the total national production value during the 1990s when China became the world's largest apparel exporter.[58] In 1979, the Shanghai Clothing Research Institute was created to support the growth of this industry.[59]

The first generation of Chinese designers emerged in this context. However, some entrepreneurs gradually started to consider the domestic market. Foreign designers and apparel makers were invited to China—Pierre Cardin had his first shows in Beijing and Shanghai in 1979—while young Chinese designers were trained abroad, particularly in Japan and Western countries. In 1980, the State Bureau of Standards introduced a standardized size system based on the data of 400,000 people throughout the country.[60] Numerous organizations have been set up since the mid-1980s to support the development of knowledge related to apparel manufacturing and design in order to increase cooperation with foreign companies, including the Shanghai Garment Trade Association in 1986, the China National Garments Association in 1991, and the China Fashion Designers Association (CFDA) in 1993.[61] These organizations also stimulated the development of a local fashion market. The first Chinese Fashion Week was organized in 1997 by CFDA.

The domestic apparel and fashion market began to develop rapidly, particularly after 2000. A new generation of private companies invested massively in branding and retail, some even starting to outsource their production to other Chinese companies. For example, Shanshan Company, a major men's suit manufacturer in the 1980s, began to outsource its production in the 1990s and refocused on designing and selling

Figure 8.8 Chaoyue Sportswear—China Fashion Week, 2007. kris krüg via Flickr.

Source: Preproduced under a CC BY-SA 2.0 license.

foreign fashion brands in the Chinese market. It cooperated notably with the Japanese trading company Itochu, which owned the distribution rights of many brands, like Marco Azzali, Le Coq Sportif, Pinky & Dianne, Callaway, and Smalto. It engaged its own Chinese designers, some trained by French companies, and launched its own brands in 2002.[62]

Although China's trajectory was unique in the extraordinarily rapid growth of its garment industry, a domestic fashion industry also emerged in many non-Western countries during the 1970s and 1980s. In general, it was the domestic market that underpinned the emergence of local fashion systems. They were supported by a new institutional environment. The case of India, known thanks to the work of Tereza Kuldova, is an excellent illustration.[63] This country had a long tradition of manufacturing traditional clothing, which continued into the twentieth century despite the influence of Western clothing culture. Following the country's independence, the rise of Indian fashion benefited from Bollywood, which, since the 1960s, had given a certain fame to the designers who dressed the film stars, following the American model. However, it was mainly in the 1980s that fashion designers made their mark on Indian fashion. Until then, Indian designers were mainly trained in Britain or the United States. The opening of the National Institute of Fashion Technology (NIFT) in 1986, based on the New York FIT model, enabled fashion designers to be trained in India, leading to the emergence of a new generation of creators. Their activities have led to the creation of a genuine Indian fashion industry. In 1987, a group of designers trained in London and India co-founded Ensemble, the first modern couture store in the country. This private company is nonetheless much more than a store; it works as a platform that welcomes a broad range of designers to advertise their labels and organize fashion shows.[64] Their style is often characterized by a fusion of Indian craftsmanship and modern design, with the widespread use of embroidery, for example. The number of independent designers and fashion boutiques has continued to grow strongly since the 1990s.

Conclusion

The 1970s and 1980s represented a phase of fundamental change that saw the emergence of the modern-day fashion business. The massive relocation of clothing production activities to China and other emerging countries had a major impact on what fashion was. From the point of view of the richest countries—the United States, Western Europe, and Japan—direct control of the production apparatus was no longer a prerequisite for fashion design. Fashion had freed itself from material constraints. Contemporary fashion systems were, therefore, being recomposed with new practices that involved creating emotional value around fashion creations. Designers, supported by the media industry, were becoming celebrities who created concepts and seduced consumers. This attraction made it possible to sell cheap accessories and clothing, manufactured mainly in emerging countries, to the mass market.

Figure 8.9 Model Naomi Campbell backstage at the Donna Karan Spring 1997 Ready to Wear Runway Show on November 1, 1996, in New York City.

Source: Photo by Kyle Ericksen/Penske Media via Getty Images.

For the most part, this new business model had been created and developed by small- and medium-sized companies, which enjoyed dazzling success, such as Giorgio Armani and Chanel. These were examples of the opportunities offered by the new global fashion industry. Bernard Arnault, who quickly understood the extraordinary potential of fashion, bought Christian Dior in 1984. It was on the foundations laid in these two decades that the global fashion industry entered a phase of tremendous growth after 1990.

Chapter 9

Fashion conglomerates and fast fashion

In LVMH's 2007 annual report, Managing Director Antonio Belloni summarized the company's recruitment strategy and the basis for its tremendous success as a luxury conglomerate. This strategy was based not only on the creativity of designers, but also on attracting excellent marketing, communications, financial, and legal teams.

> We often say that our designers and our artisans are the soul of our companies, but we can also state that our marketing and communications teams give our brands their modernity, that our sales teams are the artisans of our successes in the field, that our financial and legal teams ensure good governance and the power of the Group. I would like to insist on this point: within LVMH, all the businesses are businesses of excellence, and it is strategic to recruit, find and develop the best talent in each position.[1]

In the late 1980s, the European fashion industry began to transform itself from an industry dominated by small- and medium-sized family companies to a few multinational conglomerates or groups, mostly financed through capital markets. Two new and dominant business models emerged around the globe in the 1990s: luxury fashion conglomerates and fast-fashion groups. The first model is exemplified by multinationals such as LVMH (founded in 1987), Richemont (1988), and Kering (founded in 1962 but moved to luxury fashion through the takeover of Gucci in 1999). These firms merged fashion and luxury companies from various European countries and built and managed a portfolio of global brands.

The fast-fashion model is based on the idea that fashion constantly changes, moving away from the idea of two (sometimes four) collections presented each year, as Paris had imposed since the late nineteenth century. New information technology, including online fashion forecasting (WGSN), and the control of global supply chains, made it possible to know nearly instantly what consumers wanted and would eventually buy. As a result, they could respond rapidly to fast-changing consumer preferences. Companies like Inditex (Spain), H&M (Sweden), Fast Retailing (Japan), and, more recently, Shein (China) have become the most competitive actors in this sector. They own a dense network of mono-brand stores worldwide from where they gather instant information about consumption.

A wide range of actors between these two dominant models tried to survive and find ways to produce fashion differently. For some independent luxury fashion brands (e.g., Burberry and Hugo Boss), entering stock exchanges was necessary to acquire enough capital to control their presence on the global market and remain independent from these large conglomerates. Others, like Chanel and Armani, are still privately family-owned or partly owned by a foundation in the case of the latter.[2] For department stores, competition from mono-brand stores and the dramatic rise of e-commerce has had a strongly negative impact on their sales, as their own private labels have suffered reputational damage. Meanwhile, the Japanese apparel industry has tried since the late 1990s to invest in branding and retail but has suffered due to its inability to expand into foreign markets.

This chapter explores why and how these two global business models arose in the 1990s. What were the business strategies of the different organizational models? What are the consequences of global fashion and its impact on the environment and labor relations?

The rise of LVMH

The French holding company Moët Hennessy Louis Vuitton (LVMH) is the world's largest fashion and luxury group. It was the first European company to reach total market capitalization of $500 billion on 23 April 2023.[3] Market capitalization is a measurement of the size of a company, which changes daily and is based on the number of stocks multiplied by the price on the stock exchange.[4] Whatever its exact value on the French stock market index CAC 40, which constantly changes, it was clear by the 2020s that LVMH had become, by far, the largest European business conglomerate. Total revenue in 2023 amounted to €86.2 billion. The group operated 6,000 mono-brand stores worldwide and had 213,000 employees, of which only 40,000 were in France.[5] The question is: How did the merger of two medium-sized family firms evolve into one of the largest companies in the world since 1987?

LVMH resulted from the 1987 amalgamation of two companies: Louis Vuitton SA and Moët-Hennessy SA. Both were family firms with strong brands that expanded successfully from the 1960s. As the growth potential of their respective brands and markets was limited, both firms invested in other French companies and diversified into other products. Moët Hennessy was founded in 1971 through a merger of producers of Champagne (Moët & Chandon) and Cognac (Hennessy). The expansion of Moët Hennessy was based on takeovers of other Champagne producers (Ruinart in 1962 and Mercier in 1970) and diversification to other goods, including a takeover of cosmetics maker RoC and Parfums Christian Dior (1971). Louis Vuitton focused on leather goods (such as high-end purses, bags, and luggage) until it started to diversify into accessories in 1986. In the first half of the 1980s, Louis Vuitton showed exceptional growth. Its retained profits were re-invested in 1986 and used for the purchase of the Veuve Clicquot group, which held several Champagne brands, as well as the company Parfums Givenchy.

The families behind both groups, Moët Hennessy and Louis Vuitton, needed more cash to grow. Therefore, the groups merged to create LVMH in 1987 with the financial support of two major French banks: Lazard Frères and Paribas. However, shortly after the merger, a conflict between Henri Racamier, the CEO of Louis Vuitton, and Alain Chevalier, the CEO of Moët-Hennessy created the opportunity for a minority shareholder, Bernard Arnault, to acquire Racamier's shares, with the financial support of the British beverage group Guinness, and ultimately to control LVMH through the financial company Jacques Rober. A few years earlier, Arnault had taken control of the textile group Boussac, which had owned the house of Christian Dior since 1946, and the classic Paris department store Le Bon Marché since 1984 (see Chapter 7). Arnault had also acquired the leather goods manufacturer Céline in 1987 and funded the establishment of a company by the couturier Christian Lacroix the same year. Hence, Arnault's idea was to merge these brands and companies into one large group that would dominate the consumer goods luxury sector in France.[6] The organization of LVMH was still decentralized. Louis Vuitton and Moët-Hennessy continued to control and manage their own subsidiaries, except Parfums Dior.

From the late 1980s to the mid-1990s, LVMH began to rationalize the group's organization. Louis Vuitton oversaw subsidiary companies active in fashion, while Moët Hennessy managed subsidiaries in beverages. As late as 1997, however, the rationalization process remained incomplete. The first wave of acquisitions was realized within this organizational framework. For example, Louis Vuitton acquired the couturier Givenchy in 1988, the fashion company Kenzo in 1993, and the perfume Guerlain in 1994.[7] In the same year, it changed its financial relations with Guinness. The British firm had acquired 34 percent of Moët-Hennessy and continued to cooperate with LVMH for the worldwide distribution of its beverages. Guinness now withdrew from LVMH's capital, and LVMH, in turn, reduced its stake in Guinness (merged into Diageo in 1997) from 24 to 20 percent. These transactions generated nearly €3 billion in cash for LVMH, which enabled the group to acquire more brands in the highly profitable luxury and fashion industries. It divested brands that were not profitable enough and focused after the late 1990s much more on luxury and fashion brands. Important fashion acquisitions included the French shoemaker Berluti in 1996, the Spanish fashion company Loewe in 1996, the British shirtmaker Thomas Pink in 1999, the US ready-to-wear brand DKNY in 2001, and the Italian luxury ready-to-wear Fendi in 2002, among others. Meanwhile, it also diversified into watches and jewelry with the takeovers of French companies Fred (1995) and Chaumet (1999), Swiss companies TAG Heuer (1999), Zénith (1999), and Hublot (2008), Italian company Bulgari (2011), and Tiffany (2020).[8] In 2023, it owned seventy-five global brands, now called *houses*.[9]

LVMH further rationalized its organizational structure in 1998. The group introduced a central management structure and multidivisional organization based on different product divisions for leather goods, perfumes and cosmetics, fashion, wine and spirits, and selective distribution. This multidivisional structure changed in due course, but in the end, it was the basis for LVMH's staggering global expansion and financial success until today. The direct control of distribution was key to developing strong control of brand management and internalizing profits. The diversification in distribution opened the opportunity to create synergies between different departments and brands. External growth—that is, growth through acquiring other brands (and selling underperforming brands)—has been the main driver of LVMH's expansion since the latter part of the 1990s. Gross sales went from €4.5 billion in 1995 to €11.6 billion in 2000, €30.6 billion in 2014, and €86.2 billion in 2023. This international acquisition strategy turned LVMH into the largest global luxury business. The number of employees grew from about 14,000 in 1990 to 213,000 worldwide in 2023, including 40,000 in France.[10] Arnault permanently retained control over the group thanks to his preference shares (47.2 percent of the capital and 63.4 percent of the votes in 2018).[11]

LVMH's success, however, cannot be explained by its strategy alone. Clearly, Arnault introduced a new business model for the French luxury and fashion business and even claimed that he invented and created the luxury industry.[12] His business methods were indeed foreign to the French business system, which was more based on coordination than the liberal market behavior of aggressively buying and selling brands without taking the social consequences into account. Before he got a significant stake in LVMH, he had acquired the textile and retail business Boussac Saint-Frères in 1984, which included the fashion house Christian Dior and Le Bon Marché department store. He then sold the textile part in the north of France and dismissed 9,000 workers, which gave him a bad name in France. Nevertheless, Arnault and LVMH would continue to buy and sell brands aggressively, and this made Arnault one of the richest men on Earth and the group the largest luxury conglomerate.[13]

Another explanation for LVMH's success lies beyond the group's ability to bend the world to its will. On the contrary, the fast-changing global markets, particularly the rise of Asian markets, gave global luxury and fashion a tremendous boost. After the Plaza Accord in 1985, Japanese retailers increased imports of European luxury products. Also, South Korea and Hong Kong became important markets. But when China entered the World Trade Organization (WHO) in 2001, Japan's economy had been in a long phase of economic stagnation following the burst of the financial bubble of the late 1980s. Hence, China became the main buyer of European luxury products, particularly fashion and leather goods. The growing disposable income of the Asian middle and upper classes created a huge market for European luxury goods.[14] Moreover, the rise of prosperity in Asia and income inequality not only in Asia but also Europe and North America have been driving forces for luxury consumption. Thomas Piketty shows that income inequality within countries dropped in the period 1910–1980 but rose again after 1980, while inequality between countries declined in the latter period. As a result, the early twenty-first century showed similar levels of inequality within countries as during early twentieth-century global capitalism.[15]

Financialization of luxury fashion brands

The motto "Passionate about Creativity" has appeared in all LVMH's annual reports since 2002. LVMH emphasizes its role as a big supporter of creation, crafts, and creativity, but at the end of the day, this story also adds value to its brands and finally to the staggering market value of the group. An important development since the 1980s is the rise of big multinational conglomerates in fashion and luxury based on capital markets. LVMH is admittedly the largest company in this global business but certainly not the only example. Two other big luxury and fashion groups are Richemont and Kering, which, to a certain

Fashion conglomerates and fast fashion

extent, imitated the LVMH model. Both are also family businesses governed by very complex ownership relationships.[16]

In 1988, Anton Rupert, a South African investor in mining, tobacco, finance, media, and luxury goods, bought the French jeweler Cartier and decided to set up Compagnie Financière Richemont in the Swiss tax haven Zug to organize his foreign investments. The company was listed on the Zurich Stock Exchange, but the Rupert family owned preferred shares and had 50 percent of the voting rights. During the 1990s, Richemont was a diversified company with five unrelated divisions: luxury, tobacco, finance, natural resources, and consumer goods. The luxury division controlled several luxury brands and acquired new luxury brands, including the British firearms manufacturer Purdey (1994), the watch companies Vacheron & Constantin in Switzerland (1996), and Officine Panerai in Italy (1996), as well as the French leather goods company Lancel (1996) and the Hong Kong fashion brand Shanghai Tang (1998). However, a transformation occurred after 2005 when the company decided to focus on the highly profitable luxury business and divest its television, tobacco, and clothing interests. It also moved its headquarters from the tax haven Zug to Geneva, a city closer to the Parisian luxury and fashion ecosystem.[17]

In 2008, Richemont reorganized the holding company into five divisions: jewelry, watches, online distribution, fashion, and accessories. Its earlier divestments had provided the capital for major acquisitions in the luxury watch industry. In the fashion business, it acquired Parisian house Azzedine Alaïa (2007) and the American brand Peter

Figure 9.1 Johann Rupert the CEO of the Richemont group lines up a putt on the first hole during the third round of the 2018 Alfred Dunhill Links Championship on The Old Course at St Andrews on October 6, 2018 in St Andrews, Scotland.

Source: Photo by David Cannon/Getty Images.

Millar (2012). In 2010, it took a majority stake in the Net-A-Porter Group (online luxury retailer) and later, in 2018, signed a joint venture with Alibaba to sell fashion directly online in China. Owning fashion companies and direct sale possibilities gave Richemont and the other conglomerates a competitive advantage. By controlling the distribution and sales via their own mono-brand stores or online retail, they could bypass the wholesale business.[18]

The third-largest luxury conglomerate in the world is the French retail company Kering. In 1963, François Pinault set up a timber and building materials trading company, which was listed on the Paris Stock Exchange (Euronext Paris) in 1988. After a major acquisition in 1992 of the Au Printemps Group, which included the mail-order house La Redoute, the company was renamed Pinault-Printemps-Redoute (PPR). It would become the largest retail group in France, controlled through preferred stock by the Pinault family via a financial holding company, Artemis SA, which eventually became the main shareholder of PPR.[19]

In 1999, PPR acquired Gucci, the Florentine leather-goods company, which had opened its business in fascist Italy and expanded rapidly on the global luxury market after the war, particularly in the United States. However, Gucci fell into financial difficulties in the 1980s, and the family sold it to a Bahraini investment company, Investcorp, which reorganized the company. Tom Ford, a successful young American designer, became the new creative director and improved the brand's reputation and balance sheet. In 1995, Gucci was brought to the New York and Amsterdam stock exchanges. This attracted the attention of large luxury conglomerates. By 1999, LVMH had secretly acquired 34.4 percent of the stocks. At this point, Gucci's management turned to PPR, which proposed an increase in Gucci's capital and bought 40 percent of its shares. PPR thus outmaneuvered LVMH, and to this day, the French billionaires Pinault and Arnault are archenemies. With the influx of fresh capital, Gucci bought many famous fashion brands, including the French fashion houses Yves Saint Laurent (1999) and Balenciaga (2001), the Italian shoe manufacturer Sergio Rossi (1999), the French jeweler Boucheron (2000), the Swiss watchmaker Bedat & Co. (2000), British fashion houses Alexander McQueen (2000) and Stella McCartney (2001), and Italian leather-goods manufacturer Bottega Veneta (2001).[20] Since the end of 2004, Gucci has no longer been a listed company but a full part of PPR.

As a result of the high margins in luxury and fashion, Pinault decided to focus on these markets and divest its original retail business. Between 2007 and 2011, PPR acquired a 70 percent stake in Puma, a German sportswear business. The idea was to copy Nike's and adidas' massive success in the sports and leisurewear business (see Chapter 10). However, this move was not as profitable as expected; therefore, PPR sold its majority interest in Puma to focus exclusively on the luxury and fashion business. In 2005, François-Henri Pinault, son of the founder, continued the new path of acquiring highly profitable luxury brands and changed PPR's name to the fancier-sounding Kering in 2013.[21]

Despite differences, there are great similarities between these three large conglomerates. All three are listed on the stock exchange and own global luxury brands. All three are controlled by the founding families while at the same time attracting external investors and capital. The three family firms focus on global luxury markets, including fashion, and combine high-profitability brands with self-financing, which means they have huge internal reserves to acquire new profitable brands (and sell less profitable ones), in this way actively managing a brand portfolio.[22] In a way, luxury goods and high-end fashion are just a means to make these families richer and accumulate more capital. They are excellent examples of the financialization of the global fashion business at the end of the twentieth and early twenty-first centuries.

Fast fashion—retail and production

Not only has the luxury fashion industry shown a high degree of concentration of capital, but also big fast-fashion groups have conquered world markets with their relatively cheap clothing. Since the end of the twentieth century, the so-called fast-fashion groups, with companies like H&M, Inditex, and Fast Retailing, have been highly successful with their business model. In 2019, H&M and Zara (the most important Inditex brand) were ranked in the top five global fashion brands, after Louis Vuitton, Chanel, and Hermès.

Fast fashion is often described as cheap and unsustainable fashion, but this is a gross simplification of this market segment. According to José Antonio Miranda and Alba Roldán, fast fashion can be defined as quickly produced clothing that follows the current trends in fashion. It is driven by consumer demand, and its production is often outsourced to low-cost countries, even by groups with their own production lines, like Inditex. The fast-fashion companies that do their own design and marketing usually sell the product in their own physical stores or online.[23]

The fast-fashion model started in the 1980s and became a dominant model in the 1990s when the production of garments was relocated and competition between the big fashion brands increased dramatically. The new model has also radically changed the traditional fashion cycle, which was based on two seasons, spring/summer and autumn/winter, which meant that production had to take place at least six months in advance. The new model constantly requires new product lines to be created according to the latest trends.[24] As a result of the internet and decreasing transport costs via containers, it became easier and much faster to order garments in, for example, Southeast Asia, although the more fashionable clothes were often ordered in production locations closer to the markets. Heavy investments in information technology have led to greatly improved logistics, insights into rapidly changing consumer preferences, and stocks.[25] Despite the many similarities of fast-fashion companies, at least three different business models have developed in the world since the 1990s, exemplified by the Swedish H&M, the Spanish Inditex, and the Japanese Fast Retailing. Different company histories and path dependencies have led to variations in the business model.

H&M was founded after the Second World War by Erling Persson, who was inspired during his trip to the United States by the affordable and fashionable ready-to-wear in New York.[26] In 1947, he opened his first low-priced shop in Västerås, 100 kilometers from

Stockholm, and called it Hennes (Swedish for "hers") because it only sold women's clothing. From the start, it was a retail company that purchased from Swedish ready-to-wear manufacturers but later also from abroad, first within Europe but then from Asia too. During the 1960s and 1970s, Swedish clothing manufacturing declined and companies like H&M were sourced more and more globally with low-priced imports.[27] H&M's retail business expanded rapidly, first in Sweden and then in Scandinavia during the 1960s. In 1968, Persson bought a hunting and fishing store called Mauritz in Stockholm, diversified to men's and children's clothing, and changed the name to Hennes & Mauritz. In 1974, the retailer made its Initial Public Offering (IPO) at the Stockholm stock exchange, and its stores were rebranded to H&M. Two years later, it opened its first shop outside Scandinavia, in London, which marked the beginning of a European retail network. In the 2000s, H&M expanded globally; in 2000, it opened its first flagship store in New York, two more in 2007 (in Hong Kong and Shanghai), and a fourth in Japan in 2008.

H&M's business model remained the same as at the beginning, creating identical shops selling fashionable clothes at the best price, and spending 3 to 4 percent of its revenue on advertising.[28] In 2004, the company made an unexpected marketing move by connecting to Karl Lagerfeld (see Box 9.1), which would be the first collaboration with high-fashion designers. More collaborations followed, including Stella McCartney, Roberto Cavalli, Versace, and Alexander Wang. In the 2000s, low and high fashion became more connected and started collaborations ("collabs"). In 2023, H&M worked with 574 sub-contractors in more than 1,000 factories in Europe, North America, and Asia; however, China and Bangladesh were the most important production locations.[29] In that same year, total sales realized in 4,369 stores in seventy-eight markets, amounted to €20.2 billion and the company had 143,000 employees worldwide. H&M owned eleven brands, including COS, Weekday, Monki, and Cheap Monday.[30] The vast majority of the shares were still in Swedish hands. The Stefan Persson family (Stefan Persson was the son of Erling Persson) and related companies own 58.65 percent of the shares and have 80.51 percent of the voting rights.[31]

Box 9.1 H&M's collaboration with Karl Lagerfeld: High end meets fast fashion

In 2004, fast-fashion retailer H&M launched a line of clothing designed by the famous haute couture designer Karl Lagerfeld, best known as the creative director behind the modern revival of Chanel. In an interview with the British magazine *Fashion United*, Karl Lagerfeld stated that his intentions behind collaborating with H&M were to make his designs available to the broader public, allowing individuals with a smaller budget to access his designs. But why did H&M approach Karl Lagerfeld to start this collaboration in the first place?

From the beginning of the retail company, marketing has been an essential part of its business strategy. Innovative advertising campaigns were important tools to expand its market share, first nationally and later globally. At the end of the 1990s, H&M started a global advertising campaign, showing world-famous female models in sexy lingerie on huge outdoor billboards. Although the campaign was a huge success, female employees, particularly at the headquarters in Stockholm, began to raise complaints about the sexist character of the advertisements and demanded an end to the overexposure of the female body on billboards in the world's biggest cities. In addition, the message—"fashion and quality at the best price"—was getting blurred. It was more and more about the models and not about the H&M brand. The marketing team came up with a new idea: why not approach Karl Lagerfeld, the most famous Parisian fashion designer, and ask him to collaborate? Lagerfeld immediately agreed. When H&M's head of marketing, Jörgen Anderson, told him that his company "sells fashion at a cheap price," Lagerfeld replied: "I would prefer to call it affordable."

Figure 9.2 People awaited the arrival of British Queen Elizabeth II near a giant 1,500 square meter advertisement for Swedish fashion retailer H&M that shows German-born fashion designer Karl Lagerfeld and U.S. model Erin Wasson November 2, 2004 in central Berlin, Germany.
Source: Photo by Sean Gallup/Getty Image.

The collaboration of the high-end designer and the fast-fashion retailer was a huge success for the latter. Karl Lagerfeld, however, was less satisfied. In the end, H&M created an exclusive line with only small production numbers. Consequently, the Karl Lagerfeld designs were sold out in a matter of hours and resold for higher prices on the internet immediately. As many people had missed out on purchasing Lagerfeld's designs, the aim of creating accessible designer clothes within a fast-fashion brand had

> failed. Due to Lagerfeld's reputation of producing high-quality products, customers believed the joint H&M product to also be of high quality. However, while H&M was associated with higher quality in the luxury market, downgrading strategies may have been harmful to Lagerfeld's brand image. Here Lagerfeld was running the risk of losing prestige and exclusivity; as well, doubts about quality might have arisen. Despite these risks, luxury brands and famous designers continued to collaborate successfully with H&M after this first experiment, including Versace, Comme des Garçons, and Balmain.
>
> *Sources*: Ingrid Giertz-Mårtenson, "H&M: How a Swedish Entrepreneurial Culture and Social Values Created Fashion for Everyone," in *European Fashion: The Creation of a Global Industry*," eds Regina Lee Blaszczyk and Veronique Pouillard (Manchester: Manchester University Press, 2018), 201–219; Mona Mrad, Maya Farah, and Stephanie Haddad, "From Karl Lagerfeld to Erdem: A Series of Collaborations between Designer Luxury Brands and Fast-Fashion Brands," *Journal of Brand Management* 26 (1 September 2019), 567–582; Bin Shen, Tsan-Ming Choi, and Pui-Sze Chow, "Brand Loyalties in Designer Luxury and Fast Fashion Co-Branding Alliances," *Journal of Business Research* 81 (1 December 2017): 173–80.

Inditex is a North Spanish apparel manufacturer and fashion retail company. The story begins when Amancio Ortega and his wife Rosalia Mera opened a small garments factory in A Coruña, in Galicia in northern Spain. In 1975, they opened a store called Zara in the same city. The business expanded nationally to forty-one stores and seven factories, brought under the holding company Diseño Textil SA (Inditex) in 1985. Soon afterward, the company began to expand internationally in retail, in Portugal (1988), the United States (1989), and France (1990). By the end of the twentieth century, Inditex had expanded to thirty-three countries with 1,000 stores and a total revenue of €2.6 billion.[32] In 2001, Inditex was floated on the stock exchange in Madrid. Its founder, Amancio Ortega, via his investment vehicle Pontegadea Inversiones S.L, held 50.1 percent of the stocks and became one of the richest men in the world.[33] According to Bloomberg, he is the third-richest person in Europe after Arnault (LVMH) and Francoise Bettencourt Meyers (L'Oreal). In 2023, the company operated on five continents, owned 4,589 stores and 1,103 franchises, had 161,282 employees, and a total revenue of nearly €36 billion, making it the largest fast-fashion company in the world.[34]

Inditex's main brands, Zara, Pull&Bear, Massimo Dutti, Bershka, Stradivarius, Oysho, and Zara Home, are often seen as typical fast fashion. However, Zara's business model differed. It sold and designed clothes and outsourced production, but some more fashionable items were produced nearby in Portugal or Galicia.[35] It changed its collections rapidly and constantly and no longer followed the biannual rhythm of the traditional fashion industry. Of all fast-fashion companies, it invested the most in information technology which provided the data on stock and sales in the shops to underpin decisions on production and orders with subcontractors. It was a relative latecomer in the global fashion business and could therefore invest in the latest technology, which created a competitive advantage. At the same time, the company followed trends in high-fashion

Figure 9.3 Oscar Garcia Maceiras, chief executive officer of Inditex SA, during a full year earnings news conference at the company's headquarters in Arteixo, Spain, on Wednesday, March 13, 2024.
Source: Photo by Brais Lorenzo/Bloomberg via Getty Images.

brands and copied the silhouettes and colors. Inditex could make copies that resembled high-end brands within a few weeks and display the fashion items in Zara shop windows.[36] According to Miranda, Inditex's success can be explained by its flexibility—on the one hand, the result of the application of the latest information technology in design, stock, and sales information, and logistics with its global business operations, and on the other hand, the ability to adapt quickly to changing consumer preferences. The company has an entire team of designers who are concerned with observations and predictions about the latest trends, information that is also obtained through their own sales results.[37]

The company Fast Retailing started out the same way as H&M. In 1949, Hitoshi Yanai set up a menswear shop called *Ogori Shōji* in Yamaguchi Prefecture in the south of Honshu, Japan's main island. In 1963, it was incorporated as Ogori Shoji Co., Ltd.[38] In 1984, his son, Tadashi, opened a garment store named Unique Clothing Warehouse in Hiroshima. Soon the name was shortened to Uniqlo, which became the company's main brand. This store was not only for men but also for women, and that was why it was called "unique clothing." He expanded the sales networks into the suburbs in the early 1990s. He also changed the business structure of the company and introduced self-service, which created higher efficiency in the casual-clothing chain stores; self-service soon expanded all over Japan. In the 1994–2001 period, Uniqlo increased the number of self-service stores in Japan from 100 to 500.[39] In 1991, Ogori Shoji Co. changed its name to Fast Retailing Co. and three years later, this company was floated in the Hiroshima Stock

Exchange. In 1997, Fast Retailing was listed for the first time on the Tokyo Stock Exchange.[40] In 1998, it opened its first urban store in Tokyo and had its first overseas opening in London in 2001. New York and Paris would soon follow suit. It also started the Uniqlo Design Center, with fifty designers and a subsidiary in New York, which not only showed ambition to move more toward fashion but also to create affordable clothes and timeless designs.[41] Meanwhile, the stores grew bigger and bigger in Japan and abroad.

In the 1980s, Uniqlo had mainly stocked its shops via Japanese manufacturers, but as of the middle of that decade, Japanese retailers began to import more and more textiles from Hong Kong and China. As a result of China's open-door policy and the revaluation of the yen after the Plaza Accord of 1985, imports became much cheaper, and Japanese garment manufacturers were outcompeted. Uniqlo increasingly sourced its garments via Chinese producers, but a lack of quality was a major problem. Therefore, in 1999, it opened production offices in Shanghai and Guangzhou to control the quality of the fibers and textile products. It also went into collaborative partnerships with suppliers in Japan to develop highly functional and comfortable fibers—for example, in 2006, with Toray Industries, a large multinational chemical company.[42] For a long time, Uniqlo still depended on the Japanese market, but as of 2018, international sales had become more important than domestic sales. In 2023, Uniqlo had 800 stores in Japan with a total revenue of 890 billion Yen (€5.9 billion) and 1,634 stores outside the country with a total revenue of 1,437 billion Yen (€8.7 billion). China, meanwhile, had become, by far, the most important foreign market. Fast Retailing shows many similarities with the other big fashion conglomerates, in both the fast-fashion and luxury segments. Bringing the original family

Figure 9.4 UNIQLO store in Okeaniya Shopping and Entertainment Complex, Slavyanka, Russia, representative of the breakthrough of the Japanese apparel industry outside of Japan, 2016.

Source: Фред-Продавец звёзд via Wikimedia Commons.

Fashion conglomerates and fast fashion

Table 9.1 Largest Listed Companies Worldwide within the Apparel and Fashion Industry, in Billion Dollars

Symbol	Name	Market Cap
EPA:MC	LVMH	$181.13 b
NYSE:NKE	Nike	$107.83 b
BME:ITX	Inditex	$100.41 b
EPA:CDI	Dior	$78.73 b
EPA:KER	Kering	$75.93 b
EPA:RMS	Hermès	$71.49 b
NYSE:TJX	TJX	$51.01 b
VTX:CFR	Richemont	$46.16 b
ETR:ADS	Adidas	$45.33 b
TYO:9983	Fast Retailing	$42.96 b
BIT:LUX	Luxottica	$30.53 b
NASDAQ:ROST	Ross Stores	$29.80 b
NYSE:VFC	VF	$29.07 b
STO:HM-B	H&M	$23.81 b

Source: Adapted from Fashion United, "Top 100 Companies," https://fashionunited.com/i/top100 (accessed July 27, 2024).

businesses to the stock markets generated ample capital to expand the business; simultaneously, it made the founders billionaires. Tadashi Yanai, who is still president of Fast Retailing, has been the richest person in Japan since 2021.[43]

Table 9.1 shows the market capitalization of the fourteen largest stock-listed apparel companies in the world. All the companies mentioned in this chapter are included in this table. Data on the Fashion United site is updated on the first day of every month. As the share prices vary from day to day and hour to hour, this is only an indication of the market value; however, the table clearly shows that luxury fashion and fast-fashion conglomerates are equally important listed companies on different stock exchanges in the world.

(Un)sustainability and fashion

Fast fashion is often associated with environmental and social problems and is deemed an unstainable model.[44] The fashion industry is one of the most polluting industries in the world. According to some estimates, this industry is responsible for 20 percent of all pollution. To produce, for example, a pair of jeans made of cotton (a natural fiber) takes around 3,600 liters of water and 3 kilos of pesticides and synthetic indigo.[45] Woolen clothes production also causes CO_2 emissions, chemical dying waste, wool transport from the other side of the world, manure surpluses from sheep, etc. Although natural fibers are not environmentally friendly at all, the use of synthetic fibers is a greater threat to life on Earth. Synthetic fibers end up as microfibers in rivers and oceans after clothes

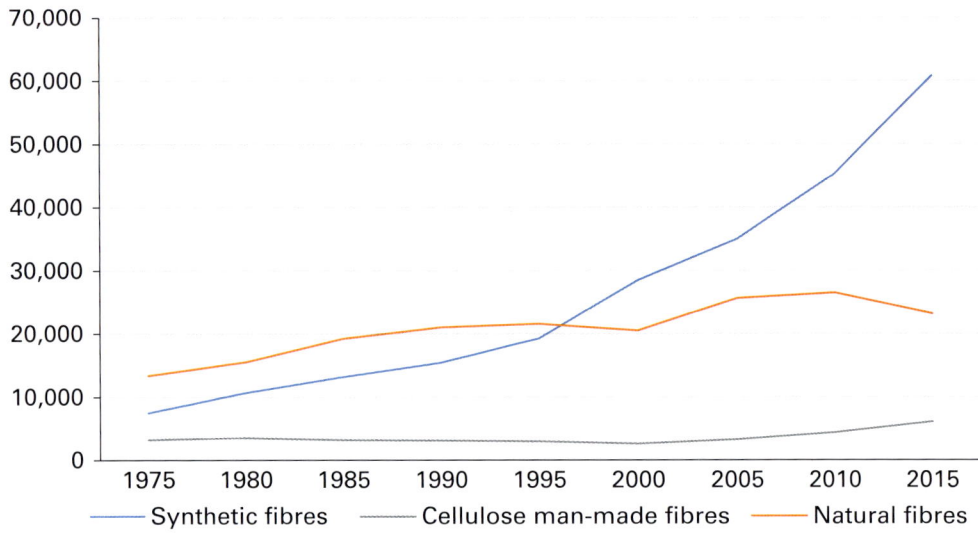

Figure 9.5 World Production of Man-made and Natural Fibers, 1975–2015 (in 1,000 Tons)
Source: Industrievereinigung Chemiefaser e.V., Production since 1975, World Production Man-made Fibers, Wool, and Cotton, https://www.ivc-ev.de/live/index.php?page_id=87 (accessed October 28, 2018).

are washed and enter the food chain of fishes, other animals, and eventually humans.[46] As shown in earlier chapters, man-made fiber production, first rayon and later fully synthetic, started at the beginning of the twentieth century and has increased spectacularly since then. Around 1995, synthetic fiber production overtook natural fiber production globally (see Figure 9.5).

Fast fashion, which uses a lot of man-made fibers, has speeded up apparel production and distribution. However, it is not only production and distribution that are fast; the consumption of these cheap items is also fast. As many clothes nowadays are of low quality and cheaply made, they generally do not last very long and quickly end up in landfills, or they are intentionally burned so as not to undercut the prices in the fast-fashion stores.[47] To produce these cheap fashion items, water, soil, energy, chemicals, and raw materials, either natural or synthetic, are required. The faster the consumption, the more these ingredients are needed, and the more are ultimately lost.

The Rana Plaza accident in Bangladesh opened the eyes of many consumers in the West to the social cost involved in global fashion and textile manufacturing. On April 24, 2013, an eight-story commercial building, Rana Plaza, collapsed just outside Dhaka. The building contained five clothing factories. Most of the people in the building at the time were female garment workers, and more than 1,100 people died.[48] Through this fatal accident, the consumers in the Global North suddenly realized how closely global production networks were integrated and that negative external effects of apparel and textile production had been externalized from the developed to the developing countries of the Global South, particularly Southeast Asia. Before the Second World War, apparel manufacturing in the West had also been done under bad social conditions in sweatshops in Berlin, London, and New York, but after the relocation of the production networks in the

Fashion conglomerates and fast fashion

Figure 9.6 European and Chinese textile and plastic waste at Dandora dump site in Nairobi.
Source: Kevin McElvaney / Greenpeace.

1960s, most consumers had not asked themselves why they could buy clothes so cheaply. The big fashion retailers, who profited most, did not tell them, either.

This is changing, particularly since the Rana Plaza disaster. Fashion brands, under pressure from non-government organizations (NGOs) and increasing consumer awareness, have begun to inform their customers about their often-hidden supply chains and the social and environmental costs of global apparel production. But will consumers in developed countries change their purchasing patterns, and to what extent do these initiatives stem more from marketing departments ("greenwashing") than from genuine concern about poor social and environmental conditions worldwide? In early 2000, H&M was the first to take action to improve its reputation when it started conducting inspections of the social conditions in subcontractors' sweatshops and showed more transparency in its annual reports about social and environmental impacts. Other fast-fashion groups followed suit. They supported all kinds of initiatives of NGOs to reduce waste and pollution and improve social conditions; they also supported independent audits. In 2019, Inditex, H&M, and The Gap were applauded in the Dow Jones Sustainability Index and the Ethical Fashion Report.[49] However, the question remains whether anything will really change without fundamentally changing the fast-fashion business model.[50]

Nevertheless, it is too easy to hold fast fashion responsible for everything wrong in the industry. What about the luxury fashion groups? Bernard Arnault claims that "a good product can last forever" and probably he is right. But does this also refer to the products of LVMH? In the 2023 Social and Environmental Responsibility Report, LVMH's chairman stated:

Building a fairer and more inclusive society, attempting to usher in a future in which desirability and sustainability are interwoven, keeping our cultural heritage alive and resolutely encouraging artists' creativity . . . That's how the LVMH Group wants to leave its mark on the world, turning its commitment into action for the common good.[51]

On every other page of LMVH's annual reports for a few years, claims have been made about sustainability and environmentally friendly production. Such claims, however, are hard to prove or disprove because nobody can verify them. There are no independent quality controls and very little transparency on the production methods of these products. The marketing of luxury products is indeed based on quality and craftsmanship, but are these products not also part of what Veblen once called "conspicuous consumption," and are they not based on a social stratification model and a way of emphasizing social inequality? According to Veblen, the production of luxury goods requires more resources than the production of nonluxury goods and, in that sense, creates more waste.[52] Inclusivity and sustainability have become the new buzzwords in the narratives of the big fashion conglomerates. But fast or slow, cheap or expensive, the profit motive is still what matters most.

Conclusion

During the 1980s and 1990s when scholars, journalists, and politicians began to use the word "globalization," the fashion industry was already global. It was the first industry to outsource most of its production to other nations and continents, where factor prices, mainly labor, were lower than at home. Also, transport prices began to drop dramatically with the introduction of containers. Relocating production in the textile and apparel industries made economic sense because making clothes with a sewing machine is labor intensive. Fiber and fabric production are much more capital intensive and more difficult to move to other continents unless the investors have local advantages, including less taxation, less regulation, and nearby markets. The rise of big fast-fashion retailing groups fits very well in this general evolution of global production networks. Most fashion retailers outsourced clothing production to other continents when these became highly competitive locations, often working through subcontractors, which pushed prices down further. New information technology supported the global production networks and made it easier to control stocks, design, and logistics. However, the rise of luxury fashion groups in the same period demands a different explanation.

In this case, it is not the production location that matters but the rise of big consumer markets for luxury products, particularly in Asia—first in Japan and later in China. The rise of new middle classes and their hunger for luxury fashion items created a demand for mainly European, French, and Italian fashion items. While the conditions for the rise of fast and luxury conglomerates differ, there are also similarities between the big fashion groups, one of which is that most are family-controlled, but they are also floated on the stock markets. This generated ample capital to expand the business via the acquisition of brands. The financialization of these business groups was essential for their growth strategies. They operate on global markets and often through their ever-growing retail outlets. The founding families have become the richest people on the planet, showing that fashion, high-end or low-end, is still a very good business opportunity. It is, however, highly unlikely that these business models, with all their variations and even good intentions, will be sustainable in the long run. The large fashion groups are mainly driven by the profit motive of family owners and other shareholders, even when they tell wonderful stories about corporate social responsibility. The fashion industry creates too much waste globally and is driven by conspicuous consumption.

Box 9.2 Issey Miyake's fashion business

Issey Miyake (1938–2022) belonged to the generation of Japanese designers who left their country to make a career in Paris in the 1960s. After graduating from Bunka Fashion College, in Tokyo, he moved to Paris and studied at the school of the *Chambre Syndicale de la Couture Parisienne*, before working for the haute couture houses Guy Laroche and Hubert de Givenchy. He would explain later that he found the styles of these traditional couturiers too bourgeois and wanted to create garments for students participating in the May 68 movement in Paris. He then went to New York in 1969 to learn from artists and designers. In 1970, he returned to Tokyo and founded his own design company, opening his first store in Aoyama, Tokyo, in 1974.

Figure 9.7 Behind the bar during a party to celebrate the one year anniversary of Studio 54, with special decorations from fashion designer Issey Miyake (apple blossom-like plants and gold screens) along with a combination entertainment/fashion show with an "East meets West" theme on April 26, 1978 in New York.

Source: Photo by Fairchild Archive/Penske Media via Getty Images.

Although he was based in Japan, Miyake pursued an international career, showing his creations in a broad range of fashion shows and events in Japan, Western Europe, and the United States. He opened sales subsidiaries and was in charge of opening and managing boutiques in France (1979), the United States (1982), and the UK (1983). He was inspired by Japanese traditional materials, techniques, and products, notably kimonos. The cultural dimension of his fashion attracted the attention of Western media, but he argued his clothing was "neither Western nor Japanese but beyond nationality." He was indeed inspired as much by Western designers and artists, like Madeleine Vionnet and Alberto Giacometti, as by Japanese tradition. He developed fashion products for many Western customers during the 1980s and 1990s, including Steve Jobs, and became one of the most globally known Japanese fashion designers.

Despite this worldwide success, Miyake did not transform his enterprise into a multinational big business, unlike most European and American brands at that time. While he diversified to a few types of accessories, such as perfumes (1992), watches (2001), and bags (2010), his core business remained garments. After 1994, Miyake gradually withdrew from the design of some collections, appointing new designers who were mostly Japanese. The company has never been listed. Although it does not disclose the value of its sales, the few data available in Japanese business media make it possible to highlight its limited development. The cumulated sales of the two distribution companies, Issey Miyake International and Issey Miyake On Limit, amounted to about 12 billion Yen in 1988 (about $96 million at that time). In 2014, the gross sales of the group reached 37.6 billion Yen (about $338 million). Sales figures tripled in twenty-five years, but this growth has been very limited when you consider the spectacular development of luxury conglomerates and fast fashion companies.

Sources: *Yomiuri Shimbun*, December 15, 2015; Bonnie English, *Japanese Fashion Designers: The Work and Influence of Issey Miyake, Yohji Yamamoto, and Rei Kawakubo* (London: Bloomsbury, 2018); Official website of Issey Miyake, https://www.isseymiyake.com/blogs/corporate/history (accessed June 24, 2024); *Nihon Keizai Shimbun*, August 11, 1988; *Kaisha shikiyo: Gyokaiban: Kouri* (Tokyo: Toyo Keizai, 2015).

Chapter 10

Sports to fashion

Herzogenaurach, July 11, 2002—adidas-Salomon AG has completed its revolutionary three divisional structure for its core brand, adidas, and will position its third division as "adidas Sport Style—the future in sportswear." The world-famous Japanese designer Yohji Yamamoto will be the Creative Director of this division. With this move, adidas and Yohji Yamamoto have intensified their relationship with a unique co-operation to explore new dimensions in sportswear. adidas represents sport, Yohji Yamamoto represents design, both symbolize true craftsmanship—together they aim to develop the future of sportswear. The first adidas Sport Style products designed by Yohji Yamamoto and the name of the collection will be presented in October 2002. The collection will hit retail in Spring/Summer 2003.[1]

With this press release, adidas announced not only its new divisional structure but also its official transformation to a fashion company, "a new dimension in sportswear." This development, however, did not start in July 2002. It was a long-term development in the global fashion industry whose beginning is impossible to determine, and it was obviously not limited to the German sportswear manufacturer. Moreover, for a long time, the "fashionalization" of the sportswear industry was not a conscious marketing-driven process invented by some clever managers in the headquarters of sports shoe manufacturers like adidas, Nike, Converse, or Reebok.[2] On the contrary, the cool kids in the New York outer boroughs created a new style, beginning with basketball shoes but also including sportswear, which shortly others would copy around the globe.[3] At the same time, the role of marketers, advertising agencies, and corporate strategies should not be underestimated. Fashion is only partly a spontaneous process, particularly in the twentieth century. The element that Simmel mentioned as driving fashion is still there: the simultaneous human drive to uniqueness and uniformity. But the question in this chapter is: What followed what? Was it the industry that followed the street style? That would mean fashion is not a trickling-down but a trickling-up phenomenon. Or was it a kind of circular process in which the industry followed the street style and then took the initiative again and spread the new style through vast investments in marketing? What was the role of intermediaries and financial markets? And finally, what role did outsourcing production from the West to the global South play? This chapter tells the long-term history of the sports shoe ("sneakers") and the sportswear industry. Since the early twentieth century, the term "sneakers" was used in the United

States to refer to the quiet rubber soles that made it possible to sneak up on a person. Nowadays, wearing sneakers has become mainstream, and even the most exclusive designer brands are selling them. This chapter will also show that the meaning of sportswear has changed, as well as its function. The boundaries between sportswear and casual leisurewear have become blurred, illustrated by the modern word "athleisure."[4] It focuses on the histories and strategies of the most important sportswear companies, which can now also be counted among the largest fashion companies in the world.

Sportswear and casual style in the United States

Sportswear is not a twentieth-century phenomenon. It goes back to the nineteenth century and perhaps even earlier, according to Jean Williams. She places the beginning of special sportswear somewhere in the middle of the eighteenth century but also mentions the example of the special football boots made for the sports fanatic Henry VIII in 1526. However, she sees the real breakthrough in sportswear in Britain as occurring at the end of the nineteenth century with the development of the ready-to-wear industry, the growing middle class, and the popularity of sports and associated clothing. Yet the industry mainly focused on the upper class and the way they spent their leisure time. Redfern, for example,

Figure 10.1 Men's Leisure wear. Fashion plates, men's 1880–1939.

Source: Costume Institute Fashion Plates, Metropolitan Museum of Art.

was the most successful British manufacturer of women's sportswear for riding, cycling, tennis, and yachting, with stores in London, New York, and Paris during the 1890s.[5] Also, the French elite enjoyed their ample leisure time at the Cote d'Azur or visiting the racecourse at Longchamp wearing sportswear designed and tailored by Parisian couture houses. In 1925, the French designer Jean Patou opened a sportswear corner in his couture house in Paris after he had visited the United States a few months earlier.[6]

Nonetheless, the beginning of sportswear for the masses is a phenomenon that originated in the United States.[7] The word, however, had several meanings and was used for different things. During the 1920s and the 1930s, particularly in America's growing middle-class culture, it became a popular word for relaxed, casual, less formal leisurewear. The term was, of course, also used for active sports, like swimming, yachting, or ball games. However, in the interwar period, the first meaning was more dominant and closely linked to the new American way of dressing and designing clothes: less elitist, more democratic, and an independent style from Paris.[8] The American fashion nationalists ultimately got their way but in a completely different way than they had envisioned before the First World War (see Chapter 5). The rise of sportswear for the masses in the United States was the result of rising incomes, increased leisure time after the general introduction of the five-day workweek in 1938 (Ford had already introduced it in 1926), man-made fibers (rayon, nylon and later polyester) that could be used for these new types of clothes, the popularity and accessibility of

Figure 10.2 Vintage color historic souvenir photo postcard published circa 1942 as part of a series titled, "Greetings from California," depicting the vibrant beach and boardwalk and amusements pier, here showing an aerial view of the crowded beach boardwalk and amusements of Santa Cruz beach and boardwalk.

Source: Photo by Nextrecord Archives / Getty Images.

California and Florida as holiday destinations, and female customers who demanded more comfortable clothes and American (female) designers who met these needs.[9]

According to William Scott, the Second World War was a pivotal moment for the development of the Californian sportswear industry. Los Angeles had become one of the main centers for the American armaments industry and attracted workers from everywhere. In their free time, these male workers were wearing casual leisurewear that was produced in California, including denim. This trend spread first on the West Coast but a little later also to the Mid-West and East Coast. The medium-sized factories on the West Coast were very flexible in their offers and excellent marketers. During the war, they established the Palm Springs Roundup, which would be renamed MAGIC after the war and would become the largest men's fashion fair in the world. It not only promoted California-made sportswear but also a lifestyle. The fashion industry on the East Coast, still producing more formal clothes, like three-piece suits, was organized in much larger production facilities and was, therefore, less flexible to market changes.[10] Some New York clothing manufacturers had moved away from New York's Seventh Avenue to open new production facilities in Miami, Florida, where sportswear production and consumption had become increasingly important from the 1930s onward. After the war, this industry grew rapidly due to the influx of capital from New York and cheap labor from Cuba. Miami would become one of the main production clusters of sportswear in the United States.[11] Although the term "sportswear" referred to much more than the clothes worn for a particular sport, the American casual trend opened new avenues for the fashion and sportswear industry all over the world.

A German sports-shoemaker conquers Germany—and then the world

Schuhfabrik Gebrüder Dassler was officially registered on July 1, 1924, but the manufacturing of shoes had already begun in 1920, right after the First World War. Although they started by making street shoes, after 1925, they entered an undeveloped niche market of sports shoes, still meaning something completely different from what we mean by it nowadays. There was still a world to win and to innovate, and that is exactly what the brothers Dassler did: Rudolf (Rudi) more as the businessman and Adolf as the technical craftsman, full of new ideas. During the Amsterdam (1928) and Los Angeles (1932) Olympic Games, the company equipped most of the German athletes, an important success factor for the Dasslers. The Nazi years, with their strong emphasis on physical training and sports, were extremely good for the bottom-line. By 1936, the company had become one of Germany's largest sports shoemakers. Despite the Dassler's membership of the racist Nazi party, they convinced the black American runner Jesse Owens, like many other national and international athletes, to run in their shoes. During the war, the company was ordered to discontinue the production of sports shoes and began to produce military goods.[12] After the war, a fraternal feud came to catharsis and lasted until the end of both brothers' lives. It would lead the company to be split into two: adidas (Adi's) and Puma (Rudi's).[13] Both headquarters would remain in Herzogenaurach, a small town in Bavaria.

The company adidas, founded in 1949, led sportswear in the world during the 1950s and 1960s. Exports increased also to the United States and Canada. The three-stripes company's success was based on innovative sports shoes and direct sponsoring of soccer teams and athletes. In the beginning, sponsoring was mainly in kind; however, in due course, bigger sums were involved to win the endorsement of the athletes and whole national teams. It was even called the "Adi and Käthe Dassler system," in which there was permanent contact with sports coaches and teams. Adidas shoes were not cheap, but they were worn by the best athletes; therefore, the demand from amateurs increased. In 1959, the oldest son, Horst Dassler, was sent to Landersheim in the French Alsace to take over an old factory and run the foreign subsidiary. From here, the entrepreneurial son started his own French business empire, whose main activities were, for the greater part, hidden from the headquarters in Germany. He also began to compete with the German parent company, exporting basketball shoes to the United States and conquering the American professional market with the adidas Superstar, beating the trusted American brand Converse (All Star) in its domestic market.[14] He also acquired the French apparel brand Le Coq Sportif and began to export its sportswear to Japan. Even the Dassler family in Germany didn't know that Horst owned all the shares. The acquisition, however, fitted

Figure 10.3 View of the Dassler shoe factory, 1928.
Source: Public Domain via Wikimedia Commons.

well with the strategy of adidas to diversify into sports apparel. In 1972, around 85 percent of all athletes at the Olympic Games were wearing adidas trainers. Horst further expanded and professionalized adidas' sponsoring system and became heavily involved in the commercialization of the FIFA World Soccer championships and the Olympic Games.[15]

Japan was one of the first non-Western markets where adidas expanded. It accessed this market through a contract signed in 1967 with Kanematsu Sports, a subsidiary of the trading company Kanematsu Corporation, to import shoes into Japan. The contract was extended over the following years to the production of shoes under license.[16] Three years later, in 1970, a second contract for the production under the license of sportswear and other sports goods was signed with Descente Ltd. This company had a strategy to produce under license sports shoes and sportswear for foreign brands on the Japanese market: Arena, 1976; Pony, 1984; and Le Coq Sportif, 1986. In 1984, Descente took over the production of shoes from Kanematsu and became adidas' only partner in Japan.[17]

By the end of the 1970s, adidas was the largest sportswear company in the world, with twenty-four factories in seventeen countries, including Germany and France, and subcontractors in Eastern Europe behind the Iron Curtain.[18] In 1978, adidas' founder Adi Dassler passed away, and Käthe took over his position as CEO. She had always been more entrepreneurial than her husband and the actual leader of the company. From the start, Adi was the shoemaker and inventor, so his death was not a rupture from a management perspective. However, six years later, Käthe died too, and Horst had to take over her position as CEO of the group. Unfortunately, in 1987, Horst suddenly died, and René Jäggi, a marketing manager, took over his position. Within ten years, the family had disappeared from the company, and for the first time, a non-family member came to the top[19]—adidas was heading for tough times.

Game changers—the rise of Nike and Reebok

The biggest threat for adidas came from a young Stanford MBA graduate, Phil Knight, who had this "crazy idea" to import high-quality sports shoes from Japan—at the time, a low-labor-cost country that was already competing successfully with American firms in the domestic electronics market.[20] He aimed to outsource production and undersell the German sports shoe company with cheaper high-end products.[21] Adidas shoes were mainly produced in countries with rising labor costs, so his idea was not that crazy. During his visit to Japan in 1962, he convinced the management of Onitsuka (now Asics) to become the representative of their Tiger brand in the United States. Unprepared and inexperienced, he came up with a name on the spot: Blue Ribbon Sports (BRS). In 1964, he partnered with his former runner coach, Bill Bowerman, who showed great interest in athletic shoe design. He would, for example, order adidas shoes from Germany and take them apart to analyze how they were made. BRS sales increased during the 1960s. In 1966, the company opened its first brick-and-mortar store. New designs were developed in close collaboration with the Japanese partners. However, when sales figures reached $2 million, BRS broke with Onitsuka in 1971 and began collaborating with two other Japanese subcontractors, Nippon

Rubber and Nihon-Koyo. BRS began to design its own shoes and ordered them still in Japan. One of the product lines was coined "Nike," after the Greek goddess of victory. An art student developed the now iconic swoosh logo for $35.[22]

During the 1970s, the company expanded to the United States, Canada, and Australia and invested heavily in research and development and marketing. It copied adidas' method of sponsoring successful athletes, who, in turn, endorsed the Nike sports shoes in their advertising campaigns. In 1978, it surpassed adidas on the American market and changed its name to Nike, Inc. Two years later, it went public on the New York Stock Exchange, where it sold 2 million shares. The money was used to finance further international expansion on all continents, which was managed via a newly established international holding: Nike International Ltd.[23] Nike completely changed the rules of the game, which would later be called "Nikefication" by economists. The company outsourced production to a low-cost country and used the savings on manufacturing for marketing and design, while its competitor adidas was stuck in old supply chains in high-labor cost countries and faced fierce competition in the US market during the 1980s. Nike was one of the first American companies to realize it was more profitable to specialize on that part of the supply chain with the highest value-added—that is, marketing and design—leaving manufacturing and distribution to low-cost countries. Nikefication was emulated soon by other companies and other sectors in the United States and Europe.[24] The problem with this model, however, was that

Figure 10.4 Nike factory workers take a nap at lunchtime below the conveyor belt where they work. Ho Chi Minh City, Vietnam, 1997.

Source: Photo by Peter Charlesworth/LightRocket via Getty Images.

relative production costs were not static. In the case of Nike, Japan became too expensive as labor costs increased and the yen appreciated compared to the dollar at the end of the 1970s. New subcontractors were found in South Korea and Taiwan, which delivered 86 percent of all Nike shoes in 1982. However, when these countries, in turn, became too expensive, manufacturing was again relocated via Korean and Taiwanese subcontractors to cheaper locations in Southeast Asia, including Indonesia, China, and Vietnam. The factories were monitored by Nike employees to guide production and guarantee quality.[25]

In the early 1980s, Nike also faced some serious issues in the home market. Consumer taste in amateur sports had changed, so there was less interest in running and running shoes. Moreover, Nike underestimated the female sports market, particularly the new aerobics trend.[26] This market was completely taken over by a British sportswear company, Reebok, which had relocated the company to the flourishing US market. In 1984, it moved its headquarters and design to Boston and, a year later, issued an IPO. It copied Nike's business model and manufactured its shoes in South Korea, Taiwan, and China.[27] Reebok anticipated the new trend that athletic shoes had become streetwear. Reebok sales went up from $13 million in 1983 to $919 million in 1986. In 1987, Reebok sales were $1.4 billion, and it had overtaken Nike, whose total sales figures amounted to $900 million.[28]

In response to the new competition, Nike took several drastic measures, including corporate restructuring, diversification, and an even greater focus on marketing.[29] In 1985, it signed a sponsoring contract with Michael Jordan and launched Air Jordan, which

Figure 10.5 Michael Jordan sits in a space ship being filmed with a camera on a crane arm against a green screen on a soundstage for a Nike "Aerospace Jordan" television commercial for Super Bowl XXVII in September, 1992 in Los Angeles, California.

Source: Photo by Roxanne McCann/Getty Images.

would become an unexpected success in the professional but also the casual and streetwear market. It boosted Nike's sales again and made Michael Jordan the richest sportsman in the world.[30] Nike could not even fulfill market demand, and the company learned that the sneaker market was much larger than the active sports market. First, it was related to basketball but shortly also to hip hop, the new underground music and street culture movement. So, it was not just a clever marketing strategy but a bottom-up fashion movement that Nike was tapping into. Nike also learned that if it could increase the prices of the shoes while keeping supply artificially low, demand would become even higher, reaching crazy levels—kids were even killed for a pair of Air Jordans. The company profited tremendously from Michael Jordan's rising star. It was not the only reason, but an important one, that in 1990, Nike took over the top position from Reebok with $2.24 billion in sales compared to Reebok's $2.16 billion in sales.[31] During the 1990s, Reebok's ambition to become the largest sportswear company in the world finally failed. Meanwhile, adidas was suffering, too, but it would make a comeback.

Table 10.1 shows the global market shares of the largest sports shoe companies in the 1990s. Clearly, Nike had become the largest sports shoe brand in the world. Reebok lost market share during this decade, while Nike became even bigger. Adidas overtook Reebok at the end of the 1990s and would become the second-largest sports shoemaker. In addition, Nike diversified into apparel in this period, as adidas had already done during the 1970s. Acquisitions of various sports apparel brands, including Cole Haan, Bauer, Starter, and Umbro, would give Nike know-how and increase its market share in this sector. Nike also expanded strongly internationally, particularly into Europe and Asia. In Europe, it would enter, for example, the lucrative soccer market and would even challenge adidas in this game.[32]

Table 10.1 Global Sports Shoe Market and Market Shares, 1991–1999

Market Share	1991	1992	1993	1994	1995	1996	1997	1999*
Nike	22.5	25.4	24.4	22.7	27.1	32.1	35.3	30.4
Reebok	18.8	20.0	18.9	18.3	17.4	14.7	14.5	11.2
adidas	13.6	10.0	9.3	10.3	9.9	10.2	10.3	15.5
Fila	0.9	2.1	2.7	3.0	4.1	6.0	5.7	3.9
Converse	3.4	3.5	4.0	4.2	3.3	2.7	3.2	2.2
New Balance	1.8	1.8	2.1	2.2	2.5	2.9	3.1	3.8
ASICS	4.7	5.4	5.2	4.7	4.2	3.5	3.0	2.5
Puma	4.6	3.8	4.3	3.1	2.4	2.4	2.1	2.1
Top 8	70.3	72.0	70.9	68.5	70.9	74.5	77.2	71.6
Others	29.7	28.0	29.1	31.5	29.1	25.5	22.8	28.4
Total	100	100	100	100	100	100	100	100

*No figures for 1998.

Source: Adapted from and based on: Richard M. Locke, "The Promise and Perils of Globalization: The Case of Nike," *Management: Inventing and Delivering Its Future* 39 (2003): 3.

Near-death experience and revival of adidas

In the outer boroughs of New York, the upcoming hip-hop culture, based on rap music, graffiti, and breakdancing, had introduced sports shoes and sportswear as a street style from the late 1970s. This new style would have a tremendous impact on the fashion world, which nobody could have predicted at the time, especially not the conservative adidas managers in Germany and France. Adidas' Superstar, however, which had conquered the NBA market during the 1970s, had also become part of this new street outfit because the best basketball players wore them as well.[33] The street, in a way, endorsed the three-stripes brand in the US market—particularly, when Run DMC produced the hit "My Adidas" in 1986. The initiative for the song had come from these most famous rappers, but an American adidas manager convinced Horst Dassler to sign the first non-sports promotional deal with the hip-hop stars. Adidas ultimately paid Run DMC's asking price of approximately $1 million.[34]

Box 10.1 Hip hop, sportswear, and fashion

Popular music and fashion were always an inseparable combination in the twentieth century. Think of the tango, jazz, rock and roll, and punk styles that populated the dance floors. This was no different with hip hop, based on rap music, graffiti, and breakdancing. The three most important music styles of the African American youth during the 1970s were funk, disco, and rap. Hip hop arose out of social and racial tensions in African American, Caribbean, and Puerto Rican subcultures in the outer boroughs of New York. Like all subcultures, it created an individual but also specific sartorial style based on denim workwear, army clothing, and sportswear. Sneakers, often worn with loose laces, became popular among kids in the hip-hop scene and are nowadays worn by all generations around the world. Many elements of the hip-hop style have become commonplace, but it is often forgotten that the style and subculture were born out of frustration with a marginalized position. Only during the late 1980s did it spread to other parts of the United States when MTV began to broadcast rap videos. In the 1990s, it became one of the dominant music and fashion styles in the world.

It was not only the music industry that recognized the potential of the new music scene; fashion and sportswear companies also saw the rising popularity of hip hop. Adidas was confronted with the popularity of their "Superstar" in the hip-hop scene when Run-D.M.C. launched their hit "My Adidas" in 1986. The most successful hip-hop band of the time copied the street style and stuck to the old-school adidas, while everyone else was wearing Reebok and Nike. At the time, adidas was struggling in the American market and Run D.M.C.'s hit was a bright spot. The early 1990s saw an explosion of hip-hop clothing brands like Karl Kani and FUBU, often endorsed by hip-hop artists. However, big brands, like Ralf Lauren, Calvin Klein, and Tommy Hilfiger, with big

Figure 10.6 Joseph Simmons, Darryl McDaniels and Jam Master Jay of the hip-hop group "Run DMC" pose for a portrait session wearing Addidas sweat suits in front of the Empire State Building in May 1985 in New York, New York.
Source: Photo by Michael Ochs Archives/Getty Images.

advertising budgets, also entered the market. MTV aired more and more hip-hop videos, and everything the artists wore sold like crazy. Tommy Hilfiger persuaded Snoop Dog to wear their clothes during his performance on *Saturday Night Live* in 1994. It became a huge success for Snoop Dog but also for the brand, which was now closely linked to the most popular music culture. Overall, hip hop changed the fashion world immensely. In California, MAGIC, the largest B2B fashion trade show for casual and streetwear in North America, turned into a hip-hop festival with loud music, dancers, and hip-hop celebrities. This was the result of the increasing space occupied by sporty urban clothing brands during the fair.

Hip hop not only had a major impact on the casual wear market but also incrementally entered the high-end fashion world. For example, in 1984 the American designer Norma Kamali used hip-hop music to show her new collection, and the 1987 Chanel collection was heavily influenced by the hip-hop style, including oversized baseball jackets.

However, high-end fashion brands like Gucci and Louis Vuitton did not focus on the hip-hop market then. Dapper Dan copied the logos of luxury designer brands like Louis Vuitton, Gucci, Chanel, Fendi, and MCM. Since 1982, Dapper Dan's Boutique, open twenty-four hours a day, tailored unique clothes out of it, creating an expensive style for drug dealers, hustlers, hip-hop stars, and athletes. In 1992, Dapper Dan's Boutique was

> closed for good after a counterfeiting lawsuit. Although he brought new ideas to designer brands, he was viewed with disdain by high-end fashion brands for years. But how things can change. In 2017, Gucci and Dapper Dan jointly started a men's clothing line. A year later, they opened a luxury fashion store in Harlem, New York.
>
> *Sources*: Elena Romero, *Free Stylin': How Hip Hop Changed the Fashion Industry*, Hip Hop in America (Santa Barbara, California: Praeger, 2012); Thomas Turner, "German Sports Shoes, Basketball, and Hip Hop: The Consumption and Cultural Significance of the Adidas 'Superstar' 1966–1988," *Sport in History*, 35:1 (2015): 127–155; Thomas Turner, "Adidas and the Creation of a Transnational Market for German Athletic Shoes, 1948–1978," *Consumer Engineering, 1920s–1970s. Marketing between Expert Planning and Consumer Responsiveness*, ed. Jan Logemann, Gary Cross, Ingo Köhler (Cham: Palgrave Macmillan, 2019).

Nevertheless, this endorsement deal could not turn the tide for the Adidas Group worldwide. In 1988, the new CEO, Jäggi, hired McKinsey to make a critical business analysis. *Defining the Future Product/Market Strategy*, as the critical report was called, stated that the brand's market position and pricing were too heterogeneous in different markets, too weak in the lifestyle segment, and the group had quality, sales, and services problems in various countries. As a result, adidas needed to improve its marketing and communication strategies and have a stronger media presence than competitors Nike and Reebok on the one hand, but also Benneton, Esprit, and Lacoste on the other. In addition, adidas was advised to professionalize its management and information systems.[35]

In the same year the critical report was made, Jäggi began a debate on the Executive Board about the legal structure of the company. If the company wanted to survive the cut-throat competition in the international sports market, it needed fresh capital; therefore, it had to change from a foundation to a joint stock company. Despite the differences in opinion and interests between the different branches of the surviving Dassler family members, adidas was transformed into a joint stock company (*Aktiengesellschaft, AG*) in 1989. When, a year later, the Dassler sisters wanted to sell their shares, the French entrepreneur Bernard Tapie, protégé of President François Mitterrand, acquired majority stock with borrowed money from a German, Japanese, and French banking consortium. Tapie, who was also the president of Olympique de Marseille, had built a business empire in France based on buying bankrupt firms. In 1990, adidas was loss-making and almost bankrupt. Nevertheless, the arrival of Tapie via his highly indebted holding company BTF turned out to be an even greater financial disaster for adidas; the direly needed capital injection did not materialize. Interestingly, Tapie proposed that adidas enter the world of haute couture and fashion. This unconventional idea, however, was not taken very seriously by the other board members at the time.

In 1993, Tapie was forced to sell his shares when he could not repay his debt to a French banking consortium that included Credit Lyonnais, Banque Worms, Assurance Générales de France, and some private investors. Robert Louis-Dreyfus, a Harvard

Business School graduate from a Parisian banker's family, was appointed CEO. He succeeded Jäggi, who had led the company during its most difficult period. Louis-Dreyfus also brought his experience in advertising from the London-based Saatchi & Saatchi. In 1995, Dreyfus decided to issue an IPO of 50.1 percent of the company's shares on the Frankfurt and Parisian stock exchanges. The revenue of the share issue was mainly used to repay the company's debts. As a result of the IPO, adidas eventually came into the hands of German, British, American, French, and Swiss investors.[36] Within a few years, the company had changed from a German family firm into an international company based on stocks. Financialization has since become an integral aspect of the global sportswear business.

Marketing of sportswear

Adidas not only followed Nike's example of outsourcing production more and more to low-cost countries but also adopted the American company's strong focus on marketing. The number of employees worldwide dropped from 12,000 in 1986 to around 5,000 seven years later. Production of apparel and shoes was, for the greater part, outsourced to Asia. In 1993, Rob Strasser and Peter Moore, founders of marketing company Sports Inc., were appointed CEO and Creative Director, respectively, of the US subsidiary Adidas America Inc. From 1976 to 1987, they had been the marketeers behind Nike's stunning success with "Air" products. Clearly, Nike had outperformed adidas in the American market and now adidas needed at least to learn from its main competitor. In 1990, the unconventional Strasser was appointed director of marketing for the whole Adidas Group. However, he did not propose to copy Nike's marketing strategy but to go back to adidas' roots and heritage and use the company's longstanding tradition of working together with athletes in the development of new products.[37] "The market was the aim and the product the key" to open the door to the sports goods market to beat the competition.[38] Strasser was thus necessary to adidas' new marketing orientation, but he passed away unexpectedly a few months after he had taken the lead in the US subsidiary.

Adidas' new CEO, Louis-Dreyfus, continued the marketing focus and signed a contract with the British advertising company Leagas Delaney to change adidas' marketing strategies to target younger consumers and have a much greater media presence. The company hired trend scouts to interview youngsters and observe hip places. TV and the movies were targeted. Between 1993 and 1998, more than 150 TV commercials were made for adidas. Active marketing had become adidas' core business, and production was, in Nike's case, outsourced to Southeast Asia.[39] Meanwhile, in 1997, the company made an important acquisition of $1.4 billion—Salomon, a French manufacturer of sky equipment, which changed its name to adidas-Salomon AG. The acquisition also included manufacturers of premium golf clubs (Taylor Made) in the United States and cycling equipment (Mavic) in France. The brand with the three stripes had come back from a deep low to regain second position in the global market for sports goods, ahead of Reebok.[40]

Meanwhile, Nike, which invested mainly in marketing, retail, and product development, faced several major reputational problems in the 1990s. While its business model was being copied by many companies in the West, it was increasingly being criticized by NGOs and consumers. Indonesian workers, for example, complained about underpayment, poor labor conditions, and the neglect of basic worker rights. Nike's initial response was to blame it on the Korean subcontractors: "[we don't] know the first thing about manufacturing. We are marketers and designers."[41] In Pakistan, Nike was accused of using child labor, and an Ernst and Young audit commissioned by the company reported serious health and safety issues in Vietnam. The audit report was leaked via an NGO to the *New York Times* and was grist to the mill for the growing anti-globalist movement. These negative stories clearly showed the other side of Nikefication, and it damaged the brand's reputation. Moreover, it affected sales. After the sales figures continued to decline—also because of the financial crisis in Southeast Asia—the company could no longer afford to blame all abuses on the subcontractors. In 1998, it introduced a minimum age for workers and American standards regarding health regulations in overseas factories. Nike began tightening controls on health and working conditions in subcontractor factories and organized compliance teams to conduct random inspections.[42]

In 2001, adidas-Salomon opened mono-brand stores in Tokyo and Berlin, copying Nike's marketing strategy, which had started Nike Town in Oregon in 1990, selling only Nike sports equipment. During the 1990s, Nike built a chain of these mono-brand stores throughout the United States.[43] Ten years later, adidas conducted a similar marketing campaign with its adidas Originals stores,[44] which targeted the leisure market: "consumers

Figure 10.7 Nike Chief Executive Officer Phil Knight at the US Open men's tennis finals, NYC, September 10, 1995.
Source: Photo by Najlah Feanny/Corbis via Getty Images.

who want to buy trend and fashion products exclusively for leisure usage but still are inspired by sports."[45] A year later, adidas-Salomon also began to compete with Nike in the United States when it opened an adidas Originals store in New York City. Twenty years later, adidas would open another 2,500 mono-brand stores all over the world. Nike also took new paths in search of new market segments. In 1999, it started direct sales via an online platform, which expanded in the 2000s. It continued to sign big endorsement deals with top athletes, but it also focused more on the apparel leisure market, like adidas. In 2002, it bought Hurley, a Californian teen lifestyle brand, and a year later Converse, the old American retro brand, whose reputation was opposed to Nike's greedy image among young Americans. Nike even established a subsidiary focusing on value-conscious consumers for sneakers and apparel. It also improved transparency about its overseas activities when it published, for the first time, a list of 700 subcontractors in 2005. These moves were intended to improve the brand's reputation and boost revenues globally. In that year, Nike surpassed $1 billion in profits (revenues $13.7 billion) and confirmed its number one position in the global sports goods market. Its founder, Phill Knight, had just given up his position as CEO and transferred to William D. Perez, who came from S.C. Johnson & Son. He would stay for just one year, showing that the packaged goods business was a different ball game than the sports goods business.[46]

Fashionalization of adidas

In 2001, Herbert Hainer took over the CEO position of a now financially flourishing adidas from Robert Louis-Dreyfus. According to Karlsch et al., this marked the end of the "Horst Dassler era," which had been characterized by a management style that lasted until the end of the millennium.[47] However, this study suggests that the 1990s marked a landslide in all significant aspects. The company changed its legal basis, capital foundation, and marketing approach. Adidas had become, wittingly or unwittingly, a fashion company. It is difficult to identify when exactly adidas entered the fashion arena because it is hard to pinpoint when sportswear became fashionable. Clearly, there is a link with hip-hop culture, which is now mainstream, but it also influenced haute couture and the catwalks.[48]

In 2002, adidas announced that it had completed its "revolutionary" three-divisional structure: adidas Sport Performance, adidas Sport Heritage, and adidas Sport Style. The Japanese designer, Yohji Yamamoto, was appointed Creative Director of the last division. The first division, Sport Performance, developed products for the sports market that had "design appeal, encouraging consumers to wear the products both on and off the court or playing field."[49] The second division, Sport Heritage, contained products that sought "to extend the unique and authentic heritage of adidas to the lifestyle market."[50] This press release clearly showed that the company was conscious of the great value of design, heritage, and fashion to add value to its products. By adding a third division,

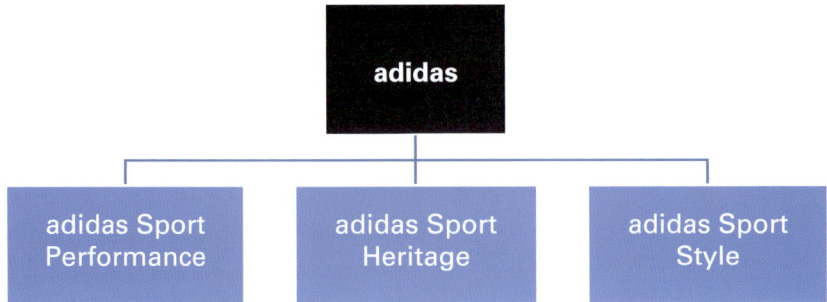

Figure 10.8 Three-Divisional Structure of adidas, 2002

Source: "Adidas Strengthens Three-Divisional Structure: Adidas Sport Style Designed by Yohji Yamamoto," Press Release: Thursday, July 11, 2002.

Sport Style, and hiring a famous Japanese designer as creative director, adidas also saw the potential to sell its sports products in high-end luxury fashion markets.

In 2004, adidas-Salomon announced a long-term partnership with British high-end fashion designer Stella McCartney. Symbolically, the announcement was made in New York, one of the global fashion capitals. The United States was still the most important market where adidas wanted to score, although the Chinese market was also growing strongly. The women's collection was created as part of the Sport Performance division and would be available in the United States, Japan, and Europe by 2005.[51] It was not presented as part of Yamamoto's Y-3 collection or under the umbrella of the Sport Style division. Apparently, adidas wanted to integrate fashion into the high-end sports market.

In 2005, adidas sold Salomon because it recognized that winter sports goods did not fit very well within its brand portfolio, and it continued as adidas AG. In the same year, it acquired one of its main competitors, Reebok, strengthening its second position in the global sporting goods market, after Nike. After this major acquisition of $3.8 billion, the adidas Group reported $12 billion in revenues. The idea behind the acquisition was that adidas could continue to grow in the leisure market in China and other emerging markets.[52] Reebok was also integrated into the new fashion strategy. In 2010, for example, Giorgio Armani S.p.A. and Reebok International Ltd announced a "global alliance to create a special collection, combining active style with sport and technology." The co-creation collection was presented at Milan Fashion Week. According to Giorgio Armani:

> Today sportswear and active wear have become really important parts of our wardrobes. I wanted to offer my customers the possibility of wearing sports clothes that were stylish and comfortable. My new alliance with Reebok is a natural consequence of this philosophy. As with all my collaborations, I am delighted to be working with experts in their field.[53]

Figure 10.9 Zinedine Zidane and Yohji Yamamoto attend a cocktail reception celebrating the opening of the new Y-3 Flagship store hosted by Yohji Yamamoto and adidas on March 10, 2011 in London.
Source: Photo by Dave M. Benett/Getty Images.

Stella McCartney was the UK team's creative director during the Olympic Summer Games in London and designed the sports outfits of the British team in 2012. This shows that the company still adhered to Dassler's marketing method but also actively linked sportswear to fashion. In 2021, adidas announced that it had sold Reebok to Authentic Brands Group (ABG) at a loss of €2.1 billion because it had not brought the profits it was expected to bring. The brand did not live up to the expectation that it could beat Nike in its own home market as it once did in the 1980s. Meanwhile, luxury fashion brands began to offer sneakers and other sportswear, sometimes in collaborations—fashionably called *collabs*—with the big sports brands: Dior with Nike and adidas with Gucci.

Nike and adidas are ultimately the winners, number one and number two in a tough competition, and have also become active in the global fashion market. In 2024, they were the number one and number two sportswear companies in the world. Puma was bought by luxury group Kering but also sold again as a management buyout in 2023. Japan's Asics, Mizuno, and Onitsuka Tiger, Nike's first supplier in the 1960s, all remained manufacturers of sportswear but never achieved the status of a competitive global fashion brand. In 2023, Nike ranked number one as the most valuable fashion brand in the world by brand value, before Louis Vuitton, Chanel, and Gucci; adidas ranked number five.[54]

Table 10.2 Fashion Brand Position and Brand Value, in Million US Dollars

Position	Brand	Brand value
1	Nike	31,306
2	Louis Vuitton	26,289
3	Chanel	19,386
4	Gucci	17,839
5	adidas	15,659
6	Hermès	14,165
7	Dior	13,152
8	Cartier	12,538
9	Zara	11,049

Source: Brand Finance, "Apparel 50 Brand Ranking," https://brandirectory.com/rankings/aparel/table (accessed July 29, 2024).

Conclusion

Sportswear and sneakers became fashionable in the twenty-first century. However, this was a long-term process that had started a hundred years earlier in the United States and incrementally spread to other continents. While fashion nationalists in the United States failed before the First World War, sportswear realized American dominance not only in global style but also the global industry. Nike, which started just with the crazy idea of one person, Phill Knight, had become the largest sportswear company in the world by the 1990s, and by 2023 the most valued fashion or apparel brand. The question was how these sportswear brands, like Nike, adidas, or Reebok, eventually also became fashion. Or, in other words, how this *fashionalization*, as we have called it, took place.

Simmel argues that fashion is a trickling-down process. The masses follow the upper class (nowadays celebrities or sports heroes), but this chapter shows that the rise of sportswear as fashion was also a bottom-up process, following hip-hop kids in the streets of New York. Then the sportswear companies used the new trends to expand their business into the leisure market as, for example, McKinsey advised adidas to do. Intermediaries like consultancy firms thus played a role in showing where there were new avenues for growth. In the end, it was much less of a spontaneous movement than the result of the active marketing strategies and huge budgets of the biggest sportswear companies in the world.

It was not an invention or innovation that transformed sportswear into fashion. It took years of adaptation to rapidly change market conditions and copy competitors' business models. Eventually, the most successful business model was introduced by Nike, which, from the start, outsourced its production to low-wage countries and focused entirely on design and marketing. Nikification, as this model was called, was copied by Reebok first and later by adidas, among others. The expansion to global markets, product innovation, and extensive marketing had only been possible after investments through the capital markets. The financialization of the biggest sports brands made this expansion possible and simultaneously necessary, as investors wanted to see the value of their shares increase. As markets had become global since the 1980s, this new trend was regarded as a lucrative investment. All over the world, people began wearing sneakers and sportswear daily—it had become a lifestyle and global fashion.

Box 10.2 Soccer shirts as fashion items

The football shirt, with its bright colors and popular team name, can today be found in places far from the football pitch: the beach, the supermarket, or the cafe. Even though some styling decisions by fans raise eyebrows, wearing a football jersey in public is socially accepted and has developed into a crucial aspect of fashion. Yet, this has only been for about three decades.

In 1973, the British sportswear brand Admiral launched its first replica kits of a Leeds United shirt. A year later, it had also made a deal with the Football Association to use its own logo on the shirt of the national team of England. In the beginning, the football shirt was exclusively for children. Then Admiral launched a revolutionary advertising campaign in the 1978/9 season in which they presented their products in adult sizes, combining the shirts with casual clothes. Simultaneously, sportswear brands and clubs began, in collaboration, to produce adult-sized club final editions as a means of commemoration, creating a legitimate reason for adults to purchase them. Combined with the loosening of societal norms as to what constituted respectable clothing, a soccer casual style emerged in England but also in other European cities. This new aestheticization of soccer was facilitated in the 1980s by a fitness boom in which sportswear as leisurewear became fashionable. While the replica shirts on match days only amounted to about 3 percent to 4 percent in the 1980s, they surged in the 1990s, reaching 25 percent and 30 percent. This can be explained by the new consumption of soccer in the 1990s, when security measures were tightened, stadiums were rebuilt, and teams were increasingly run as commercial enterprises.

In fashion, soccer shirts have now been integrated into daily style and attire. However, before the 1970s, the owner of a soccer shirt would only wear it to play the game. The bright colors of the shirts were considered unmanly and garish, as British men's fashion had not used bright colors for decades. Nowadays, the football shirt in fashion is more than just a change in taste. The shirt is not only a canvas for marketing but also socially identifies the fan. Personal taste is communicated, making a distinction between different fan groups and non-fans. In a world where fashion and clothing are a means of expressing individuality, and uniformity has a negative connotation, soccer shirts are an exception to this social trend. They are uniforms in which the consumer is dependent on the club colors, aesthetics, and commercial partners.

Besides their stylistic implications, soccer shirts have created their own space in the fashion industry. They are not subject to fashion shows or extraordinary designs but are incorporated into clubs' annual budgets. They are not designed for the sake of fashion and consumption but serve as a marketing and merchandise tool. The once small shops that sold replica shirts as souvenirs have now grown into stadium shops with products ranging from shirts to scarves, skirts, and hats. The collective TV rights sold abroad made soccer accessible worldwide and, with it, the shirts. In 2021, Bayern Munich (adidas) achieved the highest sales of soccer shirts, with 3.25 million units. Real Madrid (adidas) came in second with three million shirts sold, and Liverpool (Nike) came in third with 2.45 million shirts sold. Football shirts have not only become fashionable but also a lucrative source of income for the world's biggest soccer teams and sportswear brands.

Sources: Christopher Stride, Jean Williams, David Moor, and Nick Catley, "From Sportswear to Leisurewear: The Evolution of English Football League Shirt Design in the Replica Kit Era," *Sport in History* 35, no. 1 (2 January 2015): 156–94; Christopher Stride, Nick Catley, and Joe Headland, "Shirt Tales: How Adults Adopted the Replica Football Kit," *Sport in History* 40, no. 1 (2 January 2020): 106–146; Alexandra Schwell, Michal Buchowski, Malgorzata Kowalska, and Nina Szogs, eds, *New Ethnographies of Football in Europe* (London: Palgrave Macmillan UK, 2016). Statista, "Soccer (football) shirt sales worldwide in 2021, by club," https://www.statista.com/statistics/1118294/football-shirt-sales-by-club/ (accessed September 29, 2024).

Chapter 11

Digital fashion and global production networks

The Post-Millennial Generation is looking at three screens all the time. So they are looking at information and thinking, "I want to be surprised. I want someone to surprise me, then I'll read what they are doing, or I'll buy what they are trying to sell me." The Post-Millennial Generation is going to be difficult to sell to. So fast fashion is not just about speed to market. It's about the speed in the whole world, and the whole way we are living in that world. Everything has become seamless and integrated. It's more of a business model, a way of selling, than the fashion itself.[1]

Catriona Macnab, Vice-president WGSN, May 2016

Digitalization and artificial intelligence (AI) have entered global fashion in all possible ways and changed every step of the value chain, including design, manufacturing, logistics, marketing, and retail. The rise of the World Wide Web has linked global markets and manufacturing. Outsourcing of apparel and textile manufacturing from the Global North to the Global South (or East) began at the end of the 1960s but was boosted as a result of the introduction of the internet during the early 1990s. Communication between North and South (West and East), between designers, producers, the headquarters of large firms, retailers, and contractors made a hitherto unthinkable division of labor possible between different parts of the world. In combination with the introduction of container shipping and plummeting transport costs, a new global fashion system arose.

However, it was not only global production conditions that changed tremendously. The way ready-made fashion products were sold in different markets was revolutionized. From the end of the 1990s to the early 2000s, major online platforms and social media arose. E-commerce transformed consumers' interaction with fashion, as they got used to their ability to buy anything they wanted from anywhere in the world and to do it quickly. The way people communicated about fashion also changed dramatically. In the 2000s, young fashion bloggers conquered the internet and created a new business model, sometimes even more successful than traditional fashion magazines. Social media affected both market and consumer behavior, and fashion trends became obsolete much faster; fashion cycles have, therefore, become much shorter. Global influencers and celebrity culture nonetheless could only rise because of high-speed internet.

This chapter focuses on the transitions in the global fashion industry after 2000. It addresses the following key questions: how and why has the digitalization of the economy and AI changed global fashion over the past twenty-five years? What are the implications for global production networks, and how has digitalization affected the local fashion industry? This chapter is probably the least historical, as digitalization is an ongoing process that is still radically changing the fashion industry as we are finishing this book. It is, however, an opportunity to discuss recent changes in the fashion industry from a historical perspective.

Globalization and global production networks

In their seminal article, Robert Keohane and Joseph Nye defined what globalization was and questioned to what extent it was a new phenomenon.[2] The article was published in 2000 when the word "globalization" had just become a buzzword, and the process was not particularly well understood. According to them, it was better to use the word "globalism," which they defined as "a state of the world involving networks of interdependence at multicontinental distances."[3] Thus, globalization means an increase in globalism. Economic globalism (which is most relevant for this chapter):

> involves long-distance flows of goods, services, and capital, as well as the information and perceptions that accompany market exchange. It also involves the organization of the processes that are linked to these flows, such as the organization of low-wage production in Asia for the U.S. and European markets.[4]

In the earlier chapters, we showed that economic globalism was not new to the twentieth century. The second half of the nineteenth century and the early twentieth century until the First World War is often referred to as the first wave of globalization (also known as the "Great Wave of Globalization"). The period of the two world wars and the aftermath were periods of decreasing globalism and deglobalization. During the 1960s, the flows of goods, services, and capital began to increase again, and the fashion and apparel industries were at the forefront of this global trend. But even this trend was not new. The Silk Route, which began well before our era and was named after the most expensive and luxurious fabric, created economic exchanges between Asia and Europe. However, during those two thousand years, only a limited amount of goods and people were involved.

Therefore, according to Keohane and Nye, what matters is the thickness of the connection. The Silk Route is an example of thin globalization. What happened in the 1990s was thick globalization. Many more people were involved in this process and were directly affected by it. Economic and financial interdependence increased to unprecedented heights and at an unprecedented pace. The information technology revolution not only sped up global communication but also diminished the cost of information exchange.[5] Again, it was the fashion industry that profited from these new possibilities.

The new information technology also created a new kind of economy based on networks rather than hierarchies.[6] We have used many examples of traditional fashion firms and the growing size and influence of big fashion groups like LVMH, Kering, Inditex, Fast Retailing, Nike, and adidas, but in the 2000s, networks began to play an important role in the global fashion industry as well. Neil Coe et al. define a global production network as a "nexus of interconnected functions, operations and transactions through which a specific product or service is produced, distributed and consumed [that] extend[s] spatially across national boundaries and, in so doing, integrates parts of disparate national and subnational territories."[7] The global production networks included different kinds of networks, and they went beyond firm actors and linear processes to reveal interdependencies between and within production networks.[8] It also showed the global economy's asymmetric power relations, which exist in the global fashion and apparel industries.[9] Buyers from developed countries were in a strong power position because they could relocate from one low-cost developing country to the next. However, economic power relations were not static and changed in due course.[10]

In the 2000s, it was no longer just about outsourcing apparel production from the West to the East (or Global North to the Global South). It was more and more about changing positions within the global production networks. China is a good example. In the 1980s and 1990s, China became the world's apparel factory, but after the turn of the millennium, operations began to be reorganized on a multinational level. Digitalization helped to manage these operations and created huge digital platforms like Alibaba with two-sided markets, linking retail and production. The online wholesaler Alibaba was set up in 1999 by Jack Ma and seventeen others and became one of the largest online business-to-business (B2B) retail platforms in the world. Its IPO on the New York Stock Exchange in 2014 was the largest IPO ever.[11] At the same time, the Chinese fashion market grew enormously, and local sales, including sales of luxury fashion, became increasingly important. Western high-end and fast-fashion conglomerates benefited greatly from these growing sales opportunities, but Chinese manufacturers also increasingly focused on their own local markets, creating enormous opportunities. In addition, online retail outlets developed in China faster than in Europe and the United States, making the Chinese particularly competitive in the global online market.[12]

The rise of global production networks was not just a result of technical innovations and the digital revolution but also the result of institutional changes. In 2001, China became a member of the World Trade Organization. After years of international negotiations and major adaptations of China's economic structures, it became a member of a global rules-based trading system, creating huge opportunities for the Chinese economy and turning it into the largest exporter of goods, including apparel and fashion, and the second-largest service provider in the world.[13] In addition, the end of the multi-fiber arrangement (MFA) in 2005 meant that China and other developing countries, like Bangladesh, India, and Pakistan, could export textiles and garments more freely to the West. It was the end of the quota system, which had existed since 1974 (see Chapter 8). The end of the MFA triggered a new major wave of relocation of garment production from the developed world to the developing world.[14] Other free trade and preferential treaties were signed in the 1990s and 2000s between US, African, and Caribbean economies. In 1994, the North American Free Trade Agreement (NAFTA) was signed, which eliminated tariffs on the US market for Mexican apparel manufacturers. In 2002, the Caribbean Trade Partnership Act (CTBA) was signed, allowing nineteen countries to export freely to the United States, and two years later, the Central American Free Trade (CAFTA) Agreement was signed. In 2000, the Africa Growth Opportunity Act was signed. Some twenty-seven African countries could now export tariff- and quota-free apparel to the US market. In the same year, the European Union (EU) signed the Cotonou agreement with Africa, which had the same effect as the US agreement.[15] Both agreements attracted many investors from China, India, and Bangladesh to Africa to enter the American and European markets.[16] The Euro-Mediterranean Association Agreements signed between 1998 and 2004 with various Mediterranean countries, including Algeria, Egypt, Israel, Jordan, Morocco, Tunisia, and Syria, regulated free trade between these countries and the EU. Turkey had already entered a customs union with the EU in 1996.[17] All these bilateral and multilateral agreements, mostly signed in the early 2000s, led to a radical shift in global garment and textile production. These major institutional changes, combined with increasing digitalization, thus resulted in profound changes in global production networks.

Fashion forecasting: WGSN (London) and Stylesight (New York)

Fashion forecasting was one of the first parts of the global production networks where digitalization brought about radical changes. Fashion forecasting or prediction is a hidden practice in the fashion industry for most consumers, yet an essential business service for the global fashion system. It reduces risks for manufacturers and retailers because it allows them to know better what will be fashionable next. Fashion forecasters gather and share intelligence about colors, silhouettes, and fabrics. This information is communicated to manufacturers and retailers via trend books, seminars, trend talks, or online reports on a subscription basis. Fashion forecasters are part of trend agencies or consultancy bureaus that provide B2B services.

Since the 2000s, the nature of fashion forecasting has changed significantly due to the influx of capital and technology into the sector. The 1970s and 1980s were the heyday for trend forecasters as the business environment in the fashion industry became more competitive, and companies started looking for trends. These were also the years that well-known international fashion-forecasting agencies, such as Peclers, Nelly Rodi, and Lidewij Edelkoort's Trend Union, were established in Paris. These style bureaus were small- and medium-sized companies, personally managed by the founders, and rather capital extensive. The forecasting methodology was mostly based on lifelong experience in the fashion industry and intuition. They sold handmade trend books and mood boards to their clients in Europe, the United States, and Japan. Technological advancements, however, changed how trends were analyzed and communicated.

The rise of new and influential trend forecasting agencies in the early 2000s, such as Worth Global Style Network (WGSN) in London and Stylesight in New York, coincided with the digital transformation of society.[18] The limitations of traditional fashion forecasting, dismissed by some as a self-fulfilling prophecy and crystal ball witchcraft, along with the

Digital fashion and global production networks

rise of big data, inspired newcomers to explore novel ways of trend forecasting.[19] The datafication of fashion made it easier to monitor and analyze consumer behavior. "Big data" refers to large datasets that require AI to analyze them. One of the most recent developments in the fashion-trend forecasting industry is the gradual adoption of AI systems in trend analysis. Recently, new AI collaborative projects have been launched by Big Tech firms and fashion brands (see Box 11.1 on IBM Watson).

The London-based WGSN was founded in 1998 by brothers Julian and Marc Worth. They saw the opportunities of the World Wide Web to innovate and modernize fashion forecasting, which was until then low-tech and old-fashioned in their view. They set up a website with high-quality images based on earlier experiences with graphic design and applied it to fashion. Their online trend-forecasting business, based on subscription, was a huge success; by 2005, it already had 1,500 clients. In that year, it was acquired by EMAP (East Midland Allied Press), a large publishing and exhibitions group, for £140 million. For EMAP, it was just one business unit within the bigger picture, but it turned out to be a good investment. By 2011, WGSN had 38,000 users for a subscription rate of £16,500 for five users per company. The online fashion forecasting company simultaneously served high-end and fast-fashion customers.[20] WGSN was part of a new generation of fashion-trend agencies that provided an increasing amount of online trend information to designers, manufacturers, and retailers worldwide. In 2013, the company "merged"

Figure 11.1 WGSN senior director Greer Hughes is seen on stage during the Texhibition Istanbul 2023 at Istanbul Expo Center on March 10, 2023 in Istanbul, Turkey.

Source: Photo by Ferda Demir/Getty Images for Texhibition Istanbul.

with the New York-based Stylesight, which had been set up by Frank Bober, a menswear designer from the Seventh Avenue fashion district, under the name Primatech Corporation in 2003.[21] He started the business similarly to WGSN: an online collection of images that could predict future fashion trends. By 2011, the website contained eight million images.[22] The Platinum clients paid a $16,500 annual subscription fee, but it gave full access to twenty-five users within the company. In addition, these clients would also get two live presentations, a service WGSN did not offer. Moreover, the company offered clients customized trend reports. Ultimately, Stylesight proved to be a serious and cheaper competitor to WGSN, with superior technology. As a result, it was acquired by the media group EMAP (since 2015, Ascential), which also owned WGSN, for around $100 million, and was regarded as a merger for strategic reasons.[23] The company continued under the name of WGSN and formed the largest fashion trend-forecasting business in the world. In 2016, Ascential shares were listed on the London Stock Exchange after an IPO of £800 million. Trend and fashion forecasting was no longer a small- and medium-sized business. In 2024, WGSN was sold to Apax Partners, a global private equity advisory firm, for $700 million.[24] In the digital era, fashion forecasting has become big business.

Box 11.1 IBM Watson and fashion forecasting

IBM (International Business Machines), headquartered in New York, is one of the largest information technology companies in the world. In the 1920s, the main business model was leasing Hollerith punch-card machines to the US government and large corporations. Its first president, Thomas J. Watson (1874–1956), aimed for the best staff and latest technology. After the war, IBM became the leading firm (nicknamed the Big Blue) in the global computing industry and stayed focused until the 1990s on mainframes, software, and services. The introduction of the personal computer caused IBM to experience a deep financial crisis and to restructure the firm into a global information consultancy firm. By the 2000s, IBM was again one of the largest computer firms on the globe. In 2023, it employed more than 300,000 staff in 175 countries with a total revenue of $61.9 billion.

The business consists of three pillars: software, consulting, and infrastructure. IBM offers AI and hybrid cloud services to the biggest companies in the world, and these technologies "continue to drive value creation." In 2023, IBM introduced Watson, a "comprehensive AI and data platform, built to deliver AI models and give our clients the ability to manage the entire lifecycle of AI for business, including the training, tuning, deployment, and ongoing governance of those models."

IBM, however, has been developing AI since the 1950s. In the 1980s, they introduced a supercomputer, named Deep Blue in 1989, which finally defeated world chess champion Garry Kasparov in 1997. In 2011, IBM introduced a supercomputer that could answer questions raised in natural languages. It was first used on the popular American quiz show Jeopardy and was won by Watson, as the machine was called, named after the first president of IBM. In the 2010s, developments in AI moved faster and faster, and Watson was trained for new challenges, one of which was fashion forecasting.

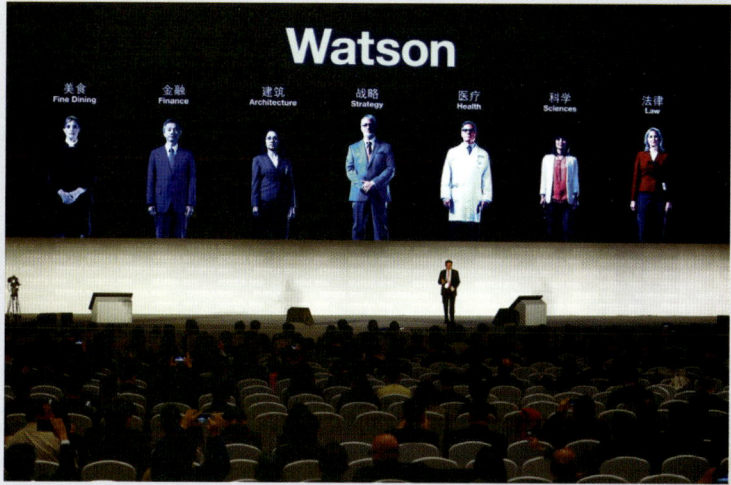

Figure 11.2 A speech about IBM Watson is delivered during the Release Ceremony for World Leading Internet Scientific and Technological Achievements as part of the third World Internet Conference (WIC) at Wuzhen Internet International Conference and Exhibition Center on November 16, 2016 in Jiaxing, Zhejiang Province of China.
Source: Photo by Visual China Group via Getty Images/Visual China Group via Getty Images.

The fashion industry, one of the largest and most polluting industries in the world, wastes huge amounts of unsold clothing and is in dire need of more accurate forecasting. Therefore, IBM began several collaborations with big retail brands. One example is its partnership with Tommy Hilfiger and the Fashion Institute of Technology (FIT) in New York in 2018 to identify future fashion trends better and improve its designs. FIT students were given access to IBM's AI capabilities and Tommy Hilfiger's stock of product images, which were then combined with massive amounts of available runaway images and fabric sites. From there, they could distillate the company's "DNA" regarding silhouettes, colors, and patterns and create new designs. Thanks to AI, it was possible to quickly analyze this large database of both textual and visual data, which would have been nigh impossible for an individual designer or even a design team to do.

Another example is IBM's collaboration with Bestseller, a Danish family-owned fashion retailer, which operates more than 9,000 shops worldwide and more than twenty brands, including Jack & Jones, Only, and Vera Moda. The company concept is based on quality clothes at affordable prices. In 2020, Bestseller India began collaborating with IBM to launch an AI project called Fabric.ai to make more accurate trend forecasts and reduce unsold apparel stock. In 2023, Bestseller announced a global corporate digital transformation based on IBM's Watson technology and cloud services.

Sources: IBM, "2023 IBM Annual Report," https://www.ibm.com/annualreport/ (accessed August 2, 2004); Rachel Arthur, "Artificial Intelligence Empowers Designers In IBM, Tommy Hilfiger And FIT Collaboration" https://www.forbes.com/sites/rachelarthur/2018/01/15/ai-ibm-tommy-hilfiger/ (accessed August 2, 2024); IBM, "Bestseller and IBM Garage bring Sustainable Fashion Forward with Fashion.ai," https://www.ibm.com/blog/bestseller-and-ibm-garage-bring-sustainable-fashion-forward-with-fashion-ai/ (accessed August 2, 2024); Ben Wubs, "US Multinationals in the Netherlands – Three Cases: IBM, Dow Chemical, and Sara Lee," in *Four Centuries of Dutch-American Relations 1609-2009*, eds Hans Krabbendam, Cornelis A. van Minnen, Gilles Scott-Smith (Boom Amsterdam and State University of New York Press Albany, New York 2009): 785–796.

E-commerce, fast fashion, and the destruction of traditional retail

The fast-fashion model is based on the idea that fashion constantly changes and is a move away from the idea of two (sometimes four) collections presented each year, as Paris had imposed since the late nineteenth century. New information technology and the control of global production networks have made it possible to know nearly instantly what consumers want and will eventually buy. Companies like Inditex (Spain), H&M (Sweden), and Fast Retailing (Japan) have become the most competitive actors in this sector (see Chapter 9). They own a dense network of mono-brand stores globally, from where they gather instant information about the preferences of consumers.

The rise of these mono-brand stores has put a heavy burden on traditional department stores, which have always strongly focused on fashion. For more than a hundred years, the department store had been a successful concept in the United States, Europe, and Asia, but department stores, especially in the mid-range segment, are losing market share to these new mono-brand stores. Business historian Ralf Banken clearly shows that German department stores, which traditionally served the middle segment, were already losing market share and turnover in the late 1970s and were losing ground in two directions: in the higher segment to the more luxurious mono-brand stores and in the lower segment to the discounters. According to Ralf Banken, department stores, such as Herti, Karstadt, and Kaufhof, focused for too long on offering a complete range and on the shopping experience.[25] Although the German experience cannot be generalized, an international trend was noticeable at the end of the twentieth century despite differences in the speed of national trends.[26] Full-fledged department stores in the mid-market segment were making losses or going bankrupt. Since the 1990s, they have been losing ground rapidly to fast-fashion chains like H&M, Zara, and Uniqlo.[27] High-end department stores, however, have benefited since the 1990s from the success of the luxury industry, with luxury fashion playing a major role in it from the 2000s.[28] Fierce competition for the department stores and the mono-brand stores of the fast-fashion conglomerates came nonetheless from a completely different angle—the rapidly developing online retail business. In the early days of e-commerce, fashion did not play a role at all.

Jeff Bezos, for example, started Amazon, an online bookstore, in 1994. E-bay, an online auction platform, was set up a year later. The biggest problems, next to technical ones, were consumer trust and online payments. After eBay acquired PayPal, the latter problem was partly solved.[29] Nike began to invest in online marketing and opened an e-commerce platform in 1999 and was one of the first movers in online fashion retail.[30] In general, the fashion industry was later than other sectors to introduce e-commerce because clothing is a personal item that people want to feel, try on, and see before they buy it. It was also difficult to replicate a live in-store experience online,[31] which was why fast-fashion brands like H&M, Zara, and Uniqlo were certainly not pioneers in e-commerce. On the contrary, in the 2000s, they continued their successful strategy and opened one store after another all over the world. Only in the 2010s did they adjust that strategy and start to focus more on online sales when the competition from fashion platforms like ASOS and Zalando, and later Shein, became fiercer.[32]

ASOS was one of the first movers in online-only fashion retail. Established by Nick Robertson and Quentin Griffiths in London in 2000, it was listed one year later on the London Stock Exchange as ASOS Plc.[33] The basic idea of the company was to offer glamorous clothes "as seen on screen" (ASOS) for an affordable price.[34] In 2004, ASOS launched its first own label and, in due course, would create seven own brands, which by 2018 were generating 40 percent of total revenue. In 2010, the online retailer expanded overseas to the United States, the EU, and Australia, where it opened offices. By 2015, it had 4,000 staff,

Figure 11.3 Logistic distribution center of the Zara Company. Sabon. Arteixo. la Coruna. The Spanish Fashion Company, INDITEX, owned by Amancio Ortega.
Source: Photo by Xurxo Lobato/Cover/Getty Images.

who worked in the headquarters in London and warehouses in Barnsley, Berlin, and Atlanta. By the 2000s, ASOS had become the UK's largest online retailer and one of the biggest e-commerce platforms in the world. The main advantages that ASOS offered to the online consumer were free shipping and returns. In this way, it wanted to eliminate the biggest disadvantages for the online fashion consumer: the delivery time and the risk that the garment would not fit.[35] ASOS now offers 850 different brands of women's and men's clothing, accessories, and beauty products, primarily targeting young adults (20+).[36] In 2023, ASOS had 23.3 million active customers on its platform and a total revenue of £3.5 billion.[37]

Meanwhile, consumers and governments have become more critical of the polluting effects of online fashion deliveries and returns, putting further pressure on the fast-fashion model.[38] In 2022, the UK government (Competition and Markets Authority) launched an investigation into British online fashion retailers ASOS and Boohoo and British fast-fashion brand George at Asda to "scrutinize their 'green' claims."[39] Two years later, in 2024, all three companies signed a formal agreement with the UK government "to change the way they display, describe, and promote their green credentials, meaning millions of customers can expect to see clear and accurate green claims."[40]

Zalando (see Box 11.2) and Shein were both founded in 2008 in Germany and China, respectively. Shein was set up in Nanjing by search engine specialist Chris Xu (Xu Yangtian). Originally, the company was called ZZKKO and sold wedding dresses online. In 2011, the online business was registered as SheInside.com and had also begun to sell womenswear worldwide. The fashion items were sourced at the wholesale clothing market in Guangzhou.[41] In 2012, the company diversified into other products like beauty products, footwear, handbags, and jewelry. It also entered markets in Europe and launched a new website, which was advertised on social media platforms like Facebook and Instagram and promoted by international fashion bloggers. The fast international expansion was financed via Chinese "top institutional investors."[42] In 2014, the Chinese e-commerce platform Romwe was acquired, which further diversified the product offerings and directly linked the company to Chinese manufacturers. A year later, the name was simplified for internet search engines to Shein. In addition, Shein acquired the California-based women's online fashion store MakeMeChic, which improved its market position in the United States. Since then, it has expanded aggressively to almost every country in the world, targeting the digitally literate Generation Z (born in the late 1990s).[43] In 2022, it became the largest (online) fashion retailer in the world.[44]

Shein's strategy is based on low-cost manufacturing, improved online technology, and localization. While all fast-fashion companies are based on cheap production and outsourcing to low-wage countries, Shein undercuts the retail prices of Inditex and H&M and has even been called the "low edition ZARA." It also claims to be faster than other fast-fashion companies (ultra-fast fashion).[45] Most of the production takes place in China. Moreover, as an online retailer, it has no physical stores like the other fast-fashion companies, which makes a huge cost difference. In addition, Shein has developed its own tracking system to predict the next style and color and become a great user of Google Trends Finder. About 75 million users of its app and websites are provided with useful data from their algorithms, helping them plan the latest trends and production. Furthermore, it extensively uses social media like TikTok, Facebook, Instagram, and Google and its own platform to advertise the brand. Shein is also better able than other fast-fashion retailers to adapt to local markets. Its apps and websites are aimed at local consumers. Its distribution centers are spread across the world, with the lion's share in China, of course, but also logistic warehousing centers in the United States, the Middle East, and Europe.[46]

During the Covid-19 crisis, due to lockdowns and social distancing, Shein's global sales increased 44 percent from $15.7 billion in 2021 to $22.7 billion. In the same period, the company's value doubled from $15 billion to $30 billion. Meanwhile, Shein moved its headquarters from Guangzhou to Singapore in 2022.[47] However, the company has increasingly come under scrutiny, especially since it was revealed that it has been quietly working on an IPO on Wall Street in 2024.[48] Criticism in the media varies from Shein's return rate being too high to its creation of huge pollution concerns as a result of low-quality clothing. It also uses toxic fabrics and there are large quantities of unsold products in its warehouses. Moreover, the labor rights of Shein's subcontractors in China are very poor, including the use of Uygur's forced labor, and there are severe data security problems with its websites and apps.[49] The poor working conditions in the contractors' factories have also been in the news in recent years.

Figure 11.4 Shein pop-up store at the Square One Shopping Centre, December 2023 in Mississauga. Source: Raysonho @ Open Grid Scheduler / Scalable Grid Engine.

Despite all these shortcomings, the company still grows, particularly in overseas markets. The United States, Europe, and the Middle East account for more than 70 percent of its revenue. In the United States, it is the second-largest retail platform after Amazon.[50] In 2022, the company launched evoluSHEIN, a "strategy for delivering positive impact across key social, environmental and governance issues, and making continuous improvements across its value chain."[51] Shein is clearly trying to adapt to the demands of Western financial markets. Currently, Shein has serious plans to launch the largest-ever IPO on the London Stock Exchange in 2025, with a total valuation of $50 billion, after encountering serious problems with its planned IPO in New York.[52]

Mediatization, bloggers, and influencers

The mass media has always played an important role in the dissemination of fashion through magazines, newspapers, radio, film, and television. All these different media have influenced the image that consumers have of fashion and their buying behavior accordingly. At the end of the twentieth century, however, we saw the emergence of a new medium: the internet. This new technology changed both how fashion was produced and consumed, and how fashion would be communicated. Agnes Rocamora called this the mediatization of fashion.[53] According to Rocamora:

> Investigating the mediatization of fashion, then, means looking at the ways fashion practices have adapted to, and been transformed by, the media. It does not mean focusing on the media themselves, but on the ways people and institutions in the field of fashion have changed their practices for and with the media.[54]

As a fashion researcher, she is interested in how the fashion industry has adapted to the ways communication has been transformed in the digital age. She focuses on three parts of the fashion industry: fashion shows, design, and retail.

Fashion shows were originally organized for elite customers in the nineteenth century but became commercial events during the twentieth century where professionals of the fashion industry, including brands, buyers, journalists, designers, forecasters, and celebrities, met twice a year. In the digital age, shows during fashion weeks became media spectacles with photos, videos, and livestreams for global audiences via different digital platforms like Facebook, Twitter, YouTube, and Instagram, with fashion bloggers in the front row, next to traditional fashion journalists.[55] Due to the Covid-19 crisis, famous brands at fashion weeks were forced to move their events online. Fashion weeks in London, New York, Paris, and Milan, among others, switched entirely to livestreams for a global audience in 2022.[56] This mediatization, according to Rocamora, has also led to clothes being designed more for the picture and video than the visual experience and touch of the fashion item:

> The ultimate audience is those people [. . .] whose understanding of designer fashion, luxury and style has been shaped not by seeing couture craftsmanship up close but by

the images of celebrities on the red carpet, the postings of celebrities on Instagram, the website advertising of luxury brands, the hyper-reality of the Kardashians [. . .][57]

The mediatization of fashion also influences how fashion is marketed. In the former section, we discussed the rise of online-only fast-fashion platforms, but also high-end brands and offline stores have adapted to the new reality. When Burberry opened its flagship store in Regent Street in London in 2012, it designed how one would navigate a website. Throughout the shop, you could find touch screens. You could collect the items you bought in the store or just order them online in the shop. In fact, a kind of hybrid reality was created in which online and offline experiences were blurred.[58] Many brands have followed the example of Burberry or come up with other innovative solutions, but clearly digitalization has changed consumers' perception of fashion and has fundamentally changed the way it is sold and bought.

The rise and fall of blogs played a revolutionary role in changing the way fashion was viewed in the 2000s. Marco Pedroni, based on an extensive list of interviews with bloggers, identifies four stages in the history of blogs.[59] In the first stage, from 2000 to 2005, fashion blogs started popping up. There was still a reasonable number of amateur bloggers who got their own sub-genre with independent voices. Most bloggers claimed they were giving a personal view of fashion and had no commercial interest in the fashion industry. A famous example is the street-style blog, the Sartorialist, launched by Scott Schumann in 2005.

During the second stage, in the second half of the 2000s, more and more blogs emerged, which became more professional as they started collaborating with brands and gained some recognition in the fashion industry. Bloggers were increasingly invited to catwalks. In 2010, Bryanboy and Tommy Ton, for example, were invited to sit in the front row next to Anna Wintour (Condé Nast) and Susy Menkes (Vogue), among other famous and established journalists at the Dolce & Gabbana show in the Milan Fashion Week.[60]

During the third stage (2010–2015), bloggers still struggled for legitimacy; however, they had overall gained a more institutionalized role within the fashion industry. Brands began to realize that bloggers could play a beneficial role in their marketing strategy. Some blogs were very successful commercially. Although many blogs still pretended to be independent, it was clear who was paying the bills. Famous bloggers like Chiara Ferragni ("The Blonde Salad") and Nicole Warne ("Gary Pepper") even started their own fashion businesses. The former launched her own shoe brand using her name, and the latter launched an online vintage clothing platform ("Gary Pepper Girl").[61]

The fourth stage is when Instagram became popular among bloggers. In 2012, Instagram had been acquired by Facebook (now Meta Platforms, Inc.), and the ever-adapting app had rapidly developed into a user-friendly, multi-media platform. Bloggers shifted from their own blogs to Instagram. In the later part of the 2010s, Instagram had developed into the most important media tool for fashion influencers.[62] Blogs did not disappear completely, and TikTok became a competitor, particularly for younger consumers. However, Instagram has become the most influential platform for the fashion industry so far, with the number of followers exceeding anything that has existed in fashion media. Nicole Warne, for example, has 2.3 million followers on Instagram[63] and is described as an "Australian fashion blogger, brand consultant, and social media guru"[64]—a job description unthinkable twenty years ago.

The Fourth Industrial Revolution in fashion

Textiles and garments played an indispensable role during the first, second, and third industrial revolutions. During the First Industrial Revolution, from the late eighteenth century, mechanized spinning and weaving of textiles in factories, especially cotton and wool, became a dynamic force in capitalism.

During the Second Industrial Revolution, in the second half of the nineteenth and early twentieth centuries, electricity and chemistry became drivers of change in textile and garment production. The introduction of the sewing machine would have been impossible without electricity, and the synthetic turn created artificial dyes and fibers, which changed the textile and fashion industries forever.

The Third Industrial Revolution, also called the Digital Revolution, began after the Second World War with the advent of mainframe computers and, later, personal computers in the late 1970s, and eventually the internet in 1991. The fashion industry has been a global industry since the nineteenth century, as we have shown in this book. However, the Digital Revolution made the rise of genuine global production networks possible, outsourcing labor-intensive parts of the supply chain to low-cost countries and keeping design, marketing, and logistics in the developed world.

Despite all the technological innovations and digital tools, the garment and fashion industries still use a nineteenth-century invention: the sewing machine. Garment production still needs human hands as it is technically complicated. More importantly, it is too expensive to produce garments with robots. The reason it was easy to outsource garment manufacturing from Europe and North America to the Global South (East) was the low investment cost. To start a garment factory, you only needed a space, sewing machines, and lots of cheap labor. At the same time, the reason there is very little room for innovation in this industry is the existence of cheap labor around the globe. Certain parts of the supply chain can be automatized and robotized—for example, spinning and weaving—but sewing is much more complicated and would make the process much more capital intensive. However, the key elements of the next technological revolution, which we are in now, are robotics and intelligent manufacturing.

The Fourth Industrial Revolution (Industry 4.0 or I4.0) is based on the Digital Revolution. In the 2010s, this term became a buzzword among economists, management scholars, and industry practitioners. There are many definitions, and it is hard to draw the line between the third and fourth industrial revolutions. However, it is obvious that industrial production is changing rapidly on a global scale because of major technological innovations. Suaad Jassem and Mohammad Rezaur Razzak define Industry 4.0 as follows:

> The basic idea behind I4.0 is the application of advanced process management especially in manufacturing driven by emergent technologies such as digitalization, robotics, artificial intelligence, internet of things, additive manufacturing, etc.; completely transforming how products are made.[65]

What we have shown in this book, however, is the way it is transforming the fashion industry now and how new technologies such as robotics, augmented and virtual reality, and artificial intelligence are being applied to the industry. What are the main issues for the fashion industry that can be solved with these new technologies?[66] The rise of fast-fashion companies like Inditex, H&M, and Shein, and their increasing speed and turnover, has made the industry barely sustainable on a global scale, as production and consumption are closely linked through global production networks. Moreover, it is very hard to forecast demand in the fashion industry; the supply-push strategy constantly leads to overstocking. The discrepancy between estimated supply and demand forces the retail sector to continually sell out clothing. According to Ellie Jin Byoungho and Daeun Chloe Shin, the forecast error in fashion production is between 40 and 100 percent.[67] This is bad for profitability but especially for the environment. New technologies of Industry 4.0 could help to match supply and demand much better, one of which is AI. Leanne Luce defines it as:

> computer science that looks at the logic behind human intelligence. The field seeks ways to understand how we think and to re-create this intelligence in machines. Because of its nature, AI extends across human activities, making it relevant in different ways to every industry. (. . .) The intersection of fashion and AI is a rich and expansive space that is just beginning to be explored.[68]

AI is closely related to machine learning, which is the most relevant part of AI for the fashion industry. The aim of machine learning is to automate processes and to "discover complex patterns that humans cannot interpret on their own."[69] AI is now more and more applied by brands and retail platforms and can also help to make more personalized decisions about sizes and consumer preferences and predict future styles. Fashion forecasting increasingly uses real-time big data and algorithms to make predictions and business decisions, which potentially can reduce overstocking. Google and IBM provide programs for the industry to make predictions, which has already been mentioned. However, there are also more specialized US companies—like True Fit, Stich Fix, and Anomoli—using AI to personalize the online customer experience and provide their services to large brands or directly to consumers. Another example is the online menswear company Indochino, the fastest-growing Canadian online retailer in 2019, which offers personalized, custom-made menswear for international clients.[70]

Other technologies that can potentially reduce waste are 3D printing and 3D knitting. Until now, 3D printing technology has been used to produce athletic shoes. 3D printers use powder that is slowly built into a designed shoe layer-by-layer.[71] As it is based on plastics, it is rarely used for apparel manufacturing. Nike and adidas are using 3D printing technology to produce special sports shoes. This has reduced the production time of models extensively. 3D knitting, however, is used to produce garments and has the great advantage of being producible in small batches or even on demand, which reduces waste and excessive stock. A B2B example is Tailored Industries in New York, which produces sweaters, among other items, for small- and medium-sized retailers. However, there are a growing number of B2C examples where consumers can directly order knitted clothes on demand.[72] Knitting is even seen as representing a move toward more sustainable, environmentally friendly, and circular fashion because it produces much less waste.[73]

Robotics in the fashion industry is the last example of the future of fashion and the application of Industry 4.0 technologies. They are already applied but usually at the initial stages. Combined with other AI technologies, robotics can create data-driven smart factories that produce garments on demand and thus reduce waste. Robots also reduce labor costs as they can work more efficiently. In 2017, the Chinese company Tianyuan Garments, for example, opened a factory in Arkansas in the United States with 330 "sewbots" that produce T-shirts for brands like adidas, Armani, and Reebok. Each robot can produce a T-shirt within twenty-six seconds. The robots are supplied by the American

Figure 11.5 Computerized Flat Knitting Machine (Jacquard Machine), Japan.
Source: Asivechowdhury via Wikimedia Commons.

Figure 11.6 Paris—3D Printed Stilettos for Dyson Showroom Exhibition. Jiri Evenhuis via Wikimedia Commons.

company SoftWear Automation, which was originally funded by the Pentagon (DARPA) because the American government wanted to bring back home the production of uniforms, which had been outsourced to China and Vietnam.[74] At the moment, however, using sewing robots is still in the infancy phase because even when combined with AI, they still have problems dealing with flexible materials like fabrics. Plastics, sometimes used for haute couture creations but mostly for sneakers, are a much more suitable material for robotics. In 2016 and 2017, adidas opened fully automated sneaker factories in Germany and the United States. The factories combined robotics, 3D knitting, 3D printing, and AI to design the shoes. The factories were, however, closed as they were not competitive. The technology is now applied in factories in Asia, where they can use economies of scale.[75]

In this section, we have only been able to give a few examples of the application of these new technologies. Moreover, these examples are strongly focused on environmental sustainability and the positive effects of these applications. As with any technology, there are certainly also negative effects. The clothing and textile industry has been one of the largest employers since the nineteenth century. According to a 2019 report by the International Labour Organization (ILO), around 60 million workers in the textile, garment, leather, and footwear industries, especially in developing countries, are at high risk of losing their jobs due to automation and digitalization.[76] Employment in the fashion industry has largely shifted to the Global South over the past fifty years. Digitalization and the adoption of Industry 4.0 technologies only accelerated during the Covid-19 crisis, with employment in these sectors, particularly in the Global South, under even greater pressure than five years ago.

Figure 11.7 Young girls working in a sweatshop in Bangladesh, November 18, 2015. Solidarity Center via Flickr.

Source: Reproduced under a CC BY 2.0 license.

Conclusion

In the last twenty-five years, digitalization and the introduction of Industry 4.0 technologies have profoundly changed the global production networks of the fashion industry. They have altered the division of labor globally. Outsourcing of textile and apparel manufacturing was done on another level, based on global connections via the internet. However, they have not only created global production networks but also, for example, around 2,000 online fashion forecasting platforms. The birth of WGSN coincided with the digital transformation of society. The nature of fashion and color forecasting altered from a small intermediary business (often located in Paris or Milan) to part of larger business groups in London or New York, based more on big data than human intuition. Also, online-only retail platforms became possible after 2000 because of high-speed internet and the application of AI technologies. Companies like ASOS, Zalando, and Shein began to compete with the older fast-fashion companies like H&M, Inditex, and Fast Retailing, which were also forced in the 2010s to adapt their original strategy and pursue business expansion via offline shops. They also applied digital strategies and included AI technologies in their business models. Luxury fashion companies needed to adapt to this new reality as well. As we are still amid the Fourth Industrial Revolution, we cannot forecast all the social and economic consequences of applying these new technologies globally. As innovation has been the main driver for change in the fashion industry, will these latest innovations make the fashion industry more sustainable and circular, or will capitalism's favorite child focus on the profits and leave the social consequences to society? It is, however, crystal clear that these new technologies have already profoundly changed the way humanity makes, communicates, designs, understands, sells, and consumes fashion.

Box 11.2 Zalando: Europe's leading online fashion platform

Zalando is a German-based e-commerce company that started in 2008 and expanded rapidly to other European countries. The platform gives access to a seemingly unlimited selection of clothing, shoes, perfume, and jewelry in just a few clicks. The turnover figures show explosive growth, from €150 million in 2010 to €10.4 billion in 2022. This firm has become Europe's leading online fashion platform, with annual revenue growth rates of 24 percent, on average, between 2014 and 2019, and an even steeper increase caused by the Covid-19 pandemic. Zalando was founded in a Berlin living room only a few days before the financial crisis in 2008. Offering free delivery and a 100-day right of return was celebrated by their customers. By 2010, Zalando had expanded to Austria, Switzerland, and the Netherlands. Today, the company is active in twenty-five European markets, connecting all major players in the fashion industry, including customers, retailers, brands, stylists, factories, and advertisers.

Even though the fashion industry was comparatively slow to adopt e-commerce, Zalando created an innovative business model. Through chatbots that respond to specific requests on their website or a mobile app, Zalando can offer a personalized customer experience, imitating the interaction with the clothing and staff in the store. Using the consumer's digital footprint, Zalando has been able to develop big data capability to mine customer preference data. Thus, by analyzing customers' behavior on the screen and interacting with them, the platform can survey consumer preferences to

Figure 11.8 Picture taken on December 12, 2012 shows employees of the internet retail company Zalando working at a logistics center in Erfurt, Eastern Germany. Zalando, is facing criticism after the broadcast of a television documentary in Germany denouncing working conditions in one of its logistics centers.

Source: Photo by MARTIN SCHUTT/DPA/AFP via Getty Images.

improve the shopping experience. Through the detailed information on each customer, Zalando distributes personalized offers and messages about their favorite brands. Therefore, the e-commerce platforms have significant marketing capabilities, which are further enhanced by social media influencers. They not only advertise for Zalando, but their channels also generate a network effect of increased demand within the digital community. Zalando has responded to the increased demand by investing in digital technologies to shorten the marketing time. Speed and scale are essential to fashion e-commerce platforms. The rapid response to new trends and adaptation of GenZ consumer needs, as well as at the large-scale e-commerce platforms, invest and create output, making it a highly dynamic industry.

This trend has significantly impacted the fashion industry. In 2022, an average of 35 percent of a company's global revenue was digitized, such as supply chain automation, platforms for customer engagement, or virtual products. E-commerce helped minimize the inventory and lower risks, simultaneously building brand loyalty. Due to the fast-growing number of platforms and offers—many fashion consumers compare multiple channels through which they access a brand prior to their purchase—a highly competitive market environment was created. This led to even more and faster innovations in the sector. Moreover, e-commerce enabled luxury fashion to be widely accessible while allowing the brands to obtain wider audiences and a larger market share. The direct contact between the online shopper and the fashion company facilitated by the e-commerce platforms has benefited brand recognition, its image, and its innovative capabilities. Digital innovations like e-commerce have profoundly changed the fashion industry in all its facets, and the end of this revolution is not yet in sight.

Sources: Laura Macchion et al., "International E-Commerce for Fashion Products: What Is the Relationship with Performance?" *International Journal of Retail & Distribution Management* 45, no. 9 (1 January 2017): 1011–31; Katarzyna Bilińska-Reformat and Anna Dewalska-Opitek, "E-Commerce as the Predominant Business Model of Fast Fashion Retailers in the Era of Global Covid-19 Pandemics,"¹ *Procedia Computer Science* 192 (1 October 2021): 2479–2490; Zalando, "Our History: From Start-Up to Grown-Up," https://corporate.zalando.com/en/about-us/our-history (accessed November 5, 2024).

Conclusion

> Hence the widespread desire of entrepreneurs to at least stay up to date, to always have the latest sample collections and the latest templates. This explains the generalization of fashion. And insofar as a whole category of businesses must aim to surpass the above "minimum" and to persuade customers to buy from them by offering attractive new products, capitalist competition creates the second tendency of modern fashion: the tendency towards rapid change.[1]

According to Werner Sombart, with whom we started this book, one of the defining elements (tendencies) of fashion—namely, constant change—arises not so much in the minds of consumers but from the need for entrepreneurs and businesses to keep up with and offer the latest fashion trends. However, not only do the trends constantly change, but the global production networks or supply chains change in form and direction. The fashion industry—consisting of fiber producers, fabric and clothing manufacturers, fashion fairs and shows, fashion journals, designers, retailers, etc.—has had to adapt to these constantly changing conditions or perish.

This book has focused on the role entrepreneurs and corporations have played in the long-term evolution of the fashion industry. Many studies have been published on costume, social, and cultural history; however, the contribution of businesses has been under-researched until now, particularly from a global perspective. One of the key questions we ask in this book is what the main drivers of these changes are. We certainly do not deny that technology is an important one, but we also observed others.

Since the beginning of the First Industrial Revolution, textile and clothing supply chains have always been global, and the production networks of the fashion industry were connected. The English cotton factories were sourced from American raw cotton. The English Industrial Revolution was not only based on capital, technology, and cheap labor but also on slave labor and a plantation economy, which were again financed via capital markets in Europe. These global connections go further back than the nineteenth century, and cotton production was not something practiced in the West. For a long time, it was concentrated in the East, and printed cotton was exported to the West. But by the mid-nineteenth century, the massive increase in the scale and scope of cotton production in Britain, and later in Continental Europe and the United States, changed the direction of global supply chains for more than a century in favor of the West.[2] The increase in cotton fabric production was a result of the introduction of mechanical spinning, power looms, and factory production. The introduction of the sewing machine, first in the United States and later in Britain and Continental Europe, was another giant technological leap in clothing production and market domination by Western manufacturers.

The first country in Asia to follow the path of the Industrial Revolution was Japan. The country was so successful that by the 1930s, Japanese power looms outproduced British cotton manufacturers, and the American silk industry had become largely dependent on Japanese raw silk exports. During the 1980s, other Asian countries, particularly China, South Korea, and India, would follow, eventually outproducing Europe, the United States, and Japan, which, for the greater part, outsourced fiber, fabric, and clothing manufacturing to these countries. Rising factor costs, particularly labor costs per worker, forced the industry to relocate manufacturing or completely outsource clothing, fabric, and fiber production.

Next to all these changes, continuity matters in the global textile and fashion industries since the 1850s. The sewing machine is still the basis of fashion and apparel manufacturing. Therefore, the industry is still labor-intensive, which means it is prone to relocation to where labor can be hired at the lowest price. Other parts of the industry, such as the production of synthetic fibers, are capital intensive and, therefore, less likely to move to locations with low labor costs. However, the synthetic fiber industry has also moved to Asia in the wake of the production locations for clothing manufacturing.

Distribution, design, and sales for a long time were still in the hands of Western companies, which targeted markets in developed countries. However, global markets have changed rapidly since the 1980s. First, Japan evolved from a low-labor-cost manufacturing base into a rich market for luxury goods, leading to the rise of luxury fashion conglomerates in France, Italy, and Switzerland. Then, since the 2000s, China has taken over Japan's position and, after two decades of unprecedented growth, has become the main market for high-end luxury brands. China has also developed into the main production location for global fashion and no longer only for Western companies. It has begun to develop its own fashion companies and brands in different segments of the markets. Recently, Shein has become a serious competitor of, for example, fast-fashion companies H&M and Inditex. This Chinese ultra-fast fashion company can produce faster and cheaper garments than European retail multinationals and can better tap into the new possibilities of AI to reach consumers around the world. Fast Retailing (Uniqlo) is an exceptional Japanese fast-fashion company and a brand that operates in global markets.

Capital and capital markets have always played an important role in the rise of the global fashion industry. Although the fashion industry consisted of both small workshops and medium-sized studios, it required huge capital investment to purchase looms, factory buildings, spinning mills, and chemical plants for artificial dyes and synthetic fibers. It also required large investments in the commodity markets to purchase raw materials such as cotton, wool, and silk. As companies in the West increasingly focused on branding, marketing, and design, capital markets were tapped to finance international expansion. Getting listed on stock exchanges in New York, Paris, or Tokyo was often a major step in the development of fashion companies. Nike and adidas are important examples of companies able to expand internationally thanks to enormous capital injections. These sports brands are now among the largest fashion companies in the world. Another recent example of a company that owes its growth largely to the capital markets is LVMH. The conglomerate has grown into the largest luxury company, in which high-end fashion plays an important role as well. Its founder, Bernard Arnault, is now among the richest people on Earth. The founders of Inditex, Amancio Ortega Gaona, and Fast Retailing, Tadashi Yanai, can also join this club.

Governments have also played a significant role in the development of a global fashion industry, sometimes in a supporting role, sometimes in their conspicuous absence. In the case of the United States, the emerging industry was protected by high import duties in the nineteenth and early twentieth centuries. Even imports of French couture were subject to high import duties. In Japan, the silk industry was supported by various government agencies and by encouraging a scientific approach to silk production. This enabled Japan to surpass China in the global silk market before the Second World War. Nazi Germany and Fascist Italy endeavored to create a national fashion and, as part of autarchy policy, stimulated the production of artificial fibers. Directly after the liberation, haute couture was protected by French law, and a list of haute couture houses had to be submitted to the Ministry of Industry every year. Furthermore, during the 1950s, the French state subsidized haute couture to promote French exports generally, including the French ready-to-wear industry, and gave the industry serious tax exemptions.[3] Yet, twenty years later, European governments, particularly German, French, and British, did not resort to protectionism when manufacturers began to outsource production and large retailers bought clothes outside Europe. This led to mass unemployment, mainly of female workers, in certain textile regions. Other industries, such as shipbuilding, automotive, and electronics, were protected during this period. Apparently, the textile and fashion industries were not considered to be among the sectors with a future. The same thing happened in the United States, where a new company like Nike didn't have a single local factory from the start. "Nikification" even became a term in economics, where a multinational company outsourced all production processes to low-wage countries and kept only design, marketing, and other essential business processes in the home country. During the 1980s, neo-liberal governments, led by the US government, did nothing to counter this. On the contrary, it was seen as a way for companies to reduce costs and increase their profitability and shareholders' value.

Quite recently, the rise of the fast-fashion industry is often presented as the cause of ecological disaster. The global production fashion network has created pollution on a massive scale because of overproduction, overconsumption, and out-of-control transport flows. Fast fashion has become one of the most polluting industries in the world and a system hard to change despite good intentions. It is the result of a long-term evolution of a global fashion system, but the question is where and when the problem started.

The previous chapters have shown that since the middle of the nineteenth century, textile and fashion production became increasingly integrated. Although the flows of goods went in different directions and the supply chains were structured differently from how they are nowadays, the movement of raw materials and clothing on a global scale did not get going until the second half of the nineteenth century. This movement was part of the industrialization of the West and the colonization of much of Africa and Asia. The production and transport of these flows of goods were probably just as polluting then as they are now, although the quality was usually better and significantly less waste was produced.

And with that, we immediately encounter several problems with the current fashion industry. Too much poor quality is consumed at the expense of enormous amounts of raw materials, energy, and fertile land (for cotton production, for example). In addition, since the Second Industrial Revolution, all kinds of synthetic products, such as artificial dyes, rayon, and nylon, have played an increasingly important role in clothing and fashion production. At the end of the twentieth century, man-made fibers overtook natural fibers in terms of share in total textile and fiber production. Research into the damage that microfibers cause to the environment, animals, and humans is still in its infancy. While the production of natural fibers such as cotton and wool also cause significant environmental destruction, microplastics, largely from washing clothes, are now being found in ecosystems around the world. Although the global fashion industry has been a highly polluting industry for centuries, the general awareness of its unsustainable practices has increased dramatically in recent decades. Fashion brands around the world are, therefore, forced to take sustainability more seriously today. However, this does not always lead to more sustainable production methods; unfortunately, greenwashing is often seen as an alternative marketing tool.

Digitalization has changed the speed of the fashion industry tremendously, but not the fact that it is still largely based on cheap labor in low-cost countries. Despite all the new technologies, clothes are still made mostly by female workers using sewing machines in small workshops or big factories. However, digitalization has changed the global division of labor and the structure of global production networks. It has become even easier for firms in the West to order clothes in the East that were designed in the West. Marketing and sales are also done more and more online, and the nature of fashion forecasting has completely changed from small- and medium-sized businesses in Paris and Milan to much bigger online companies in London and New York serving global players in Shanghai, for example. Its methodology is increasingly based on big data instead of human intuition.

The structure of fashion retail has also changed profoundly because of the rise of e-commerce, which only became possible after the introduction of high-speed internet in the 2000s. The online fashion platforms ASOS, Zalando, and Shein have seriously started to compete with fast-fashion companies like H&M, Inditex, and Fast Retailing, their success based on the global expansion of mono-brand stores. These retail platforms apply AI technology to forecast sales and consumer preferences and therefore present themselves nowadays as the solution to the environmental problems that the fashion industry itself has created. The question, however, remains: Are these online platforms the solution to or one of the major causes of the detrimental nature of the industry? Be that as it may, digitalization has profoundly changed the fashion industry in the way it designs, manufactures, communicates, and sells its products, from the lowest to the highest segments of the global market. It is impossible to forecast now what effect the introduction, for example, of 3-D printing will have on the global division of labor and production networks, and whether the West will reindustrialize as a result of the Fourth Industrial Revolution and make its own fashion again.

Fashion is an "ideology" or a "myth," according to Yuniya Kawamura, and it is a separate thing from clothing.[4] Although we agree that the high-end fashion and apparel business can be two separate worlds, we have also shown in this book how they are often linked quite closely and can thus not be studied separately. Both contain symbolic value and express the identity of the wearer. However, the businesses were often not that far apart. For example, textile tycoon and richest man in France, Marcel Boussac, bought the old couture house Gaston in 1937 and, with the young designer Christian Dior, transformed it into a new one directly after the war. Using Dior's talent and his own capital and business managers, he probably built the most successful and epic haute couture brand in the world. Interestingly, in 1984, Bernard Arnault bought the holding company Agache-Willot, which had taken over Boussac Group after it went bankrupt in 1978. A few years later, he took control of LVMH and expanded this luxury conglomerate. Dior was part of this spectacular development and was incorporated into LVMH in 2017.

In the 1980s, the former Boussac textile factories in the north of France were all closed, but haute couture was revived. LVMH was extremely successful in Japan using storytelling—"Passionate about Creativity"—and the symbolic capital France possessed in the eyes of Japanese customers. This was repeated when the Japanese market collapsed after 2000, making China, Russia, and the Middle East the main sales areas in the 2000s.

Other high-end brands from Italy, Britain, Germany, and the United States entered the highly profitable luxury fashion market. Gucci, Prada, Burberry, Hugo Boss, and DKNY were all using the same fashion reputation that Western fashion brands had built. Apparently, the West still played an important role in the global fashion industry, despite the constantly changing economic and geopolitical conditions. Fashion, which was a European or Western invention, with symbolic value, is still the basis for the domination of Western companies. This may be challenged in the future with the rise of competitors outside the West. Chinese luxury brands, for example, are growing, and they serve a huge internal market, which means they do not need to expand to the West. The rise of Chinese fashion companies is also supported by a government that leans on nationalist sentiments and increasingly sees the value of intangible capital and cultural heritage as drivers of economic growth.

Another challenge is the recent management of the diversity of European brands, which have all become global, undermining the image and symbolic capital of European fashion brands. Simultaneously, it challenges the hierarchy of the global fashion system, reminding us that the modern fashion industry has been in a constant state of flux since its beginnings.

Notes

Introduction

1. Werner Sombart, "Wirthschaft und Mode: Ein Beitrag zur Theorie der modernen Bedarfsgestaltung Grenzfragen des Nerven-und Seelenlebens," in *Einzel-Darstellungen für Gebildete aller Stände. Zwölftes Heft*, eds, L. Loewenfeld and H. Kurella (Wiesbaden: J. F. Bergmann, 1902), 23.
2. Ibid.
3. Reiner Grundmann and Nico Stehr, "Why Is Werner Sombart Not Part of the Core of Classical Sociology? From Fame to (Near) Oblivion," *Journal of Classical Sociology* 1 (2001): 257–287.
4. This article was originally published in Germany in 1904 and translated into English in 1957 for publication in the United States. Georg Simmel, "Fashion," *American Journal of Sociology* 62, no. 6 (1957): 541–58.
5. Patrik Aspers and Frédéric Godart, "Sociology of Fashion: Order and Change," *Annual Review of Sociology* 39 (2013): 185.
6. Regina Lee Blaszczyk and Ben Wubs, eds, *The Fashion Forecasters: A Hidden History of Color and Trend Prediction* (London: Bloomsbury, 2018), 1–32.
7. Roland Barthes, *The Fashion System* (New York: Hill and Wang, 1967).
8. Yuniya Kawamura, *Fashion-ology: An Introduction to Fashion Studies*, 2nd ed. (London: Bloomsbury Visual Arts: 2018), 43.
9. Ibid., 50.
10. Ibid., 43.
11. Diana Crane, "Diffusion Models and Fashion: A Reassessment," *The Annals of the American Academy of Political and Social Science* 566, no. 1 (1999): 13–24.
12. Gilles Lipovetsky, *The Empire of Fashion: Dressing Modern Democracy* (Princeton: Princeton University Press, 1994), 55–64.
13. Christopher Breward and David Gilbert, eds, *Fashion's World Cities* (London: Bloomsbury, 2006), 177–233.
14. Sanjay Subrahmanyam, *Explorations in Connected History: From the Tagus to the Ganges* (Oxford: Oxford University Press, 2005), 1–16.
15. Giorgio Riello, *Cotton: The Fabric that Made the Modern World* (Cambridge: Cambridge University Press, 2013), 20–36; Chris Nierstrasz, *Rivalry for Trade in Tea and Textiles: The English and Dutch East India Companies* (1700–1800) (Basingstoke: Palgrave Macmillan, 2015), 124–189.
16. Sven Beckert, *Empire of Cotton: A Global History* (New York: Vintage Books, 2014), 98–135.
17. Lise Skov, "The Role of Trade Fairs in the Global Fashion Business," *Current Sociology*, 54, 5 (2006): 764–783; Ben Wubs and Thierry Maillet, "Building Competing Fashion Textile Fairs in Europe, 1970–2010: Première Vision (Paris) vs. Interstoff (Frankfurt)," *Journal of Macromarketing* 37, 1 (2017), 25–39.

18. Breward and Gilbert, eds, *Fashion's World Cities*, 177–233.
19. Naoíse Mac Sweeney, *The West: A New History of an Old Idea* (London: WH Allen, 2023), 1–11.
20. Nora Mareï and Michel Savy, "Global South Countries: The Dark Side of City Logistics. Dualisation vs Bipolarisation," *Transport Policy*, Volume 100 (2021): 150–160; Stewart Patrick and Alexandra Huggins, "The Term 'Global South' Is Surging: It Should Be Retired," https://carnegieendowment.org/posts/2023/08/the-term-global-south-is-surging-it-should-be-retired?lang=en (accessed October 15, 2024).
21. According to the fashion intelligence website, Fashion United, "Global Fashion Industry Statistics," https://fashionunited.com/global-fashion-industry-statistics (accessed October 21, 2024).
22. According to the consulting company, Business Research Insights, "Automative Market Report Overview," https://www.businessresearchinsights.com/market-reports/automotive-market-102183 (accessed October 21, 2024).
23. Tony Hines and Margaret Bruce, eds, *Fashion Marketing* (London: Routledge, 2007); Mike Easey, ed., *Fashion Marketing* (John Wiley & Sons, 2009); Mandy Sheridan, Christopher Moore, and Karinna Nobbs, "Fast Fashion Requires Fast Marketing: The Role of Category Management in Fast Fashion Positioning," *Journal of Fashion Marketing and Management: An International Journal* 10, no. 3 (2006): 301–315; Christopher Breward, *Fashion* (Oxford: Oxford University Press, 2003); Kawamura, *Fashion-ology*; Valerie Steele, *Paris Fashion: A Cultural History* (Oxford: Oxford University Press, 1988); Diana Crane, *Fashion and Its Social Agendas: Class, Gender, and Clothing* (Chicago: The University of Chicago Press, 2000).
24. Regina Lee Blaszczyk, ed., *Producing Fashion: Commerce, Culture, and Consumers* (Philadelphia: University of Pennsylvania Press, 2008); Regina Lee Blaszczyk, *The Color Revolution* (Cambridge, MA: MIT Press, 2012; Blaszczyk and Wubs, eds, *The Fashion Forecasters*; Wubs and Maillet, "Building Competing Fashion Textile Fairs in Europe; Elisabetta Merlo and Francesca Polese, "Turning Fashion into Business: The Emergence of Milan as an International Fashion Hub," *Business History Review* 80, no. 3 (2006): 415–447; Pierre-Yves Donzé and Rika Fujioka, "The Formation of a Technology-based Fashion System, 1945–1990: The Sources of the Lost Competitiveness of Japanese Apparel Companies," *Enterprise & Society* 22, no. 2 (2021): 438–474.
25. Véronique Pouillard, "Managing Fashion Creativity: The History of the Chambre Syndicale de la Couture Parisienne during the Interwar Period," *Investigaciones de Historia Económica-Economic History Research* 12, no. 2 (2016): 76–89; José Antonio Miranda and Alba Roldán, "Spanish Fashion without the Country-of-origin Effect," in *National Brands and Global Markets* (London: Routledge, 2023), 152–167; Sonnet Stanfill, "The Role of the Sartoria in Postwar Italy," *Journal of Modern Italian Studies* 20, no. 1 (2015): 83–91.
26. Véronique Pouillard, "Design Piracy in the Fashion Industries of Paris and New York in the Interwar Years," *Business History Review* 85, no. 2 (2011): 319–344; Véronique Pouillard, *Paris to New York: The Transatlantic Fashion Industry in the Twentieth Century* (Cambridge MA: Harvard University Press, 2021); Regina Lee Blaszczyk and Véronique Pouillard, eds, *European Fashion: The Creation of a Global Industry* (Manchester: Manchester University Press, 2018); Elisabetta Merlo, "Italian Fashion Business: Achievements and Challenges (1970s–2000s)," *Business History* 53, no. 3 (2011): 344–362; Pierre-Yves Donzé and Ben Wubs, "Storytelling and the Making of a Global Luxury Fashion Brand: Christian Dior," *International Journal of Fashion Studies* 6, no.

1 (2019): 83–102; Rika Fujioka and Jon Stobart, "Global and Local: Retail Transformation and the Department Store in Britain and Japan, 1900–1940," *Business History Review* 92, no. 2 (2018): 251–280; Roman Köster, *Hugo Boss, 1924–1945: die Geschichte einer Kleiderfabrik zwischen Weimarer Republik und 'Drittem Reich,'* vol. 23 (München: CH Beck, 2011); Mark Spoerer, *C&A: A Family Business in Germany, the Netherlands and the UK 1911–1961* (München: CH Beck, 2016); Yoko Isozaki and Pierre-Yves Donzé, "Dominance Versus Collaboration Models: French and Italian Luxury Fashion Brands in Japan," *Journal of Global Fashion Marketing* 13, no. 4 (2022): 394–408; Juxuan Zhang and Pierre-Yves Donzé, "Knowledge Upgrade in the Chinese Apparel Industry, 1980–2020," *Enterprise & Society* (2023): 1–30.

Chapter 1

1. Quoted by Andrew Gordon, *Fabricating Consumers: The Sewing Machine in Modern Japan* (Berkeley: University of California Press, 2012), 25.
2. Jennifer Craik, *Fashion: The Key Concepts* (Oxford: Berg Publishers, 2009), 19–47.
3. Linda Welters and Abby Lillethun, *Fashion History: A Global View* (London: Bloomsbury Publishing, 2018), 1–10.
4. Geoffrey Jones, *Multinationals and Global Capitalism: From the Nineteenth to the Twenty-First Century* (Oxford: Oxford University Press, 2005), 45–75; Beckert, *Empire of Cotton*, 199–241.
5. Pat Hudson, "The Limits of Wool and the Potential of Cotton in the Eighteenth and Early Nineteenth Centuries," in *The Spinning World: A Global History of Cotton Textiles, 1200–1850* (Oxford: Oxford University Press, 2009), 327–350
6. Riello, *Cotton*, 95.
7. B. R. Mitchell, *European Historical Statistics, 1750–1970* (Berlin: Springer, 1975), 427–433.
8. Beckert, *Empire of Cotton*, Illustrated edition (New York: Vintage, 2015), 104–106.
9. Ibid., 274–311.
10. Ibid., 278.
11. Nigel Hall, "Liverpool's Cotton Importers c. 1700 to 1914," *Northern History*, 54, no. 1 (January 2, 2017): 79–93; Christof Dejung, *Die Fäden des globalen Marktes: Eine Soziale- and Kulturgeschichte des Welthandels am Beispiel der Handelsfirma Gebrüder Volkart 1851–1999* (Köln: Böhlau Verlag, 2013), 47–73.
12. Ibid., 112–117.
13. Beckert, *Empire of Cotton*, 320.
14. Giovanni Federico, *An Economic History of the Silk Industry, 183–1930*, vol. 5 (Cambridge: Cambridge University Press, 2009), 3–4.
15. Richard von Glahn, *The Economic History of China: From Antiquity to the Nineteenth Century* (Cambridge: Cambridge University Press, 2016), 392–393.
16. Ibid., 398.
17. Takasaki City University of Economics, ed., *Tomioka seishijo to gunma no sanshigyo* (Tokyo: Nihon Keizai hyoronsha, 2016), 110–111.
18. Kanji Ishii, *Kindai Nihon to Igirisu shihon* (Tokyo: Tokyo University, 1984), 182–183.
19. Hiroaki Yamazaki, ed., *Nihon keieishi no kisochishiki* (Tokyo: Yuhikaku, 2004), 44–45.
20. Christopher Howe, *The Origins of Japanese Trade Supremacy* (London: Hurst & Company, 1996), 323–325.

21. Jürgen Osterhammel, *The Transformation of the World: A Global History of the Nineteenth Century* (Princeton: Princeton University Press, 2014), 719.
22. Daniel R. Headrick, *The Tentacles of Progress: Technology Transfer in the Age of Imperialism, 1850–1940* (Oxford University Press, 1988), 39.
23. Pierre-Yves Donzé and Julia Yongue, *Japanese Capitalism and Entrepreneurship: A History of Business from the Tokugawa Era to the Present* (Oxford: Oxford University Press, 2024), 57.
24. Paul Ceruzzi, "Jacquard's Web: How a Hand-loom Led to the Birth of the Information Age," *Technology and Culture* 47 (1 January 2006): 197–198.
25. Fernand Rude, *Les révoltes des canuts (1831–1834)* (Paris: La Découverte, 2020) 111.
26. D. A. Farnie, "The Textile Machine-Making Industry and the World Market, 1870–1960," *Business History*, 32.4 (1990): 150–170.
27. Janet Hunter and S. Sugiyama, "Anglo Japanese Economic Relations in Historical Perspective, 1600–2000: Trade and Industry, Finance, Technology and the Industrial Challenge," in *The History of Anglo-Japanese Relations, 1600–2000: Volume 4 Economic and Business Relations*, eds Janet E. Hunter and S. Sugiyama (London: Palgrave Macmillan UK, 2002), 1–109; Kristine Bruland, *British Technology and European Industrialization: The Norwegian Textile Industry in the Mid-Nineteenth Century* (Cambridge: Cambridge University Press, 1989); Headrick, *The Tentacles of Progress,* 361.
28. David A. Hounshell, *From the American System to Mass Production, 1800–1932: The Development of Manufacturing Technology in the United States* (Baltimore: Johns Hopkins University Press, 1984), chapter 2.
29. Ibid., 89.
30. R. B. Davies, *Peacefully Working to Conquer the World: Singer Sewing Machines in Foreign Markets* (London: Arno Press, 1976), 140.
31. Regina Lee Blaszczyk and Uwe Spiekermann, "Bright Modernity: Color, Commerce, and Consumer Culture," in *Bright Modernity: Color, Commerce, and Consumer Culture*, eds Regina Lee Blaszczyk and Uwe Spiekermann (Cham: Springer, 2017), 1.
32. Blaszczyk, *The Color Revolution*, 25–26.
33. Alexander Engel, "Coloring the World: Marketing German Dyestuffs in the Late Nineteenth and Early Twentieth Centuries," in *Bright Modernity: Color, Commerce, and Consumer Culture,* eds Regina Lee Blaszczyk and Uwe Spiekermann (Cham: Springer, 2017), 43.
34. Ibid., 37–53.
35. Hitoshi Tamura, "Zairai orimonogyō no gijutsu kakushin to kagakusenryō. Dentō iro kara ryūkō iro he," *Shakaikeizaishi gaku*, vol. 69, 2004, 3–28.
36. Ibid., 648–651.
37. Tomoko Hashino, *Keizai hatten to sanchi – shijo – seido: Meijiki kinuorimogyo no shinka to dainamizumu* (Kyoto: Minerva, 2007), 143–168.
38. Blaszczyk*, Color Revolution*, 127–130.
39. Blaszczyk and Wubs, *The Fashion Forecasters*, 47–50.
40. Andrew Godley, "The Development of the Clothing Industry: Technology and Fashion," *Textile History*, vol. 28, no. 1 (1997): 3–10.
41. Hounshell, *From the American System to Mass Production,* 15–215.
42. Godley, "The Development of the Clothing Industry," 4.
43. Nancy L. Green, *Ready-to-Wear, Ready-to-Work: A Century of Industry and Immigrants in Paris and New York* (Durham: Duke University Press, 1997), 45.

44. Laura A. Jones, "E. Moses and Son – the Tailors who Pioneered Mass-market Men's Tailoring?" *Fashion, Style & Popular Culture* 5.1 (2018): 97–115.
45. Ibid., 98.
46. Godley, "The Development of the Clothing Industry," 6.
47. E. Moses & Son, *The Growth of an Important Branch of British Industry* (London: no name, 1860), 4.
48. Ibid., 5–6.
49. Jones, "E. Moses and Son," 100.
50. Quoted from Jones, "E. Moses and Son," 101.
51. Shmuel Feiner, *The Jewish Enlightenment* (Pennsylvania: University of Pennsylvania Press, 2004).
52. Godley, "The Development of the Clothing Industry," 6.
53. Vicki Howard, ed., *History of Retailing and Consumption*, Special Issue on Department Stores, 2021, vol. 7, 1–114.
54. Claire Walsh, "The Newness of the Department Store: A View from the Eighteenth Century," in *Cathedrals of consumption*, eds Geoffrey Crossick and Serge Jaumain (London: Routledge, 2019), 46–71.
55. Michael Barry Miller, *The Bon Marché: Bourgeois Culture and the Department Store,* 1869–1920 (Princeton: Princeton University Press, 1981), 5.
56. Ibid., 39–40 and 43.
57. Ibid., 46.
58. Ibid., 62.
59. Ibid., 49.
60. Ibid., 50.
61. Ibid., 57–58.
62. Elisabetta Merlo and Ivan Paris, *The Italian Fashion System: The Role of Institutions and Institutional Change, 1940s–1980s* (Cham: Palgrave Macmillan, 2024), 15–16.
63. Andrew C. Godley and Haiming Hang, "Collective Financing among Chinese Entrepreneurs and Department Store Retailing in China," *Business History*, 58.3 (2016): 367.
64. Paul Lerner, *The Consuming Temple: Jews, Department Stores, and the Consumer Revolution in Germany, 1880–1940* (Cornell: Cornell University Press, 2017), 212–215.
65. Rika Fujioka, "Japanese Department Stores," in *Oxford Research Encyclopedia of Business and Management* (Oxford: Oxford University Press 2018). Available online: https://doi.org/10.1093/acrefore/9780190224851.013.95 (accessed November 18, 2024).
66. Rika Fujioka, *Hyakkaten no seisei katei* [The Development of Department Stores] (Tokyo: Yuhikaku, 2006), 101–110.
67. Godley and Hang, "Collective Financing," 364–377.

Chapter 2

1. *Journal des Dames et des Modes* ("Journal of Ladies' Fashion"), vol. 42, no. 1, January 5, 1838, 14.
2. Blaszczyk and Wubs, *The Fashion Forecasters*, 9.
3. Uche Okonkwo, *Luxury Fashion Branding: Trends, Tactics, Techniques* (Berlin: Springer, 2016), 24; Didier Grumbach, *History of International Fashion* (Northampton: Interlink Books, 2014), 13–15.

4. Corinne Walker, *Une Histoire du Luxe à Genève: Richesse et Art de Vivre aux XVIIe et XVIIIe Siècles* (Genève: La Baconnière, 2018).
5. Simmel, "Fashion," 557–559.
6. Penelope Francks, *The Japanese Consumer: An Alternative Economic History of Modern Japan* (Cambridge: Cambridge University Press, 2009), 31.
7. Chantal Trubert-Tollu, Françoise Tétart-Vittu, Jean-Marie Martin-Hattemberg, and Fabrice Olivieri, *The House of Worth, 1858–1954: The Birth of Haute Couture* (London: Thames & Hudson, 2017), 16.
8. Breward, *Fashion*, 29.
9. Ibid.
10. Grumbach, *History of International Fashion*, 16.
11. Trubert-Tollu et al., *The House of Worth*, 26.
12. Ibid., 93.
13. Grumbach, *History of International Fashion*, 19.
14. Emile Zola, *La Curée* ["The Kill"] (Paris: G. Charpentier et E. Fasquelle, 1895), 128.
15. Trubert-Tollu et al., *The House of Worth*, 28.
16. Ibid., 30.
17. Ibid., 93.
18. See, for example, Diana de Marly, *Worth: Father of Haute Couture* (London: Elm Tree Books, 1990), 1.
19. Diana de Marly, *The History of Haute Couture, 1850–1950* (Manchester: Anchor Press, 1980), 18.
20. Ibid.
21. Trubert-Tollu et al., *The House of Worth*, 102.
22. Caroline Evans, *The Mechanical Smile: Modernism and the First Fashion Shows in France and America, 1900–1929* (New Haven and London: Yale University Press, 2013), 12–14.
23. Trubert-Tollu et al., *The House of Worth*, 157–158.
24. Ibid., 93.
25. De Marty, *The History of Haute Couture*, 1850–1950, 46–47.
26. Trubert-Tollu et al., *The House of Worth*, 258.
27. Ibid., 298.
28. Johanna Zanon, "Reawakening the 'Sleeping Beauties' of Haute Couture: The Case of Guy and Arnaud de Lummen," in *European Fashion: The Creation of a Global Industry*, eds Blaszczyk and Pouillard (Manchester: Manchester University Press, 2018), 86–88.
29. Grumbach, *History of International Fashion*, 31.
30. De Marly, *The History of Haute Couture, 1850–1950*, 50–59.
31. Ibid., 53.
32. Ibid., 46.
33. Buenos Aires is mentioned in Paquin's advertisements for the first time in 1911. Véronique Pouillard, and Waleria Dorogova, "Couture Ltd: French Fashion's Debut in London's West End," *Business History* 2022, vol. 64, issue 3 (2022), 606.
34. De Marly, *The History of Haute Couture, 1850–1950*, chapter 5; Grumbach, *History of International Fashion*, 28.
35. Ibid., 83.
36. Steele, *Paris Fashion,* 248.

37. Geoffrey Jones, *Beauty Imagined: A History of the Global Beauty Industry* (Oxford: Oxford University Press, 2010), 106.
38. Jay P. Pederson, "Chanel SA," *International Directory of Company Histories.* Volume 49 (Detroit, Mich.: St. James Press, 2003).
39. Pouillard, "Managing Fashion Creativity," 78.
40. Véronique Pouillard and Johanna Zanon, "Wholesale Couture: Jean Patou's Jane Paris Line (1929)," *Dress* (2019): 1–13.
41. Pouillard and Zanon, "Wholesale Couture," 1–13.
42. Lourdes M. Font, "International Couture: The Opportunities and Challenges of Expansion, 1880–1920," *Business History*, 54.1 (2012): 30–47.
43. Grumbach, *History of International Fashion*, 33.
44. Font, "International Couture," 47.
45. Quoted from Font, "International Couture," 35.
46. Pouillard and Dorogova, "Couture Ltd," 587–609.
47. Ibid., 596–597.
48. Ibid., 598–599.
49. Font, "International Couture," 39.
50. Pouillard, "Design Piracy in the Fashion Industries," 319–344.
51. Pouillard, "Managing Fashion Creativity," 76–89.
52. Ibid., 78.
53. Pouillard, "Design Piracy in the Fashion Industries," 331–337.
54. Ibid., 337–343.
55. François-Marie Grau, *La Haute Couture* (Paris: PUF, 2000), 24.

Chapter 3

1. Karl Marx, *Capital: A Critique of Political Economy,* Volume One (London: Penguin Books, 1990 [1867]), 600.
2. Ibid.
3. Simmel, "Fashion," 130–155.
4. Paul Bairoch, *Cities and Economic Development: From the Dawn of History to the Present* (Chicago: University of Chicago Press, 1991), 290.
5. Mary Louise Roberts, "Gender, Consumption, and Commodity Culture," *The American Historical Review* 103.3 (1998): 819.
6. Lori Anne Loeb, *Consuming Angels: Advertising and Victorian Women* (Oxford: Oxford University Press, 1994), 3–26.
7. Sarah Levitt, "Cheap Mass-Produced Men's Clothing in the Nineteenth and Early Twentieth Centuries," *Textile History,* 22.2 (1991): 179–192.
8. The name changed to *Harper's Bazaar* in 1929–1930.
9. For the case of Britain, see Howard Cox and Simon Mowatt, "*Vogue* in Britain: Authenticity and the Creation of Competitive Advantage in the UK Magazine Industry," *Business History* 54.1 (2012): 67–87.
10. Francks, *The Japanese Consumer*, 31–35.
11. Ibid., appendix, table 3.

12. Katrina Honeyman, *Well Suited: A History of the Leeds Clothing Industry, 1850–1990* (Edinburgh: Pasold Research Fund, 2000), 11.
13. Green, *Ready-to-Wear, Ready-to-Work*, 46.
14. Ibid., 80.
15. P. G. Hall, "The Location of the Clothing Trades in London, 1861–1951," *Transactions and Papers (Institute of British Geographers)* 28 (1960): 155–178.
16. Green, Ready-to-Wear, Ready-to-Work, 79.
17. Alice Janssens, "Fashioning Interwar Berlin: Conceptualising the German Capital's Clothing Industry," unpublished paper given at the annual conference of the European Business History Association, Vienna University of Economics and Business, August 2017.
18. Honeyman, *Well Suited*, 1–19.
19. Ibid.,14.
20. Ibid., 111–113.
21. Rachel Worth, *Fashion for the People: A History of Clothing at Marks & Spencer* (Oxford: Berg Publishers, 2007), 28.
22. Honeyman, *Well Suited*, 261.
23. Ibid., 29.
24. Ibid., 281 and 288–289.
25. Ibid., 45.
26. Ibid., 56.
27. Ibid., 3.
28. Ibid., 72.
29. Ibid., 267–268.
30. Grumbach, *History of International Fashion*, 182–186.
31. Aimée Moutet, *Les Logiques de l'Entreprise: La Rationalisation dans l'Industrie Française de l'Entre-deux-guerres* (Paris: EHESS, 1997), 233.
32. Grumbach, *History of International Fashion*, 180.
33. Riello, *Cotton*, 80–82 and 119.
34. Ibid., 95.
35. Geoffrey Owen, *From Empire to Europe: The Decline and Revival of British Industry Since the Second World War* (New York: Harper Collins, 1999), 60.
36. Honeyman, *Well Suited*, 48.
37. Jacques Marseille, *Empire Colonial et Capitalisme Français: Historie d'un Divorce* (Paris: Seuil, 1984), 53–57.
38. Spoerer, *C&A*, 31–36.
39. Ibid., 37.
40. Ibid., 65.
41. Ibid., 85.
42. Ibid., 82 and 114.
43. Ibid., 96.
44. Ibid., 97–99.
45. Florence Brachet-Champsaur and Ludovic Cailluet, "The Great Depression? Challenging the Periodization of French Business History in the Interwar Period," in *The Business History of*

Everything, vol. 8 (Business History Conference, Athens, Georgia: Business and Economic History on-line, 2010).
46. Moutet, *Les Logiques de l'Entreprise*, 233.
47. Grumbach, *History of International Fashion*, 178.
48. Ibid., 181.
49. Ibid.
50. Blaszczyk, *Fashionability: Abraham Moon*, 129.
51. Asa Briggs, *Marks & Spencer, 1884–1984* (London: Octopus Books, 1984).
52. Ibid., 23 and 113.
53. Ibid.,115.
54. Quoted from Ibid., 53–54.
55. Ibid., 65; Honeyman, *Well Suited*, 272–273.
56. Worth, *Fashion for the People*, 34.
57. Briggs, *Marks & Spencer, 1884–1984*, 67.
58. Worth, *Fashion for the People*, 68.
59. Ibid., 70.
60. Ibid., 39.
61. Ibid., 113.
62. François Jequier, *Charles Veillon (1900–1971): Essai sur l'émergence d'une éthique patronale* (Zurich : Société d'études en matière économique, 1985), 31–68.
63. Ellen Israel Rosen, *Making Sweatshops: The Globalization of the U.S. Apparel Industry* (Berkeley: University of California Press, 2002), 96–98.
64. Donzé and Fujioka, "The Formation of a Technology-based Fashion System," 438–474.

Chapter 4

1. Quoted in Yoshinori Osakabe, "Dressing Up During the Meiji Restoration: A Perspective on Fukusei (Clothing Reform)," in *Fashion, Identity, and Power in Modern Asia*, eds Kyunghee Pyun and Aida Yuen Wong (Cham: Palgrave Macmillan, 2018), 29.
2. Kyunghee Pyun and Aida Yuen Wong, *Fashion, Identity, and Power in Modern Asia* (Cham: Palgrave Macmillan, 2018), 8.
3. Riello, *Cotton*, 89–91.
4. Adam Clulow and Tristan Mostert, "Introduction: The Companies in Asia," in *The Dutch and English East India Companies: Diplomacy, Trade and Violence in Early Modern Asia*, eds Adam Clulow and Tristan Mostert (Amsterdam University Press, 2018), 17.
5. Ann M. Carlos and Stephen Nicholas, "Giants of an Earlier Capitalism: The Chartered Trading Companies as Modern Multinationals," *Business History Review* 62, 3 (1988): 398–419.
6. Nierstrasz, *Rivalry for Tade in Tea and Textiles*, passim; Martha Chaiklin, "Surat and Bombay: Ivory and Commercial Networks in Western India," in *The Dutch and English East India Companies:* Diplomacy, Trade and Violence in Early Modern Asia, eds Adam Clulow and Tristan Mostert (Amsterdam University Press, 2018), 101–124.
7. Tonio Andrade, "The Dutch East India Company in Global History: A Historiographical Reconnaissance," in *The Dutch and English East India Companies: Diplomacy, Trade and*

Violence in Early Modern Asia, eds Adam Clulow and Tristan Mostert (Amsterdam University Press, 2018), 239–56.
8. Anthony Reid, "Southeast Asian Consumption of Indian and British Cotton Cloth, 1600–1850," in *How India Clothed the World: The World of South Asian Textiles, 1500–1850,* eds Giorgio Riello and Tirthankar Roy (Leiden: Brill, 2009), 31–52.
9. Riello, *Cotton*, 92.
10. Nierstrasz, *Rivalry for Tade in Tea and Textiles*, 194–195.
11. Riello, *Cotton*, 264–272.
12. Ibid., 203–214.
13. Prasannan Parthasarathi, "Historical Issues of Deindustrialization in Nineteenth-Century South India," in *How India Clothed the World: The World of South Asian Textiles, 1500–1850,* eds Giorgio Riello and Tirthankar Roy (Leiden: Brill, 2009), 415–435.
14. Ibid.
15. Joseph A. Schumpeter, *Capitalism, Socialism and Democracy* (London: Routledge, 1994), 82–83.
16. Riello, *Cotton*, 278.
17. George Feifer, *Breaking Open Japan: Commodore Perry, Lord Abe, and American Imperialism in 1853* (New York: Smithsonian Books 2006), 38–41.
18. See, for example, Hoshimi Uchida, "The Spread of Timepieces in the Meiji Period," *Japan Review* 14 (2002): 174–175.
19. Donzé and Yongue, *Japanese Capitalism and Entrepreneurship*, 60–62.
20. Tomoko Okawa, "Imitating Authentic Clothing through Technology Transplantation," unpublished paper given at the *East Asian Business History Workshop* (online), September 2022.
21. Yoshinori Osakabe, *Yofuku, sanpatsu, datto: fukusei no meiji isshin* (Tokyo: Kodansha, 2014), 48–115.
22. Shibusawa Shasi Database, "Shibusawa Eiichi Memorial Foundation," https://shashi.shibusawa.or.jp, quoted by Okawa in "Imitating Authentic Clothing through Technology Transplantation."
23. Ibid.
24. Donzé and Fujioka, "The Formation of a Technology-based Fashion System," 456–457.
25. Gordon, *Fabricating Consumers*, 65.
26. Iwamoto Shinichi, *Mishin to ifuku no keizaishi: chikyu kibo keizai to kanai seisan* (Kyoto: Shibunkaku, 2014), Chapter 4.
27. C. F. Remer, *Foreign Investments in China* (New York: Howard Fertig, 1968), 45.
28. Christian Henriot, Shi Lu, and Charlotte Aubrun, *The Population of Shanghai (1865–1953): A Sourcebook* (Leiden: Brill, 2018), 96–97.
29. Mina Roces, "Gender, Nation, Fashion, and Modernities in the Asia-Pacific, 1900 to the Present," in *The Cambridge History of Fashion*, vol. 2, eds Christopher Breward, Beverly Lemire, and Giorgio Riello (Cambridge: Cambridge University Press, 2023), 1104.
30. Juanjuan Wu, *Chinese Fashion from Mao to Now* (Oxford and New York: Berg, 2009), 103.
31. Ibid., 105–106.
32. Davies, *Peacefully Working to Conquer the World*, Chapter 7.
33. Christopher Breward, "Fashionable Masculinities in England and Beyond: Renunciation and Dandyism, 1800–1939," in *The Cambridge History of Fashion* vol. 2, eds Christopher Breward, Beverly Lemire and Giorgio Riello (Cambridge: Cambridge University Press, 2023), 761–762.
34. Godley and Hang, "Collective Financing," 364–377.

Notes

35. Ibid., 107–109.
36. Sandy Ng, "Clothes Make the Woman: Cheongsam and Chinese Identity in Hong Kong," *Fashion, Identity, and Power in Modern Asia* (2018): 357–378.
37. Qing Huang, "Fashioning Modernity and Qipao in Republican Shanghai (1910s–1930s)" (MA diss., Ohio University, 2015), 30.
38. Angelina Illes, "The Fascination with Japanese-Styled Gowns: A Quantitative Perspective on Ready-Made Garments at the Beginning of the Eighteenth Century," *Journal of Historians of Netherlandish Art* 15:1 (Winter 2023): 2–6.
39. Akiko Fukai, "Japonism in Fashion" [*Mo-do no japonizumu*] (Kyoto: The Kyoto Costume Institute, 1996), https://www.kci.or.jp/en/research/dresstudy/pdf/e_Fukai_Japonism_in_Fashion.pdf (accessed November 17, 2024).
40. Richard Martin and Harold Koda, *Orientalism: Visions of the East in Western Dress* (New York: The Metropolitan Museum of Art, 1994), 31 and 36.
41. Heather Chan, "From Costume to Fashion: Visions of Chinese Modernity in *Vogue* Magazine, 1892–1943," *Ars Orientalis* 47 (2017), 210–232.
42. Gabriel P. Weisberg, *Japonisme: Japanese Influence on French Art 1854–1910* (Cleveland: Kent State University Press, 1975), 2–9.
43. Fukai, "Japonism in Fashion," 6.
44. Ibid., 1 and 7.
45. Ibid., 2–3.
46. Pierre-Yves Donzé, "From the 'Yellow Peril' to 'Cool Japan': Country's Image and Global Competitiveness of the Japanese Manufacturing Industry Since the Meiji Period," in *National Brands and Global Markets: An Historical Perspective*, eds Nikolas Glover and David M. Higgins (New York: Routledge, 2023), 168–184.
47. Anne Grosfilley, "The Global Trade of the Wax Fabric," in *The Routledge History of Fashion and Dress, 1800 to the Present*, eds Veronique Pouillard and Vincent Dubé-Senécal (London: Routledge 2023), 81–98.
48. Elise van Nederveen Meerkerk, Corinne Boter, Sarah Carmichael, and Katharine Frederick, "Global Shifts and Local Actors: Revising Macro-Level Theories on the Relocation of Textile Production from the Lens of the Household in the Netherlands and Java, c. 1820–1940," *BMGN – Low Countries Historical Review*, 138 (2023): 12–20.
49. Vlisco, "The Founding of Vlisco," https://www.vlisco.com/heritage/the-founding-of-vlisco (accessed September 15, 2024).
50. Grosfilley, "The Global Trade of the Wax Fabric," 82.
51. Ibid., 82–87.
52. Willem Ankersmit, "The Waxprint: Its Origin and Its Introduction on the Gold Coast" (MA diss., University Leiden, 2010), 58.
53. Ankersmit, "Ankersmits Textielfabrieken NV. Een Historisch Overzicht," https://ankersmit.info/Geschiedenis.php (accessed September 21, 2024).

Chapter 5

1. Edward Bok, "Paris Fashions and Our's: Mr. Bok Says Modest Women Look Askance at French Designs," *New York Times*, September 6, 1912, *ProQuest Historical Newspapers*, 8.

2. Marlis Schweitzer, "American Fashion for American Woman: The Rise and Fall of Fashion Nationalism," in *Producing Fashion: Commerce, Culture, and Consumers*, ed. Regina Lee Blaszczyk (Philadelphia, Pennsylvania: University of Pennsylvania Press, 2008), 142.
3. John E. Foster and William John Eccles, "Fur Trade in Canada," *The Canadian Encyclopedia*, 2013, https://www.thecanadianencyclopedia.ca/en/article/fur-trade#:~:text=The%20fur%20trade%20was%20a,European%20demand%20for%20felt%20hats.
4. Beckert, *Empire of Cotton*, 84–85.
5. Beckert, *Empire of Cotton*, 85–97.
6. Ibid., 103–105.
7. Ibid., 243.
8. George C. Herring, *From Colony to Superpower: U.S. Foreign Relations since 1776* (Oxford: OUP, 2011), 240–241.
9. David Reynolds, *America, Empire of Liberty: A New History* (London: Allen Lane, 2009), 243.
10. Bruce Stokes, "Protectionism and Politics," *EJournal USA, Economic Perspectives* (2007): 7–8.
11. Kevin H. O'Rourke, "Tariffs and Growth in the Late Nineteenth Century," in *Classical Trade Protectionism 1815–1914*, eds Jean-Pierre Dormois and Pedro Lains (Abingdon: Routledge, 2006), 133.
12. Alfred D. Chandler, *Scale and Scope: The Dynamics of Industrial Capitalism* (Cambridge MA: The Belknap of Harvard University Press, 1994), 4.
13. Alfred D. Chandler, *The Visible Hand: The Managerial Revolution in American Business* (Cambridge MA: The Belknap of Harvard University Press, 1999), 498–499.
14. Ibid., 57–58
15. Ibid., 58–59.
16. Kenton Beerman, "The Beginning of a Revolution: Waltham and the Boston Manufacturing Company," *The Concord Review* (1994): 141–157.
17. Ibid., 151–152.
18. Chandler, *The Visible Hand*, 60–62.
19. Hounshell, *From the American System to Mass Production*, 68.
20. Anne Hollander, "The Modernization of Fashion," *Design Quarterly*, Winter, 1992, No. 154 (Winter, 1992): 27–33.
21. Herring, *From Colony to Superpower*, 127–133.
22. Green, *Ready-to-Wear and Ready-to-Work*, passim.
23. Azam Gandchi Kassirzadeh, "Selected Factors that Influence the Mass-Production of Misses' High-fashion and Popular-Priced Ready-to-Wear Apparel in the United States" (PhD diss., Texas Woman's University, 1978), 15–18.
24. Norma M. Rantisi, "The Ascendance of New York Fashion," *International Journal of Urban and Regional Research* Volume 28.1 (March 2004): 90–91.
25. Elizabeth Ewing and Alice Mackrell, *History of Twentieth Century Fashion* (London: Crysalis Books Group, 2005), 60–61.
26. Rantisi, "The Ascendance," 91.
27. Schweitzer, "American Fashion," 132–136.
28. Rantisi, "The Ascendance," 91.
29. Schweitzer, "American Fashion," 132.
30. Pouillard, *Paris to New York*, 26–27.

31. Ibid., 35–36.
32. Ibid., 29–30.
33. Rantisi, "The Ascendance," 92.
34. Lynn Downey, "Levi Strauss: A Short Biography" (Levi Strauss & Co, 2008) http://www.levistrauss.com/sites/default/files/librarydocument/2010/4/History_Levi_Strauss_Biography.pdf (accessed October 5, 2024).
35. Levi Strauss, "We have . . . Been innovating since the birth of the blue jean in 1873" https://www.levistrauss.com/levis-history/ (accessed December 16, 2021).
36. Ninke Bloemberg, "Dutch Jeans," in *Blue Jeans*, eds Ninke Bloemberg and Hans Schopping (Utrecht: Centraal Museum, 2012), 7.
37. James Sullivan, *Jeans: A Cultural History of an American Icon* (New York: Gotham, 2007), 36.
38. Thomas Stege Bojer, Josh Sims, Sven Ehmann and Robert Klanten, eds, *Blue Blooded: Denim Hunters and Jeans Culture* (Berlin: Gestalten, 2016), 184–185.
39. Sandra Curtis Comstock, "The Making of an American Icon: The Transformation of Blue Jeans during the Great Depression," in *Global Denim*, eds, Daniel Miller and Sophie Woodward (New York: Berg, 2011), 23.
40. Comstock, "The Making of an American Icon," 35–38.
41. Ewing and Mackrell, *History of Twentieth Century Fashion*, 99–101.
42. Emmanuelle Polle, *Jean Patou, A Fashionable Life* (Paris: Flammarion, 2013), 96.
43. Pouillard, *Paris to New York*, passim.
44. Sonnet Stanfill, *New York Fashion* (London V&A Publications, 2007), 28–49.
45. William R. Scott, "California Casual: Lifestyle Marketing and Men's Leisurewear, 1930–1960," in *Producing Fashion: Commerce, Culture, and Consumers*, ed., Regina Lee Blaszczyk (Philadelphia, Pennsylvania: University of Pennsylvania Press, 2008), 170.
46. Quoted in: Department of City Planning Office of Historic Resources, *Los Angeles Citywide Historic Context Statement. Context: Industrial Development, 1850–1980* (Los Angeles: City of Los Angeles, 2018), 142.
47. Joanna Jana Laznicka, "The Boss Workwear Buttons: Unveiling the History Behind Them," https://focusspeed.com/the-boss-workwear-buttons-history-behind-them/ (accessed October 6, 2024).
48. Jewish Museum of the American West, "The Brownstein-Louis Company Catalog of 1918: Men's Furnishing Goods in Los Angeles," https://www.jmaw.org/brownstein-louis-los-angeles-2/ (accessed October 6, 2024).
49. Encyclopedia.com. "Catalina Sportswear," https://www.encyclopedia.com/fashion/news-wires-white-papers-and-books/catalina-sportswear (accessed October 6, 2024).
50. Scott, "California Casual,"173–174.
51. Department of City Planning Office, *Los Angeles Citywide Historic Context Statement*, 142–144.
52. Scott, "California Casual," 170.
53. In 1979, MAGIC opened its exhibition spaces for international manufacturers. Ten years later, the fair was relocated to Las Vegas because it needed more space. Since 1995, it has also invited women's apparel producers to show their products. MAGIC Marketplace, https://www.apparelsearch.com/trade_shows/magic_fashion_fabric_trade_show.htm and https://www.magicfashionevents.com/en/home.html (accessed December 19, 2021).

Chapter 6

1. Quoted in Irene Guenther, *Nazi Chic: Fashioning Women in the Third Reich* (Oxford: Berg Publishers, 2004), 151.
2. Larissa Zakharova, *S'habiller à la soviétique: La mode et le Dégel en USSR* (Paris: CNRS Éditions 2011), 36–49.
3. Robert O. Paxton, *The Anatomy of Fascism* (London: Penguin Books: 2004), 58–64.
4. Ibid., 109–110. Mussolini was executed by Italian communist partisans at the end of the war on April 28, 1945.
5. Emanuela Scarpellini, *Italian Fashion since 1945. A Cultural History* (Cham: Palgrave Macmillan: 2019), 63.
6. Ibid., 63. Simmel, "Fashion," 541–558.
7. Eugenia Paulicelli, *Fashion under Fascism: Beyond the Black Shirt* (London: Bloomsbury: 2004), 147–154.
8. Elisabetta Merlo and Francesca Polese, "Italy," in *Berg Encyclopedia of World Dress and Fashion: West Europe*, ed. Lise Skov (Oxford: Berg, 2010), 254–255.
9. Elisabetta Merlo and Mario Perugini, "The Determinants of the Emergence of Turin as the First Capital of Italian Fashion Industry (1900–1960)," *Fashion Theory* 24:3 (2020): 335–336.
10. Cinzia Capalbo, "Creativity and Innovation of the Italian Fashion System in the Inter-war Period (1919–1943)" *Investigaciones de Historia Económica* ["Economic History Research"], 12:2 (2016): 92–93.
11. Merlo and Perugini, "The Determinants of the Emergence of Turin," 337–348.
12. Capalbo, "Creativity and Innovation of the Italian Fashion System," 90–99; Valerio Cerretano, "Autarky, Market Creation and Innovation: Snia Viscosa and Saici, 1933–1970," *Business History*, 64:6 (2022): 1110–1130.
13. Geoffrey Owen, *The Rise and Fall of Great Companies: Courtaulds and the Reshaping of the Man-made Fiber Industry* (Oxford: Oxford University Press, 2010), 19.
14. Valerio Cerretano, "European Cartels and Technology Transfer: The Experience of the Rayon Industry, 1920 to 1940," *Zeitschrift für Unternehmensgeschichte* ["Journal of Business History"], 56 Jahrg., H. 2. (2011): 206–224.
15. Valerio Cerretano, "Multinational Business and Host Countries in Times of Crisis: Courtaulds, Glanzstoff, and Italy in the Interwar Period," *Economic History Review*, 71, 2 (2018): 552–555.
16. Ibid., 553.
17. Cerretano, "Autarky, Market Creation and Innovation," 1114–1118.
18. Ferragamo Archives, https://archive.ph/z7PlY (accessed July 27, 2024); Stefania Ricci, *Walking Dreams: Salvatore Ferragamo, 1898–1960* (Editorial RM 2006).
19. Merlo and Polese, "Italy," 256.
20. Museo Ferragamo and LIFE Photocollection, "Made in Italy: Salvatore Ferragamo's Ideas, Models and Inventions," *Google Arts & Culture*, https://artsandculture.google.com/story/made-in-italy-salvatore-ferragamo-s-ideas-models-and-inventions/UQWRSqxpWZsfIg (accessed June 18, 2024),
21. John Armitage and Joanne Roberts, "The Globalisation of Luxury Fashion: The Case of Gucci" *Luxury*, 6:3 (2019): 227–246.

22. Deirdre Pirro, "Guccio Gucci: A Leather Lineage," *The Florentine,* https://www.theflorentine.net/2009/06/18/guccio-gucci/ (accessed April 4, 2024).
23. Quoted in: Guenther, *Nazi Chic,* 170.
24. Ibid., 167–201.
25. Ibid., 200–201.
26. Jonas Scherner, "The Beginnings of Nazi Autarky Policy: The 'National Pulp Programme' and the Origin of Regional Staple Fiber Plants," *The Economic History Review*, New Series, 61:4 (2008): 869.
27. Köster, *Hugo Boss*, 39.
28. Köster, *Hugo Boss*, 44–50.
29. Scherner, "The Beginnings of Nazi Autarky Policy," 868–871.
30. Ibid., 870–871.
31. Owen, *The Rise and Fall of Great Companies*, 19–20.
32. Christian Marx and Ben Wubs, "National Conflicts in a Multinational: The Case of the Dutch–German AKU/VGF/Akzo, 1920s to 1970s," *Business History* 64: 9 (2022): 1709–1734.
33. Theodor Langenbruch, *Glanzstoff 1899–1949* (Wuppertal: Enka AG, 1985), 64.
34. Ibid., 126–127.
35. Marx and Wubs, "National Conflicts in a Multinational," 1709–1734.
36. Andrew Gordon, *A Modern History of Japan from Tokugawa Times to the Present* (Oxford: Oxford University Press, 2003), 196–203.
37. Donzé and Yongue, *Japanese Capitalism and Entrepreneurship*, chapter 6.
38. Abe Takeshi and Kyohei Hirano, *Sen'i sangyo* (Tokyo: Nihon keieishi kenkyujo, 2013), 71–75.
39. Yamazaki, *Nihon Kasen Sangyo*, 299 and 337.
40. Hiroaki Yamazaki and Takeshi Abe, *Orimono kara apareru he: bingo orimonogyo to sasaki shoten* (Osaka: Osaka University Press, 2012), 105–158.
41. Ibid., 151–152.
42. Ibid., 286.
43. Francks, *The Japanese Consumer*, 132–133.
44. *Zeitaku ha teki da: senji keizai toseika no tokyo* (Tokyo: Tokyo Metropolitan Archives, 2012), 31, 35, 46, 81.
45. Ewing and Mackrell, *History of Twentieth Century Fashion*, 141.
46. Lou Taylor, "From Berlin to Paris," in *Paris Fashion and World War Two Global Diffusion and Nazi Control*, ed. Lou Taylor and Marie McLoughlin (London: Bloomsbury, 2020), 40.
47. Ibid., 14–16.
48. Ibid., 38–39.
49. Grumbach, *History of International Fashion*, 37.
50. Ibid., 51.
51. Lou Taylor, "The Lyon Haute Nouveauté Fashion Textile Industry During World War Two; Design Making, Exhibition and International Diffusion," in *Paris Fashion and World War Two Global Diffusion and Nazi Control*, eds Lou Taylor and Marie McLoughlin (London: Bloomsbury, 2020), 54–60.
52. Ewing and Mackrell, *History of Twentieth Century Fashion*, 141–142.
53. Bethan Bide, "London Leads the World: The Reinvention of London Fashion in the Aftermath of the Second World War," *Fashion Theory* 24, 3 (2020): 352–356.
54. Ewing and Mackrell, *History of Twentieth Century Fashion*, 145–146; 152–154.

55. Michelle Jones, *London Couture and the Making a Fashion Centre* (Cambridge MA: MIT Press 2022), 3–12.
56. Owen, *The Rise and Fall of Great Companies*, 15–16.
57. Ibid., 25–30.
58. Pouillard, *Paris to New York*, 129.
59. Ibid., 119.
60. Ibid., 130.
61. Ewing and Mackrell, *History of Twentieth Century Fashion*, 147–148; 152–154.
62. Owen, *The Rise and Fall of Great Companies*, 23–31.
63. Scott, "California Casual," 172.
64. Los Angeles Almanac, "General Population," http://www.laalmanac.com/population/po26.php (accessed December 19, 2021).
65. Scott, "California Casual," 172–173.

Chapter 7

1. *Les Echos*, August 6, 1999.
2. Marie France Pochna, *Bonjour, Monsieur Boussac* (Paris: R. Laffont, 1980), 138–139.
3. "Portraitist in France," *Life* 37:14 (1954): 133.
4. Pouillard, *Paris to New York*, 138–142.
5. Yuniya Kawamura, *The Japanese Revolution in Paris Fashion* (Oxford: Berg, 2004), 44. The decline continued (18 houses in 1995 and 11 in 2002).
6. Grau, *La Haute Couture*, 12. The decline continued in the following years (200 customers in 1990).
7. Vincent Dubé-Senécal, "Fashion, Industry and Diplomacy: Reframing Couture–Textile Relations in France, 1950s–1960s," *Enterprise & Society,* 24:2 (2023): 459.
8. Ibid.
9. Tomoko Okawa, "Licensing Practices at Maison Christian Dior," in *Producing Fashion. Commerce, Culture and Consumers,* eds Regina Lee Blaszczyk (Pennsylvania: University of Pennsylvania Press, 2011), 82–108; Pouillard, *Paris to New* York, 138–166.
10. Pouillard, *Paris to New York*, 139.
11. *Le Monde*, 8 September 2023.
12. Pouillard, *Paris to New York*, 150–152.
13. Ibid.,153.
14. Okawa, "Licensing Practices at Maison Christian Dior," 96.
15. Ibid., 104.
16. Okawa also published data for 1973 and 1975, during which fur was profitable and ready-to-wear loss-making in 1973 but profitable in 1975. Data for other years are not available. Okawa, "Licensing Practices at Maison Christian Dior," 103.
17. Grumbach, *History of International Fashion*,124.
18. Teri Agins, *The End of Fashion: How Marketing Changed the Clothing Business Forever* (New York: Harper Collins, 1999), 30.
19. David Zajtmann, "Une révolution dans la mode: le prêt-à-porter des couturiers parisiens (1965–2000)" *Entreprises et histoire* 3 (2022): 52–63.
20. Grumbach, *History of International Fashion*, 248–249.

21. Alicia Drake, *Beautiful People: Saint Laurent, Lagerfeld: Splendeurs et misères de la mode* (Paris: Denoël, 2008), 121–125.
22. Regina Lee Blaszczyk and Ben Wubs, "Beyond the Crystal Ball," In *The Fashion Forecasters: A Hidden History of Color and Trend Prediction*, eds Regina Lee Blaszczyk and Ben Wubs (London: Bloomsbury, 2018), 16–17.
23. Grumbach, *History of International Fashion*, 254.
24. Ibid., 257–259; Drake, *Beautiful People*, 84–85.
25. Drake, *Beautiful People*, 185.
26. *The New York Times*, July 29, 1976.
27. Drake, *Beautiful People*, 310.
28. *The New York Times*, July 29, 1976.
29. Drake, *Beautiful People*, 176.
30. Pouillard, "Recasting Paris Fashion," 41.
31. Ibid., 170–176.
32. Francesca Sterlacci and Joanne Arbuckle, *Historical Dictionary of the Fashion Industry* (Lanham, Maryland: Rowman & Littlefield, 2017), 22–23, 36, 97 and 127–129.
33. Scott, "California Casual,"169.
34. Ibid., 170.
35. Ibid.
36. Ibid., 179–180.
37. Rosen, *Making Sweatshops*, 103.
38. Ibid.,104.
39. Ibid.,184.
40. Ibid., 106.
41. Jay P. Pederson, ed., "Phillips-Van Heusen," *International Directory of Company Histories*, Vol. 24 (Michigan: St. James Press, 1998), 383–385.
42. Rosen, *Making Sweatshops*, 139.
43. Pierre-Yves Donzé, *Selling Europe to the World: The Rise of the Luxury Fashion Industry, 1980–2020* (London: Bloomsbury Publishing, 2023), 130–131.
44. Elisabetta Merlo and Valeria Pinchera, "Configuring Cultural Emerging Industries: A Comparison of the French and Italian Fashion Industries," *Business History Review* 97: 4 (2023): 779–807 (here 795).
45. Nicola White, *Reconstructing Italian Fashion: America and the Development of the Italian Fashion Industry* (London: Bloomsbury Academic, 2000), 24.
46. Merlo and Polese, "Turning Fashion into Business," 424–428.
47. Quoted by Merlo and Polese, "Turning Fashion into Business," 427.
48. Ibid., 432.
49. Elisabetta Merlo and Mario Perugini, "Making Italian Fashion Global: Brand Building and Management at Gruppo Finanziario Tessile (1950s–1990s)" in *The Brand and Its History: Trademarks, Branding and National Identity*, ed. Patricio Sáiz and Rafael Castro (London: Routledge, 2022), 250–277, 55.
50. Merlo and Polese, "Turning Fashion into Business," 432.
51. Elena Cedrola and Ksenia Silchenko, "Ermenegildo Zegna: When Family Values Guide Global Expansion in the Luxury Industry," *Fashion Brand Internationalization* (New York: Palgrave Pivot, 2016), 31–64.

52. European Fashion Heritage Association, "Tales of Italian Style: Biki," https://fashionheritage.eu/tales-of-italian-style-biki/ (accessed June 21, 2024).
53. Elisabetta Merlo, "When Fashion Met Industry: Biki and Gruppo Finanziario Tessile (1957–72)," *Journal of Modern Italian Studies* 20:1 (2015): 92–110.
54. Ibid.,107.
55. Household expenses statistics, quoted by Donzé and Fujioka, "The Formation of a Technology-based Fashion System, 449.
56. Ibid., 454–457.
57. Gordon, *Fabricating Consumers*, 230–231.
58. Census of Manufacture (MITI), quoted by Donzé and Fujioka, "The Formation of a Technology-based Fashion System," 448.
59. Ibid., 456.
60. Pierre-Yves Donzé, "Fashion Prediction and the Transformation of the Japanese Textile Industry: The Role of Kentaro Kawasaki (1950–1990)," in *The Fashion Forecasters: A Hidden History of Color and Trend Prediction*, eds Regina Lee Blaszczyk and Ben Wubs (London: Bloomsbury, 2018), 149–166.
61. *Kaiin meibo* (Tokyo: Fashion Editors Club, 1991) 1–5.
62. Kawamura, *The Japanese Revolution in Paris Fashion*, 91–112.
63. Donzé and Fujioka, "The Formation of a Technology-based Fashion System," 440.
64. Isozaki and Donzé, "Dominance Versus Collaboration Models," 394–408.
65. Tomoko Okawa, "Licensing and the Mass Production of Luxury Goods," in *Oxford Handbook of Luxury Business,* eds Pierre-Yves Donzé, Véronique Pouillard, and Joanne Roberts (Oxford: Oxford University Press, 2022), 173 and 193.
66. Spoerer, *C&A*, 243–244 and 285–291.
67. *New York Times*, September 5, 1983.
68. Spoerer, *C&A*, 281–282.
69. Ibid., 79–81.
70. Ibid., 244.
71. Ibid., 290.
72. Jay P. Pederson, ed., "Benetton Group," *International Directory of Company Histories*, Vol. 67 (Michigan: St. James Press, 2005), 47–49.
73. Briggs, *Marks & Spencer, 1884*–1984, 67–68.
74. Ibid., 65.
75. Ibid., 117.
76. Pederson, Jay P., "The Gap, Inc.," *International Directory of Company Histories*, Vol. 18 (Michigan: St. James Press 1997), 191–194.

Chapter 8

1. Jan-Otmar Hesse, "The German Textile Puzzle: Selective Protectionism and the Silent Globalization of an Industry," *Business History Review* 93, no. 2 (2019): 233.
2. Ibid., 225 and 227.
3. Stéphane Marchand, *Les guerres du luxe* (Paris: Fayard, 2001), 78–80.

4. Peter Dicken, *Global Shift: Mapping the Changing Contours of the World Economy* (London: Sage, 2015), 451–476.
5. Donzé and Fujioka, "The Formation of a Technology-based Fashion System," 10–13.
6. Christel Lane and Jocelyn Probert, *National Capitalisms, Global Production Networks: Fashioning the Value Chain in the UK, US, and Germany* (Oxford: OUP, 2009), 106 –108.
7. Leonard K. Cheng and William K. Fung, "The Globalization of Trade and Production: A Case Study of Hong Kong's Textile and Clothing Industries," in *Global Production and Trade in East Asia*, eds Leonard K. Cheng and Henryk Kierzkowski (Boston, MA: Springer, 2001), 227–243.
8. Zhang and Donzé, "Knowledge Upgrade," 1–2.
9. Bangyan Feng, *100 Years of Li & Fung: Rise from Family Business to Multinational* (Thomson Learning, 2007), 56–92.
10. Tina Grant and Thomas Derdak, "Esprit de Corp.," *International Directory of Company Histories*, Vol. 29 (St. James Press, 1999), 180–182.
11. Lane and Probert, *National Capitalisms*, 137.
12. Mushtaq H. Khan, "Technology Policies and Learning with Imperfect Governance," in *The Industrial Policy Revolution I: The Role of Government beyond Ideology*, eds Joseph E. Stiglitz and Justin Yifu Lin, Basingstoke: Macmillan, 2013, 109.
13. Hanako Nagata, *990 en no jinzu ga tsukurareru no ha naze?* (Tokyo: Godo, 2016), 60–64.
14. Khan, "Technology Policies and Learning with Imperfect Governance," 112.
15. Hesse, "The German Textile Puzzle," 225.
16. Ibid., 240.
17. Jean-Claude Daumas, ed., *Dictionnaire Historique des Patrons Français* (Paris: Flammarion, 2010), 121–122 and 724–725.
18. For the British case, see the example of the decline of the Leeds clothing industry discussed by Honeyman, *Well Suited*, chapter 11.
19. Dicken, *Global Shift*, 463.
20. Adele Hast et al., "Levi Strauss & Co," *International Directory of Company Histories*, Vol. 5 (St. James Press, 1992), 362–365.
21. Donzé, *Selling Europe to the World*, 90.
22. Blaszczyk, *Fashionability*, 236–284.
23. Ibid., 270.
24. Ibid., 263–264.
25. Ben Wubs, "Interstoff's Fashion Table: The Internalization of Fashion Forecasting in the World's Most Important Fashion Fabric Fair," in *The Fashion Forecasters: A Hidden History of Color and Trend Forecasting,* eds Regina Lee Blaszczyk and Ben Wubs (New York: Bloomsbury Academic, 2018), 167–190.
26. Alicia Drake, *Beautiful People*, 287 and 374–375.
27. Ibid., 376–377.
28. Donzé, *Selling Europe to the World*, 102–105.
29. Drake, *Beautiful People*.
30. Agins, *The End of Fashion*, 83.
31. John Potvin, *Giorgio Armani: Empire of the Senses* (London & New York: Routledge, 2013), 79–127.
32. Potvin, *Giorgio Armani*, 44.

33. Merlo and Perugini, "Making Italian Fashion Global," 58.
34. Potvin, *Giorgio Armani*, 105.
35. Merlo, "Italian Fashion Business," 353.
36. Djurdja Bertlett, Shaun Cole, and Agnès Rocamora, eds, *Fashion Media: Past and Present* (London: Bloomsbury, 2013), 13–72; Roland Barthes, *Système de la Mode* (Paris: Le Seuil, 1967).
37. Breward, *Fashion*, 126.
38. Catherine Dior and Jean-Pierre Teto, *Dior by Dior* (London: V&A Publishing, 2007), 28.
39. Pamela Church Gibson, *Fashion and Celebrity Culture* (London: Bloomsbury, 2013), 5 and 177.
40. Alberto Oliva, Norberto Angeletti, and Anna Wintour, *In Vogue: An Illustrated History of the World's Most Famous Fashion Magazine* (New York: Rizzoli International, 2012).
41. Grant McCracken, "Who Is the Celebrity Endorser? Cultural Foundations of the Endorsement Process," *Journal of Consumer Research*, 16, 3 (1989): 310–321.
42. Kawamura, *Fashion-ology*, 64; Elizabeth Wissinger, *This Year's Model: Fashion, Media, and the Making of Glamour* (New York: New Word University Press, 2015), 236.
43. Wissinger, *This Year's Model*, 81–82.
44. Bibia Pavard, Sandrine Lévêque, and Claire Blandin, "Elle et Marie Claire dans les années 1968: une 'parenthèse enchantée'?" *Le Temps des médias* 2 (2017): 65–78.
45. On the history of *Vogue*, see Oliva and Angeletti, *In Vogue*, 1–13.
46. Mariko Morimoto and Susan Chang, "Western and Asian Models in Japanese Fashion Magazine Ads: The Relationship with Brand Origins and International Versus Domestic Magazines," *Journal of International Consumer Marketing* 21.3 (2009): 173–187.
47. According to Wikipedia, https://en.wikipedia.org/wiki/Category:Lists_of_Vogue_cover_models (accessed November 18, 2024).
48. Donzé and Fujioka, "The Formation of a Technology-based Fashion System," 446–454.
49. Tsutomu Yagi, *Wacoal to Renown* (Tokyo: Tokyo Keizai, 1978), 209–210.
50. Ibid., 179.
51. Isozaki and Donzé, "Dominance Versus Collaboration Models," 394–408.
52. For the example of American brands, see W. David Marx, *Ametora: How Japan Saved American Style* (New York: Basic Books, 2015), 123–150.
53. Kawamura, *The Japanese Revolution in Paris Fashion*, 105.
54. Lise Skov, "Fashion-Nation: A Japanese Globalization Experience and a Hong Kong Dilemma," *Re-Orienting: The Globalization of Asian Dress,* eds Sandra Niessen, Ann Marie Leshkowich, and Carla Jones (Oxford and New York: Berg, 2003), 216.
55. Ibid., 219.
56. Wu, *Chinese Fashion from Mao to Now*, chapter 7.
57. Ibid., p. 131.
58. Zhang and Donzé, "Knowledge Upgrade," 1.
59. Wu, *Chinese Fashion from Mao to Now*, 136.
60. Ibid., 137.
61. Ibid., 138–139.
62. Zhang and Donzé, 20–21.
63. Tereza Kuldova, *Luxury Indian Fashion: A Social Critique* (London: Bloomsbury Publishing, 2016), 19–41.
64. Ibid., 76.

Chapter 9

1. LVMH, Annual Report 2007, 8. Quote from Pierre-Donzé and Ben Wubs, "LVMH: Storytelling and Organizing Creativity in Luxury and Fashion," in *European Fashion. The Creation of a Global Industry*, eds Regina Lee Blaszczyk and Veronique Pouillard (Manchester: Manchester University Press, 2018), 78.
2. Chanel. "Chanel Limited Financial Results for the Year Ended 31 December 2023," https://www.chanel.com/puls-img/ 1716301904618-pressrelease 2023resultsengfinalpdf.pdf (accessed 26 June, 2024). Deborah Ball, "Giorgio Armani Lays Groundwork for Future of His Fashion House." *Wall Street Journal*, August 1, 2016, https://www.wsj.com/articles/giorgio-armani-announces-foundation-to-protect-his-house-1470068542
3. *Financial Times*, "LVMH Becomes First European Company to Hit $500bn Market Value," https://www.ft.com/content/ 1f40342f-5075-47ba-ae86-7728b410bc30 (accessed November 3, 2024).
4. YCharts, "Lvmh Moet Hennessy Louis Vuitton Market Cap," https://ycharts.com/companies/LVMUY/market_cap (accessed April 11, 2024).
5. LVMH, "2023: New Record Year for LVMH," January 25, 2024, https://www.lvmh.com/news-documents/press-releases/2023-new-record-year-for-lvmh/ (accessed April 12, 2024).
6. This section is partly based on Donzé and Wubs, "LVMH," 63–85.
7. LVMH, Lettre aux Actionnaires, February 1994.
8. Pierre-Yves Donzé, *A Business History of the Swatch Group: The Rebirth of Swiss Watchmaking and the Globalization of the Luxury Industry* (Basingstoke: Palgrave Macmillan, 2014), 117–120.
9. LVMH. "Our 75 Maisons," https://www.lvmh.com/houses/ (accessed April 14, 2024).
10. Donzé and Wubs, "LVMH," 71; LVMH, "2023: New Record Year for LVMH," January 25, 2024 https://www.lvmh.com/news-documents/press-releases/2023-new-record-year-for-lvmh/ (accessed April 12, 2024).
11. Donzé, *Selling Europe to the World*, 65–66.
12. Bernard Arnault and Yves Messarovitch, *La Passion Créative* (Paris: Plon, 2000), 9.
13. Giacomo Tognini said of Arnault in *The World's Richest Person 2024*, "This French tastemaker came from a wealthy family and turned millions into hundreds of billions over nearly four decades." https://www.forbes.com/sites/giacomotognini/2024/04/03/the-worlds-richest-person-2024/ (accessed April 13, 2024).
14. Pierre-Yves Donzé and Rika Fujioka, "European Luxury Big Business and Emerging Asian Markets, 1960–2010," *Business History*, 57: 6 (2015): 10–14.
15. Lucas Chancel and Thomas Piketty, "Global Income Inequality, 1820–2020: The Persistence and Mutation of Extreme Inequality," *Journal of the European Economic Association* 19: 6 (2021): 3026.
16. Donzé, *Selling Europe to the World*, 28–35.
17. Ibid., 69.
18. Ibid., 71.
19. Ibid., 72.
20. Ibid., 74.
21. Ibid.,75–76.

22. Hubert Bonin, "Luxury, Banking, and Finance," in *The Oxford Handbook of Luxury Business*, eds Pierre-Yves Donzé, Véronique Pouillard, and Joanne Roberts (Oxford: Oxford University Press 2020), 83–92.
23. José Antonio Miranda and Alba Roldán, "Fast Fashion: A Successful Business Model Forced to Transform," in *The Routledge History of Fashion and Dress, 1800 to the Present*, eds Veronique Pouillard and Vincent Dubé-Senécal (London: Routledge 2023), 266–267.
24. Ibid., 267–268.
25. Ibid., 271–272.
26. Ingrid Giertz-Mårtenson, "H&M: How Swedish Entrepreneurial Culture and Social Values Created Fashion for Everyone," in *European Fashion: The Creation of a Global Industry*, eds Regina Lee Blaszczyk and Veronique Pouillard (Manchester: Manchester University Press, 2018), 201–219.
27. Elisa Arrigo, "Offshore Outsourcing in Fast Fashion Companies: A Dual Strategy of Global and Local Sourcing?" in *Eurasian Business and Economics Perspectives. Eurasian Studies in Business and Economics*, eds M.H. Bilgin, H. Danis, E. Demir, and C.D. García-Gómez, vol 19. (Berlin: Springer 2021), 73–86; Giertz-Mårtenson, "H&M," 206.
28. Nebahat Tokatli, "Global Sourcing: Insights from the Global Clothing Industry—The Case of Zara, a Fast Fashion Retailer," *Journal of Economic Geography* 8: 1 (January 2008): 30.
29. H&M Group, "Our Supply Chain in Numbers, https://hmgroup.com/sustainability/leading-the-change/transparency/supply-chain/ (accessed April 17, 2024).
30. H&M Group, Annual and Sustainability Report 2023, https://hmgroup.com/investors/annual-and-sustainability-report/ (accessed July 27 2024).
31. H&M Group, "Shareholders: The 20 Largest Shareholders as at 28 March 2024," https://hmgroup.com/investors/shareholders/ (accessed April 17, 2024).
32. José Antonio Miranda, "The Country-Of-Origin Effect and the International Expansion of Spanish Fashion Companies, 1975–2015," *Business History* 62:3 (2017): 499–500.
33. Bloomberg, "Bloomberg Billionaires Index," https://www.bloomberg.com/billionaires/profiles/amancio-ortega-gaona/ (accessed April 17, 2024). On this day, he was ranked fifteenth with a total net worth of $92.6 billion.
34. Inditex, "Statement of Non-financial Information 2023," https://annualreport2023.inditex.com/en/centro-de-descarga (accessed April 17, 2024).
35. Miranda, "The Country-of-Origin Effect," 501.
36. Tokatli, "Global Sourcing," 27–31.
37. Miranda, "The Country-of-Origin Effect," 501–502.
38. M. Mirza, A. Verma, D. M. H. Kee, and A. Suffi, "The Key Success Factors: A Case Study of UNIQLO," *Journal of the Community Development in Asia* 3:2 (2020): 1–10; T. Usui, M, Kotabe, and J. Y. Murray, "A Dynamic Process of Building Global Supply Chain Competence by New Ventures: The Case of Uniqlo," *Journal of International Marketing* 25:3 (2017): 1–20; Hongjoo Woo and Byoungho Jin," Asian Apparel Brands Internationalization: The Application of Theories to the Cases of Giordano and Uniqlo," *Fashion and Textiles*, 1 (2014): 1–14.
39. Akihiro Kinoshita, "How is a Retail Business Brand Embedded in Social Structures, Networks, and Territories? A Historical Case of Uniqlo," *Ryutsu*, 2018:41 (2018): 6–7.
40. Fast Retailing, "1949–2003," https://www.fastretailing.com/eng/about/history/2003.html (accessed April 18, 2024).

41. Frederike Schulz-Müllensiefen and Aenne Stöckmann, "Uniqlo: A Case Study on Creating Market Share with Affordable and Timeless Designs," in *Multinational Management: A Casebook on Asia's Global Market* Leaders, ed. R.T. Segers (Cham: Springer International Publishing Switzerland, 2016), 222–223.
42. Ibid., 229.
43. Bloomberg, "#30 Tadashi Yanai $40.3," https://www.bloomberg.com/billionaires/profiles/tadashi-yanai/, (accessed April 18, 2024).
44. Andrew Brooks, Kate Fletcher, Robert A. Francis, Emma Dulcie Rigby, and Thomas Roberts, "Fashion, Sustainability, and the Anthropocene," *Utopian Studies* 28:3 (2017): 482–504.
45. Miranda and Roldán, "Fast Fashion," 276.
46. Brooks et al., "Fashion, Sustainability, and the Anthropocene," 486.
47. Miranda and Roldán, "Fast Fashion," 275–277.
48. Foreign & Commonwealth Office and Department for International Development, "The Rana Plaza Disaster," https://www.gov.uk/government/case-studies/the-rana-plaza-disaster (accessed April 20, 2024).
49. Miranda and Roldán, "Fast Fashion," 277.
50. Brooks et al., "Fashion, Sustainability, and the Anthropocene," 498.
51. LVMH, "2023 Social and Environmental Responsibility Report, Chairman's Message," https://r.lvmh-static.com/uploads/2024/04/lvmh_committed_to_positive_impact_2023.pdf (accessed April 21, 2024), 12.
52. Thorstein Veblen, *The Theory of the Leisure Class* (New York: Macmillan, 1899), passim.

Chapter 10

1. Adidas Group, "Adidas Strengthens Three-Divisional Structure: Adidas Sport Style Designed by Yohji Yamamoto," Press Release: Thu, July 11, 2002, https://www.proquest.com/docview/443832472?sourcetype=Wire percent20Feeds (accessed May 11, 2024).
2. Geoffrey Jones, Michael Norris, and Sophi Kim, "Horst Dassler, Adidas, and the Commercialization of Sport," *Harvard Business School Case*, 9-316-007, December 7, 2015; Phil Knight, *Shoe Dog: A Memoir by the Creator of Nike* (London: Simon & Schuster, 2016); Rainer Karlsch, Christian Kleinschmidt, Jörg Lesczenski and Anne Sudrov, *Playing the Game: The History of Adidas* (Munich: Siedler Verlag, 2018); Kim Minhong, "How Phil Knight Made Nike a Leader in the Sport Industry: Examining the Success Factors," *Sport in Society* 23: 9 (2020): 1512–1523; Thomas Turner, "Adidas and the Creation of a Transnational Market for German Athletic Shoes, 1948–1978," in *Consumer Engineering, 1920s–1970s. Marketing between Expert Planning and Consumer Responsiveness,* ed. Jan Logemann, Gary Cross, Ingo Köhler (Cham: Palgrave Macmillan, 2019).
3. Crane, "Diffusion Models and Fashion," 13–24; Crane, Fashion and Its Social Agendas; Derrick P. Alridge and James B. Stewart, "Introduction: Hip Hop in History: Past, Present, and Future," The Journal of African American History 90: 3 (2005): 190–195; Elena Esposito, "Originality through Imitation: The Rationality of Fashion," Organization Studies 32: 5 (2011): 603–13; Tasha Lewis and Natalie Gray, "The Maturation of Hip-Hop's Menswear Brands: Outfitting the Urban Consumer," Fashion Practice 5: 2 (2013): 229–43; Yuniya Kawamura, Sneakers, Fashion, Gender, and Subculture (London: Bloomsbury, 2016); Thomas Turner, "German Sports Shoes,

Basketball, and Hip Hop: The Consumption and Cultural Significance of the Adidas 'Superstar' 1966–1988," *Sport in History* 35:1 (2015): 127–155.
4. Mette Bielefeldt Bruun and Michael A. Langkjær, "Sportswear: Between Fashion, Innovation and Sustainability," *Fashion Practice* 8, 2 (2016): 181–188.
5. Jean Williams, "Sport from Mr and Mrs Andrews Circa 1750 to Dior x Air Jordan 1," in *The Routledge History of Fashion and Dress, 1800 to the Present*, eds Veronique Pouillard and Vincent Dubé-Senécal (London: Routledge 2023), 377–390.
6. Polle, *Jean Patou*, 96.
7. Scott, "California Casual," 169–186; Deirdre Clemente, "Made in Miami: The Development of the Sportswear Industry in South Florida, 1900–1960," *Journal of Social History*, 41:1 (Fall, 2007): 127–148.
8. Richard Martin, *American Ingenuity: Sportswear 1930s–1970s: Exhibition Catalogue* (New York: Metropolitan Museum of Art, 1998), 8–17.
9. Scott, "California Casual," 169–186; Clemente, "Made in Miami," 127–148.
10. Scott, "California Casual," 172–173; 182–186.
11. Clemente, "Made in Miami," 139–143.
12. Karlsch et al., *Playing the Game*, 20–75.
13. Barbara Smit, *Sneaker Wars: The Enemy Brothers Who Founded Adidas and Puma and the Family Feud that Forever Changed the Business of Sports* (New York: Harper Collins, 2008), passim.
14. Turner, "Adidas and the Creation of a Transnational Market," 176–178.
15. Jones, Norris, and Kim, "Horst Dassler, Adidas, and the Commercialization of Sport," 5–8.
16. KG 100, *Kanematsu kabushiki kaisha sogyo 100 shunen kinenshi* (Kobe: Kanematsu, 1990), 106–109.
17. *Nikkei Sangyo Shimbun*, June 12, 1984.
18. Jones, Norris, and Kim, "Horst Dassler, Adidas, and the Commercialization of Sport," 7.
19. Karlsch et al., *Playing the Game*, 149–166.
20. Knight, *Shoe Dog*, 9–38.
21. Richard M. Locke, "The Promise and Perils of Globalization: The Case of Nike," *Management: Inventing and Delivering Its Future*, 39 (2003): 4.
22. Michelle Childs and Byoungho Jin, "Nike: An Innovation Journey," in *Product Innovation in the Global Fashion Industry. Palgrave Studies in Practice: Global Fashion Brand Management*, eds B. Jin and E. Cedrola (New York: Palgrave Pivot, 2018), 86.
23. Ibid., 87–88.
24. George P. Huber, "Changes in the Structures of US Companies: Action Implications for Executives and Researchers," *Journal of Organization Design* 5:1 (2016): 3–4.
25. Locke, "The Promise and Perils of Globalization," 4–5.
26. Childs and Jin, "Nike," 88.
27. Patricia A. Turner, "Ambivalent Patrons: The Role of Rumor and Contemporary Legends in African-American Consumer decisions," *Journal of American Folklore* 105: 418 (1992): 433.
28. Robert F. Hartley, *Management Mistakes and Successes* (New York: John Wiley & Sons, 1997), 158.
29. Childs and Jin, "Nike," 88.
30. Douglas Kellner, "The Sports Spectacle, Michael Jordan, and Nike: Unholy Alliance?" in *Michael Jordan, Inc. Corporate Sport, Media Culture, and Late Modern America*, ed. David L. Andrews (Albany: State University of New York Press, 2001).

31. Hartley, *Management Mistakes and Successes*, 158.
32. Childs and Jin, "Nike," 104.
33. Turner, "German Sports Shoes, Basketball, and Hip Hop," 139–141.
34. Yuniya Kawamura, *Sneakers: Fashion, Gender, and Subculture* (London: Bloomsbury, 2016); Turner, "German Sports Shoes, Basketball, and Hip Hop," 144–147.
35. Karlsch et al., *Playing the Game*, 285–286.
36. Ibid., 178–190.
37. Ibid., 290–291.
38. Rob Strasser, "Mit Business Units den Markt erobern," in *Playing the Game: The History of Adidas,* eds Rainer Karlsch, Christian Kleinschmidt, Jörg Lesczenski, and Anne Sudrov (Munich: Siedler Verlag, 2018), 291.
39. Karlsch et al., *Playing the Game*, 290–296.
40. Dave Mote et al., "Adidas AG," in *International Directory of Company Histories*, ed. Steven Long, et al., vol. 256 (Michigan: St. James Press, 2023), 9.
41. Quote from Locke, "The Promise and Perils of Globalization," 11.
42. Ibid., 10–15.
43. Maura Troester, et al., "NIKE, Inc.," in *International Directory of Company Histories*, edited by Steven Long, et al., vol. 248 (Michigan: St. James Press, 2023), 366.
44. Mote et al., "Adidas AG," 363–370.
45. Adidas Group, "Adidas-Salomon to Open Original Stores," Press Release Adidas-Salomon, 21 May 2001 https://www.adidas-group.com/en/media/press-releases (accessed June 8, 2019).
46. Troester, et al., "NIKE, Inc.," 367–368.
47. Karlsch et al., *Playing the Game*, 11.
48. Alridge and Stewart, "Introduction: Hip Hop in History"; Elena Romero, *Free Stylin: How Hip Hop Changed the Fashion Industry* (Santa Barbara, California: Praeger, 2012). Turner, "German Sports Shoes, Basketball, and Hip Hop."
49. Adidas Group, "Adidas Strengthens Three-Divisional Structure."
50. Ibid.
51. Adidas-Solomon AG, "Adidas by Stella McCartney: Introducing the first true sport performance design collection for women," Press Release, September 8, 2004 https://www.kanzownet.de/projekte/_adidas/press.pdf (accessed November 4, 2024).
52. Mote et al., "Adidas AG," 10.
53. Adidas Group, "Giorgio Armani S.p.A. and Reebok International Ltd.," Press Release January 15, 2010, https://www.adidas-group.com/en/media/press-releases (accessed June 26, 2019).
54. Brand Finance, "Apparel 50 Brand Ranking," https://brandirectory.com/rankings/apparel/table (accessed May 29, 2024).

Chapter 11

1. Quoted in Blaszczyk and Wubs, eds, *The Fashion Forecasters*, 246.
2. Robert O. Keohane and Joseph S. Nye, "Globalization: What's New? What's Not? (And So What?)," *Foreign Policy*, no. 118 (2000): 104–19.
3. Ibid., 105.
4. Ibid., 106.

5. Ibid., 113–114.
6. Richard N. Langlois, "The Vanishing Hand: The Changing Dynamics of Industrial Capitalism," *Industrial and Corporate Change*, volume 12, issue 2 (April 2003): 351–385; Richard N. Langlois, *The Corporation and the Twentieth Century: The History of American Enterprise* (Princeton & Oxford: Princeton University Press, 2023), 519–551.
7. Neil Coe, Peter Dicken, and Martin Hess, "Global Production Networks: Realizing the Potential," *Journal of Economic Geography* 8, no. 3 (2008): 274.
8. Ibid., 277.
9. Peter Dicken, "Geographers and 'Globalization': (Yet) Another Missed Boat?" *Transactions of the Institute of British Geographers* 29, no. 1 (March 1, 2004): 5–26.
10. Lane and Probert, *National Capitalisms*, 126–152.
11. Alibaba Group, "Milestones," https://www.alibabagroup.com/en-US/about-alibaba#history-and-milestone (accessed August 10, 2024).
12. Juanjuan Wu, Yue Hu, Lei Xu, and Marilyn R. DeLong, "Designed in China: Multiple Approaches to Fashion and Retail," in *Making Fashion in Multiple Chinas*, eds Wessie Ling and Simona Segre-Reinach (London: IB Tauris, 2018), 69–93.
13. Henry Gao, Damian Raess, and Ka Zeng, eds, *China and the WTO: A Twenty-Year Assessment* (Cambridge University Press; 2023), 1.
14. Lane and Probert. *National Capitalisms*, 106–126; Zara Liaqat, "The End of Multi-fiber Arrangement and Firm Performance in the Textile Industry: New Evidence," *The Pakistan Development Review* 52, no. 2 (2013): 97–126.
15. Lane and Probert, *National Capitalisms*, 117–118.
16. Ibid., 116–120.
17. Ibid., 118.
18. Lisa van Barneveld and Ben Wubs, "Fashion Forecasting, Gender, and Artificial Intelligence," in *The Routledge History of Fashion and Dress, 1800 to the Present*, ed. Veronique Pouillard and Vincent Dubé-Senécal (London: Routledge 2023), 247–265.
19. Mikayla DuBreuil and Sheng Lu, "Traditional vs. Big-Data Fashion Trend Forecasting: An Examination Using WGSN and EDITED," *International Journal of Fashion Design, Technology and Education*, 13:1 (2020): 68–77.
20. Blaszczyk and Wubs, *The Fashion Forecasters*, 244.
21. Ibid., 235.
22. Ibid., 239–240.
23. Ibid., 236.
24. WGSN, "WGSN announces completion of acquisition agreement with Apax Funds," https://www.wgsn.com/en/wgsn/press/press-releases/wgsn-announces-completion-acquisition-agreement-apax-funds (accessed August, 12, 2024); Apax Global Alpha, "Funds Advised by Apax Complete Acquisition of WGSN," https://www.apaxglobalalpha.com/news/funds-advised-by-apax-complete-acquisition-of-wgsn (accessed August 12, 2024).
25. Ralf Banken, "Was es im Kapitalismus gibt, gibt es im Warenhaus: Die Entwicklung der Warenhäuser in der Bundesrepublik," *Zeitschrift für Unternehmensgeschichte* ["Journal of Business History"] 57 Jahrg., H. 1. (2012): 3–30.
26. Peter Scott and Patrick Fridenson, "New Perspectives on 20th-Century European Retailing," *Business History*, 60:7 (2018): 945.

27. Ibid., 948.
28. Elisabetta Merlo, "Italian Luxury Goods Industry on the Move: SMEs and Global Value Chains," in *Global Luxury*, eds Pierre-Yves Donzé and Rika Fujioka (Singapore: Palgrave, 2018), 39–63.
29. Charles Ntumba, Samuel Aguayo, and Kamau Maina, "Revolutionizing Retail: A Mini Review of E-commerce Evolution," *Journal of Digital Marketing and Communication* 3(2) (2023): 102.
30. Childs and Byoungho, "Nike: An Innovation Journey," 90.
31. Marta Blázquez, "Fashion Shopping in Multichannel Retail: The Role of Technology in Enhancing the Customer Experience," *International Journal of Electronic Commerce* 18, no. 4 (July 2014): 97–116.
32. Emmanuel Sirima Silva, Hossein Hassani, and Dag Øivind Madsen, "Big Data in Fashion: Transforming the Retail Sector," *Journal of Business Strategy*, vol. 41, no. 4 (2020): 22; Byoungho Ellie Jin and Daeun Chloe Shin, "Changing the Game to Compete: Innovations in the Fashion Retail Industry from the Disruptive Business Model," *Business Horizons* 63 (2020): 301–311.
33. Brownlie, Douglas, Paul Hewer, and Rachel Stewart, "Keeping Fashionable Company: ASOS and the Collective Logic of Online Spaces," Academy of Marketing Conference 2013; Liying Wei, "Decision-making Behaviours toward Online Shopping," *International Journal of Marketing Studies* 8.3 (2016): 115–116.
34. Gemma-Lee Parker and Bethan Alexander, "Digital Only Retail: Assessing the Necessity of an ASOS Physical Store within Omnichannel Retailing to Drive Brand Equity," in *Bloomsbury Fashion Business Cases* (London: Bloomsbury, 2022), 2.
35. Wei, "Decision-making Behaviours," 117.
36. Parker and Alexander, "Digital Only Retail," 2
37. ASOS, "ASOS Annual Report." https://www.asosplc.com/ (accessed August 17, 2024).
38. Linglin Zhang and Yunlan Gou, "Value-Creation Strategy of Nanjing SHEIN," *International Journal of Frontiers in Sociology* 3.20 (2021): 92.
39. Competition and Market Authority Gov.UK, "ASOS, Boohoo and Asda: Greenwashing Investigation," https://www.gov.uk/cma-cases/asos-boohoo-and-asda-greenwashing-investigation (accessed August 17, 2024).
40. Ibid.
41. Arin Ria, "A Brief History of SHEIN," https://futurestartup.com/2023/11/06/a-brief-history-of-shein/ (accessed August 24, 2024).
42. Linglin Zhang and Yunlan Gou, "Value-Creation Strategy," 89–94; Han Jia, "Analysis of Business Development of a Technology Commercial Company" (MS diss., Universitat Politècnica de Catalunya, 2022).
43. Zhang and Gou, "Value-Creation Strategy," 89–92.
44. Kane Wu and Anirban Sen, "China's Shein files for US IPO in Major Test for Investor Appetite – Sources," https://www.reuters.com/markets/deals/chinese-fast-fashion-shein-files-us-ipo-wsj-2023-11-27/ (accessed August 24, 2024).
45. Ria, "A Brief History of SHEIN."
46. Zhang and Gou, "Value-Creation Strategy," 89–92.
47. Ria, "A Brief History of SHEIN."
48. Wu and Sen, "China's Shein files for US IPO."
49. Zhang and Gou, "Value-Creation Strategy," 92; Gabrielle Fonrouge, "Chair of Powerful House Committee Pushes Shein about Data Protections, China Relationship," https://www.cnbc.

com/2023/12/20/shein-grilled-on-china-relationship-data-privacy-ahead-of-ipo.html (accessed August, 24, 2024); Vauhini Vara, "Fast, Cheap, and Out of Control: Inside Shein's Sudden Rise," https://www.wired.com/story/fast-cheap-out-of-control-inside-rise-of-shein/∞tcid=_wired-verso-hp-trending_f29c2a0e-7e31-4007-9182-4d4a228ed90e_popular4-1 (accessed August 25, 2024).

50. Zhang and Gou, "Value-Creation Strategy," 91–93.
51. Shein Group, "2023 Sustainability and Social Impact Report," Shein Newsroom, https://www.sheingroup.com/corporate-news/company-updates/2023-sustainability-and-social-impact-report/ (accessed August 24, 2024).
52. Julie Zhu, Greg Roumeliotis, and Kane Wu, "Exclusive: Shein Steps Up London IPO Preparations Amid U.S. Hurdles to Listing," https://www.reuters.com/markets/deals/shein-steps-up-london-ipo-preparations-amid-us-hurdles-listing-sources-say-2024-05-10/ (accessed August 24, 2024).
53. Agnès Rocamora, "Mediatization and Digital Media in the Field of Fashion," *Fashion Theory* 21:5 (2017): 505–522. Agnès Rocamora, "The Datafication and Quantification of Fashion: The Case of Fashion Influencers" *Fashion Theory* 26:7(2022): 1109–1133.
54. Rocamora, "Mediatization and Digital Media," 509.
55. Ibid., 509–510.
56. FWO – Fashion Week Online. "Global Fashion Industry Statistics," https://fashionweekonline.com/ (accessed August 27, 2024),
57. Cited in Rocamora, "Mediatization and Digital Media," 511.
58. Rocamora, "Mediatization and Digital Media," 509–514.
59. Marco Pedroni, "Two Decades of Fashion Blogging and Influencing: A Critical Overview," *Fashion Theory* 27:2 (2023): 237–268.
60. Ibid., 264.
61. Ibid., 244–245.
62. Ibid., 237–268. Karen de Perthuis and Rosie Findlay, "How Fashion Travels: The Fashionable Ideal in the Age of Instagram," *Fashion Theory* 23:2 (2019): 219–242; Anthony Fung, "Transnational Flow of Chinese and UK Fashion Discourse: Analyses of Digital Platforms and Online Shopping in China," *Fashion Theory* 25:7 (2021): 917–930.
63. Instagram, "Nicole Warne," https://www.instagram.com/nicolewarne/ (accessed August 27, 2004).
64. Celebs Ages, "Nicole Warne," https://www.celebsages.com/nicole-warne/ (accessed August 27, 2024).
65. Suaad Jassem and Mohammad Rezaur Razzak, "Industry 4.0: The Future of Manufacturing – Foundational Technologies, Adoption Challenges, and Future Research Directions," in *Fourth Industrial Revolution and Business Dynamics: Issues and Implications*, eds Al Mawali, Nasser Rashad, Anis Moosa Al Lawati, and Ananda S. (Singapore: Palgrave Macmillan, 2021), 128.
66. Ellie Jin Byoungho and Daeun Chloe Shin, "The Power of 4th Industrial Revolution in the Fashion Industry: What, Why, and How Has the Industry Changed?" *Fash Text* 8, 31 (2021): 1–25.
67. Ibid., 4.
68. Leanne Luce, *Artificial Intelligence for Fashion: How AI is Revolutionizing the Fashion Industry* (Berkeley: CA Press, 2019), 3.
69. Ibid., 4.
70. Jin and Shin, "The Power of 4th Industrial Revolution," 13.

71. Byoungho Jin and Elena Cedrola, eds, *Product Innovation in the Global Fashion Industry,* 22–23. Lushan Sun, "3D Printing and Additive Manufacturing in Fashion," in *Leading Edge Technologies in Fashion Innovation Product Design and Development Process from Materials to the End Products to Consumers,* ed. Young-A Lee (Chan: Palgrave Macmillan 2022), 59–74.
72. Jin and Shin, "The Power of 4th Industrial Revolution," 11.
73. Alenka Pavko Čuden, "Knitting towards Sustainability, Circular Economy and Industry 4.0," *Applied Research* vol 2, issue 6 (December 2023): 1–16.
74. Alex Beall, "Chinese Factory Sets Up in Arkansas to Make T-Shirts Using U.S. Robots," https://www.therobotreport.com/chinese-factory-sets-arkansas-make-t-shirts-using-u-s-robots/ (accessed August 31, 2024).
75. Jin and Shin, "The Power of 4th Industrial Revolution," 9.
76. International Labour Office, Sectoral Policies Department, "The Future of Work in Textiles, Clothing, Leather and Footwear," Working Paper: No. 326 (Geneva: ILO, 2019).

Conclusion

1. Sombart, "Wirtschaft und Mode," 20.
2. Riello, *Cotton*, 288–295.
3. Pouillard, *Paris to New York*, 142–147.
4. Kawamura, *Fashion-ology*, 43.

References

Adidas Group. "Giorgio Armani S.p.A. and Reebok International Ltd." Press Release, January 15, 2010. Available online: https://www.adidas-group.com/en/media/press-releases (accessed June 26, 2019).

Adidas Group. "Adidas-Salomon to Open Original Stores." Press Release Adidas-Salomon, May 21, 2001. Available online: https://www.adidas-group.com/en/media/press-releases (accessed June 8, 2019).

Adidas Group. "Adidas Strengthens Three-Divisional Structure: Adidas Sport Style Designed by Yohji Yamamoto." Press Release July 11, 2002. Available online: https://www.proquest.com/docview/443832472?sourcetype=Wire percent20Feeds (accessed May 11, 2024).

Adidas-Solomon AG. "Adidas by Stella McCartney: Introducing the First True Sport Performance Design Collection for Women." Press Release September 8, 2004. Available online: https://www.kanzownet.de/projekte/_adidas/press.pdf (accessed November 4, 2024).

Agins, Teri. *The End of Fashion: How Marketing Changed the Clothing Business Forever*. New York: Harper Collins, 1999.

Alibaba Group. "Milestones." Available online: https://www.alibabagroup.com/en-US/about-alibaba#history-and-milestone (accessed August 10, 2024).

Alridge, Derrick P., and James B. Stewart. "Introduction: Hip Hop in History: Past, Present, and Future." *The Journal of African American History* 90: 3 (2005): 190–195.

Andrade, Tonio. "The Dutch East India Company in Global History: A Historiographical Reconnaissance." In *The Dutch and English East India Companies. Diplomacy, Trade and Violence in Early Modern Asia*, edited by Adam Clulow and Tristan Mostert. Amsterdam University Press, 2018.

Ankersmit, Willem. "The Waxprint: Its Origin and Its Introduction on the Gold Coast." MA diss., University Leiden, 2010.

Apax Global Alpha. "Funds Advised by Apax Complete Acquisition of WGSN." Available online: https://www.apaxglobalalpha.com/news/funds-advised-by-apax-complete-acquisition-of-wgsn (accessed August 12, 2024).

Armitage, John, and Joanne Roberts. "The Globalisation of Luxury Fashion: The Case of Gucci." *Luxury*, 6:3 (2019): 227–246.

Arnault, Bernar, and Yves Messarovitch. *La Passion Créative*. Paris: Plon, 2000.

Arrigo, Elisa. "Offshore Outsourcing in Fast Fashion Companies: A Dual Strategy of Global and Local Sourcing?" In *Eurasian Business and Economics Perspectives: Eurasian Studies in Business and Economics*, vol. 19, edited by M. H. Bilgin, H. Danis, E. Demir, and C. D. García-Gómez. Berlin: Springer 2021.

Arthur, Rachel. "Artificial Intelligence Empowers Designers in IBM, Tommy Hilfiger and FIT Collaboration." Available online: https://www.forbes.com/sites/rachelarthur/2018/01/15/ai-ibm-tommy-hilfiger/ (accessed August 2, 2024).

ASOS. "ASOS Annual Report." Available online: https://www.asosplc.com/ (accessed August 17, 2024).

Aspers, Patrik, and Frédéric Godart. "Sociology of Fashion: Order and Change." *Annual Review of Sociology* 39 (2013): 185.

Bairoch, Paul. *Cities and Economic Development: From the Dawn of History to the Present*. Chicago: University of Chicago Press, 1991.

Ball, Deborah. "Giorgio Armani Lays Groundwork for Future of His Fashion House." *Wall Street Journal*, August 1, 2016. Available online: https://www.wsj.com/articles/giorgio-armani-announcCs-foundation-to-protect-his-house-1470068542

Banken, Ralf. "Was es im Kapitalismus gibt, gibt es im Warenhaus: Die Entwicklung der Warenhäuser in der Bundesrepublik," *Zeitschrift für Unternehmensgeschichte* ["Journal of Business History"] 57 Jahrg., H. 1. (2012): 3–30.

Barthes, Roland. *The Fashion System*. New York: Hill and Wang, 1967.

Barthes, Roland. *Système de la Mode*. Paris: Le Seuil, 1967.

Beall, Alex. "Chinese Factory Sets Up in Arkansas to Make T-Shirts Using U.S. Robots." Available online: https://www.therobotreport.com/chinese-factory-sets-arkansas-make-t-shirts-using-u-s-robots/ (accessed August 31, 2024).

Beckert, Sven. *Empire of Cotton: A Global History*. New York: Vintage Books, 2014.

Beckert, Sven. *Empire of Cotton: A Global History*. Illustrated edition. New York: Vintage, 2015.

Beerman, Kenton. "The Beginning of a Revolution: Waltham and the Boston Manufacturing Company." *The Concord Review* (1994): 141–157.

Bertlett, Djurdja, Shaun Cole, and Agnès Rocamora, eds. *Fashion Media: Past and Present*. London: Bloomsbury, 2013.

Bide, Bethan. "London Leads the World: The Reinvention of London Fashion in the Aftermath of the Second World War." *Fashion Theory* 24, 3 (2020): 352–356.

Bide, Betha, and Lucie Whitmore. *Fashion City: How Jewish Londoners Shaped Global Style*. London: Bloomsbury, 2023.

Bilińska-Reformat, Katarzyna, and Anna Dewalska-Opitek. "E-Commerce as the Predominant Business Model of Fast Fashion Retailers in the Era of Global Covid-19 Pandemics,'" *Procedia Computer Science* 192 (1 October 2021): 2479–2490.

Blaszczyk, Regina Lee, and Ben Wubs, eds. *The Fashion Forecasters: A Hidden History of Color and Trend Prediction*. London: Bloomsbury, 2018.

Blaszczyk, Regina Lee, ed. *Producing Fashion: Commerce, Culture, and Consumers*. Philadelphia: University of Pennsylvania Press, 2008.

Blaszczyk, Regina Lee. *The Color Revolution*. Cambridge, MA: MIT Press, 2012.

Blaszczyk, Regina Lee, and Ben Wubs. "Beyond the Crystal Ball." In *The Fashion Forecasters: A Hidden History of Color and Trend Prediction*, edited by Regina Lee Blaszczyk and Ben Wubs. London: Bloomsbury, 2018.

Blaszczyk, Regina Lee, and Véronique Pouillard, eds. *European Fashion: The Creation of a Global Industry*. Manchester: Manchester University Press, 2018.

Blaszczyk, Regina Lee, and Uwe Spiekermann. "Bright Modernity: Color, Commerce, and Consumer Culture." In *Bright Modernity: Color, Commerce, and Consumer Culture*, edited by Regina Lee Blaszczyk and Uwe Spiekermann. Cham: Springer, 2017.

Blázquez, Marta. "Fashion Shopping in Multichannel Retail: The Role of Technology in Enhancing the Customer Experience." *International Journal of Electronic Commerce* 18, no. 4 (July 2014): 97–116.

Bloemberg, Ninke. "Dutch Jeans." In *Blue Jeans*, edited by Ninke Bloemberg and Hans Schopping. Utrecht: Centraal Museum 2012.

Bloomberg. "Bloomberg Billionaires Index." Available online: https://www.bloomberg.com/billionaires/profiles/amancio-ortega-gaona/ (accessed April 17, 2024).

Bloomberg. "#30 Tadashi Yanai $40.3." Available online: https://www.bloomberg.com/billionaires/profiles/tadashi-yanai/ (accessed April 18, 2024).

Bojer, Thomas Stege, Josh Sims, Sven Ehmann, and Robert Klanten, eds. *Blue Blooded: Denim Hunters and Jeans Culture*. Berlin: Gestalten, 2016.

Bok, Edward. "Paris Fashions and Our's: Mr. Bok Says Modest Women Look Askance at French Designs." *New York Times*, September 6, 1912, *ProQuest Historical Newspapers*, 8.

Boles, Elson E. "Critiques of World-Systems Analysis and Alternatives: Unequal Exchange and Three Forms of Class and Struggle in the Japan? US Silk Network, 1880? 1890." *Journal of World-Systems Research* (2002): 150–212.

Bonin, Hubert. "Luxury, Banking, and Finance." In *The Oxford Handbook of Luxury Business*, edited by Pierre-Yves Donzé, Véronique Pouillard, and Joanne Roberts. Oxford: Oxford University Press 2020.

Brachet-Champsaur, Florence, and Ludovic Cailluet. "The Great Depression? Challenging the Periodization of French Business History in the Interwar Period." In *The Business History of Everything*, vol. 8. Business History Conference, Athens, Georgia: Business and Economic History online, 2010.

Brand Finance. "Apparel 50 Brand Ranking." Available online: https://brandirectory.com/rankings/apparel/table (accessed May 29, 2024).

Breward, Christopher. *Fashion*. Oxford: Oxford University Press, 2003.

Breward, Christopher. "Fashionable Masculinities in England and Beyond: Renunciation and Dandyism, 1800–1939." In *The Cambridge History of Fashion* vol. 2, edited by Christopher Breward, Beverly Lemire, and Giorgio Riello. Cambridge: Cambridge University Press, 2023.

Breward, Christopher, and David Gilbert, eds. *Fashion's World Cities*. London: Bloomsbury, 2006.

Briggs, Asa. *Marks & Spencer, 1884–1984*. London: Octopus Books, 1984.

Brooks, Andrew, Kate Fletcher, Robert A. Francis, Emma Dulcie Rigby, and Thomas Roberts. "Fashion, Sustainability, and the Anthropocene." *Utopian Studies* 28, 3 (2017): 482–504.

Brownlie, Douglas, Paul Hewer, and Rachel Stewart. "Keeping Fashionable Company: ASOS and the Collective Logic of Online Spaces." Academy of Marketing Conference, 2013.

Bruland, Kristine. *British Technology and European Industrialization: The Norwegian Textile Industry in the Mid-Nineteenth Century*. Cambridge: Cambridge University Press, 1989.

Bruun, Mette Bielefeldt, and Michael A. Langkjær. "Sportswear: Between Fashion, Innovation and Sustainability." *Fashion Practice* 8, 2 (2016): 181–188.

Bunka Fukuso Gakuin: 40 nen no ayumi ["Bunka Fashion College: 40th Anniversary"]. Tokyo: Bunka Fukuso Gakuin, 1963.

Business Research Insights. "Automotive Market Report Overview." Available online: https://www.businessresearchinsights.com/market-reports/automotive-market-102183 (accessed October 21, 2024).

Byoungho, Ellie Jin, and Daeun Chloe Shin. "The Power of 4th Industrial Revolution in the Fashion Industry: What, Why, and How Has the Industry Changed?" *Fash Text* 8, 31 (2021): 1–25.

Byoungho, Ellie Jin, and Daeun Chloe Shin. "Changing the Game to Compete: Innovations in the Fashion Retail Industry from the Disruptive Business Model." *Business Horizons* 63 (2020): 301–311.

Byoungho, Jin and Elena Cedrola, eds. *Product Innovation in the Global Fashion Industry.* New York: Palgrave 2018.

Bytheway, Simon James. *Investing Japan: Foreign Capital, Monetary Standards, and Economic Development, 1859–2011*. Cambridge University Press, 2014.

Capalbo, Cinzia. "Creativity and Innovation of the Italian Fashion System in the Inter-war Period (1919–1943)." *Investigaciones de Historia Económica* ["Economic History Research"], 12, 2 (2016): 92–93.

Carlos, Ann M., and Stephen Nicholas. "Giants of an Earlier Capitalism: The Chartered Trading Companies as Modern Multinationals." *Business History Review* 62, 3 (1988): 398–419.

Cedrola, Elena, and Ksenia Silchenko. "Ermenegildo Zegna: When Family Values Guide Global Expansion in the Luxury Industry." *Fashion Brand Internationalization*. New York: Palgrave Pivot, 2016.

Celebs Ages. "Nicole Warne." Available online: https://www.celebsages.com/nicole-warne/ (accessed August 27, 2024).

Cerretano, Valerio. "Autarky, Market Creation and Innovation: Snia Viscosa and Saici, 1933–1970." *Business History* 64, 6 (2022): 1110–1130.

Cerretano, Valerio. "European Cartels and Technology Transfer: The Experience of the Rayon Industry, 1920 to 1940." *Zeitschrift für Unternehmensgeschichte* ["Journal of Business History"], 56. Jahrg., H. 2. (2011): 206–224.

Cerretano, Valerio. "Multinational Business and Host Countries in Times of Crisis: Courtaulds, Glanzstoff, and Italy in the Interwar Period." *Economic History Review*, 71, 2 (2018): 552–555.

Ceruzzi, Paul. "Jacquard's Web: How a Hand-loom Led to the Birth of the Information Age." *Technology and Culture*, 47 (January 1, 2006): 197–198.

Chaiklin, Martha. "Surat and Bombay: Ivory and Commercial Networks in Western India." In *The Dutch and English East India Companies: Diplomacy, Trade and Violence in Early Modern Asia*, edited by Adam Clulow and Tristan Mostert. Amsterdam University Press, 2018.

Chan, Heather. "From Costume to Fashion: Visions of Chinese Modernity in *Vogue* Magazine, 1892–1943." *Ars Orientalis* 47 (2017), 210–232.

Chancel, Luca, and Thomas Piketty. "Global Income Inequality, 1820–2020: The Persistence and Mutation of Extreme Inequality." *Journal of the European Economic Association*, 19:6 (2021): 3026.

Chanel. "Chanel Limited Financial Results for the Year Ended 31 December 2023." Available online: https://www.chanel.com/puls-img/1716301904618-pressrelease2023resultsengfinalpdf.pdf (accessed June 26, 2024).

Chandler, Alfred D. *Scale and Scope: The Dynamics of Industrial Capitalism*. Cambridge MA: The Belknap of Harvard University Press, 1994.

Chandler, Alfred D. *The Visible Hand: The Managerial Revolution in American Business*. Cambridge MA: The Belknap of Harvard University Press, 1999.

Cheng, Leonard K., and William K. Fung. "The Globalization of Trade and Production: A Case Study of Hong Kong's Textile and Clothing Industries." In *Global Production and Trade in East Asia*, edited by Leonard K. Cheng and Henryk Kierzkowski. Boston, MA: Springer, 2001.

Childs, Michell, and Byoungho Jin. "Nike: An Innovation Journey." In *Product Innovation in the Global Fashion Industry*: Palgrave Studies in Practice: Global Fashion Brand Management, edited by B. Jin, B. and E. Cedrola. New York: Palgrave Pivot, 2018.

Clemente, Deirdre. "Made in Miami: The Development of the Sportswear Industry in South Florida, 1900–1960." *Journal of Social History* 41:1 (Fall, 2007): 127–148.

Clulow, Adam, and Tristan Mostert. "Introduction: The Companies in Asia." In *The Dutch and English East India Companies*, edited by Adam Clulow and Tristan Mostert, *Diplomacy, Trade and Violence in Early Modern Asia*. Amsterdam University Press, 2018.

Coe, Neil, Peter Dicken, and Martin Hess. "Global Production Networks: Realizing the Potential." *Journal of Economic Geography* 8, no. 3 (2008): 274.

Competition and Market Authority Gov.UK. "ASOS, Boohoo and Asda: Greenwashing Investigation." Available online: https://www.gov.uk/cma-cases/asos-boohoo-and-asda-greenwashing-investigation (accessed August 17, 2024).

Comstock, Sandra Curtis. "The Making of an American Icon: The Transformation of Blue Jeans during the Great Depression." In *Global Denim*, edited by Daniel Miller and Sophie Woodward. New York: Berg, 2011.

Cox, Howard, and Simon Mowatt, "*Vogue* in Britain: Authenticity and the Creation of Competitive Advantage in the UK Magazine Industry." *Business History* 54.1 (2012): 67–87.

Craik, Jennifer. *Fashion: The Key Concepts*. Oxford: Berg Publishers, 2009.

Crane, Diana. "Diffusion Models and Fashion: A Reassessment." *The Annals of the American Academy of Political and Social Science* 566, no. 1 (1999): 13–24.

Crane, Diana. *Fashion and Its Social Agendas: Class, Gender, and Clothing*. Chicago: The University of Chicago Press, 2000.

Cruz-Fernandez, Paula de la. "Manufacturing and the Importance of Global Marketing." In *The Routledge Companion to the Makers of Global Business*, edited by Teresa da Silva Lopes, Christina Lubinski and Heidi J. S. Tworek. New York: Routledge, 2020.

Čuden, Alenka Pavko. "Knitting towards Sustainability, Circular Economy and Industry 4.0." *Applied Research* vol 2, issue 6 (December 2023): 1–16.

Dalton, Lauren, Pauline Sullivan, Jeanne Heitmeyer, and Ann DuPont. "Robertson's Model: A Framework for Exploration of the Second World War Conservation Consumption Policy Influence on Fashion in the US." *International Journal of Consumer Studies* 36, no. 6 (2012): 611–621.

Daumas, Jean-Claude, ed. *Dictionnaire Historique des Patrons Français*. Paris: Flammarion, 2010.

Davies, R. B. *Peacefully Working to Conquer the World: Singer Sewing Machines in Foreign Markets*. London: Arno Press, 1976.

Dejung, Christof. *Die Fäden des globalen Marktes: Eine Soziale- and Kulturgeschichte des Welthandels am Beispiel der Handelsfirma Gebrüder Volkart 1851–1999*. Köln: Böhlau Verlag, 2013.

de Marly, Diana. *The History of Haute Couture, 1850–1950*. Manchester: Anchor Press, 1980.

de Marly, Diana. *Worth: Father of Haute Couture*. London: Elm Tree Books, 1990.

Department of City Planning Office of Historic Resources. *Los Angeles Citywide Historic Context Statement. Context: Industrial Development, 1850–1980*. Los Angeles: City of Los Angeles, 2018.

de Perthuis, Karen, and Rosie Findlay. "How Fashion Travels: The Fashionable Ideal in the Age of Instagram." *Fashion Theory* 23:2 (2019): 219–242.

Dicken, Peter. "Geographers and 'Globalization': (Yet) Another Missed Boat?" *Transactions of the Institute of British Geographers* 29, no. 1 (March 1, 2004): 5–26.

Dicken, Peter. *Global Shift: Mapping the Changing Contours of the World Economy*. London: Sage, 2015.

Dior, Catherine, and Jean-Pierre Teto, *Dior by Dior*. London: V&A Publishing, 2007.

Donzé, Pierre-Yves. *A Business History of the Swatch Group: The Rebirth of Swiss Watchmaking and the Globalization of the Luxury Industry*. Basingstoke: Palgrave Macmillan, 2014.

Donzé, Pierre-Yves. "From the 'Yellow Peril' To 'Cool Japan': Country's Image and Global Competitiveness of the Japanese Manufacturing Industry Since the Meiji Period." In *National Brands and Global Markets: An Historical Perspective*, edited by Nikolas Glover and David M. Higgins. New York: Routledge, 2023.

Donzé, Pierre-Yves. *Selling Europe to the World: The Rise of the Luxury Fashion Industry, 1980–2020*. London: Bloomsbury Publishing, 2023.

Donzé, Pierre-Yves, and Ben Wubs. "LVMH: Storytelling and Organizing Creativity in Luxury and Fashion." In *European Fashion: The Creation of a Global Industry*, edited by Regina Lee Blaszczyk and Veronique Pouillard. Manchester: Manchester University Press, 2018.

Donzé, Pierre-Yves, and Ben Wubs. "Storytelling and the Making of a Global Luxury Fashion Brand: Christian Dior." *International Journal of Fashion Studies* 6, no. 1 (2019): 83–102.

Donzé, Pierre-Yves, and Julia Yongue. *Japanese Capitalism and Entrepreneurship: A History of Business from the Tokugawa Era to the Present*. Oxford: Oxford University Press, 2024.

Donzé, Pierre-Yves, and Rika Fujioka. "European Luxury Big Business and Emerging Asian Markets, 1960–2010." *Business History* 57: 6 (2015): 10–14.

Donzé, Pierre-Yves, and Rika Fujioka. "The Formation of a Technology-based Fashion System, 1945–1990: The Sources of the Lost Competitiveness of Japanese Apparel Companies." *Enterprise & Society* 22, no. 2 (2021): 438–474.

Downey, Lynn. "Levi Strauss: A Short Biography." Levi Strauss & Co, 2008. Available online: http://www.levistrauss.com/sites/default/files/librarydocument/2010/4/History_Levi_Strauss_Biography.pdf (accessed October 5, 2024).

Drake, Alicia. *Beautiful People: Saint Laurent, Lagerfeld: Splendeurs et misères de la mode*. Paris: Denoël, 2008.

Dubé-Senécal, Vincent. "Fashion, Industry and Diplomacy: Reframing Couture–Textile Relations in France, 1950s–1960s." *Enterprise & Society* 24:2 (2023): 459.

DuBreuil, Mikayla, and Sheng Lu. "Traditional vs. Big-Data Fashion Trend Forecasting: An Examination Using WGSN and EDITED." *International Journal of Fashion Design, Technology and Education* 13:1 (2020): 68–77.

Easey, Mike, ed. *Fashion Marketing*. John Wiley & Sons, 2009.

Encyclopedia.com. "Catalina Sportswear." Available online: https://www.encyclopedia.com/fashion/news-wires-white-papers-and-books/catalina-sportswear (accessed October 6, 2024).

Engel, Alexander. "Coloring the World: Marketing German Dyestuffs in the Late Nineteenth and Early Twentieth Centuries." In *Bright Modernity: Color, Commerce, and Consumer Culture*, edited by Regina Lee Blaszczyk and Uwe Spiekermann. Cham: Springer, 2017.

English, Bonnie. *Japanese Fashion Designers: The Work and Influence of Issey Miyake, Yohji Yamamoto, and Rei Kawakubo*. London: Bloomsbury, 2018.

Entwistle, Joanne, and Elizabeth Wissinger, eds. *Fashioning Models: Image, Text and Industry*. London: A&C Black, 2013.

Esposito, Elena. "Originality through Imitation: The Rationality of Fashion." *Organization Studies* 32: 5 (2011): 603–613.

European Fashion Heritage Association. "Tales of Italian Style: Biki." Available online: https://fashionheritage.eu/tales-of-italian-style-biki/ (accessed June 21, 2024).

Evans, Caroline. *The Mechanical Smile: Modernism and the First Fashion Shows in France and America, 1900–1929*. New Haven and London: Yale University Press, 2013.

Ewing, Elizabeth, and Alice Mackrell. *History of Twentieth Century Fashion*. London: Crysalis Books Group, 2005.

Faraut, François. *Histoire de "La Belle Jardinière."* Paris: Belin, 1987.

Farnie, D. A. "The Textile Machine-Making Industry and the World Market, 1870–1960." *Business History* 32.4 (1990): 150–170.

Fashion United. "Global Fashion Industry Statistics." Available online: https://fashionunited.com/global-fashion-industry-statistics (accessed October 21, 2024).

Fast Retailing. "1949–2003." Available online: https://www.fastretailing.com/eng/about/history/2003.html (accessed April 18, 2024).

Federico, Giovanni. *An Economic History of the Silk Industry, 183–1930*. Vol. 5. Cambridge: Cambridge University Press, 2009.

Feifer, George. *Breaking Open Japan: Commodore Perry, Lord Abe, and American Imperialism in 1853*. New York: Smithsonian Books, 2006.

Feiner, Shmuel. *The Jewish Enlightenment*. Pennsylvania: University of Pennsylvania Press, 2004.

Feng, Bangyan. *100 Years of Li & Fung: Rise from Family Business to Multinational*. Thomson Learning, 2007.

Ferragamo Archives. Available online: https://archive.ph/z7PIY (accessed July 27, 2024)

Financial Times. "LVMH becomes First European Company to Hit $500bn Market Value." Available online: https://www.ft.com/content/1f40342f-5075-47ba-ae86-7728b410bc30 (accessed November 3, 2024).

Fonrouge, Gabrielle. "Chair of Powerful House Committee Pushes Shein about Data Protections, China Relationship." Available online: https://www.cnbc.com/2023/12/20/shein-grilled-on-china-relationship-data-privacy-ahead-of-ipo.html (accessed August 24, 2024).

Font, Lourdes M. "International Couture: The Opportunities and Challenges of Expansion, 1880–1920." *Business History* 54.1 (2012): 30–47.

Foreign & Commonwealth Office and Department for International Development. "The Rana Plaza Disaster." Available online: https://www.gov.uk/government/case-studies/the-rana-plaza-disaster (accessed April 20, 2024).

Foster, John E., and William John Eccles. "Fur Trade in Canada." *The Canadian Encyclopedia*. 2013. Available online: https://www.thecanadianencyclopedia.ca/en/article/fur-trade#:~:text=The%20fur%20trade%20was%20a,European%20demand%20for%20felt%20hats.

Francks, Penelope. *The Japanese Consumer: An Alternative Economic History of Modern Japan*. Cambridge: Cambridge University Press, 2009.

Fujioka, Rika. "Japanese Department Stores." In *Oxford Research Encyclopedia of Business and Management*. Oxford: Oxford University Press 2018. Available online: https://doi.org/10.1093/acrefore/9780190224851.013.95 (accessed November 18, 2024).

Fujioka, Rika. *Hyakkaten no seisei katei* ["The Development of Department Stores"]. Tokyo: Yuhikaku, 2006.

Fujioka, Rika, and Ben Wubs. "Competitiveness of the Japanese Denim and Jeans Industry: The Cases of Kaihara and Japan Blue, 1970–2015." In *European Fashion: The Creation of a Global Industry*, edited by Regina Lee Blaszczyk and Véronique Pouillard. Manchester: Manchester University Press, 2018.

Fujioka, Rika, and Jon Stobart. "Global and Local: Retail Transformation and the Department Store in Britain and Japan, 1900–1940." *Business History Review* 92, no. 2 (2018): 251–280.

Fujioka, Rika, Zhen Li, and Yuta Kaneko. "The Democratization of Luxury and the Expansion of the Japanese Market, 1960–2010." In *Global Luxury: Organizational Change and Emerging Markets since the 1970s*, edited by Pierre-Yves Donzé and Rika Fujioka. Basingstoke: Palgrave Macmillan, 2018.

Fukai, Akiko. "Japonism in Fashion" [*Mo-do no japonizumu*]. Kyoto: The Kyoto Costume Institute, 1996. Available online: https://www.kci.or.jp/en/research/dresstudy/pdf/e_Fukai_Japonism_in_Fashion.pdf. (accessed November 17, 2024).

Fung, Anthony. "Transnational Flow of Chinese and UK Fashion Discourse: Analyses of Digital Platforms and Online Shopping in China." *Fashion Theory* 25:7 (2021): 917–930.

FWO – Fashion Week Online. "Global Fashion Industry Statistics." Available online: https://fashionweekonline.com/ (accessed August 27, 2024).

Gao, Henry, Damian Raess, and Ka Zeng, eds. *China and the WTO: A Twenty-Year Assessment*. Cambridge University Press, 2023.

Gibson, Pamela Church. *Fashion and Celebrity Culture*. London: Bloomsbury, 2013.

Giertz-Mårtenson, Ingrid. "H&M: How Swedish Entrepreneurial Culture and Social Values Created Fashion for Everyone." In *European Fashion: The Creation of a Global Industry*, edited by Regina Lee Blaszczyk and Veronique Pouillard. Manchester: Manchester University Press, 2018.

Godley, Andrew. "The Development of the Clothing Industry: Technology and Fashion." *Textile History* 28, no. 1 (1997): 3–10.

Godley, Andrew C., and Haiming Hang. "Collective Financing among Chinese Entrepreneurs and Department Store Retailing in China." *Business History*, 58.3 (2016): 367.

Gordon, Andrew. *Fabricating Consumers: The Sewing Machine in Modern Japa*. Berkley, California: University of California Press, 2012.

Gordon, Andrew. *A Modern History of Japan from Tokugawa Times to the Present*. Oxford: Oxford University Press, 2003.

Grant, Tina, and Thomas Derdak. "Esprit de Corp." *International Directory of Company Histories*. Vol. 29. St. James Press, 1999, 180–182.

Grau, François-Marie. *La Haute Couture*. Paris: PUF, 2000.

Green, Nancy L. *Ready-to-Wear, Ready-to-Work: A Century of Industry and Immigrants in Paris and New York*. Durham: Duke University Press, 1997.

Grosfilley, Anne. "The Global Trade of the Wax Fabric." In *The Routledge History of Fashion and Dress, 1800 to the Present*, edited by Veronique Pouillard and Vincent Dubé-Senécal. London: Routledge 2023.

Grumbach, Didier. *History of International Fashion*. Northampton: Interlink Books, 2014.

Grundmann, Reiner, and Nico Stehr. "Why Is Werner Sombart Not Part of the Core of Classical Sociology? From Fame to (Near) Oblivion." *Journal of Classical Sociology* 1 (2001): 257–287.

Guenther, Irene. *Nazi Chic: Fashioning Women in the Third Reich*. Oxford: Berg Publishers, 2004.

Hall, Nigel. "Liverpool's Cotton Importers c. 1700 to 1914." *Northern History* 54, no. 1 (2 January 2017): 79–93.

Hall, P. G. "The Location of the Clothing Trades in London, 1861–1951." *Transactions and Papers (Institute of British Geographers)* 28 (1960): 155–178.

Handley, Susannah. *Nylon: The Story of a Fashion Revolution: A Celebration of Design from Art Silk to Nylon and Thinking Fibers*. Baltimore: Johns Hopkins University Press, 1999.

Hartley, Robert F. *Management Mistakes and Successes*. New York: John Wiley & Sons, 1997.

Hashino, Tomoko. *Keizai hatten to sanchi – shijo – seido: Meijiki kinuorimonogyo no shinka to dainamizumu*. Kyoto: Minerva, 2007.

Hast, Adele et al. "Levi Strauss & Co," *International Directory of Company Histories*. Vol. 5 (St. James Press, 1992).

Headrick, Daniel R. *The Tentacles of Progress: Technology Transfer in the Age of Imperialism, 1850–1940*. Oxford University Press, 1988.

Henriot, Christian, Shi Lu, and Charlotte Aubrun. *The Population of Shanghai (1865–1953): A Sourcebook*. Leiden: Brill, 2018.

Herring, George C. *From Colony to Superpower. U.S. Foreign Relations since 1776*. Oxford: OUP, 2011.

Hess, Heather. "The Wiener Werkstätte and the Reform Impulse." In *Producing Fashion: Commerce, Culture, and Commerce*, edited by Regina Lee Blaszczy. Philadelphia: University of Pennsylvania Press, 2008.

Hesse. Jan-Otmar. "The German Textile Puzzle: Selective Protectionism and the Silent Globalization of an Industry." *Business History Review* 93, no. 2 (2019): 233.

Hines, Tony, and Margaret Bruce, eds. *Fashion Marketing*. London: Routledge, 2007.

H&M Group. "Annual and Sustainability Report 2023." Available online: https://hmgroup.com/investors/annual-and-sustainability-report/ (accessed July 27, 2024).

H&M Group. "Our Supply Chain in Numbers." Available online: https://hmgroup.com/sustainability/leading-the-change/transparency/supply-chain/ (accessed April 17, 2024).

H&M Group. "Shareholders: The 20 Largest Shareholders as at 28 March 2024." Available online: https://hmgroup.com/investors/shareholders/ (accessed April 17, 2024).

Hollander, Anne. "The Modernization of Fashion." *Design Quarterly*, No. 154 (Winter, 1992): 27–33.

Honeyman, Katrina. *Well Suited: A History of the Leeds Clothing Industry, 1850–1990*. Edinburgh: Pasold Research Fund, 2000.

Hounshell, David A. *From the American System to Mass Production, 1800–1932: The Development of Manufacturing Technology in the United States*. Baltimore: Johns Hopkins University Press, 1984.

Howard, Vicki, ed. *History of Retailing and Consumption*. Special Issue on Department Stores, vol. 7 (2021), 1–114.

Howe, Christopher. *The Origins of Japanese Trade Supremacy*. London: Hurst & Company, 1996.

Huang, Qing. "Fashioning Modernity and Qipao in Republican Shanghai (1910s–1930s)." MA diss., Ohio University, 2015.

Huber, George P. "Changes in the Structures of US Companies: Action Implications for Executives and Researchers." *Journal of Organization Design* 5:1 (2016): 3–4.

Hudson, Pat. "The Limits of Wool and the Potential of Cotton in the Eighteenth and Early Nineteenth Centuries." In *The Spinning World: A Global History of Cotton Textiles, 1200–1850*. Oxford: Oxford University Press, 2009.

Hunter, Janet, and S. Sugiyama. "Anglo Japanese Economic Relations in Historical Perspective, 1600–2000: Trade and Industry, Finance, Technology and the Industrial Challenge." In *The History of Anglo-Japanese Relations, 1600–2000: Volume 4 Economic and Business Relations*, edited by Janet E. Hunter and S. Sugiyama. London: Palgrave Macmillan UK, 2002.

IBM. "Bestseller and IBM Garage Bring Sustainable Fashion Forward with Fashion.ai." Available online: https://www.ibm.com/blog/bestseller-and-ibm-garage-bring-sustainable-fashion-forward-with-fashion-ai/ (accessed August 2, 2024).

IBM. "2023 IBM Annual Report." Available online: https://www.ibm.com/annualreport/ (accessed August 2, 2004).

Illes, Angelina. "The Fascination with Japanese-Styled Gowns: A Quantitative Perspective on Ready-Made Garments at the Beginning of the Eighteenth Century." *Journal of Historians of Netherlandish Art* 15:1 (Winter 2023): 2–6.

Inditex. "Statement of Non-financial Information 2023." Available online: https://annualreport 2023.inditex.com/en/centro-de-descarga (accessed April 17, 2024).

Industrievereinigung Chemiefaser e.V. *Production since 1975, World Production Man-made Fibers Wool, and Cotton*. Available online: https://www.ivc-ev.de/live/index.php?page_id=87 (accessed October 28, 2018).

International Labour Office, Sectoral Policies Department. "The Future of Work in Textiles, Clothing, Leather and Footwear." Working Paper: No. 326 (Geneva: ILO, 2019).

Instagram. "Nicole Warne." Available online: https://www.instagram.com/nicolewarne/ (accessed August 27, 2004).

Ishii, Kanji. *Kindai Nihon to Igirisu shihon*. Tokyo: Tokyo University, 1984.

Isozaki, Yoko, and Pierre-Yves Donzé. "Dominance Versus Collaboration Models: French and Italian Luxury Fashion Brands in Japan." *Journal of Global Fashion Marketing* 13, no. 4 (2022): 394–408.

Janssens, Alice. "Fashioning Interwar Berlin: Conceptualising the German Capital's Clothing Industry." Unpublished paper given at the annual conference of the European Business History Association. Vienna University of Economics and Business, August 2017.

Jassem, Suaad and Mohammad Rezaur Razzak. "Industry 4.0: The Future of Manufacturing –Foundational Technologies, Adoption Challenges, and Future Research Directions." In *Fourth Industrial Revolution and Business Dynamics: Issues and Implications*, edited by Al Mawali, Nasser Rashad, Anis Moosa Al Lawati, and Ananda S. Singapore: Palgrave Macmillan, 2021.

Jequier, François. *Charles Veillon (1900–1971): Essai sur l'émergence d'une éthique patronale*. Zurich: Société d'études en matière économique, 1985.

Jewish Museum of the American West. "The Brownstein-Louis Company Catalog of 1918: Men's Furnishing Goods in Los Angeles." Available online: https://www.jmaw.org/brownstein-louis-los-angeles-2/ (accessed October 6, 2024).

Jia, Han. "Analysis of Business Development of a Technology Commercial Company." MS diss., Universitat Politècnica de Catalunya, 2022.

Jones, Geoffrey. *Beauty Imagined: A History of the Global Beauty Industry*. Oxford: Oxford University Press, 2010.

Jones, Geoffrey. *Multinationals and Global Capitalism: From the Nineteenth to the Twenty-First Century*. Oxford: Oxford University Press, 2005.

Jones, Geoffrey, Michael Norris, and Sophi Kim. "Horst Dassler, Adidas, and the Commercialization of Sport." *Harvard Business School Case*, 9-316-007, December 7, 2015.

Jones, Laura A. "E. Moses and Son – the Tailors who Pioneered Mass-Market Men's Tailoring?" *Fashion, Style & Popular Culture* 5.1 (2018): 97–115.

Jones, Michelle. *London Couture and the Making a Fashion Centre*. Cambridge MA: MIT Press 2022.

Journal des Dames et des Modes, 42, no. 1, January 5, 1838, 14.

Kaigai raisensu burando no genkai to kongo no kadai. Osaka: Yano Institute, 1984.

Karlsch, Rainer, Christian Kleinschmidt, Jörg Lesczenski, and Anne Sudrov. *Playing the Game: The History of Adidas*. Munich: Siedler Verlag, 2018.

Kassirzadeh, Azam Gandchi. "Selected Factors that Influence the Mass-Production of Misses' High-Fashion and Popular-Priced Ready-to-wear Apparel in the United States." PhD diss., Texas Woman's University, 1978.

Kawamura, Yuniya. *Fashion-ology: An Introduction to Fashion Studies*. Second Edition. London: Bloomsbury Visual Arts: 2018.

Kawamura, Yuniya. *The Japanese Revolution in Paris Fashion*. Oxford: Berg, 2004.

Kawamura, Yuniya. *Sneakers, Fashion, Gender, and Subculture*. London: Bloomsbury, 2016.

Kellner, Douglas. "The Sports Spectacle, Michael Jordan, and Nike: Unholy Alliance?" In *Michael Jordan, Inc. Corporate Sport, Media Culture, and Late Modern America*, edited by David L. Andrews. Albany: State University of New York Press, 2001.

Keohane, Robert O., and Joseph S. Nye. "Globalization: What's New? What's Not? (And So What?)." *Foreign Policy*, no. 118 (2000): 104–119.

KG 100. *Kanematsu kabushiki kaisha sogyo 100 shunen kinenshi*. Kobe: Kanematsu,1990.

Khan, Mushtaq H. "Technology Policies and Learning with Imperfect Governance." In *The Industrial Policy Revolution I: The Role of Government beyond Ideology*, edited by Joseph E. Stiglitz and Justin Yifu Lin, Basingstoke: Macmillan, 2013.

Kinoshita, Akihiro. "How is a Retail Business Brand Embedded in Social Structures, Networks, and Territories? A Historical Case of Uniqlo." *Ryutsu*, 2018:41 (2018): 6–7.

Knight, Phil. *Shoe Dog: A Memoir by the Creator of Nike*. London: Simon & Schuster, 2016).

Köster, Roman. *Hugo Boss, 1924–1945: Die Geschichte einer Kleiderfabrik zwischen Weimarer Republik und 'Drittem Reich,'* vol. 23. München: CH Beck, 2011.

Kremer, Roberta S. ed. *Broken Threads: The Destruction of the Jewish Fashion Industry in Germany and Austria*. Oxford and New York: Berg, 2007.

Kuldova, Tereza. *Luxury Indian Fashion: A Social Critique*. London: Bloomsbury Publishing, 2016.

Lane, Christe, and Jocelyn Probert. *National Capitalisms, Global Production Networks: Fashioning the Value Chain in the UK, US, and Germany*. Oxford: OUP, 2009.

Langenbruch, Theodor. *Glanzstoff 1899–1949*. Wuppertal: Enka AG, 1985.

Langlois, Richard N. *The Corporation and the Twentieth Century: The History of American Enterprise*. Princeton & Oxford: Princeton University Press, 2023.

Langlois, Richard N. "The Vanishing Hand: The Changing Dynamics of Industrial Capitalism." *Industrial and Corporate Change*, volume 12, issue 2 (April 2003): 351–385.

Laznicka, Joanna Jana. "The Boss Workwear Buttons: Unveiling the History Behind Them." Available online: https://focusspeed.com/the-boss-workwear-buttons-history-behind-them/ (accessed October 6, 2024).

Lerner, Paul. *The Consuming Temple: Jews, Department Stores, and the Consumer Revolution in Germany, 1880–1940*. Cornell: Cornell University Press, 2017.

Les Echos, August 6, 1999.

Levi Strauss & Co. "We have . . . Been innovating since the birth of the blue jean in 1873." Available online: https://www.levistrauss.com/levis-history/ (accessed December 16, 2021).

Levitt, Sarah. "Cheap Mass-Produced Men's Clothing in the Nineteenth and Early Twentieth Centuries." *Textile History* 22.2 (1991): 179–192.

Lewis, Tasha, and Natalie Gray. "The Maturation of Hip-Hop's Menswear Brands: Outfitting the Urban Consumer." *Fashion Practice* 5: 2 (2013): 229–243.

Li, Lillian M. "Silks by Sea: Trade, Technology, and Enterprise in China and Japan." *The Business History Review*, vol. 56, no. 2 (Summer, 1982): 192–217.

Liaqat, Zara. "The End of Multi-fiber Arrangement and Firm Performance in the Textile Industry: New Evidence." *The Pakistan Development Review* 52, no. 2 (2013): 97–126.

Lipovetsky, Gilles. *The Empire of Fashion: Dressing Modern Democracy*. Princeton: Princeton University Press, 1994.

Locke, Richard M. "The Promise and Perils of Globalization: The Case of Nike." *Management: Inventing and Delivering Its Future* 39 (2003): 4.

Lockwood, William W. "Japanese Silk and the American Market." *Far Eastern Survey*, 5.4 (1936): 31–36.

Loeb, Lori Anne. *Consuming Angels: Advertising and Victorian Women*. Oxford: Oxford University Press, 1994.

Los Angeles Almanac. "General Population." Available online: http://www.laalmanac.com/population/po26.php (accessed December 19, 2021).

Luce, Leanne. *Artificial Intelligence for Fashion: How AI is Revolutionizing the Fashion Industry*. Berkeley: CA Press, 2019.

LVMH. "2023: New Record Year for LVMH," January 25, 2024. Available online: https://www.lvmh.com/news-documents/press-releases/2023-new-record-year-for-lvmh/ (accessed 12 April 2024).

LVMH. "2023 Social and Environmental Responsibility Report, Chairman's Message." Available online: https://r.lvmh-static.com/uploads/2024/04/lvmh_committed_to_positive_impact_2023.pdf (accessed April 21, 2024).

LVMH. "Our 75 Maisons." Available online: https://www.lvmh.com/houses/ (accessed April 14, 2024).

Ma, Debin. "The Modern Silk Road: The Global Raw-Silk Market, 1850–1930." *The Journal of Economic History* 56.2 (1996).

Macchion, Laura et al. "International E-Commerce for Fashion Products: What Is the Relationship with Performance?" *International Journal of Retail & Distribution Management* 45, no. 9 (1 January 2017): 1011–1031

McCracken, Grant. "Who Is the Celebrity Endorser? Cultural Foundations of the Endorsement Process." *Journal of Consumer Research* 16, 3 (1989): 310–321.

MAGIC Marketplace. Available online: https://www.apparelsearch.com/trade_shows/magic_fashion_fabric_trade_show.htm (accessed December 19, 2021).

Marchand, Stéphane. *Les Guerres du Luxe*. Paris: Fayard, 2001.

Mareï, Nora, and Michel Savy. "Global South Countries: The Dark Side of City Logistics. Dualisation vs Bipolarisation." *Transport Policy*, Volume 100 (2021): 150–160.

Marseille, Jacques. *Empire Colonial et Capitalisme Français: Historie d'un Divorce*. Paris: Seuil, 1984.

Martin, Richard. *American Ingenuity: Sportswear 1930s–1970s: Exhibition Catalogue*. New York: Metropolitan Museum of Art, 1998.

Martin, Richard, and Harold Koda. *Orientalism: Visions of the East in Western Dress*. New York: The Metropolitan Museum of Art, 1994.

Marx, Christian, and Ben Wubs. "National Conflicts in a Multinational: The Case of the Dutch–German AKU/VGF/Akzo, 1920s to 1970s." *Business History* 64: 9 (2022): 1709–1734.

Marx, Karl. *Capital: A Critique of Political Economy*. Volume One. London: Penguin Books, 1990 [1867].

Marx, W. David. *Ametora: How Japan Saved American Style*. New York: Basic Books, 2015.

Merlo, Elisabetta. "Italian Fashion Business: Achievements and Challenges (1970s–2000s)." *Business History* 53, no. 3 (2011): 344–362.

Merlo, Elisabetta. "Italian Luxury Goods Industry on the Move: SMEs and Global Value Chains." In *Global Luxury*, edited by Pierre-Yves Donzé and Rika Fujioka. Singapore: Palgrave, 2018.

Merlo, Elisabetta. "When Fashion Met Industry: Biki and Gruppo Finanziario Tessile (1957–72)." *Journal of Modern Italian Studies* 20:1 (2015): 92–110.

Merlo, Elisabetta, and Francesca Polese. "Italy." In *Berg Encyclopedia of World Dress and Fashion: West Europe*, edited by Lise Skov. Oxford: Berg, 2010.

Merlo, Elisabetta, and Francesca Polese. "Turning Fashion into Business: The Emergence of Milan as an International Fashion Hub." *Business History Review* 80, no. 3 (2006): 415–447.

Merlo, Elisabetta, and Ivan Paris. *The Italian Fashion System: The Role of Institutions and Institutional Change, 1940s–1980s*. Cham: Palgrave Macmillan, 2024.

Merlo, Elisabetta, and Mario Perugini. "The Determinants of the Emergence of Turin as the First Capital of Italian Fashion Industry (1900–1960)." *Fashion Theory* 24:3 (2020): 335–336.

Merlo, Elisabetta, and Mario Perugini. "Making Italian Fashion Global: Brand Building and Management at Gruppo Finanziario Tessile (1950s–1990s)." In *The Brand and Its History: Trademarks, Branding and National Identity*, edited by Patricio Sáiz and Rafael Castro. London: Routledge, 2022.

Merlo, Elisabett, and Valeria Pinchera. "Configuring Cultural Emerging Industries: A Comparison of the French and Italian Fashion Industries." *Business History Review* 97: 4 (2023): 779–807.

Miller, Michael Barry. *The Bon Marché: Bourgeois Culture and the Department Store*, 1869–1920. Princeton: Princeton University Press, 1981.

Minhong, Kim. "How Phil Knight Made Nike a Leader in the Sport Industry: Examining the Success Factors." *Sport in Society* 23: 9 (2020): 1512–1523.

Miranda, José Antonio. "The Country-of-Origin Effect and the International Expansion of Spanish Fashion Companies, 1975–2015." *Business History* 62:3 (2017): 499–500.

Miranda, José Antonio, and Alba Roldán, "Fast Fashion: A Successful Business Model Forced to Transform." In *The Routledge History of Fashion and Dress, 1800 to the Present*, edited by Veronique Pouillard and Vincent Dubé-Senécal. London: Routledge, 2023.

Miranda, José Antonio, and Alba Roldán. "Spanish Fashion without the Country-of-origin Effect." In *National Brands and Global Markets*. London: Routledge, 2023.

Mirza, M., A. Verma, D. M. H. Kee, and A. Suffi. "The Key Success Factors: A Case Study of UNIQLO." *Journal of the Community Development in Asia* 3:2 (2020): 1–10.

Mitchell, B. R. *European Historical Statistics, 1750–1970*. Berlin: Springer, 1975.

Mokyr, Joë. *Economic History of the United States Since 1865*. Lecture Notes Economics Northwestern University. Available online: https://faculty.wcas.northwestern.edu/~jmokyr/Graphs-and-Tables.PDF (accessed December 15, 2021).

Moore, Christopher M., and Grete Birtwistle. "The Burberry Business Model: Creating an International Luxury Fashion Brand." *International Journal of Retail & Distribution Management* 32, no. 8 (2004): 412–422.

Morimoto, Mariko, and Susan Chang. "Western and Asian Models in Japanese Fashion Magazine Ads: The Relationship with Brand Origins and International Versus Domestic Magazines." *Journal of International Consumer Marketing* 21.3 (2009): 173–187.

Moses, E., & Son. *The Growth of an Important Branch of British Industry*. London: no name, 1860.

Mote, Dave, et al., "Adidas AG." In *International Directory of Company Histories*, edited by Steven Long, et al., vol. 256. Michigan: St. James Press, 2023.

Moutet, Aimée. *Les Logiques de l'Entreprise: La Rationalisation dans l'Industrie Française de l'Entre-deux-guerres*. Paris: EHESS, 1997.

Mrad, Mona, Maya Farah, and Stephanie Haddad. "From Karl Lagerfeld to Erdem: A Series of Collaborations between Designer Luxury Brands and Fast-Fashion Brands." *Journal of Brand Management* 26 (1 September 2019), 567–582.

Museo Ferragamo and LIFE Photocollection. "Made in Italy: Salvatore Ferragamo's Ideas, Models and Inventions." *Google Arts & Culture*, Available online: https://artsandculture.google.com/story/made-in-italy-salvatore-ferragamo-s-ideas-models-and-inventions/UQWRSqxpWZsfIg (accessed June 18, 2024)

Nagata, Hanako. *990 en no jinzu ga tsukurareru no ha naze?* Tokyo: Godo, 2016.

The New York Times, July 29, 1976.

The New York Times, September 5, 1983.

Ng, Sandy. "Clothes Make the Woman: Cheongsam and Chinese Identity in Hong Kong." *Fashion, Identity, and Power in Modern Asia* (2018): 357–378.

Nierstrasz, Chris. *Rivalry for Tade in Tea and Textiles: The English and Dutch East India Companies (1700–1800)*. Basingstoke: Palgrave Macmillan, 2015.

Nihon Keizai Shimbun. August 11, 1988.

Nikkei Sangyo Shimbun. June 12, 1984.

Ntumba, Charles, Samuel Aguayo, and Kamau Maina. "Revolutionizing Retail: A Mini Review of E-commerce Evolution." *Journal of Digital Marketing and Communication* 3(2) (2023): 102.

Ohkita, Kenichi. "Coopetition through International Luxury Brand Licensing: Burberry in Japan." In *Global Opportunities for Entrepreneurial Growth: Coopetition and Knowledge Dynamics within and across Firms*. Bingley: Emerald Publishing Limited, 2017.

Okawa, Tomoko. "Imitating Authentic Clothing through Technology Transplantation." Unpublished paper given at the *East Asian Business History Workshop* (online), September 2022.

Okawa, Tomoko. "Licensing and the Mass Production of Luxury Goods." In *Oxford Handbook of Luxury Business*, edited by Pierre-Yves Donzé, Véronique Pouillard, and Joanne Roberts. Oxford: Oxford University Press, 2022.

Okawa, Tomoko. "Licensing Practices at Maison Christian Dior." In *Producing Fashion. Commerce, Culture and Consumers*, edited by Regina Lee Blaszczyk. Pennsylvania: University of Pennsylvania Press, 2011.

Oliva, Alberto, Norberto Angeletti, and Anna Wintour. *In Vogue: An Illustrated History of the World's Most Famous Fashion Magazine*. New York: Rizzoli International, 2012.

O'Rourke, Kevin H. "Tariffs and Growth in the Late Nineteenth Century." In *Classical Trade Protectionism 1815–1914*, edited by Jean-Pierre Dormois and Pedro Lains. Abingdon: Routledge, 2006.

Osakabe, Yoshinori. "Dressing Up During the Meiji Restoration: A Perspective on Fukusei (Clothing Reform)," In *Fashion, Identity, and Power in Modern Asia*, edited by Kyunghee Pyun and Aida Yuen Wong. Cham: Palgrave Macmillan, 2018.

Osakabe, Yoshinori. *Yofuku, sanpatsu, datto: fukusei no meiji isshin*. Tokyo: Kodansha, 2014.

Okonkwo, Uche. *Luxury Fashion Branding: Trends, Tactics, Techniques*. Berlin: Springer, 2016), 24.

Osterhammel, Jürgen. *The Transformation of the World: A Global History of the Nineteenth Century*. Princeton: Princeton University Press, 2014.

Owen, Geoffrey. *From Empire to Europe: The Decline and Revival of British Industry Since the Second World War*. New York: Harper Collins, 1999.

Owen, Geoffrey. *The Rise and Fall of Great Companies: Courtaulds and the Reshaping of the Man-made Fiber Industry*. Oxford: Oxford University Press, 2010.

Parker, Gemma-Lee and Bethan Alexander. "Digital Only Retail: Assessing the Necessity of an ASOS Physical Store within Omnichannel Retailing to Drive Brand Equity." In *Bloomsbury Fashion Business Cases*. London: Bloomsbury, 2022.

Parthasarathi, Prasannan. "Historical Issues of Deindustrialization in Nineteenth-Century South India." In *How India Clothed the World*: *The World of South Asian Textiles, 1500–1850*, edited by Giorgio Riello and Tirthankar Roy. Leiden: Brill, 2009.

Patrick, Stewart, and Alexandra Huggins. "The Term 'Global South' Is Surging: It Should Be Retired." Available online: https://carnegieendowment.org/posts/2023/08/the-term-global-south-is-surging-it-should-be-retired?lang=en (accessed October 15, 2024).

Paulicelli, Eugenia. *Fashion under Fascism: Beyond the Black Shirt*. London: Bloomsbury: 2004.

Pavard, Bibia, Sandrine Lévêque, and Claire Blandin. "Elle et Marie Claire dans les Années 1968: Une 'parenthèse enchantée'?" *Le Temps des Médias* 2 (2017): 65–78.

Paxton, Robert O. *The Anatomy of Fascism*. London: Penguin Books, 2004.

Pederson, Jay P. ed. "Benetton Group." *International Directory of Company Histories*. Vol. 67. Michigan: St. James Press, 2005.

Pederson, Jay P. ed. "The Gap, Inc." *International Directory of Company Histories*. Vol. 18. Michigan: St. James Press, 1997.

Pederson, Jap P. ed. "Phillips-Van Heusen." *International Directory of Company Histories*, Vol. 24. Michigan: St. James Press, 1998.

Pedroni, Marco. "Two Decades of Fashion Blogging and Influencing: A Critical Overview." *Fashion Theory* 27:2 (2023): 237–268.

Pederson, Jay P. "Chanel SA." *International Directory of Company Histories*. Volume 49. Detroit, Mich.: St. James Press, 2003,

Pirro, Deirdre. "Guccio Gucci: A Leather Lineage." *The Florentine*. Available online: https://www.theflorentine.net/2009/06/18/guccio-gucci/ (accessed April 4, 2024).

Pochna, Marie France. *Bonjour, Monsieur Boussac*. Paris: R. Laffont, 1980.

Polle, Emmanuelle. *Jean Patou: A Fashionable Life*. Paris: Flammarion, 2013.

"Portraitist in France." *Life* 37:14 (1954): 133.

Potvin, John. *Giorgio Armani: Empire of the Senses*. London & New York: Routledge, 2013.

Pouillard, Véronique. "Design Piracy in the Fashion Industries of Paris and New York in the Interwar Years." *Business History Review* 85, no. 2 (2011): 319–344.

Pouillard, Véronique. "Managing Fashion Creativity: The History of the Chambre Syndicale de la Couture Parisienne during the Interwar Period." *Investigaciones de Historia Económica-Economic History Research* 12, no. 2 (2016): 76–89.

Pouillard, Véronique. *Paris to New York: The Transatlantic Fashion Industry in the Twentieth Century*. Cambridge MA: Harvard University Press, 2021.

Pouillard, Véronique, and Johanna Zanon. "Wholesale Couture: Jean Patou's Jane Paris Line (1929)." *Dress* (2019): 1–13.

Pouillard, Véronique, and Waleria Dorogova. "Couture Ltd: French Fashion's Debut in London's West End." *Business History* 2022, vol. 64, issue 3 (2022), 606.

Pyun, Kyunghee, and Aida Yuen Wong. *Fashion, Identity, and Power in Modern Asia*. Cham: Palgrave Macmillan, 2018.

Rantisi, Norma M. "The Ascendance of New York Fashion." *International Journal of Urban and Regional Research* 28.1 (March 2004): 90–91.

Reid, Anthony. "Southeast Asian Consumption of Indian and British Cotton Cloth, 1600–1850." In *How India Clothed the World: The World of South Asian Textiles, 1500–1850*, edited by Giorgio Riello and Tirthankar Roy. Leiden: Brill, 2009.

Remer, C. F. *Foreign Investments in China*. New York: Howard Fertig, 1968.

Reynolds, David. *America, Empire of Liberty: A New History*. London: Allen Lane, 2009.

Ria, Arin. "A Brief History of SHEIN." Available online: https://futurestartup.com/2023/11/06/a-brief-history-of-shein/ (accessed August 24, 2024).

Ricci, Stefania. *Walking Dreams: Salvatore Ferragamo, 1898–196*. Editorial RM, 2006.

Riello, Giorgio. *Cotton: The Fabric that Made the Modern World*. Cambridge: Cambridge University Press, 2013.

Roberts, Mary Louise. "Gender, Consumption, and Commodity Culture." *The American Historical Review* 103.3 (1998): 819.

Rocamora, Agnès. "The Datafication and Quantification of Fashion: The Case of Fashion Influencers." *Fashion Theory* 26:7 (2022): 1109–1133.

Rocamora, Agnès. "Mediatization and Digital Media in the Field of Fashion." *Fashion Theory* 21:5 (2017): 505–522.

Roces, Mina. "Gender, Nation, Fashion, and Modernities in the Asia-Pacific, 1900 to the Present." In *The Cambridge History of Fashion*, vol. 2, edited by Christopher Breward, Beverly Lemire, and Giorgio Riello. Cambridge: Cambridge University Press, 2023.

Romero, Elena. *Free Stylin: How Hip Hop Changed the Fashion Industry*. Santa Barbara, California: Praeger, 2012.

Rosen, Ellen Israel. *Making Sweatshops: The Globalization of the U.S. Apparel Industry*. Berkeley: University of California Press, 2002.

Rude, Fernand. *Les révoltes des canuts (1831–1834)*. Paris: La Découverte, 2020.

Scarpellini, Emanuela. *Italian Fashion since 1945: A Cultural History*. Cham: Palgrave Macmillan: 2019.

Schanzenbach, Wolfgang. "From Siber & Brennwald to DKSH Japan K.K.: More than 140 Years of Building Bridges between East and West." In *Handbuch Schweiz-Japan*, edited by Patrick Ziltener. Zurich: Chronos, 2010.

Scherner, Jonas. "The Beginnings of Nazi Autarky Policy: The 'National Pulp Programme' and the Origin of Regional Staple Fiber Plants." *The Economic History Review*, New Series, 61:4 (2008): 869.

Schumpeter, Joseph A. *Capitalism, Socialism and Democracy*. London: Routledge, 1994.

Schulz-Müllensiefen, Frederike, and Aenne Stöckmann. "Uniqlo: A Case Study on Creating Market Share with Affordable and Timeless Designs." In *Multinational Management: A Casebook on Asia's Global Market Leaders*, edited by R.T. Segers. Cham: Springer International Publishing Switzerland, 2016.

Schweitzer, Marlis. "American Fashion for American Woman: The Rise and Fall of Fashion Nationalism." In *Producing Fashion: Commerce, Culture, and Consumers*, edited by Regina Lee Blaszczyk. Philadelphia: University of Pennsylvania Press, 2008.

Schwell, Alexandra, Michal Buchowski, Malgorzata Kowalska, and Nina Szogs, eds. *New Ethnographies of Football in Europe*. London: Palgrave Macmillan UK, 2016.

Scott, Peter, and Patrick Fridenson. "New Perspectives on 20th-Century European Retailing." *Business History* 60:7 (2018): 945.

Scott, William R. "California Casual: Lifestyle Marketing and Men's Leisurewear, 1930–1960." In *Producing Fashion: Commerce, Culture, and Consumers*, edited by Regina Lee Blaszczyk. Philadelphia: University of Pennsylvania Press, 2008), 170.

Shein Group. "2023 Sustainability and Social Impact Report." Shein Newsroom. Available online: https://www.sheingroup.com/corporate-news/company-updates/2023-sustainability-and-social-impact-report/ (accessed August 24, 2024).

Shen, Bin, Tsan-Ming Choi, and Pui-Sze Chow. "Brand Loyalties in Designer Luxury and Fast Fashion Co-Branding Alliances." *Journal of Business Research* 81 (1 December 2017): 173–180.

Sheridan, Mandy, Christopher Moore, and Karinna Nobbs. "Fast Fashion Requires Fast Marketing: The Role of Category Management in Fast Fashion Positioning." *Journal of Fashion Marketing and Management: An International Journal* 10, no. 3 (2006): 301–315.

Shibusawa Shasi Database. "Shibusawa Eiichi Memorial Foundation." Available online: https://shashi.shibusawa.or.jp.

Shigeichi Sugino, Shigaku keiei no ikiru: watashino seikatsu to kangae [The Management of Private School] Tokyo: Nihon shobo, 1958.

Shinichi, Iwamoto. *Mishin to ifuku no keizaishi: chikyu kibo keizai to kanai seisan*. Kyoto: Shibunkaku, 2014.

Silva, Emmanuel Sirima, Hossein Hassani, and Dag Øivind Madsen. "Big Data in Fashion: Transforming the Retail Sector." *Journal of Business Strategy* vol. 41, no. 4 (2020): 22.

Simmel, Georg. "Fashion." *American Journal of Sociology* 62, no. 6 (1957): 541–558.

Skov, Lise. "Fashion-Nation: A Japanese Globalization Experience and a Hong Kong Dilemma." In *Re-Orienting: The Globalization of Asian Dress*, edited by Sandra Niessen, Ann Marie Leshkowich and Carla Jones. Oxford and New York: Berg, 2003.

Skov, Lise. "The Role of Trade Fairs in the Global Fashion Business." *Current Sociology* 54, 5 (2006).

Smit, Barbara. *Sneaker Wars: The Enemy Brothers Who Founded Adidas and Puma and the Family Feud that Forever Changed the Business of Sports* (New York: Harper Collins, 2008), passim.

Sombart, Werner. "Wirthschaft und Mode: Ein Beitrag zur Theorie der modernen Bedarfsgestaltung Grenzfragen des Nerven- und Seelenlebens." In *Einzel-Darstellungen für Gebildete aller Stände. Zwölftes Heft*, edited by L. Loewenfeld and H. Kurella. Wiesbaden: J. F. Bergmann, 1902.

Spoerer, Mark. *C&A: A Family Business in Germany, the Netherlands and the UK 1911–1961*. München: CH Beck, 2016.

Spoerer, Mark. *C&A: Ein Familienunternehmen in Deutschland, den Niederlanden und Großbritannien, 1911–1961*. Munich: Verlag C. H. Beck, 2016.

Stanfill, Sonnet. "The Role of the Sartoria in Postwar Italy." *Journal of Modern Italian Studies*, 20, no. 1 (2015): 83–91.

Stanfill, Sonnet. *New York Fashion*. London V&A Publications, 2007.

Steele, Valerie. *Paris Fashion: A Cultural History*. Oxford: Oxford University Press, 1988.

Sterlacci, Francesca, and Joanne Arbuckle. *Historical Dictionary of the Fashion Industry*. Lanham, Maryland: Rowman & Littlefield, 2017.

Stokes, Bruce. "Protectionism and Politics." *EJournal USA, Economic Perspectives* (2007): 7–8.

Strasser, Rob. "Mit Business Units den Markt erobern." In *Playing the Game: The History of Adidas*, edited by Rainer Karlsch, Christian Kleinschmidt, Jörg Lesczenski, and Anne Sudrov. Munich: Siedler Verlag, 2018.

Stride, Christopher, Jean Williams, David Moor, and Nick Catley. "From Sportswear to Leisurewear: The Evolution of English Football League Shirt Design in the Replica Kit Era." *Sport in History* 35, no. 1 (2 January 2015): 156–194.

Stride, Christopher, Nick Catley, and Joe Headland. "Shirt Tales: How Adults Adopted the Replica Football Kit." *Sport in History* 40, no. 1 (2 January 2020): 106–146.

Statista. "Soccer (Football) Shirt Sales Worldwide in 2021, by Club." Available online: https://www.statista.com/statistics/1118294/football-shirt-sales-by-club/ (accessed September 29, 2024).

Subrahmanyam, Sanjay. *Explorations in Connected History: From the Tagus to the Ganges*. Oxford: Oxford University Press, 2005.

Sullivan, Jame. *Jeans: A Cultural History of an American Icon*. New York: Gotham, 2007.

Sun, Lushan. "3D Printing and Additive Manufacturing in Fashion." In *Leading Edge Technologies in Fashion Innovation Product Design and Development Process from Materials to the End Products to Consumers*, edited by Young-A Lee. Chan: Palgrave Macmillan 2022.

Sweeney, Naoíse Mac. *The West: A New History of an Old Idea*. London: WH Allen, 2023.

Takasaki City University of Economics, ed. *Tomioka seishijo to gunma no sanshigyo*. Tokyo: Nihon Keizai hyoronsha, 2016.

Takeshi, Abe, and Kyohei Hirano. *Sen'i Sangyo*. Tokyo: Nihon keieishi kenkyujo, 2013.

Tamura, Hitoshi. "Zairai orimonogyō no gijutsu kakushin to kagakusenryō. Dentō iro kara ryūkō iro he." *Shakaikeizaishi gaku*, vol. 69, 2004, 3–28.

Taylor, Lou. "From Berlin to Paris." In *Paris Fashion and World War Two Global Diffusion and Nazi Control*, edited by Lou Taylor and Marie McLoughlin. London: Bloomsbury, 2020.

Taylor, Lou. "The Lyon Haute Nouveauté Fashion Textile Industry During World War Two: Design Making, Exhibition and International Diffusion." In *Paris Fashion and World War Two Global Diffusion and Nazi Control*, edited by Lou Taylor and Marie McLoughlin. London: Bloomsbury, 2020.

Tognini, Giacomo. "The World's Richest Person 2024." Available online: https://www.forbes.com/sites/giacomotognini/2024/04/03/the-worlds-richest-person-2024/ (accessed April 13, 2024).

Tokatli, Nebahat. "Global Sourcing: Insights from the Global Clothing Industry—The Case of Zara, a Fast Fashion Retailer." *Journal of Economic Geography*, 8: 1 (January 2008): 30

Tregenza, Liz. *Wholesale Couture: London and beyond, 1930–70*. London: Bloomsbury, 2023.

Troester, Maura. et al. "NIKE, Inc." in *International Directory of Company Histories*, edited by Steven Long, et al., vol. 248. Michigan: St. James Press, 2023.

Trubert-Tollu, Chantal, Françoise Tétart-Vittu, Jean-Marie Martin-Hattemberg, and Fabrice Olivieri. *The House of Worth, 1858–1954: The Birth of Haute Couture*. London: Thames & Hudson, 2017.

Tsunemi, Mikiko. *Kuwasawa Yoko to modan dezain undo* ["Kuwasawa Yoko and Modern Design"] Tokyo: Kuwasawa gakuen, 2007.

Turner, Patricia A. "Ambivalent Patrons: The Role of Rumor and Contemporary Legends in African-American Consumer Decisions." *Journal of American Folklore* 105: 418 (1992): 433.

Turner, Thomas. "Adidas and the Creation of a Transnational Market for German Athletic Shoes, 1948–1978." In *Consumer Engineering, 1920s–1970s: Marketing between Expert Planning and Consumer Responsiveness*, edited by Jan Logemann, Gary Cross, Ingo Köhler. Cham: Palgrave Macmillan, 2019.

Turner, Thomas. "German Sports Shoes, Basketball, and Hip Hop: The Consumption and Cultural Significance of the Adidas 'Superstar' 1966–1988." *Sport in History* 35:1 (2015): 127–155.

Uchida, Hoshimi. "The Spread of Timepieces in the Meiji Period." *Japan Review* 14 (2002): 174–175.

Usui, T., M. Kotabe, and J. Y. Murray. "A Dynamic Process of Building Global Supply Chain Competence by New Ventures: The Case of Uniqlo." *Journal of International Marketing* 25:3, (2017): 1–20.

van Barneveld, Lisa and Ben Wubs. "Fashion Forecasting, Gender, and Artificial Intelligence." In *The Routledge History of Fashion and Dress, 1800 to the Present*, edited by Veronique Pouillard and Vincent Dubé-Senécal. London: Routledge 2023.

van Nederveen Meerkerk, Elise, Corinne Boter, Sarah Carmichael, and Katharine Frederick. "Global Shifts and Local Actors: Revising Macro-Level Theories on the Relocation of Textile Production from the Lens of the Household in the Netherlands and Java, c. 1820–1940." *BMGN – Low Countries Historical Review* 138 (2023): 12–20.

Vara, Vauhini. "Fast, Cheap, and Out of Control: Inside Shein's Sudden Rise." Available online: https://www.wired.com/story/fast-cheap-out-of-control-inside-rise-of-shein/∞tcid=_wired-verso-hp-trending_f29c2a0e-7e31-4007-9182-4d4a228ed90e_popular4-1 (accessed August 25, 2024).

Veblen, Thorstein. *The Theory of the Leisure Class*. New York: Macmillan, 1899.

Vlisco. "The Founding of Vlisco." Available online: https://www.vlisco.com/heritage/the-founding-of-vlisco (accessed September 15, 2024).

von Glahn, Richard. *The Economic History of China: From Antiquity to the Nineteenth Century*. Cambridge: Cambridge University Press, 2016.
Walker, Corinne. *Une Histoire du Luxe à Genève: Richesse et Art de Vivre aux XVIIe et XVIIIe Siècles*. Genève: La Baconnière, 2018.
Walsh, Claire. "The Newness of the Department Store: A View from the Eighteenth Century." In *Cathedrals of Consumption*, edited by Geoffrey Crossick and Serge Jaumain. London: Routledge, 2019.
Warner, Patricia Campbell. "The Americanization of Fashion: Sportswear, the Movies and the 1930s." In *Twentieth-Century American Fashion*, edited by Linda Welters and Patricia A. Cunningham. Oxford: Berg, 2008.
Wei, Liying. "Decision-making Behaviours toward Online Shopping." *International Journal of Marketing Studies* 8.3 (2016): 115–116.
Weisberg, Gabriel P. *Japonisme: Japanese Influence on French Art 1854–1910*. Cleveland: Kent State University Press, 1975.
Welters, Linda, and Abby Lillethun. *Fashion History: A Global View*. London: Bloomsbury Publishing, 2018.
Westphal, Uwe. *Fashion Metropolis Berlin 1836–1939: The Story of the Rise and Destruction of the Jewish Fashion Industry*. Leipzig: Seemann Henschel, 2019.
WGSN. "WGSN Announces Completion of Acquisition Agreement with Apax Funds." Available online: https://www.wgsn.com/en/wgsn/press/press-releases/wgsn-announces-completion-acquisition-agreement-apax-funds (accessed August 12, 2024).
White, Nicola. *Reconstructing Italian Fashion: America and the Development of the Italian Fashion Industry*. London: Bloomsbury Academic, 2000.
Wilkins, Mira. *The History of Foreign Investment in the United States 1914–1945*. Cambridge MA, Harvard University Press, 2004.
Williams, Jean. "Sport from Mr and Mrs Andrews Circa 1750 to Dior x Air Jordan 1." In *The Routledge History of Fashion and Dress, 1800 to the Present*, edited by Veronique Pouillard and Vincent Dubé-Senécal. London: Routledge 2023.
Wissinger, Elizabeth. *This Year's Model: Fashion, Media, and the Making of Glamour*. New York: New Word University Press, 2015.
Woo, Hongjoo, and Byoungho Jin. "Asian Apparel Brands Internationalization: The Application of Theories to the Cases of Giordano and Uniqlo." *Fashion and Textiles* 1 (2014): 1–14.
Worth, Rachel. *Fashion for the People: A History of Clothing at Marks & Spencer*. Oxford: Berg Publishers, 2007.
Wu, Juanjuan. *Chinese Fashion from Mao to Now*. Oxford and New York: Berg, 2009.
Wu, Juanjuan, Yue Hu, Lei Xu, and Marilyn R. DeLong. "Designed in China: Multiple Approaches to Fashion and Retail." In *Making Fashion in Multiple Chinas*, edited by Wessie Ling and Simona Segre-Reinach. London: IB Tauris. 2018.
Wu, Kane, and Anirban Sen. "China's Shein Files for US IPO in Major Test for Investor Appetite – Sources." Available online: https://www.reuters.com/markets/deals/chinese-fast-fashion-shein-files-us-ipo-wsj-2023-11-27/ (accessed August 24, 2024).
Wubs, Ben. "Interstoff's Fashion Table: The Internalization of Fashion Forecasting in the World's Most Important Fashion Fabric Fair." In *The Fashion Forecasters: A Hidden History of Color and*

Trend Forecasting, edited by Regina Lee Blaszczyk and Ben Wubs. New York: Bloomsbury Academic, 2018.

Wubs, Ben. "US Multinationals in the Netherlands – Three Cases: IBM, Dow Chemical, and Sara Lee." In *Four Centuries of Dutch-American Relations 1609-2009*, edited by Hans Krabbendam, Cornelis A. van Minnen, Gilles Scott-Smith. Boom Amsterdam and State University of New York Press Albany, New York 2009.

Wubs, Ben, and Thierry Maillet. "Building Competing Fashion Textile Fairs in Europe, 1970–2010: Première Vision (Paris) vs. Interstoff (Frankfurt)." *Journal of Macromarketing* 37, 1 (2017), 25–39.

Yagi, Tsutomu. *Wacoal to Renown*. Tokyo: Tokyo Keizai, 1978.

Yamazaki, Hiroaki. *Nihon Kasen Sangyo hattasu shiron*. Tokyo: Tokyo University Press, 1975.

Yamazaki, Hiroaki, ed. *Nihon keieishi no kisochishiki*. Tokyo: Yuhikaku, 2004.

Yamazaki, Hiroaki, and Takeshi Abe. *Orimono kara apareru he: bingo orimonogyo to sasaki shoten*. Osaka: Osaka University Press, 2012.

YCharts. "Lvmh Moet Hennessy Louis Vuitton Market Cap." Available online: https://ycharts.com/companies/LVMUY/market_cap (accessed April 11, 2024).

Yesil, Bilge. "'Who Said This Is a Man's War?': Propaganda, Advertising Discourse and the Representation of War Worker Women during the Second World War." *Media History* 10, no. 2 (August 2004): 103–117.

Yomiuri Shimbun, December 15, 2015.

Yoshimoto, Yoko. "Hana Hiraku Yosai Gakkou" ["Developing Dressmaking School"]. In *Yosai no Jidai* [The Era of Dressmaking], edited by Kazuko Koizumi. Tokyo: OM Shuppan.

Zajtmann, David. "Une révolution dans la mode: le prêt-à-porter des couturiers parisiens (1965–2000)." *Entreprises et histoire* 3 (2022): 52–63.

Zakharova, Larissa. *S'habiller à la soviétique: La mode et le Dégel en USSR*. Pais: CNRS Éditions 2011.

Zalando. "Our History: From Start-Up to Grown-Up." Available online: https://corporate.zalando.com/en/about-us/our-history (accessed November 5, 2024).

Zanon, Johanna. "Reawakening the 'Sleeping Beauties' of Haute Couture: The Case of Guy and Arnaud de Lummen." In *European Fashion: The Creation of a Global Industry*, edited by Blaszczyk and Pouillard. Manchester: Manchester University Press, 2018.

Zeitaku ha teki da: senji keizai toseika no Tokyo. Tokyo: Tokyo Metropolitan Archives, 2012.

Zhang, Juxuan, and Pierre-Yves Donzé. "Knowledge Upgrade in the Chinese Apparel Industry, 1980–2020." *Enterprise & Society* (2023): 1–30.

Zhang, Lingli, and Yunlan Gou. "Value-Creation Strategy of Nanjing SHEIN." *International Journal of Frontiers in Sociology* 3.20 (2021): 92.

Zhu, Julie, Greg Roumeliotis, and Kane Wu. "Exclusive: Shein Steps Up London IPO Preparations Amid U.S. Hurdles to Listing." Available online: https://www.reuters.com/markets/deals/shein-steps-up-london-ipo-preparations-amid-us-hurdles-listing-sources-say-2024-05-10/ (accessed August 24, 2024).

Zola, Emile. *La Curée* ["The Kill"]. Paris: G. Charpentier et E. Fasquelle, 1895.

Index

Note: References in *italic* refer to figures, **bold** refer to tables. References followed by "n" refer to notes.

3D knitting 213, 214
3D printing 213–14, *215*

Abraham Moon & Sons 147
adidas 179, 183–4, 196–7, 221
    brand position and value 195, **196**
    company structure 193–4, *194*
    fashionalization of 193–6
    marketing 191, 192–3
    "My Adidas" song (by Run DMC) 188
    vs. Nike and Reebok 184–5, 187
    Reebok ownership 194, 195
    revival 188, 190–1
    Salomon acquision 191
    sneaker factories in Germany and United States 215
    and Stella McCartney 194
    "Superstar" shoes in hip-hop culture 188
Admiral 197
Africa
    Africa Growth Opportunity Act 202
    cotton trade 63, 65–7
    wax fabrics 77, 79–80
Agache-Willot Group 49, 223
A. Girard & Cie 62
AI (artificial intelligence) 199, 213
A La Belle Jardinière (BJ) store 20, 48–9
Algemene Kunstzijde Unie (AKU) 109–10, *110*
Alibaba 201
Amazon 207
American Council for Style and Design (ACSAD) 117
American fashion industry 83–4, 96–7
    American Viscose Corporation 98, *98*, 120
    cotton textile industries and 83, 84–5, *86*, 87, **88**, 96, 97
    creativity of fashion designers 130
    denim 90–2, 97
    fashion magazines 47, 153
    foreign investments in 98–9
    fur trade 84, *84*, 96–7
    Hollywood and 94–6
    industrialization 85–9, 90, 97
    leisure and sportswear 92–4, *93*, 96, 181–2
    man-made fiber production 120–1
    Men's Apparel Guild in California (MAGIC) 96, 182, 189, 237n53
    Men's Wear Manufacturers of Los Angeles 96
    New York as fashion center 89–90, 117, *129*
    vs. Parisian influence 39, 83–4
    post-WWII 128–30, 138, 139
    ready-to-wear clothing 87–9, 90, 97
    silk industry 81–2, 220
    synthetic fiber production in 97–9
    in WWII 101, *118*, 118–20, *121*
American Gigolo (film) 149–50
Anne Klein & Co. 156–7
Apax Partners 204
Arcadia Bazaar Company 62
Armani, Giorgio 133, 135, 149–50, *151*, 160, 162
    alliance with Reebok 194
    joint ventures in Japan 150, 155
    sales **150**
Arnault, Bernard 49, 175–6, 221, 223
    Boussac Group takeover 141–2, 163
    Christian Dior takeover 160
    LVMH takeover 142, 162–4
    Willot Frères takeover 146
Asher, Jerome 130
ASOS 207–8, 216, 222–3
Aubert, Georges 38–9
Au Bon Marché in Paris 21–2
Au Mikado boutique 77
Au Printemps Group 166
Authentic Brands Group (ABG) 195

Autonomous Body for the Permanent National Fashion Exhibition (*Autonomo per la Mostra Permanente Nazionale della Moda*, EAMPNM) 103–4

B2B retail platforms (business-to-business) 201
Bader, Théophile 35
Balenciaga, Cristobal 37, 112, 127, 128, 166
Balmain, Pierre 129, 136
Bangladesh Garment Manufacturers and Exporters Association (BGMEA) 145–6
Banken, Ralf 206
Barthes, Roland 2
BASF 18, 109
Bayer 18, 109
Beer, Gustav 37
Bellezza magazine 104
Belloni, Antonio 161
Benetton company 137, 139, 190
Bergdorf Goodman (department store) 61
Bertin, Rose 25
Bestseller (fashion retailer) 205
Bezos, Jeff 207
Bide, Bethan 114
Biki. *See* Broyure, Elvira Leonardi
Birkin, Jane 153
"Blackshirts" movement 102, *103*
Blaszczyk, Regina Lee 18
bloggers, fashion 210, 211–12
Bobergh, Otto Gustav 28–9
Bocconi brothers 22
Bohan, Marcel 126
Bok, Edward 83
Borletti, Senatore 105
Boss, Hugo 108
Boston Manufacturing Company 87
Boucicaut, Aristide 21–2
Boucicaut, Marguerite 22
Boussac Group 141, 146
Boussac, Marcel 57, 123, 146, 223
Boussac Saint-Frères 164
Bowerman, Bill 184
Brenninkmeijer in Sneek 60
Brennwald, Caspar 13
Breward, Christopher 152
British fashion industry 38–9, 146
　British Industrial Revolution 67, 97
　British Nylon Spinners 115
　cotton trade 66–8
　Jewish fashion district in London 116–17
　unemployment in textile regions 221
　in WWII 101, 114–16

Brownstein-Louis Co. 94
Broyure, Elvira Leonardi *132*, 132–3
Bunka Fashion College (BFC) 71–2
Burberry (fashion brand) 61, 135, 151–2, 211, 223
　Sanyo Shokai partnership with 136
Burberry, Thomas 152
Burton, Montague 57
Business and Fashion, Sombart (*Wirtschaft und Mode*) 1

C&A 45, 59–61, 136–7
CAFTA. *See* Central American Free Trade Agreement
calico-printing 9
　Calico Printers Association 116
California Casual 97, 121
Calvin Klein 130, 145, 149, 188
Campbell, Naomi *160*
Capital (Marx) 45
Cardin High Fashion Prize 72
Cardin, Pierre 72, 136, 158
Caribbean Trade Partnership Act (CTBA) 201–2
Cartier, Louis 33, 165
Cartwright, Edmund 14
Catalina Knitting Mills 94, 130
Cavalli, Roberto 168
Céline (leather goods manufacturer) 163
Central American Free Trade Agreement (CAFTA) 202
Chanel, Gabrielle (Coco) 32, 34–6, *35*, 42, 126, 135, 149, 160
　designs for Hollywood stars 95
　garçonne style introduction 92
　Parfums Chanel company 35
　private ownership in fashion industry 162
　in WWII 112
Chevalier, Alain 162
Chinese fashion industry 73–5, 80, 157–9. *See also specific entries*; wax fabrics
　Chaoyue Sportswear *158*
　China Fashion Designers Association (CFDA) 158
　China National Garments Association 158
　department stores emergence, 24
　global trade and production 143–4, *144*, 172, 201–2, 220
　influence on Western fashions 65–6, 75–7, *76*
　nationalist sentiments in 223–4
　silk and 10–11, **11**, *76*, 81–2

Chloé (fashion brand) 127, 148
Claiborne, Liz 130
C. Mendès firm 127, 132, 138
colors/dyes
    color revolution 18–19
        artificial 18–19, 24, 108, 109–11, 113, 140, 221
Comptoir des Textiles Artificiels (CTA) 98, 105
Condé Nast (publisher) 129, 131
Cosmopolitan magazine 47, *47*, 153
cotton 8–9, 65–6, 78–9, 140, 219–20
    British cotton fabrics 58–9, 66–8
    Exchange markets 9
    in Japan 111
    Long-Term Arrangement for Cotton Textiles (LTA) 142
    and man-made fibers, 105–6
    printed cotton from India 66, 219
    role in US economic development 84–7, 97, 130
    and slavery 84–5
    sustainability 173–4, 222
    trade for modern fashion business 8–9, 14
Courtaulds 98, 105, 109, 115–16, 120
Courtauld, Samuel 115–16
couture. *See* high-end fashion
Crawford, Joan 94, 95
"cultural capital" for fashion brands 153

Daewoo 144
Daimaru (department store) 23, 135
Dali, Salvador 95
Dangel, Louis 42
Dapper Dan's Boutique 189–90
Dassler shoemaker company 182–4
Davis, Jacob 91
Davis, Tobé Coller 129
Deep Blue IBM 204–5
Delanghe 112
Delon, Alain 155
Deneuve, Catherine 153
Descente Ltd 184
Desh Garments 144, *144*
developing economies and fashion industry 157–9
Dietrich, Marlene 96
digitalization in fashion industry 199, 222
    digital platforms creation 201
    e-commerce platforms 207–10
    fashion bloggers 210, 211–12
    fashion influencers 199, 212
    and fast-fashion model 206, 207

    mediatization of fashion 210–11
    and mono-brand stores 206
Digital Revolution 212. *See also* Industrial Revolution
Dior, Christian 43, 57, 72, *72*, 123, 135, 152
    Christian Dior SA 122, 125–6, 135–6, 160
    Miss Dior perfume *125*
Diseño Textil SA 170
DKSH 13
Dolce & Gabbana 147
Donna Karan New York (DKNY) 142, 155, 156–7, 223
Doucet, Jacques 30, 32
Douglas Aircraft Company, women workers in *118, 121*
Drecoll, Christoph von 37
Dress Creators League 43
Dressmaker Gakuin designer school 72, 133
Dressmaking magazine 72
dry goods stores 22–3
Duff Gordon, Lucy Lady 37
DuPont 98, 99, 115, 120, 129
    magazine advertisement for DuPont Lycra *140*
    nylon production 139–40
D'URBAN 154–5
Dutch East India Company (*Vereenigde Oost-Indische Compagnie,* VOC) 4, 78
    adoption of Chinese and Japanese clothing culture 75
    and British cotton 66–7
    trade with Japan 68
dyes. *See* colors/dyes

East Midland Allied Press (EMAP) 203
e-commerce platforms 5, 199
    ASOS 207–8, 216, 222–3
    role in fashion industry 207
    Romwe 208
    Shein 208–10, *209*, 213, 216, 222–3
    Zalando 207, 208, 216, *217*, 217–18, 222–3
Ehrenfreund, Kurt 52
Elle magazine 153
E. Moses & Son 19–20
Engelbrecht, Kurt 101
English East India Company (EIC) 4, 9, 14, 58
    adoption of Chinese and Japanese clothing culture 75
    global trade of British cotton 66–7
English fashion industry. *See* British fashion industry
Enka 109

Ensemble (couture store) 159
Ermenegildo Zegna 132, 146, 150
Esprit 144, 146, 190
Eugénie (French Empress) 28–9
Euro-Mediterranean Association Agreements 202
evoluSHEIN 210
Ewing, Elizabeth 115

F. & A. Swanzy 79, 80
fabrics production for European colonies 58–9. *See also* cotton; silk; wool
Facebook 208–9, 210, 211
factories for textile 54–7, *55*, **56**
fascism and German fashion 101–2, 106–10
    Frauen-Warte magazine *107*
    fascism and Italian fashion 101–2, 221
    "Blackshirts" movement 102, *103*
    EAMPNM and 103–4
    ENM and 104–5
    fashion criteria 103
    Ferragamo and Gucci's role 106
    fixed code in uniforms 102–3
    Italian menswear (1930s) *104*
    Snia's role 105–6
fashion capitals 3, 220–1
    Berlin 52
    New York 194
    Paris 37, 97, 101, 107, 112, 117, 122
fashion design(er) schools
    in Japan 71–3
    in United States 90
fashion for masses 63
    advertisement for Raynster raincoats *51*
    advertisement poster *50*
    A La Belle Jardinière 48–9
    Au Pauvre Jacques Clothing Fashions Poster *58*
    change in consumption habits 46–8
    fabrics production for European colonies 58–9
    industrial factories role 54–7
    industrialization and 49–51
    internalization retail model 59–61
    outsourcing model 61–3
    small firms, networks of 51–2, 54
fashion houses 43, 147–51
fashion influencers 199, 212
Fashion Institute of Technology (FIT) 205
fashion magazines
    in Japan 70–1, 72
    in United States 94
    for women 46–7, *47*
fashion media 141, 152–4
    fashion models 31
Fashion Originators' Guild of America (FOGA) 43
fast-fashion 161, 167
    digitalization and 206, 207
    ecological impact 221–2, 173–6, *175*
    Fast Retailing Co. 167, 171–3, 206–7, 216, 220, 223
    H&M 137, 167–70, 213, 216, 220, 223
    Inditex 167, 170–1, 213, 216, 220, 223
    market capitalization 173, **173**
    Shein 208–10, *209*, 213, 216, 222–3
Fast Retailing Co. 167, 171–2, 206–7, 216, 220, 223
    business collaborations 172, 173
    store in Russia *172*
Ferragamo (luxury fashion company) 106
Ferragni, Chiara 211
Fischer, Donald 137
Fleming, Ebenezer Brown 79
Ford Model Agency 31
Ford, Tom 166
forecasting of fashion 202
    IBM Watson and 204–6
    international fashion-forecasting agencies 202
    Stylesight 202, 204
    WGSN 202–4, 216
    free trade and preferential treaties 201–2
French fashion industry 127. *See also* Parisian high-end fashion
    domination in America 89
    impact of shift in production for textile industries 146
    magazines 46
    Paris fashion during German occupation 112–13
    Paris as global fashion capital 37, 97, 101, 107, 112, 117, 122
    syndicates 29, 36, 42, 89, 124–5
    unemployment in textile regions 221
Fujin kurabu magazine 71
Fujokai magazine 71
fur trade 84, 96–7

Galeries Lafayette (department store) 35, 61
Gap, Inc. 137, 139, 142, 144, 150, 175
Garcia Maceiras, Oscar *171*
garçonne style 92
"Gary Pepper Girl" (e-commerce platform) 211

Gaultier, Jean-Paul 136
Gebrüder Volkart 9
General Motors 18
Gere, Richard 150
German fashion industry 52–3. *See also specific entries*
    artificial dyes development 18
    conservation of fur products 53
    Deutsches Mode-Institut 106–7
    German Institute for Men's Fashion 53
    outsourcing of textile production 141–2, 146
    trade associations 54
    unemployment in textile regions 221
    Viennese design influence 40–1
Gerson, Herrmann 52
G. F. Perkin & Sons company 18
Giacometti, Alberto 178
Gill & Rentner 90
Giorgini, Giovanni Battista 131
Givenchy 163, 177
    Parfums Givenchy 162
Glanzstoff (*Vereinigte Glanzstoff Fabriken*, VGF) 98
globalization 147, 176, 200
Global North/South distinction 4, 201
Google 209, 213
Great Universal Stores (GUS) 151, 152
Greenburg, Adrian Adolph 94
greenwashing 175, 222
Greta Garbo 94–5, *95*
Gualino, Riccardo 105
Gucci 106, 166, 223
Guenther, Irene 101, 107

H&M (Hennes & Mauritz) 167–8, 216, 220, 223
    business model after WWII 137
    collaboration with Karl Lagerfeld 168–70, *169*
Haarlemsche Katoen Maatschappij (HKM) *79*, 79–80
Hainer, Herbert 193
Harper's Bazaar magazine 29, 47, 90
Harrods 21–3
Haskalah movement 20
"health-dress" 40
Henry VIII 180
Hepburn, Katharine 94, 96
high-end fashion 25–6, 32–7, 44. *See also Parisian high-end fashion*
    Charles Frederick Worth 27–31
    globally 37–41
    High Fashion magazine 72
    trade associations 42–3

hip-hop culture and fashion 188–90
Hitoshi Yanai 171
Hoechst 18, 109
Hollywood 94–6
House of Gaston 123
House of Paquin 38
Howard & Bullough 15
Hughes, Greer *203*
Hugo Boss 223
Hyam & Co. 61

IBM (International Business Machines) 204, 213
    Bestseller collaborations 205
    Tommy Hilfiger and FIT collaborations 205
    Watson AI platform 204–6, *205*
IG Farben in Germany 18, 99, 109, 115
I. J. Dewhirst (clothing manufacturer) 62, 137
Imperial Chemical Industries (ICI) 115–16
Incorporated Society of London Fashion Designers (Inc. Soc.) 115
Indian fashion industry. *See also specific entries*
    cotton weighers in Bombay *10*
    modern fashion designers 159
    textile and cotton industry in 8–9, 54, 58–9, 66–8
Inditex 167, 206, 216, 220, 223
    business strategy 170–1
    Garcia Maceiras at conference *171*
    Zara 167, 170, 207
Industrial Revolution 3, 7–8, 14, 65, 67, 97, 219–20
    1st 212, 219
    2nd 212, 222
    3d 212
    4th 212–16
    in United States 85–6
Instagram 208–10, 211–12
International Labour Organization (ILO) 215
Issey Miyake 134, 155–6, *156*
    fashion business 177–8
    at Studio 54 anniversary celebration *177*
Italian fashion industry 131–3. *See also fascism and Italian fashion*
    Commentary and Italian Dictionary on Fashion 104
    Ente Italiano Moda (EIM) 105
    Ente Nazionale della Moda (ENM) 104–5
    Gruppo Finanziario Tessile (GFT) 132–3, 138, 150
    luxury wool manufacturing 146

Italian Socialist Party (PSI) 102
Itochu 155
Itokin 136

Jacques Rober (financial company) 162
Jäggi, René 184, 190
Jakob Weil 63
Jane Paris 37
Japanese fashion industry. *See also specific entries*
   artificial dyes 18
   beginnings 7
   designer schools 71–3
   DKNY 155, 156–7, 223
   fashion magazines 70–1, 72
   foreign brands and 135–6, 155, 223
   Giorgio Armani Japan 155
   independent designers, 155–6
   influence on Western fashion 75, 77, 80
   international expansion challenges 154–5
   investments 142
   military dictatorship and Japanese fashion 101, 110–2
   nationalist ideology in 101, 110–12
   in nineteenth century 47–8
   silk 10–4, 65, 81–2, 220–1
   trench coats business in 151
   westernization 65–6, 68–70, 80, 133–5, 138–9
J. C. Penney 130
J. D. Matthewman (Textile) Ltd. 147
Jean Patou Inc. 37
jeans 90–2, 97, 118–19
Jews in fashion industry 20, 22. *See also* Levi Strauss & Co
   in England 56–7, 116–17
   and fascism, 101, 107–8, 116–17
   in Germany 52–3
Jin Byoungho, Ellie 213
John Fraser & Company 9
John Hetherington & Sons 15
Jordan, Michael *186*, 186–7
Joseph Hepworth & Sons 56
Joseph May & Sons 56
Journal des Dames et des Modes magazine 25
J. Strauss Brother & Co 90

Kamakura Shobo publishing company 72
Kanebo (cosmetic firm) 135–6
Kanematsu Sports 184
Kansai Yamamoto 155
Karan, Donna 157

Karlsch, Rainer 193
Kashiyama firm 133
Kawabe 136
Kawakubo, Rei 134, 155
Kawamura, Yuniya 2–3, 153, 223
Kehrl, Hans 113
Kenzo Takada 133, 134, *134*, 155, 156
Kering 164–5, 166
kimono 47, 77
King Cotton (US) 97
Klein, Anne 157
Knight, Phil 184, *192*, 193, 196
Krum, Maria 129
Kuldova, Tereza 159
Kuwasawa Design School 72–3

Lacoste 190
Lagerfeld, Karl 127, 148
   with de la Fressange *148*
   H&M's collaboration with 168–70, *169*
   role in Chanel 149
   with Rykiel and Takada *134*
La Guardia, Fiorello 117
La Mode Illustrée magazine 47
Lanvin, Jeanne 32, 34
La Redoute 166
Lazareff, Hélène 153
Leagas Delaney (advertising company) 191
Le Bon Marché 141, 163
Lee, Henry David 91–2
leisurewear 180–2, *180*. *See also* soccer shirts
   adidas and 192–3, 194
   in American fashion 93, 94, 121, 129
   for American female workers 118–19
   Los Angeles as center of 121
Lelong, Lucien 32, 37, 112–13, *113*
Le Mercure Galant magazine 25
Le Moniteur de la Mode magazine 46
Levin, David Leib 52
Levi Strauss & Co. 90–2, *91*, 146
Li & Fung (trading company) 144
Lipovetsky, Gilles 3
Lisser, Kurt 60
L'Oréal 149
Loren, Sophia 153
Louis-Dreyfus, Robert 190–1
Louis Vuitton (LVMH) 142, 161–4, 221, 223
   DKNY acquisition by 157
   sustainability 175–6
Louis XV 25
Lowell, Francis Cabot 87
low fashion 3

Luce, Leanne 213
Lundin, Augusta 29
luxury fashion companies 106, 161–2, 176. *See also* high-end fashion; Parisian high-end fashion
    financialization of 164–7
    Kering 164–5, 166
    Louis Vuitton 162–4, 175–6, 221, 223
    ready-to-wear producers 150
    Richemont 165–6
LVMH. *See* Louis Vuitton

Macy's department stores 21, 22
Madam magazine 72
mail-order sales 22, 89, 90
MakeMeChic 208
mannequins 30
Marie–Antoinette 25, *26*
Marinotti, Franco 105
Marks & Spencer (M&S) 61–3, 136, 137
Marx, Karl 45
masses. *See* fashion for masses
Ma Ying Piu 24
McCartney, Stella 168, 194, 195
McDaniels, Darryl *189*
McKinsey 5, 190, 196
mediatization of fashion 210–1
Milan Sample Fair 131
Miranda, José Antonio 167
Mitsubishi Rayon 154
Mitsukoshi store, Japan 23, 47, 69
Moët-Hennessy SA 162–3
Molyneux 112, 114
Monet, Claude 65
mono-brand stores 146, 162, 166, 192–3, 206, 223
Monoprix 61
Moore, Peter 191
Mori, Hanae 134, 155, 156
Mrs. magazine 72
Mugler, Thierry 136
Multi-Fiber Arrangement (MFA) 142–3, 201
Mussolini, Benito 101, 102, *103*

NAFTA. *See* North American Free Trade Agreement
National Institute of Fashion Technology (NIFT) 159
Netherlands' fashion industry
    C&A stores in 45, 60, 61
    cotton export *78*, 79
    Japanese-style garments adoption 75

Kultuurstelsel 78
Nederlandsche Handel-Maatschappij N. V. (NHM) 78
NV Deventer Katoenmaatschappij (DKM) 79–80
N. V. Nationale Confectie Industrie (NCI) 60, 137
wax fabrics 66
Newton, Alfred 38
Newton, Helmut 148
New York Fashion Institute of Technology (FIT) 117
Nien Hsing Textile Co. 144
Nike, Inc. 184–7, 196, 221
    athletic shoe designs 184–5
    brand position and brand value 195, **196**
    global market shares 187, **187**
    marketing strategies 191, 192, 193
    and Michael Jordan *186*, 186–7
    Nik(e)ification 185–6, 196–7, 221
Nippon Rubber 184–5
North American Free Trade Agreement (NAFTA) 143, 201
Novità magazine 131
nylon 99, 115–16, 222
    introduction by DuPont 120, 129
    revolution 139–40
    stockings *120*

Ogori Shōji 171. *See also* Fast Retailing Co.
Ohrbach department store 136–7
Opium perfume 147–8, *147*
Ortega Gaona, Amancio 170, *207*, 221
outsourcing production 61–3, 130–2, 141–2, 146, 158, 176, 185, 216, 220, 221
Owens, Jesse 182

Paquin, Jeanne 34, 38, 76, 90
Parisian high-end fashion 3, 5, 24, 26, 32–7, 90, 97, 112
    Asian designers in Paris 155
    Chanel's role in 34–6
    Christian Dior SA foundation 125–6
    couturiers, growth of 32–3
    Dior's role 123, 125–6
    evening ensemble *28*
    female designers 34
    French exports of clothing and lingerie *36*
    haute couture houses (1954) *124*
    Mondriaan Fashion from Paris *128*
    perfume business 36
    Poiret's role in 33–4

post-WWII business model 124–5, 138
ready-to-wear business shift 36–7
Saint Laurent's role 123, 126, 127–8
summer dress design 34
trade association in 32, 42–3
transnational expansion of 37–41, 43
Worth's work of 26, 27–31
Parissot, Pierre 20, 48
Parsons School of Design 90
Patou, Jean 31, 32, 36, 37, 92–3, 181
pattern-cutting manuals 20
Pedroni, Marco 211
perfume business 36
    Chanel No. 5, 35
    Guerlain 163
    Jean Patou Inc. 37
    L'Oréal 149
    Miss Dior perfume 125
    Opium *147*, 147–8
    "Rosine" 33
Persson family 167–8
Peter Millar 165–6
Phillips, Lawrence 130
Phillips-Van Heusen (PHV) 130
Platt Brothers 15
Poiret, Paul 30, 32
    as customer of Wiener Werkstätte 41
    fashion tour in United States 90
    kimono-style coats creation 77
    modern silhouette 92
    ready-to-wear collections 37
    role in Parisian haute couture 33–4
    in Vienna *40*
polyester 116, 140
Pompadour, Madame 25
Prada 223
Pratt Institute, fashion design program 90
Premier Vision 157
Prévinaire, Jean Baptiste Theodore 79
Primavesi, Otto 40
public relations manager 153
Puma 166, 183, 195

qipao (Chinese dress) 75, 80, 157

Racamier, Henri 162–3
Radziwill, Lee 150
Raika Co. 155
Ralph Lauren 130, 149, 188
Rana Plaza disaster in Bangladesh 174–5
rayon 92, 98–9, 122, 139, 174
    in Britain during WWII 115

    in Germany 108–9
    in Japan 111
    manufacturing by Snia 105
ready-to-wear 5, 19, 45
    in American fashion industry 83–4, 87–9, 90, 97
    in Britain during WWII 115
    demand for cheap clothing 50–1
    in Paris 36–7
    production methods 20, 122
    promotions by magazines 153
Redfern & Sons 37–8, 180–1
Reebok 184–7, 190
    acquisition by adidas 194, 195
Renown (fashion company) 111, 133, 154–5
retail companies development 59–60
Richemont 164–6
robotics in fashion industry 214
Rocamora, Agnes 210
Roldán, Alba 167
Romwe e-commerce platform 208
Rosie the Riveter 118
"Rosine" perfume 33
Rubinstein, Ida Lvovna 32
Run DMC group 188–9, *189*
Rupert, Anton 165

Samuel Courtauld & Co. 98
Sanyo Shokai 70, 133
    partnership with Burberry 136, 152
    trench coats business 151–2
Schacht, Hjalmar 108–9
Schiaparelli, Elsa 37, 95, 112
Schiller, Karl 141
Schuhfabrik Gebrüder Dassler 182, *183*
Scott, William 93, 182
Seibu Department Stores 155
sewing machines 7, 15, 24, 51, 220
    advertising for Singer machines *17*
    in American fashion industry 88–9
    manufacturing in Leeds and Glasgow 54–5
    Singer in Japan 7, 15–17, *17*, 55, 70
    in Worth's modern business model 30
Shanghai Clothing Research Institute 157
Shanghai Cutting and Tailoring College 75
Shanghai Garment Trade Association 158
Shanshan Company 158–9
Shein 208–10, *209*, 216
    competing with fast-fashion companies 222–3
    sustainable growth during Industry 4.0, 213

Shin, Daeun Chloe 213
Shirokiya store, Japan 47
Shufu no tomo magazine 71
Siber & Brennwald merchant company 11, 13
silk 24
    artificial production 97–8
    Chinese silk industry 10–11, *76*, 81–2
    imported silk reeling machine *12*
    industrial development in United States 82
    Japanese silk industry 10–12, *12*, 65, 81–2
    Road/Route 10, 200
    role in modern fashion business 8, 9, 10, 14
    and Siber & Brennwald merchant company 11, 13
    stockings *120*
    world production **11**
Simmel, Georg 2, 103, 179, 196
Simmons, Joseph *189*
Sincere (department store) 24
Singer, Isaac M. 15, 16
Slater, Samuel 86–7
slavery 85
sneakers 2, 179–80, 188, 195, 196, 215. *See also* sportswear industry
Snoop Dog 189
soccer shirts 197–8
social media 199. *See also* fashion media
Societa Nationale Industrie Applicazione Viscosa (Snia Viscosa) 105–6, 109, 110
Société Parisienne de Confection (SPC) 61
Soen magazine 71
Soen Prize 72
Soeurs, Callot 76, *76*
SoftWear Automation 215
Sombart, Werner 1–2, 219
South Korean production network 144–5
Sports Inc. 191
sportswear industry 47, 180–1
    adidas 179, 183–4, 188–91, 193–5, 221
    fashionalization of 179, 196
    growth in United States 121, 181–2
    and hip-hop culture 188–90
    marketing strategies 191–3
    Nike, Inc. 184–7, 192, 195, 221
    promotion by magazines 153
    Puma 166, 183, 195
    Schuhfabrik Gebrüder Dassler 182, *183*
    sneakers and 2, 179–80, 188, 195, 196, 215
    soccer shirts 197–8
    styles in American fashion *93*, 93–4
Sportswear Round Up in Palm Springs (1942) 96

standardization of sizes 19–20, 50–1
staple fibers 105–6, 108
Steel, Valerie 35
Strasser, Rob 191
Strauss, Levi 90–2
Stylesight 202, 204
Subrahmanyam, Sanjay 3–4
Sugino, Yoshiko 72
Sulzer Brothers in Switzerland 15
sumptuary laws in Europe 25–6
Suzuki Shokai 111
Swanson, Gloria 95
syndicates
    Chambre Syndicale de la Couture et de la Confection pour Dames et Fillettes 42
    Chambre Syndicale de la Couture Parisienne (CSCP) 29, 36, 42, 89, 124–5
    International Ladies Garment Workers Union (ILGWU) 89
synthetic fibers 92, 99, 113, 122, 220. *See also* DuPont
    Germany as producer 105–6, 107–8
    global shifts in world production *143*, 143–6
    Italy as producer 101
    nylon 115–16, 139–40
    polyester 116, 140
    for sportswear mass-production 181
    sustainability of 115, 173–4
    United States as producer 97–8, 99, 120, 122
    world production of *143*, 174, *174*

Tadashi Yanai 171, 173, 221
Taiwan production 144–5
Takihyo Inc. 155, 156–7
Tapie, Bernard 190
Taylor, Elizabeth 153
textile machinery 14–15, *15*, 24
Tianyuan Garments 214
TikTok 209, 212
Tomio Taki 156–7
Tommy Hilfiger 145, 149, 188
    IBM's collaborations with 205
    Snoop Dog 189
Toray Industries 111, 172
Toshiyuki Hata 7
trench coats 151–2
Turnure, Arthur B. 90

Ungaro, Emanuel 133
uniforms 19, 69–70, 88–9, 102–3, 108, 111–2
United Africa Company (UAC) 80

United Kingdom (UK). *See* British fashion industry
United Sattes. *See* American fashion industry

van Vlissingen, Pieter Fentener 79
Vendome Syndicate Ltd 38
Vereinigte Glanzstoff Fabriken (VGF) 105, 108, 109, 110
Vernet, Marie Augustine 27, 28, 30, 31
Versace 168
Veuve Clicquot group 162
Victor Emmanuel III (King) 102
Videau brothers 21
Viennese design influence 40–1
Vionnet, Madeleine 32, 34, 178
    couture design *41*
    making Japanese technique-based dresses 77
    PAIS creation 42
Vlisco 79–81
Vogue magazine 47, 76, 90, 92
    internationalization 154
    as publications for families 153
    Vogue Italia 131

Waldman, Bernard 96
Wallas & Co. 147
Wang, Alexander 168
Warne, Nicole 211, 212
Watson, Thomas J. 204
wax fabrics. *See also* synthetic fibers
    consumption in West African market 66, 79–80
    Dutch imitation batik 79
    Indonesian batik 77–8
    production companies in Netherlands 78–9
Wertheimer, Alain 149
West Coast apparel industry 127
Wiener Werkstätte 40–1
Williams, Jean 180
Willot Frères 146
Wimmer-Wisgrill, Eduard Josef 41
wool. *See also* cotton
    environmental issues 222
    in German textile industry 108
    Industries Research Association (WIRA) 62
    jersey shorts *93*

    luxury wool manufacturing in Italy 146
    milk wool manufacturing *110*
    in modern fashion business 8, 14
    in United States 81
World War II (WWII). *See also* fascism and German fashion; fascism and Italian fashion
    American fashion style 101
    British nationalistic policies in fashion 101, 114–16
    global shifts in fashion houses 112
    military dictatorship in Japanese 101, 110–2
    rayon production in Britain 115
    restrictions in US 119–10
    sportswear industry development 182
    women fashion in wartime factories *118*, 118–19
Worth & Bobergh enterprise 28–31
Worth, Andrée Caroline 33
Worth, Charles Frederick 27–31, *27*, 33, 43. *See also* high-end fashion
    costume design for Rubinstein *32*
    using Japanese-inspired motifs and techniques 77
    trade association in haute couture, foundation of 42
Worth, Gaston-Lucien 29, 30
Worth Global Style Network (WGSN) 202–4, 216
Worth, Jean-Philippe 29, 30
Wrangler overalls 92, 130

Yohji Yamamoto 134, 179
    at opening of Y-3 Flagship store *195*
    role in adidas's Sport Style 193–4
Yves Saint Laurent (fashion house) 123, 136, 166
    dress designs on Mondriaan Fashion by 128, *128*
    at launch of Opium perfume *147*
    role in new Parisian business model 126, 127–8, 147

Zalando 207, 208, 216, *217*, 217–18, 222–3
Zara Company 167, 170, 207
    logistic distribution center *207*
Zola, Emile 21, 29